T0396535

The Great Transformation of China

China's Economic Transformation, Innovation and Development

Series Editor
Fulin Chi
China Institute for Reform and Development
Haikou, Hainan, China

China is facing unprecedented challenges in its continued modernization process. This series brings together government insiders, academics, and policymakers in articulating specific social and political issues that China is trying to resolve, offering scholars around the world insights into what China's leadership see as the biggest challenges facing the nation and how best to resolve them. The series publishes monographs and edited volumes with contributions on a global basis dedicated to ground-breaking research on the Chinese modernization process.

More information about this series at
http://www.palgrave.com/gp/series/15346

Shuzhong Gu · Meie Xie · Xinhua Zhang

Green Transformation and Development

ZHEJIANG UNIVERSITY PRESS
浙江大学出版社

palgrave
macmillan

Shuzhong Gu
Development Research Center
of the State Council (DRC)
Beijing, China

Meie Xie
Yunnan University of Finance
and Economics
Kunming, China

Xinhua Zhang
Party School of Xinjiang Uygur
Autonomous Region Committee
of C.P.C
Urumqi, China

ISSN 2509-6001   ISSN 2509-601X   (electronic)
The Great Transformation of China
ISBN 978-981-32-9494-3   ISBN 978-981-32-9495-0   (eBook)
https://doi.org/10.1007/978-981-32-9495-0

Jointly published with Zhejiang University Press
The print edition is not for sale in Mainland of China. Customers from Mainland of China
please order the print book from: Zhejiang University Press.

This Palgrave Macmillan imprint is published by the registered company Springer Nature
Singapore Pte Ltd.
The registered company address is: 152 Beach Road, #21-01/04 Gateway East, Singapore
189721, Singapore

Series Editor's Preface

The Year 2020: A Historic Choice of Economic Transformation and Upgrading

A great nation with 13 billion people is facing a changing situation it has not ever faced for a thousand years. Change, transformation, and innovation feature the main melody of the era. In this era of high integration of growth, transformation, and reform, "great transformation" is exactly what decides the destiny of China. In other words, not only will "toxic assets" left in the traditional system have to be eliminated completely but also the new way for further growth needs to be paved quickly while letting loose the new motive force of development.

The major transformation in China's "13th Five-Year Plan" (FYP) is historically decisive. With the economic transformation as the focal point, both social transformation and government transformation are in the crucial period of transition, in which innumerable thorny problems have to be tackled. Our general judgment is that the year 2020 is like a "gorge" we have to jump over. Specifically, by the end of 2020 we will have eliminated the pressure on short-term growth and changed the way for economic development while achieving a comparatively prosperous society in an all-round way and becoming one of the high-income countries in the world. If we plan well enough to make the best use of 2020, a mid-term period in the 13th FYP, we can lay a solid foundation for the medium-to-long-term peaceful and sustainable growth.

If we fail to grasp the historical opportunity of 2020, we will lose the initiative of "great transformation", thus resulting in multiple systemic economic risks.

The significant breakthrough for achieving the economic transformation and upgrading in the 13th FYP period is how to cope with "four threes". Firstly, three major trends: one for industrial transformation and upgrading from "made in China" to "intellectually made in China"; one for urbanized transformation and upgrading from scale to population; and one for consumption pattern upgrading from material to service. Secondly, three major challenges: one for achieving a major breakthrough in structural reform by enhancing the structural adjustment despite the economic downturn; one for "corner overtaking" by responding to the global new round of scientific and technological revolution and increasing the ability to innovate; and one for a real and down-to-earth reform. At present, the transformation depends more on the all-round breakthrough in reform. It couldn't move forward at all without the change in systematic structure. And the growth would suffer big pressures. Thirdly, three major goals: one for industry, namely forming the service-dominated industrial structure by accelerating the process of service in manufacture; one for a major motive force, namely forming a consumption-oriented new pattern of economic growth, in which consumption guides investment and domestic consumption becomes a main force that spurs economic growth; and one for opening-up, namely forming a new open pattern dominated by service trade so as to redouble service trade in scale. Finally, three major relationships to be handled properly: one between the short term and the medium-to-long term, in which the best job should be done for 2020 (the mid-term period) while resolving contradictions in the short term, basing ourselves on the mid-term and keeping our eyes on the long term; one between speed and structure which requires accelerating the structural adjustment while maintaining an increase by 7% or so; and one between policy and system in which the key is to gain a policy advantage in achieving institutional innovation under the economic pressure.

The past 40 years of reform and opening-up have left us numerable valuable assets. The most valuable one is that the more complex the situation may be and the more fundamental the change in environment, the more determined we will be in carrying out the reform and pushing through the transformation. All these require that the "great transformation" need overall arrangement and ambitious planning, need a significant breakthrough in the reform of industrial structure, urban–rural structure, regional structure, ownership pattern, open structure and administrative power structure, and need prospective planning in green sustainable development and "internet plus" development trends.

By judging the transformational reform in the 13th FYP period, China (Hainan) Institute for Reform and Development (CIRD) and Zhejiang University Press have jointly designed and published this set of series entitled *The Great Nation in Great Transformation—Economic Transformation and Innovative Development in China*. The book series has paid attention to readability based on being strategic, prospective and academic. It is our expectation that the series will offer enlightenment to readers who are closely watching the transformational reform in China while playing an active role in promoting the transformational reform in the 13th FYP period.

The authors of the series are mostly well-known scholars in their own subject areas, who wrote their respective books in their spare time. As the director of the editorial board of the series, I wish, first and foremost, to extend my sincere thanks to the consultants, editorial board members, authors, and the leadership and editors of the press.

Last but not least, this set of series covers a wide range of subject areas, each volume representing its author's own research conclusions and academic opinions. The set does not require consistency in terms of viewpoints. Any criticism and correction from readers are truly welcome.

September 2015   Fulin Chi

PREFACE

The 18th CPC national congress and the third, fourth and fifth plenary sessions of the 18th CPC central committee all made clear plans and requirements for ecological progress. Ecological civilization will become an important foundation and a necessary path to support the great rejuvenation of the Chinese nation and the realization of the beautiful Chinese dream. The core of ecological civilization construction is green development, low-carbon development and circular development. Green development, from a broad perspective, also includes low-carbon development and circular development. In this sense, green development will become the top priority of China's ecological civilization construction and the main direction and goal of China's social and economic development and transformation. Green transformation and development is the inevitable requirement of China's economic development, the inevitable requirement of China's social development, the inevitable requirement of the innovation of the Chinese government's governance philosophy and the inevitable requirement of the people's yearning for a better life.

China is in the stage of rapid industrialization and urbanization, as well as the upgrading stage of agricultural modernization, and is also in the crucial stage of green transformation and development. At this stage, it is necessary to sort out the scientific connotation and foreign experience of green development, is extremely necessary to sort out the driving force, resistance, effectiveness and problems of China's green transformation and development, is extremely necessary to systematically discuss the fiscal green transformation, financial green transformation, technological green transformation and consumption green transformation that support China's green transformation and development, as well as the cadre assessment system and its reform that promote green transformation and development. To this end, the book is divided into four units. The first unit (Chapters 1 and 2) focuses on the origin and connotation of green, as well as foreign green development experience. The second unit (Chapters 3, 4 and 5) focuses on the discussion on the pressure, momentum and resistance of China's green transformation and development. The third unit (Chapters 6, 7, 8, 9 and 10) discusses the main paths or key areas of China's green transformation from the five important aspects: government finance, finance, consumption, science and technology and urbanization. The fourth unit (Chapter 11) focuses on the cadre assessment system and its reform aimed at promoting green transformation and development.

The book was jointly written by Gu Shuzhong (Deputy Director, Research Fellow, Institute of Resources and Environmental Policy, Development Research Center of the State Council, and Part-Time Doctoral Supervisor, Institute of Geographic Sciences and Resources, Chinese Academy of Sciences), Xie Meie (Postdoctoral Fellow, Institute of Geographic Sciences and Resources, Chinese Academy of Sciences, Associate Professor, Yunnan University of Finance and Economics), Zhang Xinhua (Postdoctoral Fellow, Institute of Geographical Sciences and Resources, Chinese Academy of Sciences; Lecturer, Party School of Xinjiang Uygur Autonomous Region Committee of the Communist Party of China) and Wang Xingjie (Postdoctoral Fellow, Institute of Geographical Sciences and Resources, Chinese Academy of Sciences, Engineer, Environmental Engineering Evaluation Center, Ministry of Environmental Protection). Among them, Gu Shuzhong and Wang Xingjie wrote the Chapters 1 and 2, Gu Shuzhong wrote the Chapter 11, Zhang Xinhua wrote the Chapters 3, 4, 5 and 9 and Xie Meie wrote the Chapters 6, 7, 8 and 10. The framework and draft of the book was designed by Gu Shuzhong.

Beijing, China   Shuzhong Gu
Kunming, China   Meie Xie
Urumqi, China   Xinhua Zhang

CONTENTS

LIST OF FIGURES

Chapter 7

Chapter 8

Chapter 9

Chapter 10

LIST OF TABLES

Chapter 8

Chapter 9

Chapter 10

CHAPTER 1

The Origin and Connotation of Green Development

1 START WITH GREEN

1.1 The Broad Implication of Green

Between yellow and blue, and in the middle of the spectrum, green is a kind of balanced color. Today's mainstream society gives a very broad meaning of green.

First, green symbolizes life. Green is the main hue of plants; plants cannot be separated from the photosynthesis of green. Without green, there can be no plants, there can be no animals and there can be no human beings. In this sense, green is the origin of all life and is the symbol of vitality.

Second, green symbolizes health. Associated with the previous moral, green is a symbol of both life (vitality) and health.

From a medical point of view, green does contribute to health, especially to the recovery of patients. People often use green to describe healthy and safe food, which is called green food.

Third, green symbolizes hope. The tender green of plants breaking through the soil is the hope of plants to grow, bloom and bear fruit, and is the hope of the value of life. Green symbolizes hope.

Fourth, green symbolizes peace. From the perspective of psychology, green can make people calm, quiet and peaceful, so that people can get along with each other better.

© The Author(s) 2019
S. Gu et al., *Green Transformation and Development*,
The Great Transformation of China,
https://doi.org/10.1007/978-981-32-9495-0_1

1

Fifth, green symbolizes peace. Based on the meaning and role of peace, as well as the meaning that the international mainstream society gives the meaning of peace to green, green is often used to represent peace, such as Greenpeace.

Sixth, green symbolizes balance. Green itself is the transition color, harmonic color or balance color between blue and yellow. At the same time, green is also a symbol of the earth's vitality and the balanced development of man and nature.

Seventh, green symbolizes friendliness. Green is the good deeds of human beings to treat nature well, and the kindness to nature, which is the embodiment of kindness to nature; at the same time, green is often the embodiment of friendship between people.

Eighth, green is a symbol of tolerance. The green is full of vitality, and it is also an expression of all kinds of biological species. The green development, from the essence, is dynamic development, is respect for nature and the development of human tolerance.

Ninth, green symbolizes wealth. This is particularly true in Western countries such as the United States, which see green as wealth and tend to use green as the dominant color of money.

Finally, green symbolizes permission. When traffic lights are set, all countries set green to allow access, red lights to ban traffic, yellow lights as waiting lights to transition between red and green lights, so-called Stop at the red light and walk when it turns green. What's more, many countries tend to call the unimpeded passage the green passage. In early warning systems, the risk-free zone is often set to green, the danger zone to red, and the zone or interval between safety and danger to yellow.

1.2   *Wide Application of Green*

As green has many positive connotations mentioned above, modern society is often keen on using green as a prefix and modifier, so more and more modern popular words have emerged, such as the green revolution, green plan, green design, green investment, green technology, green industry, green trade, green enterprises, green consumption and green logo, green culture, green sculpture, green literature, green software, green activity, green food, green architecture, green authentication, green finance, green finance, green investment, green production, green communities, green organization, green products, green transportation, green travel, green energy, green home, green economy, green politics and green culture.

All of the above "green" terms, in essence, can be summed up as green development.

2   THE ORIGIN OF GREEN DEVELOPMENT

2.1   *Green Development Mainly Stems from the Unsustainability of Traditional Development*

Green development is mainly caused by problems in traditional development concepts, paths and models, which are mainly manifested in resource waste and exhaustion, environmental pollution and damage, ecological deterioration and deficit, and social (distribution) injustice. In short, green development mainly stems from the unsustainability of traditional development, from the reflection on traditional development concepts, traditional development paths and traditional development models, and from the search for alternative development concepts, development paths and development models.

2.2   *Green Development Mainly Stems from the Idea of Sustainable Development*

Going back to the source, green development first originates from the concept and thought of sustainable development. In 1987, the report *Our Common Future* defined the connotation of sustainable development and elaborated the theory that sustainable development is the development to meet the needs of Future generations without compromising their ability to meet their own needs. *Our Common Future* was officially released in April 1987 by the World Commission on Environment and Development under the leadership of the then Prime Minister of Norway, Mrs. Brundtland. The report is divided into three parts, namely "common problem", "common challenges" and "joint efforts", focused on the world's population, grain, species, energy, industrial and residential issues, clearly put forward that the development crisis, energy crisis and environmental crisis can't be separated up, the earth's resources and energy far cannot satisfy the needs of the development of human beings, and clearly put forward the concept of "sustainable development" through a series of distinctive judgments and viewpoints, such as the need to change the development model for the benefit of current and future generations.

2.3   Green Development Began with the Introduction of the Green Economy

Green development begins with the concept of green economy. The purpose of green economy is to promote the integration of economic development, social development and environmental protection. It is a new economic concept emerging under the influence of sustainable development theory. It was first proposed by the British economist Pierce (Pierce's *Blueprint for a Green Economy*) in 1989. Also in 1989, the United Nations Environment Programme put forward the concept of "clean production", and China introduced the idea of circular economy in the 1990s. At that time, the concept of green economy was only mentioned, but there was no in-depth study and no systematic theory. However, a series of viewpoints such as sustainable development, clean production and circular economy are intrinsically consistent with the green economy. The academic circles, countries and society of all countries have responded to the problems existing in human development.

Since the beginning of the twenty-first century, especially in recent years, a series of concepts such as circular economy, low-carbon economy, ecological economy and clean production have become increasingly difficult to cope with complex global economic, resource, energy and environmental problems. The development in the new era calls for the application of new economic theories. It was Ban Ki-Moon, the UN Secretary-General, who led the world's economic activity. At the UN climate conference in Bali at the end of 2007, Ban Ki-Moon pointed out that "mankind is facing a great change in the era of green economy". The green economy is providing a positive boost to development and innovation on a scale perhaps not seen since the "industrial revolution". In September 2008, a new international financial crisis broke out. Under the circumstances of multiple crises, such as energy, food, climate change and the financial crisis, we should vigorously develop the green economy, create a new era of green economy and achieve sustainable development of human society in order to save costs and protect the environment. Responding to the global economic recovery has become a major issue to be solved in front of the world. In October 2008, the United Nations Environment Programme (UNEP) launched the global green New Deal and green economy plan, which calls on governments to establish a "green economy" growth model featuring low energy consumption, environmental friendliness and sustainability in order to revive and upgrade the world economy. The United Nations environment program's initiative to develop a green economy and a new green deal has been well received by the international community. The United States, Japan, the European Union and other countries have put forward green economic development plans, implemented green new policies and taken the development of green industry as an important measure to promote economic restructuring, which has made green economy become a trend and trend in the field of global environment and development, so as to plan the development in the post-crisis era. In 2009, the United Nations held a special council to advocate the development of green economy: The theme is to make the world toward green economy, advocate green New Deal. The Rio +20 conference in 2012 focused on how to develop a green economy.

The new historical background and development stage endow green economy with new connotation and mission, making green economy a new economic concept emerging in the process of development mode innovation. The use of green economy as an important response to multiple crises, such as the financial crisis, energy crisis, environmental and resource crisis and climate change risk, has been recognized by all countries in the world.

2.4 Green Development Is the Sublation of China's Traditional Concept of "Unity of Man and Nature"

China's traditional culture of "the unity of man and nature", which respects, complies with and protects nature, is the natural soil for the formation and dissemination of the concept of green development in China. The Taoist culture of "Human follows land, land follows sky, sky follows Taoism, Taoism follows nature" systematically explains the relationship between man and nature, and its core idea is to respect the laws of nature. Although the concepts of resources, environment, ecology and space are not clearly put forward, they focus on the fact that we cannot sacrifice nature to satisfy the endless desires and demands of human beings.

Of course, "the unity of man and nature" is not to blindly emphasize that human beings do nothing and do not know what to do in front of nature. Human beings should not be mere conservationists, but natural knower, protectors, improvers and adaptors aiming at the unity of man and nature. To this end, we need to study and respect the laws of nature, promote scientific and technological progress and institutional innovation, and achieve sustainable development with resource conservation, environmental friendliness, ecological conservation, social harmony and political inclusiveness at its core.

3   What Is Green Development

3.1   The Basic Connotation of Green Development

Green development is an all-embracing, dynamic, evolving and complex concept. At the same time, green development is a concept with clear connotation, clear hierarchy, clear objectives and specific requirements. The core idea of green development is to protect the natural resource base on which human beings live and develop, and to realize the sustainable use of natural resources. We should protect the natural environment that is closely related to us, including the atmospheric environment, the water environment and the soil environment, and strive to achieve the beauty of the natural environment. We must protect the ecosystem that has evolved with us and strive to ensure its continued stability and enhanced service functions. In short, green development is a development (concept, path and mode) characterized by resource conservation, environmental friendliness and ecological conservation. Green development consists of green economy, green society (green communities, green institutions, green schools, etc.), green politics (green assessment, nature protection, etc.), and green culture (culture that respects, complies with and protects nature).

3.2   The Core of Green Development Is the Green Economy

Green economy is an economic pattern characterized by resource conservation, environmental friendliness and ecological conservation. Green economy, composed of green industry, green finance, green fiscal, green investment, green consumption and green trade, is a complex giant system.

The first is green industry or green production system. Emphasis is placed on greening traditional industries, vigorously developing circular economy, promoting clean production and developing green enterprises. We will focus on developing industries related to energy conservation and environmental protection, new generation information technology, biotechnology, high-end equipment manufacturing, new energy, new materials and new energy vehicles. We will energetically develop ecological agriculture, ecological tourism, green producer services and living services. We will effectively raise the efficiency of resource utilization and ensure that resources are used economically. Green label, green product (green food, green building, etc.) and green service are the important connotation of green industry system.

The second is the green circulation or green logistics system. Emphasis should be laid on improving the level of transport services, minimizing the impact of volatilization, leakage, deterioration and loss of products and raw materials on the environment and human health in the process of storage and transportation, improving the mileage utilization rate and tonnage utilization rate of freight vehicles, as well as the actual load rate and transport efficiency of passenger vehicles.

The third is the green distribution system. It emphasizes that the government and society should shoulder the responsibility of environmental renovation, protection and restoration, and the construction of new ecological environment projects through redistribution. Through the form of redistribution, the income of all social strata is balanced to ensure the consumption of green products by low-income people.

Fourth is the green consumption system. We should stress the importance of building a sound ecological civilization, advocate the concept of civilized, economical, green and low-carbon consumption, and promote the formation of a green lifestyle and consumption pattern suited to China's national conditions.

The fifth is the green market system. We will stress the importance of organizing and implementing major demonstration projects for the application of green products and technologies, support the expansion of green markets and innovation in business models and improve the green industry standard system and market access system.

The sixth is the green investment system, including green fiscal and green finance. Green investment will place greater emphasis on social investment, resource conservation, environmental conservation and ecological conservation. Among them, the green fiscal requires the government to give priority to saving water, land, energy, mineral, biological and other resources, giving priority to improving the environmental quality of water, atmosphere and soil, giving priority to the protection of natural and artificial ecosystems, and improving the service function of ecosystems. While adhering to the market orientation, green finance also adheres to the green development orientation and gives preference to green development projects in terms of loan interest rate, credit limit and repayment term.

4   TEN FEATURES OF GREEN DEVELOPMENT

First, the characteristic of humanization. Green development emphasizes putting people first. Economic growth should be subordinated to and serve the needs and development of human beings. It emphasizes the harmonious development between human beings and nature to better realize the healthy development of human beings. Green development strives for social progress at a higher level. It believes that economic and social development should emphasize the equitable distribution of wealth, benefit education, health and employment, and promote human capital. Green development, which gives consideration to individual welfare, the interests of the present and future generations, is a concept of social development at a higher level.

Second, the ecological characteristics. Green development requires the establishment of a return to nature production and lifestyle, including natural, beautiful and comfortable living environment, safe and healthy food, green and environmentally friendly home, travel and their own sustainable development. Green development seeks sustainable utilization of the ecological environment and natural resources and intergenerational equity, emphasizes that healthy economic development should be based on ecological development and the harmony between man and nature, proposes to make full use of low-carbon ecological technology in industrial production, reduces energy and resource consumption and greenhouse gas and pollutant emissions, conducts climate-friendly, ecological and environment-friendly production, follows ecological laws in the agricultural production and carries out production layout out in accordance with the natural laws of biology, constantly develops and provides green, safe, efficient and harmless products and services to improve the overall and individual welfare of human beings.

Third, the characteristic of rationalization. Green development requires that the speed of economic development should be reasonable, the scale should be reasonable, the structure should be reasonable, the process should be reasonable, and the utilization of resources and environment should be reasonable. The whole process of economic and social development should be in harmony with nature and be compatible with society. Green development requires the internalization of resource and environment utilization to obtain the maximum economic benefits with the minimum resource consumption, so as to maximize the efficiency on the basis of green, health and safety, enhance the sustainability of resources and ecological environment, and finally achieve comprehensive, coordinated and sustainable development.

Fourth, the characteristics of economy. Green development requires to carry out the conservation priority strategy and promote economy in production, circulation, distribution, conservation and consumption, full implementation of total resource and energy utilization control, two-way supply and demand regulation, and differentiated management, strengthen the reuse and comprehensive utilization of resources, greatly improve the efficiency of energy resources and utilization, improve all kinds of resources.

Fifth, the characteristic of high efficiency. Green development requires the improvement of production efficiency, economic efficiency and the utilization efficiency of resources and environment. Green development not only contains the "green" but also includes the content of the development cycle and the content of people-oriented, sustainable development with economic development, comprehensive improvement of people's living standard as the core, guaranteeing the harmonious coexistence of human and nature, human and environment, and maximizing social equity between people, and contains the content of the "economy", namely the resources with the minimum cost to obtain the biggest economic benefits. Green development is the development that maximizes the efficiency and profit of sustainable utilization and protection of natural resources and ecological environment on the basis of green, healthy and more effective development. Only when the efficiency is maximized, the ecological system can achieve harmony under new conditions or at a higher level, and the goal of social system's maximum fairness can be realized.

Sixth, the characteristics of cleanness. Green development requires cleaner production, circulation, distribution and consumption throughout the life cycle. It is required that in the whole process of production, processing, transportation and consumption of the product, there is no or little damage to human body and environment, and the product meets certain environmental protection standards. It includes clean products, new green products produced by major industrial technology innovation and ecological protection construction and service projects and works; It is required to reduce the consumption of non-renewable resources, extend the service cycle of products, adopt green design, adopt green energy, conduct green production and processing, apply green label and green packaging and implement green consumption.

Seventh, the characteristics of low carbonization. Addressing the challenge of climate change to mankind is one of the main causes of green development. Green development emphasizes the low-carbon features of social and economic development, so that social and economic development can reduce its dependence on carbon-based fuels as much as possible, realize the transformation of energy utilization and reduce greenhouse gas emissions. Green development triggers the green energy revolution, which is a new revolution to replace non-renewable fossil energy with renewable resources. It will fundamentally change the development pattern of industrial economy and promote sustainable development of mankind.

Eighth, the characteristics of security. A considerable part of the world's economic, social and resource and environmental problems are related to the security of economic operation mode. Green development requires economic security, social security, resource security, ecological security and environmental security, and controllable economic, social, resource and ecological environmental risks. Among them, resource security, ecological security and environmental security are the main goals pursued by green development.

Ninth, the characteristics of high-technicalization. The innovation and large-scale application of green technology is the key to the success of green development. Through the large-scale green technology breakthrough, the request strengthens the science and technology innovation ability construction and the science and technology infrastructure construction, carries on the second revolution, the reconstruction economic process, molds the brand-new green development form and the pattern. Without the greening of science and technology, there will be no real green development.

Finally, the characteristics of low cost. Green development requires that social and economic development be balanced with current and future needs, be combined with the construction of a resource-conserving and environment-friendly society to reduce the cost of economic transformation, economic development and resource and environment utilization, requires to reduce the cost of economic transformation, the cost of economic development, the cost of resource and environment utilization, and to reduce the cost of prosperity, so as to further strengthen the foundation for sustainable development of mankind.

5   THE RELATIONSHIP BETWEEN GREEN DEVELOPMENT, CIRCULAR DEVELOPMENT AND LOW-CARBON DEVELOPMENT

5.1   Green Development and Circular Development

Although green development and circular development have something in common in terms of "5R", which means resource conservation, pollution reduce, green living and re-evaluate, reuse, recycle and rescue, the connotation of green development also includes people-oriented, scientific and technological means to realize green production, green circulation and green distribution. In other words, it should give consideration to maximization of efficiency and social justice, realize resource substitution by means of science and technology and realize the balance between man and nature in the dynamic process. Although circular development also emphasizes "people-oriented", the "people-oriented" of circular development is mainly reflected in its concern for resources and environment. That is to say, the concern for humanity is expressed through the concern for resources and environment, which is realized through the improvement of the living environment of human beings. It does not have green distribution, which ensures that people with the lowest income can buy and consume the content of green products. Green development, on the other hand, emphasizes social equity rather than circular development.

5.2   Green Development and Low-Carbon Development

Low-carbon development is the general term for a series of human behaviors and activities characterized by low-carbon industry, low-carbon technology and low-carbon life. Low-carbon development is characterized by low energy consumption, low emissions and low pollution. It is an economic development mode evolving from the era of high carbon energy to the era of low carbon energy, with the basic requirements of coping with the impact of carbon-based energy on climate warming and the basic purpose of achieving sustainable economic and social development.

Compared with the low-carbon development, the connotation of green development is much richer, which not only includes the content of low-carbon development, but also includes energy conservation and emission reduction, resource recycling, solid and liquid waste management and other practices. In short, green development is the concept with the broadest meaning, including circular development and low-carbon development, among which circular development mainly focuses on solving environmental pollution problems, while low-carbon development mainly focuses on energy structure optimization and greenhouse gas emission reduction.

6   Why Does China Need Green Development

6.1   The Necessity of China's Green Development Is Reflected in at Least Three Aspects

First, China's traditional development mode at the cost of resources and environment needs to be transformed. Over the past 30 years of reform and opening up, China's GDP has been growing at an ultra-high speed. Economic development is driven too much by resource input and investment, rather than by technological progress and innovation in exchange for improved productivity. At present, China has become the world's largest energy consumer. China's per capita cultivated land, fresh water and forest that sustain people's basic survival are 1/3, 1/4 and 1/7 of the world average, respectively, and has always been plagued by arable land and food problems. China's industrial structure is still unreasonable. Although the industrial structure adjustment policies have achieved initial results, the proportion of resource-intensive industries, environmentally unfriendly industries and ecological non-conservation industries is still large, and the resources, environment and ecological pressure for industrial development are still large. China's energy consumption per unit of GDP is very high, much higher than that of high-income countries, and even higher than the world average. In short, China's traditional development mode at the cost of resources and environment urgently needs to be transformed.

Second, it is urgent to reverse the extremely severe situation of resources, environment and ecology in China. The rapid development of resources and the rapid growth of energy consumption are accompanied by ecological destruction and environmental pollution. At present, 1/3 of the land in China has been hit by acid rain, 70% of the river system is polluted, 1/4 of the residents do not have pure drinking water and 1/3 of the urban population have to breathe the polluted air. Resources and environment can provide resources for production activities and material basis for economic development. However, environment also has an inhibitory effect on economy, which is mainly reflected in the fact that after the environment is polluted and damaged, not only the society suffers huge economic losses, but also the sustainable development of human beings is threatened. China's natural resources and environment can no longer continue to bear and load the traditional mode of economic growth. We must seek rapid economic development in harmony with nature and build a resource-conserving and environment-friendly economic system.

Thirdly, the unbalanced development of China's economy and society and the problems caused by it need to be solved urgently. Since the reform and opening up, China's economic development has made great achievements, but social development is still lagging behind, especially in education, medical care, social security, etc., and the imbalance between economic and social development is extremely prominent. In addition, the imbalance between urban and rural development, the problem of inter-regional development imbalance, the income imbalance between social strata and the superposition of many problems and their effects have led to an increasing number of social conflicts and contradictions, aggravating them, which has shaken the foundation of economic development, and then shaken the foundation of national development. The realization of coordinated economic and social development requires more balanced development, overall development.

In a word, China is still a developing country, which is in the process of rapid industrialization and urbanization, while facing multiple pressures such as developing economy, eliminating poverty, controlling pollution and slowing down greenhouse gas emissions. Many long-standing environmental problems have yet to be resolved, and new ones keep emerging. Despite all the efforts we have made, the situation remains grim for us to conserve resources, protect the environment and tackle climate change. Promoting green development is not only China's independent action to accelerate economic restructuring and change the mode of economic development, but also an important measure for China to cope with global climate change. It is an inevitable choice and objective requirement for China, a big country with a population of 1.3 billion to achieve modernization, break the bottleneck of energy and resources and realize peaceful development.

6.2   The Significance of China's Green Development Is Reflected in at Least Three Aspects

First, green development is conducive to enhancing the capacity for sustainable economic and social development. From the perspective of long-term development, in order to enhance the sustainable development capacity of the economy and society, we must change the traditional development model of "high input, high consumption and low efficiency" and properly handle the relationship between economy, resources and environment. This requires us to find a new development model. The people-oriented, low-carbon, ecological and reduced-quantity features of green development embody the higher level social development concept of harmonious development between human and society and nature, and make human social civilization develop toward a brand-new economic form. Through the green transformation of traditional development, we can continuously reduce carbon emissions, lower the cost of resources and ecological environment, improve the coordination of economy, society and environment and enhance the ability of sustainable development of economy and society, which is in line with China's development of resource-conserving, environmentally friendly society requirements.

Second, green development will help open up new areas of growth in China. Green development, as a new development path, helps to promote the emergence of new forms of development. *The Decision of the State Council on Accelerating the Cultivation and Development of Strategic Emerging Industries* issued by the Chinese government in October 2010 clearly put forward the strategic emerging industries, including energy conservation and environmental protection, new-generation information technology, biology, high-end equipment manufacturing, new energy, new materials, new energy vehicles and other industries. These industries are characterized by low resource and energy consumption, high driving coefficient, abundant employment opportunities and good comprehensive benefits, which conform to the concept of green economic development and have become new economic growth points in China.

Third, green development helps improve China's international competitiveness and influence. The rise of the green development trend is driven by the latest practices of all countries in the context of global climate change. Developed countries, in particular, have issued major measures to develop green economy in response to climate change, making it rapidly become an important trend affecting the process of world economic development. In addition, in the process of economic globalization, the role of tariff barriers is increasingly weakened, and non-tariff barriers including "green barriers" are increasingly prominent. In recent years, some developed countries, in terms of resources and environment, require end products to meet the requirements of environmental protection, which has increasingly serious impact on China's foreign trade, especially the expansion of exports. Therefore, under the background of green international development, it is imperative and inevitable for China to promote green development. Through green development, it needs to accelerate technological innovation, improve technological level and international standards, so as to improve the international competitiveness and influence of China's economy.

In a word, green development is in line with China's national conditions of resources, environment and ecology. It is in line with the concept, objectives and requirements of China's ecological civilization building and the goals and requirements of China's national governance capacity and system building. At the same time, green development is in line with the requirements and aspirations of the people, especially the new era and new requirements for the general improvement of environmental awareness of Chinese citizens.

Green development is an inevitable choice at the current stage of China's development. The basic feature of the current stage is the development stage of the upper middle-income group. In this stage, the constraint of resources and environment on China's development has undergone six fundamental changes: (1) In terms of time, from short-term constraint to long-term constraint, the constraints of resources and environment on the sustainable development of social economy will be long term, continuous and even difficult to reverse. (2) In terms of spatial transformation from local constraint to overall constraint, resources and environment have and will have a long-term restrictive effect on the sustainable development of social economy in almost all regions of China. (3) In the field of change from a few constraints to a many constraints, resource and environment not only have significant constraints on resource-intensive industries or sectors, environmentally sensitive industries or sectors, but also have more and more significant direct or indirect constraints on more and more industries or sectors. (4) The change from a few to many constraints in terms of types, covering almost all types of resources, including water, land, energy, minerals and biological resources, and almost all environmental fields, including water environment, atmospheric environment and soil environment will have and will continue to have a significant constraints on socio-economic development. (5) From elastic constraint to rigid constraint in strength, the constraint of resources and environment on China's development has been rigid or even irreversible for a long time. In this context, it is necessary and urgent to explore the path and mode of China's sustainable development under the strong constraints of resources and environment. (6) In representation, it changes from recessive constraint to explicit constraint, the restraining effect of resources and environment on China's social and economic development and people's life is not only recognized by scientists, leading cadres and other social elites, but also widely recognized and alerted by more and more ordinary people. The consciousness of resource and environment crisis has become the mainstream of society.

In order to adapt to these changes, development transformation is necessary. Green transformation is the main direction and goal of development transformation.

7   STRATEGIC CONCEPT OF PROMOTING GREEN TRANSFORMATION AND DEVELOPMENT

7.1   General Idea

With the goal of promoting the green transformation of China's development pattern and the green adjustment of its economic structure, we should adhere to the principles of overall planning, step-by-step implementation, innovation guidance, scientific and technological support, overall promotion, key leap forward, moderate growth rate, reasonable structure, government guidance, market regulation, social participation and strengthening self-discipline, will set up nine major systems, namely the green production system, the green circulation system, the green distribution system, the green consumption system, the green construction system, the green policy system, the green market system, the green energy system and the green culture system. We should focus on key areas such as green philosophy, green transformation of traditional industries, green adjustment of industrial structure, vigorously developing green industries, steadily implementing green construction, encouraging the use of green energy, promoting energy conservation and consumption reduction, implementing green accounting as soon as possible, comprehensively strengthening environmental protection and actively participating in global cooperation. Making breakthrough in five key links, namely the innovation and large-scale application of green technology, improving the utilization efficiency of resources and energy, the extension and undertaking of producer social responsibility, construction of standard system of green economy statistics, making innovation in institutions and mechanisms for green economic development so as to promote the sustained and sound development of China's green economy.

7.2 Basic Principles

First, overall planning and step-by-step implementation. To make overall plans for the development of China's green economy, we should make a systematic layout, specify the timing, scale and structure of development, and promote coordinated development. We will actively carry out industrial demonstration, prevent overheated investment and redundant construction, and guide orderly development. Second, innovation and technology support. We will establish a system of technological innovation with enterprises as the main body, the market as the guide, and the combination of industry, academia and research institutes. We will work hard to improve the capacity for original and integrated innovation and the ability to introduce, digest and absorb new innovations, and raise the overall technological level of the industry. We will make breakthroughs in a number of key and core technologies and master relevant intellectual property rights. At the same time, we should strengthen policy support, coordination and guidance, train and give full play to the role of high-quality personnel, accelerate the transformation of innovation results and promote the industrialization process. We will continue to deepen reform, address both the symptoms and root causes and resolve deep-seated problems in redundant development through institutional innovation.

Third, overall progress and key breakthroughs. We will continue to combine improving the long-term competitiveness of the national economy with supporting current development. We need to take a long-term view, take new directions in the development of science, technology and industry, make early deployment in major frontier areas and cultivate as soon as possible a number of new pilot industries with high science and technology content, great development potential and strong driving force. At the same time, based on the current situation, we should promote the rapid development of relevant industries that play an important role in alleviating the bottleneck of economic and social development, promote the healthy development of high-tech industries, drive the transformation and upgrading of traditional industries and accelerate the formation of pillar industries. We will select the most basic and conditions of the field as a breakthrough, focusing on advancing. We will vigorously foster green industrial clusters and promote the development of advantageous regions in the first place.

Fourth, the growth rate is moderate and the structure is reasonable. We will ensure that the speed of development is consistent with the quality and efficiency of the structure. We should give top priority to development, maintain a reasonable scale and speed of development, optimize the economic structure and place greater emphasis on quality and efficiency while conserving resources and protecting the environment.

Fifth, government guidance and market regulation. We will give full play to the basic role of the market and combine it with government guidance and promotion. With the market as the guide and enterprises as the main body, we will give full play to the basic role of the market in allocating resources through deepening reform and innovating mechanisms. At the same time, for the important areas and key links of overall economic and social development, it needs to be integrated use of law, economy, technology, standards and necessary administrative means, coordinate industry, environmental protection, land and financial policies, government planning guidance, policy incentives and organizational coordinating role, formulate a special industrial policy and planning, which is conducive to develop green economy system environment, policy environment and market environment.

Sixth, social participation and self-discipline. Green development must become the consensus of the whole society, and it must be the common participation and joint efforts of the whole society. The degree of social participation in green development reflects the degree of social civilization. At the same time, every family and every social member must strengthen self-discipline, strictly restrain and regulate their own behaviors, and in particular, it is necessary to improve the ethics, morality, science and technology and cultural literacy of every social member.

Self-discipline, or not, is also an important symbol of the level of social civilization.

7.3 Key Areas

First, accelerate the green transformation of traditional industries. (1) Enhance the transformation and upgrading of traditional manufacturing industry. To develop the advanced manufacturing industry with the focus on revitalizing the equipment manufacturing industry, we need to rely on key construction projects, improve the localization of major technical equipment through independent innovation, technology introduction, cooperative development and joint manufacturing and raise the overall level of research and development and design, supporting core components, processing and manufacturing, and system integration. We will support accelerated technological upgrading in iron and steel, nonferrous metals, petrochemical, electric power and other industries to reduce energy consumption and improve the comprehensive utilization of resources. We will strictly implement the national industrial policy and project management regulations, strengthen the review of land use, energy conservation assessment and environmental impact assessment and strictly control new projects in industries with high energy consumption, high emissions and overcapacity. We will use it to drive and promote industrialization. We will encourage the use of high technology and advanced and applicable technologies to transform and upgrade the manufacturing sector and increase the proportion of independent intellectual property rights, independent brands and high-end products. (2) Promote clean production. In the production process, raw materials and energy are saved, toxic raw materials are eliminated and the quantity and toxicity of all wastes are reduced. From the acquisition of raw materials to the final treatment of products, reduce the negative impact of products on the environment. Incorporate environmental considerations into the design and delivery of services. (3) Encourage green development of enterprises. In accordance with the principles of ecology and ecological economics, an ecological production and operation management system shall be established, clean production shall be carried out, non-toxic and harmless production techniques and comprehensive utilization techniques shall be developed and ecological production or service processes shall be organized, which makes the whole enterprise technological process and management process ecological, changes the modern enterprise material production process or service process into natural ecological process or into natural ecological process, and forms the enterprise ecological pattern of ecological production and ecological life. It makes the best use of all kinds of natural resources and raw materials and energy put into the production process. It can greatly improve the utilization rate of resources and energy, reduce or even eliminate wastes and form an organic whole of ecological economy with less input, low consumption, high quality, no pollution and the production of products in line with ecological environmental standards, so as to realize the benign cycle and sustainable development of the ecological economy of enterprises.

Second, accelerate the transformation of green industrial structure. We will eliminate outdated technologies and equipment by adjusting the structure of industries, products and consumption of resources and energy. We will accelerate the development of the tertiary industry, which is mainly represented by the service sector, and the new and high technology industry, which is mainly represented by information technology. We will transform traditional industries with new and high technologies and advanced and appropriate technologies, promote the optimization and upgrading of the industrial structure and improve the overall level of technology and equipment in the industry. We will accelerate the formation of a national economic structure with high scientific and technological content, low resource consumption and good economic and environmental performance. (1) Promote the restructuring of key industries. We will promote structural adjustment in key industries such as equipment manufacturing, shipbuilding, automobile, metallurgy and building materials, petrochemical, textile, packaging, electronic information and construction. (2) Promote the development of the service industry. We will make it a strategic priority to promote the development of the service sector in optimizing and upgrading the industrial structure, foster a policy and institutional environment conducive to the development of the service sector, expand new areas, develop new forms of business and foster new hotspots. We will accelerate the development of producer services. We will deepen specialization, accelerate innovation in service products and service models, promote the integration of producer services with advanced manufacturing and accelerate the development of producer services. We will vigorously develop the domestic service industry. We will enrich the types of service products for both urban and rural residents, expand the supply of services, improve the quality of services and meet diverse needs. We will create an environment conducive to the development of the service sector. We will promote reform through opening-up and development through competition, promote institutional innovation in the service sector, improve the policy system for the service sector and improve the environment for the development of the service sector. (3) Adjust the industrial structure of raw materials. We will focus on adjusting the product mix, organizational structure and industrial layout of the raw materials industry to improve product quality and technological content in accordance with energy, resource conditions and environmental capacity. (4) Cultivate and develop strategic emerging industries. We will, on the basis of major technological breakthroughs and major development needs, promote the in-depth integration of emerging technologies with emerging industries and, on the basis of continuing to strengthen and expand high-tech industries, develop strategic emerging industries into leading and pillar industries. We will promote leapfrog development in key areas. We will vigorously develop strategic emerging industries such as energy conservation and environmental protection, new generation information technology, biotechnology, high-end equipment manufacturing, new energy, new materials and new energy vehicles. We will implement the industrial innovation and development program. With the goal of mastering core and key industrial technologies and accelerating industrial scale development, we will give full play to the leading and supporting role of major national science and technology projects. We will support business model innovation and market expansion, organize the implementation of several major industrial innovation and development projects and cultivate a number of key enterprises and demonstration bases in strategic emerging industries by relying on advantageous enterprises, industrial agglomeration zones and major projects. We will set up special funds and industrial investment funds for the development of strategic emerging industries, expand the scale of government investment in start-ups in emerging industries and bring into full play the role of the multi-level capital market in financing. We will encourage financial institutions to increase their credit support through a comprehensive use of favorable fiscal policies such as risk compensation. We will improve tax support policies that encourage innovation and encourage investment and consumption. We will accelerate the establishment of industry standards and a system of technical standards for key products that are conducive to the development of strategic emerging industries. Supporting the infrastructure construction of new product application creates a good environment for cultivating and expanding market demand.

Third, accelerate the transformation from traditional agriculture to modern agriculture. We will accelerate progress in agricultural science and technology, strengthen the building of agricultural facilities, adjust the structure of agricultural production, change the pattern of agricultural growth and increase the overall production capacity of agriculture. We will steadily develop grain production, accelerate the implementation of industrial projects to produce high-quality grain and build large commercial grain production bases to ensure food security. We will improve the distribution of agricultural production, promote the industrialized operation of agriculture, accelerate agricultural standardization, promote the processing, transformation and value-added of agricultural products, and develop agriculture with high yield, high quality, high efficiency, ecological protection and safety. We will vigorously develop animal husbandry, raise the level of scale, intensification and standardization, protect natural grasslands and build bases for feed grasslands. We will actively develop aquaculture, protect and rationally utilize fishery resources, promote green aquaculture methods and develop efficient and ecological aquaculture. We will develop raw material forest and timber forest base according to local conditions and improve the comprehensive utilization rate of wood. We will strengthen irrigation and water conservancy projects, transform medium-and low-yielding farmland and improve land consolidation. We will raise the level of agricultural mechanization and improve the systems for popularizing agricultural technologies, marketing of agricultural products, quality, safety of agricultural products and prevention and control of animal and plant diseases and insect pests. We will vigorously promote water-saving irrigation and use fertilizers and pesticides in a scientific way to promote sustainable agricultural development.

Fourth, accelerate the transformation of natural resources utilization mode. We will accelerate the transition from extensive and wasteful use of natural resources to intensive and economical use. We will vigorously promote energy conservation and consumption reduction in key areas such as industry, construction and transportation, and strengthen the conservation and intensive use of water, land and mineral resources.

Fifth, accelerate the green transformation of regional development. We will explore the path of green transformation with distinctive features in combination with the development foundation, resource and environmental characteristics, economic and social development orientation, development direction and development goals of different regions. The eastern region should play its own advantages and lead the way in green transformation. The green transformation in the central region should persist in protection during development; the green transformation in the Western region should persist in developing with protection. The green transformation of northeast China needs to persist in developing through restoration. We will adjust the layout of regional industries. We will raise the level of economies of scale and industrial concentration of enterprises, accelerate the development of large enterprises and form a number of large companies and enterprise groups with independent intellectual property rights, prominent main businesses and strong core competitiveness. We should give full play to the role of small- and medium-sized enterprises, encourage them to form a cooperative relationship with large enterprises on the basis of division of labor, raise the level of specialization in production and promote their technological progress and industrial upgrading. We should give full play to our comparative advantages, actively promote the rational flow and allocation of factors of production and guide the development of industrial clusters. Starting from the overall strategic layout of regional development and in accordance with the carrying capacity and development potential of resources and the environment, we will implement regional industrial layouts that distinguish between optimal development, key development, restricted development and prohibited development.

Sixth, accelerate the ecological construction ideas and mode transformation. We will increase forest carbon sink, continue to implement key state afforestation projects, actively implement carbon sink afforestation projects, deepen urban afforestation and strengthen forestry operations and sustainable management. With strict protection as the premise, we will ensure moderate growth of woodland scale. We will focus on increasing forest area to ensure that the goal of forest coverage is achieved. With scientific management as the core, we will improve forest quality and comprehensive benefits. To optimize the layout of the structure, we shall coordinate the regional forest land protection and utilization. With the innovation management system as the breakthrough, we shall form the new mechanism for woodland protection utilization management. Comprehensive protection of woodland: (1) strict use control. To optimize the layout of the structure, we shall coordinate the regional forest land protection and utilization, strictly restrict the conversion of forestland to construction land, strictly control the conversion of forestland into other agricultural land and strictly protect public welfare forest lands. We will intensify efforts to restore temporarily occupied forestland and catastrophic deforested land. (2) Implement hierarchical management. Scientific classification of forest protection grade; forest land protection and management by grade shall be implemented. (3) Strengthen forest protection. Strictly protect the forests; balance the forest area; curb forest degradation. (4) Actively supplement woodland. Increase the forest resources. Strengthen the regulation of idle land suitable for forestry. (5) Guide land conservation. Appropriate protection of woodland for national infrastructure and public construction use. Control the use of forest land for urban and rural construction; restrict the occupation of forestland by industrial and mining development; regulate the use of forest land for commercial operation; formulate prohibited and restricted catalogue of projects of requisition and occupation of forest land. Rational utilization of woodland: (1) Optimize the structure. Overall planning of public welfare forest land and commodity forest land; scientific adjustment of natural and artificial woodland structure. (2) Key guarantee points. Protecting land for ecological barrier; ensuring key public welfare forest lands; to safeguard the basic forestland for national timber and forest product production. (3) Scientific management. Establishing the forest land quality evaluation and grading system; implementing forest quality projects; we will implement the Woody grain and oil project. (4) Sustainable utilization. Accelerate the process of ecological restoration and afforestation; we will strengthen ecological management of degraded forest land in key regions. Overall regional management: (1) Optimize regional layout. Adjust and optimize the spatial distribution of forest land utilization. (2) Implement differential management. Actively protect and expand the green ecological space of the development zone; supporting the development of key development zones and ecological construction; ensuring and limiting the demand for ecological land in development zones; strictly protect the forest resources in development zones. (3) Strengthening macro-control. Strengthen national macro-control capability; strengthen the protection and utilization responsibility of provincial forestland; implement policies on the protection and utilization of regional forest land; continue to give top priority to conservation and natural restoration, intensify ecological protection and development, and reverse the trend of ecological and environmental degradation at its source. Build ecological security barrier, strengthen ecological protection and management and establish ecological compensation mechanism.

Seventh, accelerate the green transformation of infrastructure construction. (1) Strengthen the green transformation of energy infrastructure. We will strengthen the building of the power grid, optimize its structure and expand the transmission of electricity from west to east. We will build large coal bases, readjust and upgrade small and medium-sized coal mines, and encourage the pooling of coal and power. We will pursue simultaneous development of oil and gas, step up exploration, development and utilization of oil and gas resources, expand overseas cooperation in development and accelerate infrastructure development in the oil and gas sectors. (2) Strengthen the green transformation of transportation infrastructure. We will improve inter-regional transportation networks, build intercity rapid networks, give priority to the development of public transportation and make intensive and economical use of resources in planning, design, construction, operation, maintenance, management and service, promote resource recycling, vigorously promote energy conservation and emission reduction, and effectively protect and improve the ecological environment. Starting with the construction of an all-round sustainable transportation system, we will guide residents to adopt reasonable means of transportation, provide convenient and efficient transportation facilities, vigorously promote the development of urban buses, bicycles, electric vehicles and other means of transportation, and reduce fuel consumption and pollution emissions of the urban transportation system. (3) Strengthen the green transformation of water conservancy infrastructure. We will improve water conservancy infrastructure and, on the basis of continuing to improve large rivers, actively improve important tributaries, lakes and small- and medium-sized rivers to increase urban and rural water supply and flood control. We will improve the system for disaster prevention and reduction and strengthen our ability to withstand natural disasters. We will coordinate the allocation of groundwater resources in the upper and lower reaches of the Yangtze River, control groundwater exploitation and actively carry out desalination. We will strengthen the construction of flood control and drought relief projects, focusing on strengthening levees and controlling water conservancy hubs, strengthening weak links in flood control and disaster reduction, and continue to strengthen the main dikes of large rivers, reinforce flood storage areas, reinforce dangerous reservoirs and build key urban flood control projects. We will build the south-to-north water diversion project. We will intensify the construction and renovation of drinking water projects for people and livestock and supporting projects for irrigation areas. (4) Accelerate the green transformation of information infrastructure. We will strengthen information infrastructure such as broadband communications networks, digital television networks and the next-generation Internet, promote the integration of the three networks and improve the information security system. (5) Accelerate the green transformation of buildings. We will step up research and development of green building technologies and make innovations in building products that save energy, land, water and materials, carry out research on the green building design and construction standard system, and establish the green building evaluation index system, so as to provide people with healthy, applicable and efficient use of resources and space, and build a harmonious coexistence with nature; further strengthen oversight of energy conservation in new buildings. Check the air conditioning temperature of hotels, shopping malls, office buildings and other public places; promote the development of an energy conservation regulatory system for government offices and large public buildings and the development of energy-saving model universities; vigorously promote the energy conservation of existing buildings in northern heating areas; vigorously promote energy conservation and emission reduction in municipal public sector; study policies for energy saving and carbon reduction wastewater regeneration and sludge treatment and disposal in line with China's national conditions; actively guide the development of green buildings; promote the use of renewable energy in buildings; vigorously develop the low-carbon and green building industry and accelerate the development of energy efficient and waste industries such as recycling and treatment of construction waste, ready-mixed concrete and mortar, and bulk cement. (6) Accelerate the construction of comprehensive urban carrying capacity. We will adhere to the principles of putting people first, saving land and energy, protecting the environment, being safe and practical, giving prominence to distinctive features and protecting cultural and natural heritage. We will formulate urban plans in a scientific way, improve standards for urban development and strengthen the binding force of urban planning. We will rationally determine the boundaries of urban development, regulate the construction of new urban areas, raise the population density of built-up areas, adjust and optimize the structure of land used for construction, prevent the over-expansion of the area of megacities, and prevent and treat "urban disease". We will make overall planning for the construction of above-ground and underground municipal public facilities, improve infrastructure for transportation, communications, power supply, heat supply, gas supply, water supply and drainage, and sewage and garbage treatment, and strengthen our ability to prevent disasters such as fire fighting. We will expand urban green space and public activity space and accelerate the development of urban public cultural and sports facilities for the general public. We will promote the renovation of "villages in cities" and the urban and rural areas. We will strengthen the oversight of the construction market and standardize its order. We will deepen reform of the urban construction investment and financing system and issue bonds for the construction of municipal projects. We will strengthen comprehensive urban management, promote the construction of digital cities, improve the level of information and refined management services, pay attention to cultural inheritance and protection, improve the city's cultural environment.

Eighth, accelerate the green transformation of energy production and consumption. (1) Optimize the development of coal power generation with a focus on large and efficient units. We will develop safe and efficient coal mines, promote the integration of coal resources and the merger and reorganization of coal mining enterprises, and develop large coal enterprise groups. We will carry out research, development and demonstration of coal-to-natural gas, coal-to-liquid fuel and coal-based poly-generation in an orderly manner, and steadily advance industrialization. We will develop clean, efficient and large-capacity coal-fired power plants, give priority to the development of cogeneration units in large- and medium-sized cities and industrial parks, as well as comprehensive utilization power stations such as large coal burning power stations at pithead and coal gangues. We will strengthen clean production and utilization of coal and develop and disseminate efficient and clean combustion technologies. We will actively promote the industrialization of clean coal technology. (2) Rational utilization of oil and natural gas resources. We will step up exploration and development of oil and natural gas resources, stabilize domestic oil production, promote the rapid growth of natural gas production and promote the development and utilization of unconventional oil and gas resources such as coal-bed methane and shale gas. (3) Orderly development of hydropower on the basis of ecological protection. We will focus on the construction of large hydropower stations in southwest China, develop hydropower resources in small- and medium-sized rivers in light of local conditions, and scientifically plan and build pumped storage power stations. (4) Develop nuclear power efficiently on the basis of ensuring safety. We will accelerate the development of nuclear power in economically developed coastal areas, regions with concentrated power loads and provinces in central China that lack coal. (5) Accelerate the development of wind, solar, geothermal and biomass energy. In the "three north" and coastal areas rich in wind energy resources, build a number of 10 million kilowatt wind power base. We will strengthen the construction of supporting projects connected to the grid and effectively develop wind power. We will energetically develop solar energy, biomass energy, geothermal energy and other new energy sources, promoting the application of distributed energy systems.

Finally, accelerate the process of energy saving and consumption reduction. (1) Improve the incentive and restraint mechanism for energy conservation and emission reduction. Optimize the energy structure, reasonably control the total energy consumption, improve the pricing mechanism for resource products and environmental resources tax and fee system, and perfect the laws and regulations and standards for energy conservation and emissions reduction, strengthen energy conservation and emission reduction target responsibility appraisal, the resource conservation and environmental protection throughout the production, circulation, consumption, construction in various areas and each link and promote the sustainable development ability. (2) Adhere to and implement the policy of giving priority to energy conservation. Priority should be given to energy conservation in formulating and implementing development strategies, development plans, industrial policies, investment management and fiscal, tax, financial and pricing policies. In drawing up special plans, energy conservation should be taken as an important part and all regions should formulate medium- and long-term plans for energy conservation in light of their actual conditions. The demonstration and evaluation of energy saving should be strengthened in the project proposal and feasibility study report of the construction project; we will give high priority to energy conservation in promoting structural adjustment and technological progress. We will support energy conservation in the state's fiscal, taxation, financial and pricing policies. We will focus on the actions taken by thousands of enterprises to conserve energy, announce the assessment results, strengthen target responsibility, strengthen management of energy use, and raise the level of energy use. (3) Eliminate backward production capacity. Focusing on the steel, cement, plate glass, non-ferrous metals, coke, paper, leather, printing and dyeing industries, we will further accelerate the elimination of outdated production capacity, implement target responsibilities, improve policy constraints, establish incentive, supervision and inspection mechanisms and other comprehensive measures to ensure that tasks are completed on schedule. The people's governments at the provincial level shall be responsible for the formulation of the task of eliminating backward production capacity in their respective areas, and shall divide the task among cities, counties and relevant enterprises. Relevant departments should assign the task of eliminating backward production capacity in various regions, publish a list of enterprises to eliminate backward production capacity and ensure that backward production capacity is shut down as scheduled. We will implement a system for phasing out outdated and high-energy-consuming products and equipment, regularly publish a list of products and equipment that have been phased out and intensify supervision and inspection. Energy-consuming products or buildings that fail to meet the mandatory energy efficiency standards shall not be sold out of the factory or allowed to start construction. Penalties shall be increased for the production, sale and use of energy-consuming products and equipment that have been eliminated by the state and that consume too much energy. We will formulate development plans and policies for energy-intensive industries such as iron and steel, nonferrous metals and cement, and raise standards for industry access. We will formulate policies to restrict the use of energy in certain sectors, as well as the export of scarce domestic resources and energy-intensive products. Construction or expansion of conventional oil-fired generating sets is strictly prohibited; to limit the use and construction of gas turbines for diesel power generation and fuel oil under the condition that regional power supply is balanced and can meet the demand for electricity. (4) Comprehensively promote energy conservation and emission reduction. We will strictly control the excessive growth of industries that consume high energy and emit high emissions, focus on energy conservation in key areas such as industry, construction, transportation and public institutions, and strengthen management of energy conservation in key energy-using units. We will accelerate the implementation of key projects to conserve energy and reduce emissions. We will strengthen the assessment of energy conservation targets and improve the system of rewards and punishments. We will improve laws and regulations and standards for energy conservation, and formulate, improve and strictly enforce energy consumption quotas and energy efficiency standards for major energy-consuming products, and strengthen the assessment and review of energy conservation in fixed asset investment projects. We will improve the market-based mechanism for energy conservation, accelerate the implementation of contract energy management and power demand management, and improve energy efficiency labeling, certification of energy-efficient products and the system for mandatory government procurement of energy-efficient products. We will promote advanced energy-saving technology and products. We will strengthen capacity building for energy conservation. We will vigorously promote energy-saving technologies and products. We will launch a campaign to save energy and reduce carbon emissions in 10,000 enterprises and promote nationwide efforts to save energy and reduce emissions.

7.4   Key Measures

First, the green concept runs through the policy. The development of green economy as a major national strategy is included into the national economic and social development of the medium- and long-term planning. In the implementation of integrated environment and development decisions, economic stimulus programs and industrial restructuring and revitalization programs, we will integrate the concept, measures and actions of green economy, truly embody the scientific outlook on development and the requirements of "two-oriented" social construction, accelerate the formulation of green economy development plans and integrate the concept of green economy into the development plans of various departments and fields, and promote the comprehensive greening of all sectors of the national economy. First, formulate environmental and economic policies throughout the reproduction process, promote the price reform of resource products, promote the internalization of external costs of environmental pollution, formulate fiscal policies and tax policies conducive to environmental protection and levy environmental taxes. Second, actively study environmental policies and strengthen guidance on financial services and overseas investment in the field of environmental protection. Third, establish the statistical and evaluation mechanism of green economy, scientifically predict the development trend of green economy and provide effective support for formulating policies related to green economy development.

Second, the formulation of green economic development strategy planning. We will raise the development of the green economy to a national strategic level, formulate a strategic plan for the development of the green economy and define the strategic objectives, tasks and priorities of the development of the green economy. We will formulate a roadmap for the development of the green economy, carry out demonstration projects for the development of the green economy and ensure the development of the green economy through laws, regulations, standard systems, institutional arrangements, policies and measures.

Third, improve the green economy policy system. We will formulate and improve fiscal, tax, financial, insurance, investment and financing, industrial and other policies to promote the development of a green economy. We will increase government subsidies for the comprehensive utilization of resources, new energy, energy conservation, environmental protection and other green industries. We will implement tax policies and export tax rebates that are conducive to the comprehensive utilization of resources, new energy, energy conservation, environmental protection and other green industries. We will improve and strengthen green credit policies and give full play to the important role of finance in energy conservation, environmental protection and green industry development. Fourth, formulate supporting policies to support green development. We will give full play to the synergistic effects of addressing climate change, energy conservation and environmental protection, new energy development, and ecological improvement, actively explore institutions and mechanisms conducive to the development of a green economy, explore effective government guidance and economic incentive policies, and study the use of market mechanisms to promote the development of a green economy. Land supply according to law and regulations. Supply and use land according to laws and regulations.

Fifth, deepen reform of prices for resource products and charges for environmental protection. We will establish and improve a pricing mechanism for resource products that flexibly reflects market supply and demand, resource scarcity and environmental damage costs, and promote structural adjustment, resource conservation and environmental protection. We will improve the pricing mechanism for resource products. We will continue to reform water prices and improve the pricing policies for water resources, water conservancy projects and urban water supplies. We will actively promote the reform of electricity prices, carry out pilot projects for direct trading and bidding for electricity from large users, improve the mechanism for setting electricity prices for transmission and distribution, and reform the structure for classifying electricity prices for sale. We will actively implement a tiered pricing system for residential electricity and water. We will further improve the mechanism for setting prices for refined petroleum products and actively promote market-oriented reform, rationalize the price comparison between natural gas and alternative energy. In accordance with the linkage mechanism of price, tax, fee and rent, we will appropriately raise the resource tax burden, improve the method for calculating and levying tax, change the levying of important resource products from the levying of specific quantity and quota to the levying of specific price and fixed rate, and promote the rational development and utilization of resources. We will press ahead with the reform of the environmental fee system. We will establish and improve the polluter pays system and increase the collection rate for sewage charges. We will reform the way waste disposal fees are collected and appropriately raise the standard for waste disposal fees and government subsidies. We will improve the sewage charging system. We will energetically press ahead with the reform of environmental taxes and fees, and gradually expand the scope of environmental protection taxes by selecting items with heavy prevention and control tasks and mature technical standards. We will establish and improve the mechanism for trading resources and environmental property rights. We will introduce a market mechanism and establish a sound system for the paid use and trading of mining and pollutant discharge rights. We will standardize and develop the market for trading exploration and mining rights, develop the market for trading pollution rights, regulate the price behavior of trading pollution rights, improve the system of laws, regulations and policies, and promote the orderly flow of resources, environmental and property rights and open, fair and just trading.

Sixth, introduce a new mechanism for energy conservation based on the market mechanism. (1) Establish the energy conservation information release system, use modern information dissemination technology, timely release all kinds of energy consumption information at home and abroad, advanced energy conservation new technology, new process, new equipment and advanced management experience, guide enterprises to tap potential transformation, improve energy efficiency. (2) Comprehensive resource planning and power demand management shall be carried out, and the quantity saved shall be incorporated into the overall planning as resources to guide the rational allocation of resources. Take effective measures to improve the efficiency of terminal electricity consumption, optimize the mode of electricity consumption and save electricity. (3) Vigorously promote the implementation of energy-saving product certification and energy efficiency labeling management system and guide users and consumers to purchase energy-saving products by using market mechanism. (4) Carry out contract energy management, overcome the market barriers to the promotion of new energy-saving technologies, promote the industrialization of energy conservation and provide one-stop services of diagnosis, design, financing, transformation, operation and management for enterprises implementing energy conservation transformation. (5) Establish an investment guarantee mechanism for energy conservation and promote the development of energy conservation technology service system. (6) Voluntary agreement on energy conservation shall be implemented, that is, a voluntary agreement on energy conservation shall be signed between energy-consuming users or industry associations and the government.

CHAPTER 2

Make Full Use of the Experience of International Green Development

1 IT IS NECESSARY TO DRAW ON THE EXPERIENCE OF INTERNATIONAL GREEN DEVELOPMENT

Green development comes from green economy. The idea of a "green economy" comes from Rachel Carson's book *Silent Spring*. The purpose of green economy is to fight against the behavior of polluting environment and destroying ecology for the sake of economic development. With the increasingly obvious restriction of ecological environment on economic development, countries around the world have gradually realized the importance of living in harmony with the natural environment, and have taken measures to develop green economy. The United States, Europe, Japan and other major developed countries have taken active actions and formulated and advanced a series of plans to promote economic growth through the development of green economy. Some developing countries also have ambitious plans to create miracles in the development of "green economy".

It should be acknowledged that China, limited by its stage of development, still lags far behind many other countries, especially developed countries such as Europe, the United States and Japan, in developing green economy and promoting green development. These countries have conducted a lot of useful explorations and practices in terms of legal system building for green development, institutional transformation and institutional innovation, and have produced quite a few successful

S. Gu et al., *Green Transformation and Development*,
The Great Transformation of China,
https://doi.org/10.1007/978-981-32-9495-0_2

practices and typical experiences. As the largest developing country, China should be practical and realistic to study and draw lessons from foreign practices and experience of the development of green, combined with China's national conditions, the condition of the people, by localization transformation, the transformation and absorption, especially with the overall goal of ecological civilization construction, the overall deployment, accelerating the green transformation development in our country. It is beneficial and necessary to learn from the experience of green development abroad.

2   DRAW ON THE EXPERIENCE AND PRACTICES OF THE UNITED STATES IN GREEN ECONOMY

For a long time, the United States has been the world's largest producer, consumer and importer of energy. After a series of disasters such as resource destruction, environmental pollution and energy crisis, the United States began to take some measures and gradually embarked on the path of energy-saving and green development. In recent years, in order to cope with climate change and get rid of the economic difficulties caused by the financial crisis, the development of green economy has received unprecedented attention in the United States. At the same time, in order to promote green development and realize green recovery, the US government has introduced a lot of policies and measures to promote the economic transformation to a clean energy economy.

2.1   Pay Attention to Energy Conservation and Efficiency

On February 15, 2009, the United States enacted the *American Recovery and Reinvestment Act*, which aims to promote energy efficiency through capital investment and reduce energy consumption in multiple economic sectors. For example, the bill provides $5 billion for Weatherization Assistance, a $6500 grant to low-income homes to improve their energy efficiency; The bill also provides $3.2 billion for the Conservation BlockGrant program, most of which is used to help US states, local governments and native American tribes invest in projects to improve energy efficiency, reduce energy use and reduce fossil fuel emissions. At the same time, under the bill, the United States will focus on investing in advanced vehicle and fuel technologies, research and development and use of next-generation vehicle batteries, advanced biofuels, plug-in hybrid vehicles, all-electric vehicles and the infrastructure necessary to reduce America's dependence on oil for transportation. In addition, by improving traditional transportation and vigorously developing high-speed railways, more people are likely to choose railways or public transportation with low energy consumption. In the ACES act, it requires higher energy efficiency standards for industry, buildings, lighting, appliances, transportation, promotes energy efficiency labeling for buildings, develop smart transportation, implements energy conservation programs in the public sector, subsidizes the renovation of old buildings, rewards the recovery of electricity and heat energy and promotes contract energy management to increase energy efficiency.

2.2 Develop the Manufacturing Industry of Clean Energy and Related Equipment

In the Obama administration's proposed 2011 budget, the administration said it would invest in basic research and development in clean energy as part of a drive to transform the way energy is used and produced, while addressing climate change. At the same time, the United States is committed to developing the manufacturing of clean energy equipment, with an emphasis on manufacturing wind turbines, solar panels, electric cars, batteries, and other components of clean energy. As the United States transitions from dependence on fossil fuels to clean energy, demand for advanced energy products will increase significantly, and these investments will help clean energy manufacturers in the United States increase their manufacturing capacity to meet growing demand. The total is expected to exceed $90 billion by 2019.

2.3 Control Greenhouse Gas Emissions and Combat Climate Change

First, carbon capture and storage. Carbon capture and storage (CCS) is a method used to limit greenhouse gas emissions by capturing and sequestering carbon from the burning of fossil fuels and preventing it from entering the atmosphere. Of course, although some carbon has already been stored in the ocean or deep underground, there are still some persistent problems to be solved in terms of storage and so on. Under the *American Recovery and Reinvestment Act*, the United States invests primarily in core research, development, and demonstration of these technologies. In addition to the application of carbon dioxide capture and storage (CCS), the United States is also developing low-carbon fuels, plug-in electric vehicle infrastructure construction, promote large-scale transportation electrification, speed up the "smart grid" research and development and promotion, improve the power grid transmission and allocate, established the clean energy innovation center, etc., to reduce dependence on oil imports and ensure national energy security.

Secondly, the establishment of emissions data statistics. Since 2010, the United States has been collecting and compiling accurate greenhouse gas emissions data from various sectors of the economy, such as generators and cement producers. This statistical result provides an important basis for formulating policies to minimize carbon emissions.

Finally, clean energy and security laws. In June 2009, the US House of Representatives passed the *Clean Energy and Security Act of America* (ACES). The bill includes a cap-and-trade program and a goal of reducing greenhouse gas emissions by more than 80% by 2050.

2.4   *Establishing a Market Mechanism for Promoting the Transformation of the Clean Energy Economy*

First, establish a cap-and-trade system. The United States has used a cap-and-trade system to reduce sulfur dioxide (SO_2) emissions since 1995. According to the implementation results over the years, the cost of the total sulfur dioxide control and emission trading system has been greatly reduced compared with the expected cost and achieved good results. At the same time, a deposit and lending mechanism for emissions trading rights will be set up to make the polluter's emission reduction behavior have certain flexibility during the discharge period. Under this mechanism, with the change of transaction right price, the polluter can make a large degree of emission reduction when the transaction right price is higher and store the emission reduction right in the bank for later use. Similarly, firms can reduce their borrowing costs by future management, thus allowing them to discharge more pollution in the present. In addition, a price cap or floor has been set in the cap-and-trade system. Because while trading rights deposits and loans allow companies to control their emissions costs, they may not be able to prevent unexpected and potentially long-term changes in trading rights that could be affected by a recession or economic boom, fuel price fluctuations or technological breakthroughs. As a result, cap-and-trade schemes often include protection mechanisms to curb overpricing. For example, in the northeastern United States, the greenhouse gas trading system, when the price of a trading right exceeds a certain threshold, will enable some additional flexible terms to reduce the cost of enterprises.

Second, the establishment of offset trading system. Offset trading is also an important measure to reduce the cost of the cap-and-trade program. Offset trading refers to the "emission savings" that enterprises can purchase from other enterprises to reduce their emissions to meet their own emission needs. Since greenhouse gases are a global pollutant and have the same impact wherever they are emitted, offsetting trading strategies make it possible to achieve emission reduction targets at a lower cost.

Third, establish an international cooperation mechanism for emission reduction. Given the global nature of greenhouse gas emissions and the declining share of the United States in them, the United States alone will not be able to address the most serious risks posed by climate change. Therefore, international cooperation is extremely important in carbon emission reduction. To achieve this goal, the US government is actively working with major developed and emerging economies to reduce greenhouse gas emissions, reduce emissions intensity and promote economic development.

2.5 Formulating Relevant Laws and Regulations

In order to reduce energy consumption, the United States has promulgated the *National Energy Conservation Policies and Regulations*, *National Home Appliances Energy Conservation Act* and other bills. In order to meet the needs of the situation and strengthen energy conservation and new energy development, the United States promulgated the *National Energy Policy Act 2005* in 2005. The *Energy Policy Law*, with more than 1720 pages, 18 chapters and more than 420 clauses, is the most extensive energy law in the United States in nearly 40 years. Since taking office, US President Barack Obama has taken a more active stance on global climate issues, striving to develop a green economy as a major policy means to turn "crisis" into "opportunity" and revitalize the US economy, and pushing the controversial *US Clean Energy and Security Act* through the US congress.

3 Draw on the Experience of the EU in Green Development

The financial crisis that erupted in 2008 destroyed two decades of economic and social progress in European countries, while exposing structural flaws, slow growth, low productivity and a lack of investment in research and innovation. This eventually led to the outbreak of the European sovereign debt crisis, the rise of business bankruptcies and unemployment, and the emergence of the real economy recession. At the same time, the EU was striving to maintain its world leadership in tackling climate change and green and clean development. These problems have forced the EU to undertake reforms in the transition to a green economy.

3.1 Formulate a Green Plan or Action Plan

The EU is ahead of the world in tackling climate change and developing a low-carbon economy. In December 2008, the EU agreed on an energy and climate package covering six aspects: amendments to the emissions trading scheme, complementary measures and quota allocation directives for member states, CCS regulations, renewable energy directives, vehicle CO_2 emission regulations and fuel quality directives. In order to meet the challenge of climate change and achieve the three 20% targets (by 2020, the greenhouse gas emissions of the 15 EU countries will be cut by 20% on the basis of 1990. Renewable energy consumption will account for 20% of the total energy consumption in the EU, and energy efficiency will be improved by 20%) proposed by the EU, and drive the economic transformation toward high energy efficiency and low emissions, and to lead the world into the "post-industrial revolution" era, EU countries have developed national plans or action plans, and governments have put forward policies and measures to promote the development of low-carbon economy, so that enterprises, especially transnational corporations, can capture business opportunities.

On June 17, 2010, the leaders of the 27 EU countries formally adopted the *EU 2020 Strategy*. The main purpose of building a resource-efficient Europe is to support the transformation of the European economy into a resource-efficient and low-carbon one, achieve economic growth by reducing the use of resources and energy, and ensure energy security. The main measures include: improving energy and resource efficiency; developing new green transport modes, improving the overall efficiency of the EU transport system and stimulating the development of emerging industries; giving full play to the role of the network; accelerating the development of information and communication technology; helping small and medium-sized enterprises improve their ways of production and operation and save energy and reduce emissions.

3.2   Develop New and Renewable Energy Industries

The new energy industry is the focus of low-carbon economy and also the focus of increased investment in the world after the financial crisis. For example, the European Union has pledged to raise the share of renewable energy in energy consumption to 20% by 2020, reduce the consumption of coal, oil, natural gas and other fossil fuels by 20% and reduce the share of biofuels in transportation energy consumption by 10%. The UK leads the world in the development of low-carbon energy such as offshore wind energy and seaweed energy. In 2008, China set a target of building 33 GW of wind capacity within 10 years, which could power 25 million homes. In December 2008, the French Environment Ministry unveiled a package of 50 measures to develop renewable energy, including biofuels, wind, geothermal, solar and hydropower. In addition to the vigorous development for renewable energy, the French government spent 400 million euros in 2009 on research and development for clean energy vehicles and "low-carbon vehicles". In addition, nuclear energy has been a pillar of France's energy policy and a focus of its green economy.

3.3   Reduce the Cost of Greenhouse Gas Emission Reduction by Economic Means

The market means to reduce carbon emissions mainly include emission trading and carbon tax, etc. The EU has good experience in this respect. In carbon trading, there are plan-based and project-based emissions trading—the former is the trading market of the European Union, the United Kingdom, etc., and the latter is the voluntary emission trading of the Chicago board of trade. In the amendment to the EU Emission Trading System (EUETS) in 2008, the EU adjusted the scope of coverage, the method for determining emission caps, the allocation of quotas and the use of emission reduction credits, and setting emission caps for non-EUETS coverage and provided that by 2020, emissions from transportation, construction, agriculture and waste utilization be reduced by an average of 10% compared with that in 2005. The UK's economic policy instruments include an emissions trading scheme, a carbon fund, etc. The government also supports the establishment of a carbon credit fund to support the creation of low-carbon, high-growth enterprises. Norway, Sweden, the Netherlands, Denmark, Germany and the UK have all introduced carbon taxes. Norway has imposed a $50 per ton carbon tax on more than 60% of carbon dioxide emissions since 1991. In 1991, Sweden introduced a carbon dioxide tax on oil, coal, natural gas, liquefied petroleum gas, gasoline and domestic aviation fuel, based on the average carbon content and calorific value of the fuel. Practice shows that the adjustment of tax policy can not only promote the improvement of energy efficiency, the development of renewable energy and emission reduction, but also promote the economic development.

3.4   Promote a Low-Carbon Lifestyle

The EU attaches great importance to the construction of low-carbon lifestyle. For example, in the aspect of transportation, the EU requires the carbon emission of cars to be reduced to the level of 120 g/km by 2012. It is clearly proposed to develop decarbonized transport, develop intelligent, upgraded and comprehensively interconnected transport modes, as well as supporting infrastructure and give full play to the role of information and communication technology. It promotes the construction of hybrid infrastructure, accelerates the construction of power grid and power infrastructure, strengthens the management of intelligent transportation, launches the "green" vehicle plan to reduce carbon dioxide emissions of road vehicles, and develops hybrid electric vehicles and hybrid technology. They work together to develop new standards. Britain has a number of means to steer people towards a low-carbon lifestyle. For example, it requires all new homes to be carbon neutral by 2016, at least one-third of new homes to have a carbon footprint reduction plan, with zero disposable plastic bags, and so on. The London government believes that measures to tackle climate change, including energy conservation and energy efficiency, should not reduce the original quality of life, stressing that "it is not necessary to reduce the quality of life, but to change the way of life". Finland's low-carbon lifestyle starts with concrete energy saving actions. Without slogans or catchword, finns have many energy-saving habits, such as manual elevator doors, non-use of removable paper towel, use of peat (A coal with a low degree of metamorphism) for electricity, and wood for fuel. Also, no one leaves an office building with the lights on or over-wraps gifts. In a word, low carbon society requires people to live a good life, but not extravagant.

3.5 Strengthen International Cooperation on Carbon Emission Reduction and Low-Carbon Economy

Climate is the world's largest public good, a country is difficult to achieve carbon reduction task, so Western countries strengthen mutual cooperation. Together with eight industrial powers and EU partners, the United Kingdom is working to develop technologies to combat climate change, to meet its carbon reduction targets and to get the most out of it by helping other countries, particularly the developing countries meet their carbon reduction targets. Germany has cooperated with many countries, especially developing countries in the field of climate protection, strengthened coordination with the United States and initiated the trans-Atlantic climate and technology action between the European Union and the United States. The focus was on harmonizing standards and developing common research plans, and specific measures for this action were identified at the EU-US summit in April 2007.

4 DRAW LESSONS FROM JAPAN'S EXPERIENCE IN GREEN DEVELOPMENT

Japan is one of the earliest countries to produce the idea of green economic development, one of the earliest countries to practice the green economic development model, and one of the countries with relatively successful green economic development at present.

4.1 Development of the Green Economic Model

After the Meiji restoration in the late nineteenth century, Japan quickly embarked on the road of modern industrialization. However, due to the lack of resources, Japan has to rely on imports. The huge contradiction between the passive supply of resources and the growing demand for industrial development forces Japan to constantly explore and change its economic development model.

First, the incubation period of green economic model. The scarcity of resources in the Second World War forced Japan to seek alternatives to resources and advocate the conservation of materials and energy. In 1941, Japanese militarism launched the Pacific war in order to plunder strategic resources and realize the ambition of global hegemony. However, the war not only caused disasters and sufferings to the people of Asian countries, but also made Japan more short of resources. Subsequently, the maritime supply lines were blocked, which objectively accelerated its defeat. After the war, Japan, deeply constrained by resources, laid the foundation for the change of Japanese economic model in terms of material substitution and economy.

Second, the beginning of the green economy model. After Second World War, Japan devoted itself to economic development and achieved the rapid economic growth from the 1950s to the 1970s. By 1968, Japan's GDP ranked second in the world. However, in exchange for rapid economic growth at the expense of the environment, environmental pollution, ecological destruction and imbalance and other environmental hazards occurred frequently. During this period, Japan became a world-famous "public hazard country". In this regard, the Japanese government has put the problem of solving public hazards on the agenda and formulated and implemented a number of public hazards prevention and control laws, which effectively stimulated the development of Japan's green economy. In the mid-1970s, Japan's economic development entered a stable stage, and a resource-saving economic model was basically formed, which laid a foundation for the establishment of a green economy.

Third, the development period of green economic model. Since the 1990s, Japan has become a big waste producer in developed countries. The occurrence of dioxins from waste incineration has once again aroused people's concern about waste disposal. To this end, the Japanese government began to revise the *Waste Disposal Law* for many times in 1991, and successively introduced laws on the utilization of renewable resources, such as the *Recycling Law of Containers and Packages* and the *Recycling Law of Household Appliances*. The implementation of the policy of resource recycling has strongly promoted the development of Japan's green economy. The green economy has been slowly coming to be accepted.

Fourth, the emergence period of the green economy mode under the global financial crisis. In 2008, the subprime mortgage problem in the United States broke out and rapidly evolved into the largest global financial crisis after Second World War, which was worse than before for the long-term depressed Japanese economy, causing the Japanese economy to fall into the historical trough again. The financial crisis has renewed Japan's search for a new economic model. The green economy is gaining ground. In April 2009, Japan released a draft policy entitled *Green Economy and Social Change*, which proposed to vigorously develop green economy, increase green demand and promote green technological innovation. It will inject green vitality into the Japanese economy and help it recover from the crisis. Meanwhile, it will cope with the increasingly serious environmental crisis, promote the coordinated development of environment, resources and economy, and achieve the unity of low-carbon society, circular society and harmonious coexistence of nature.

4.2   Main Policies and Practices of Japan in Developing Green Economy

At present, the main feature of Japan's green economic development model is that the government starts from increasing the demand for green products and services and green technological innovation, gradually promotes the green awareness and ability of market players, gives full play to the role of local governments and non-governmental organizations, strengthens international cooperation and gradually creates a large and sound green market. The main policies are as follows:

Promote the "Greening" of Infrastructure Construction
First, green transformation of public infrastructure such as primary and secondary school buildings. Installing solar power installations in primary and secondary school buildings. In accordance with the *Greenhouse Gas Emission Control Measures Plan for Government Facilities* approved by the cabinet, low-carbon transformation of central government office facilities will be carried out, and local government facilities and parks and other public places under their management will be gradually transformed.

Second, strengthening the construction of compact cities and low-carbon transportation. We will build a new generation of urban basic transportation, including pedestrian spaces, bicycle spaces and rail transit systems, strengthen the intensive construction of urban functional areas and promote the economical use of untapped resources in urban rivers and groundwater.

Third, improving the quality of our land. Control illegal dumping of industrial household refuse; carry out integrated management of attached and drifting garbage across regions; carry out harmless disposal of toxic waste.

Fourth, natural disaster prevention capability. Transforming the natural environment of national parks and other places to ensure the water quality of river courses; protection of forest resources; establishing emergency facilities to respond to natural disasters caused by climate change.

Promote the "Greening" of National Living Consumption

Promote the consumption of energy-saving household appliances, rely on green points to popularize green household appliances, use green product identification, guide the consumption of energy-saving household appliances, use fiscal subsidies and tax breaks to promote the consumption of energy-efficient or new energy vehicles, promote the deployment of biofuel supply facilities and fast car charging facilities, and promote the use of biofuels. Government departments take the lead in using the new generation of automobiles; develop energy-efficient buildings, support innovation in insulation, revise LCA guidelines, implement the 200-year housing plan and develop fuel cells and heat pumps; at the national level, the government green procurement system was first introduced and then gradually promoted to the local level.

Enhance the "Greening" of Enterprises' Production and Investment

First, establishing a green economy operation system. To expand the domestic credit trading system and steadily promote the voluntary domestic carbon emission trading system (JVETS) led by the Ministry of Environment, in accordance with the provisions of the *Trial Measures for the Comprehensive Domestic Market of Carbon Trading*, which was implemented in October 2008; Promote carbon neutrality and carbon footprint.

Second, promoting green business practices. Promote the construction of ISO40001, Eco action21 and other environmental management systems to improve environmental management; accelerate the introduction of environmental management systems such as environmental reporting and environmental accounting; develop corporate biodiversity conservation responsibility guidelines.

Third, promoting the development of recycling industry. Strengthen the construction of good material recycling industry; promote low carbonization of waste disposal system.

Fourth, improving the green investment and financing system. Expand the financing of environmental equipment, invest in environment-friendly enterprises and industries, and evaluate the "environmental capability" of enterprises. For example, preferential loans for environmental protection have low interest rates and long repayment periods, with a general repayment period of 15 years, and the interest rate is 1~2% lower than the market rate: Loans to small and medium-sized enterprises amount to 520 million yen, and loans to large enterprises amount to 40% of their total environmental protection expenses. The government makes up for the shortage of funds received by enterprises from private financial institutions and makes up for the shortage of funds in long-term areas that are difficult for private financial institutions to reach. It has effectively promoted enterprises to implement environmental protection and successfully transformed enterprises into the main subject of environmental protection investment.

Fifth, the green transformation of the energy structure. We will formulate development plans for renewable energy and improve the policy for generating electricity from new energy sources. We will carry out trials for smart power grids. Making full use of local resources, such as developing small hydropower and geothermal energy; we will steadily develop nuclear power.

Strengthen Research and Development of "Green" Technologies

In the field of technology research and development, we will strengthen research and development of technologies that are both economic and environmental friendly, promote research on environmental and economic policies, and formulate a medium- and long-term roadmap for building a "low-carbon society".

Due consideration should be given to the advanced nature of technological development to develop technologies that will be popularized in 10–20 years, such as photovoltaic, solar thermal utilization, biomass energy, wind power, small hydropower and geothermal energy, LED lighting, high-performance thermal insulation materials without fluorocarbon compounds and energy-saving appliances.

We will strengthen research and development of technologies to address climate change, and study the impacts of climate change on water, food, ecosystems and disaster prevention. From a long-term perspective, we should consider the technological development of climate greenhouse gas emission reduction, and accelerate the development of solar cells, electric vehicles, CCS, methane hydrate, energy allocation system, and we shall the use of non-fossil energy to produce hydrogen and nuclear fusion energy; we will actively participate in the formulation of international standards and strengthen environmental monitoring and management and information collection and analysis.

Attach Importance to and Mobilize Local Governments and Civil Society to Develop Green Economy
To build an organizational structure centering on local public bodies (Japanese local administrative organs). Establish local green construction fund to support local green economy development; build an environmentally friendly local transportation system; prevent and control air pollution, water pollution and other public hazards. We will attach great importance to promoting the role of non-governmental organizations in protecting the natural environment and training talents and establish local organizations for the purpose of cultivating talents.

We will strengthen support for non-governmental organizations and corporate public welfare activities, construct a circular society between cities and regions and promote the recycling of renewable resources, water resources, phosphorus and other elements.

Set up corresponding environmental protection service organizations to provide technical and financial support to private enterprises and local governments. Set up JRC. Through the Japanese government's finance and investment loan program, JRC mainly engages in the construction and transfer of pollution control projects and provides loans to private enterprises and local governments. It has played a leading role in guiding investment in pollution control, successfully driving private capital in the market and guiding the majority of small and medium-sized enterprises to become the main subject of investment in pollution prevention and control: In construction and transfer projects and loan projects, JEC plays the role of technical consultant, especially in loan projects. JEC's suggestions and guidance on the technical rationality and investment scale of enterprises promote the pollution control of enterprises.

International Cooperation on Green Development
In terms of international cooperation, seek cooperation at different levels, including enhanced cooperation based on the Clean Asia Initiative; strengthen cooperation in personnel, technology and funds; developing Asian standards for green technologies; conduct extensive collaborative

research with different institutions such as universities. We will establish an information-sharing platform to promote Asia's circular economy and social development. At the same time, strengthen air pollution detection and afforestation activities.

5 DRAW ON THE EXPERIENCE OF SOUTH KOREA IN GREEN DEVELOPMENT EXPERIENCE

South Korea is a resource-poor country. Since the 1990s, due to the long-term implementation of extensive economic growth mode, resource consumption is too high. The growth mode of "high energy consumption and high pollution" is difficult to create enough jobs, and South Korea is trapped in the economic growth dilemma of "low employment rate and low growth rate". In order to accelerate the transformation of traditional energy-intensive manufacturing economy, South Korea will set green growth as the axis of future development. It is hoped that by vigorously developing the green technology industry to enhance the ability to cope with climate change, improve the rate of energy independence and national green competitiveness, and finally achieve long-term sustainable economic growth, and to this end, a series of effective measures have been taken.

5.1 *Establish a Regulatory System and New Standards to Promote the Achievement of Emission Reduction Targets*

Enhancing the ability to cope with environmental change is an important part of South Korea's green growth strategy. At the G8 Summit held in July 2008, South Korea proposed a voluntary carbon dioxide emission reduction target of 30% by 2020. In order to implement this target, South Korea adopted the following four systems:

First, South Korea requires emitters to buy emissions from a "carbon market" if they exceed the legal limit. South Korea's carbon market, which limits annual carbon dioxide emissions to 600 million tons, requires companies, construction sites and large buildings with annual emissions of more than 3000 tons to enter the market. The carbon market is managed by South Korea's environment ministry. At present, 30 large companies, factories and three supermarkets, including Hyundai Motor and Samsung Electronics, have been added to the carbon trading system.

Second, establishing a greenhouse gas inventory reporting system. The South Korean government will implement a greenhouse gas emission and energy use target management system for more than 600 enterprises with high greenhouse gas emissions nationwide. Enterprises selected by the government shall follow the emission reduction targets and energy use saving targets set by them, and report their emission reduction and energy use. The government shall supervise and inspect the target enterprises.

Third, the establishment of carbon credits system. Carbon credits system is an emission reduction system mainly aimed at national individuals. "Carbon credits" are calculated according to the saving amount of water and electricity, that is, one credit is gained for every 10 grams of carbon dioxide emission reduction. Households and businesses that save water, electricity and gas receive carbon credits, and the government awards residents and businesses based on how many carbon credits they receive in a year. Funding for the awards came from the government budget, with the central and local governments taking 50% each. Incentives will be offered in the form of cash, resident transportation cards, shopping cards, vouchers for the use of public facilities, local tax breaks and property fee waivers and so on.

Fourth, establishing an environmental risk assessment system. In order to cope with climate change, in addition to strict regulation on energy conservation and emission reduction, the government has also established an environmental risk assessment system to assess the impact of climate change, agriculture, biodiversity, health and water quality changes, so as to improve the government's ability to respond to climate change.

5.2   Improve Energy Efficiency and Increase Energy Conservation

Because of the large gap between South Korea's energy consumption and that of other OECD countries, the country's green growth strategy places great emphasis on improving energy efficiency and saving energy.

The first is to sign energy use agreements with high-energy-consuming enterprises. Companies whose energy consumption exceeded 500,000 TOE (tons oil equivalent) in 2010, 50,000 TOE in 2011 and 20,000 TOE in 2012 are all targets for the government to negotiate and sign energy consumption agreements.

Second, establishing an energy consumption reporting system for transportation enterprises, implementing new fuel efficiency standards and promoting the use of hydrogen-powered vehicles. We will promote the use of light-emitting diode (led) lighting, ban incandescent lighting, and improve the efficiency of lighting energy use.

Third, building low-carbon villages and green and energy-efficient houses, and promoting energy-saving renovation of buildings. By 2020, 600 low-carbon green villages and 1 million energy-efficient green houses will be built in South Korea, and existing houses will be retrofitted for energy conservation.

Fourth, the establishment of smart grid system. The South Korean government plans to set up a smart grid system by 2030 to improve energy production and consumption efficiency across the board.

Fifth, setting a cost-based electricity price to encourage businesses and households to change the way they consume energy. The government subsidized energy prices for low-income households, reducing the share of energy expenditures in the total income of 10% of households from 7.3% in 2009 to 5.0% in 2013.

5.3 Improve the Fuel Efficiency of Transportation and Improve the Urban Transportation Network

South Korea, the world's fifth largest auto maker, has much to do to reduce energy consumption by making transportation more fuel efficient.

First, improving automobile fuel efficiency and emission standards. In the *Green Growth Five-Year Plan* formulated in 2009, South Korea explicitly required that the fuel consumption and emission standards of automobiles be raised to 17 kilometers per liter of gasoline mileage, and all automobiles should meet the standards by 2015.

Second, actively promoting the use of renewable transport fuels. The government plans to pass a renewable fuel standard to encourage carmakers to offer dual-fuel vehicles that run on biodiesel, bioethanol and gas, and to make biodiesel use 7% of the total by 2020.

Third, investment in building a public transport system to increase the number of people who ride bicycles. The government invested in the construction of urban public transport systems and railway networks, greatly increasing the capacity of urban public transport. To promote green transportation, the government is also laying thousands of meters of bike lanes across the country. The paving of bicycle lanes will significantly increase the cycling rate.

5.4   Building Water Source Protection and Ecological Infrastructure

Due to the deterioration of the environment and climate, the incidence of drought and flood disasters is also increasing year by year. The South Korean government invests 4.3 billion us dollars annually in the construction and maintenance of disaster prevention facilities. In order to improve the ability to protect water resources and improve the ecological environment, South Korea mainly adopts the following measures:

First, the implementation of river restoration projects. The main purpose is to protect water resources, reduce the pressure of water scarcity, control the flood, improve water quality and restore ecosystems, create multi-functional space for local residents, promote regional economic development in the river center.

Second, strengthening green infrastructure. In terms of construction of sewage treatment and algae control facilities, by the end of 2009, South Korea had built 323 sewage treatment facilities and 58 wastewater treatment facilities.

Third, building an ecosystem monitoring network. Since 2007, more than 929 kilometers of small rivers in 540 regions have been included in the monitoring system. In order to promote ecosystem restoration, South Korea will also carry out 120 regional river reconstructions and rebuild 84 river coastal wetlands. Ecosystem restoration projects could create 340,000 jobs and generate $31.1 billion in local economic benefits.

5.5   Formulate Policies to Promote Green Growth

Time-limited and targeted fiscal, taxation and financial incentive policies are the basic factors to promote green economic transformation. The main policies adopted by the South Korean government are as follows:

First, increasing government green investment. The government injected $83.6 billion, or about 2% of gross domestic product, into green growth between 2009 and 2013.

Second, providing tax incentives to encourage private capital to invest in green industries. We will exempt green deposits from interest income tax and offer tax breaks on the interest earned by private individuals on bonds invested in green industries.

Third, the establishment of green funds and credit guarantee funds. The South Korean government has launched a "Green Fund" (about us $400 million) to provide financial support for SMEs to make green investments. It set up a green loan guarantee fund and the amount of guaranteed capital was increased from $1.9 billion in 2009 to $5.4 billion in 2013.

5.6 Establishing Relevant Supporting Laws and Systems

At the end of August 2008, the Republic of Korea released the *National Basic Energy Plan*, calling for increasing energy independence, reducing the proportion of coal and oil consumption and increasing the proportion of new and renewable energy. In September 2008, the *Low-Carbon and Green Growth Strategy* put forward the implementation of the "green technology and clean energy to create new growth drivers and employment opportunities" of the new development model, to achieve high energy consumption from the manufacturing economy to the service economy. On January 6, 2009, the state council of the republic of Korea adopted the "green project" plan, which proposed to provide new growth impetus for the future development of the South Korean economy through green investment, and put forward the three "green New Deal" goals of "creating jobs, expanding future growth momentum and basically establishing low-carbon growth strategy". On January 13, 2009, the *Outlook and Development Strategy for New Growth Drivers* was formulated, and 17 new growth drivers, including renewable energy, were identified to guide future development. On April 14, 2010, the *Basic Law on Green Growth* was formally implemented, further clarifying South Korea's green growth strategy in the form of national laws.

CHAPTER 3

The Pressure of Green Transformation and Development

1   INTERNAL OBJECTIVE PRESSURE ON CHINA'S GREEN TRANSFORMATION AND DEVELOPMENT

1.1   Resource Constraints

Long-Term Tight Constraints on Land Resources

China occupies 1/15 of the world's land area, ranking the third in the world. In 2012, the per capita land area was 0.0071 square kilometers, and the per capita level in the world was 0.018 square kilometers. China is 39% of the world's average. The per capita arable land is 0.08 hectares, compared with 0.2 hectares in the world. The per capita arable land in China is 40% of the world average. China has a large area of land that cannot be used, such as deserts, gobi and bare rock mountains, which account for 23.49% of the country's total land area. China has insufficient reserve land resources, with only 14.5% of the total cultivated land. According to the second national land survey, in 2009, China's arable land was 135.4 million hectares, and in 2012, it was 135.1 million hectares, with a decrease of 0.0027 million hectares. A considerable part of cultivated land in China needs to be returned to forest, grass, wet soil and fallow, and a considerable amount is not suitable for farming due to pollution. And a certain number of them have been affected by the destruction of the topsoil layer and the overexploitation of

© The Author(s) 2019   55
S. Gu et al., *Green Transformation and Development*,
The Great Transformation of China,
https://doi.org/10.1007/978-981-32-9495-0_3

groundwater and so on. Accordingly, farmland protection situation still is austere. With the development of industrialization and urbanization, construction land continues to expand. From 1996 to 2012, the area of cultivated land and garden increased, the area of grassland and forest decreased, and the area of residential and industrial land increased (see Figs. 1 and 2). China's urban built-up areas are expanding faster than its urban population. In addition, the structure and layout of urban land use are unreasonable. The proportion of industrial land in cities is too large. The proportion of land for commercial services and municipal environment is lower than that of foreign comprehensive cities (5 ~ 10%).

The Overall Constraint of Energy and Resources Is Too Tight
China's per capita coal, oil and natural gas are only 69, 6.2 and 7.7% of the world average, respectively. With the development of economy and society and the acceleration of industrialization and urbanization, the large-scale construction of infrastructure and housing in China needs a large number of energy-intensive products, and the increment of energy used by residents keeps increasing. In the past 30 years and more, China's total energy production increased from 628 million tons of standard coal in 1978 to 3.4 billion tons in 2013, and its total energy consumption increased from 571 million tons of standard coal in 1978 to 3.75 billion tons of standard coal in 2013. China is the world's largest producer and consumer of energy. China's energy consumption structure is dominated by coal. In 2013, coal accounted for 75.5% of China's

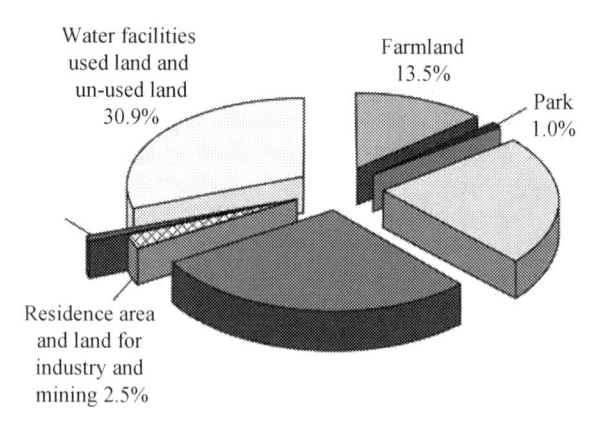

Fig. 1   General situation of land use in China in 1996

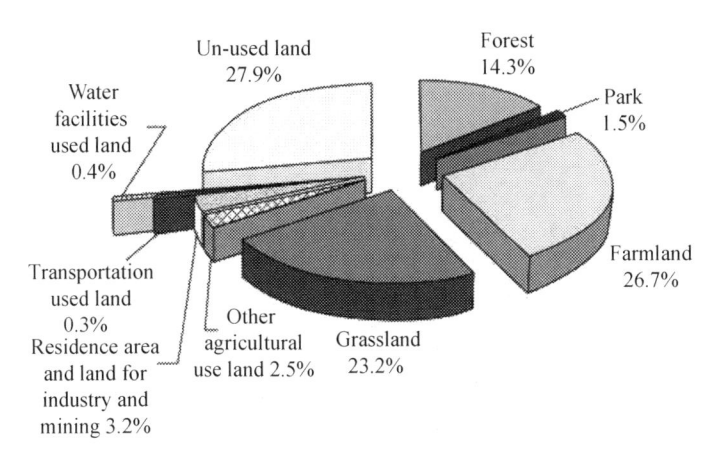

Fig. 2 General situation of land use in China in 2012

disposable energy, and China's coal consumption accounted for 50.31% of the world's total consumption. It is compiled according to the BP statistical review of world energy 2014 workbook. China's energy shortage looms large. According to the comparison between the mining amount and the proved reserves, based on the mining amount in 1950, China's coal can be mined for 3816 years. According to the amount of mining in 2000, it can be mined for 88 years. According to the amount of mining in 2011, China will be without coal in 33 years. Wang Wentao, Liu Yanhua. *China's Energy Outlet for Sustainable Development*. Chinese Society for Sustainable Development (ed.) *Green Development: A Global Perspective and China's Choice*, People's Post and Telecommunications Press, 2014, page 9. Since 1993, China has become a net importer of oil. In 2013, China imported a net 299 million tons of oil, and its dependence on foreign countries was 58.98%. Since 2007, China has become a net importer of natural gas. In 2013, China imported 446 million cubic meters of natural gas, and its dependence on foreign countries was 27.53%. Even relatively rich coal resources need to be imported in large quantities. Since 2011, China has become a net importer of coal, with a net import of 170 million tons in 2013 and dependence on foreign countries was 4.43% (see Fig. 3). The contradiction between supply and demand of energy resources is increasingly prominent in China. In 2009, the United Nations released the *World Water Development Report: Water in A Changing World*, and China was listed as a country with severe

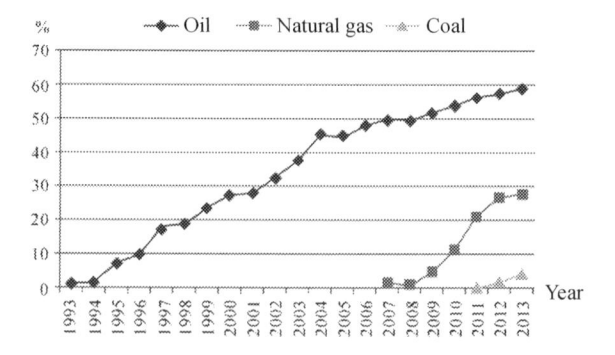

Fig. 3   China's energy dependence on foreign countries in the past 20 years

water shortage. Over the past 50 years, China has lost more than 1000 lakes, with an average of 20 lakes drying up each year. Of the 665 cities, nearly 400 are short of water, and about 200 are severely short of water. China's cities are short of water by 16 million cubic meters per day and 6 billion cubic meters per year. Water shortage has become a normal situation in China.

China's Water Shortage Has Long Restricted Social and Economic Development
In 2013, China's per capita water resources were 2059.7 cubic meters, only one-fourth of the world's per capita level, and the spatial and temporal distribution of water resources was seriously uneven.

The Problem of Resource Depletion (Region) Is Prominent
In 2008, 2009 and 2011, China identified 69 resource-exhausted cities (counties and districts) in three batches. The irrationality of the industrial structure of resource-based cities is increasingly prominent. When the pillar industry of resource-based city declines, the whole city will be in an embarrassing situation of more input, less output and poor benefit. The problem of sustained economic growth and social stability in resource-exhausted regions or cities has become an important factor affecting the sustained economic growth and social stability of the whole country. Such areas are often vulnerable to becoming "problem areas" or "trouble areas". In this regard, special attention should be given to the process of transformation and development.

1.2 Environmental Constraints

China's increasingly serious water pollution, air pollution and solid waste pollution have poisoned the ecosystem, directly affecting people's quality of life and even threatening people's life safety.

The Pressure of Water Pollution Persists

In 2013, China discharged 69.544 billion tons of wastewater, including 23.527 million tons of chemical oxygen demand (cod) and 2.457 million tons of ammonia nitrogen. The country's surface water is generally mildly polluted. Of China's top ten river systems, IV ~ V classes and poor V class water quality section ratio were 19.3 and 9.0%, respectively; part of the urban river pollution is heavier. In the water quality of provincial boundary waters, IV ~ V classes and poor V class water quality section ratio were 18.2 and 19.5%, respectively. The proportions of mild pollution, moderate pollution and severe pollution in lakes (reservoirs) were 26.2, 1.6 and 11.5%, respectively. The proportions of eutrophication, moderate nutrition and poor nutrition were 27.8, 57.4 and 14.8%, respectively. Among the monitoring points of groundwater environmental quality, the proportion of poor and extremely poor was 43.9 and 15.7, respectively, as shown in Fig. 4.

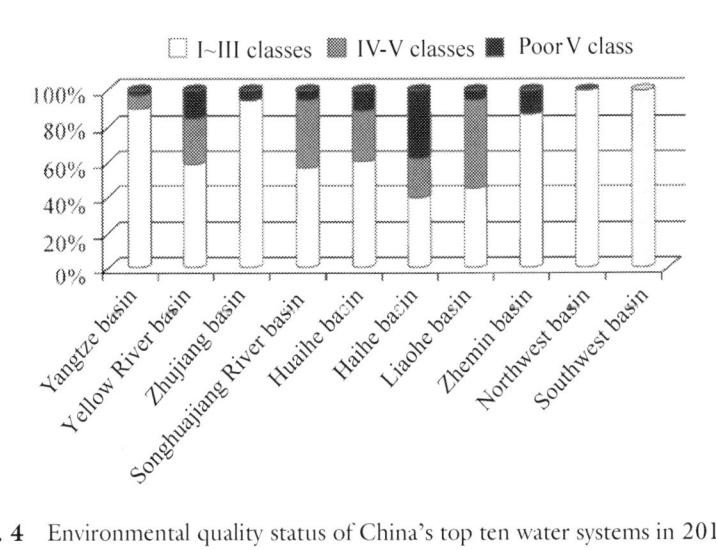

Fig. 4 Environmental quality status of China's top ten water systems in 2013

There Is a Long Way to Go in Dealing with Haze

With the further development of urban and regional economy, the fine particulate matter and ozone pollution in the atmosphere are aggravated, vehicle exhaust, dust from construction sites and other man-made emissions are seriously polluted, and the occurrence and severity of haze weather are increased. China is the world's largest emitter of sulfur dioxide and ozone-depleting substances. In 2013, it emitted 20.439 million tons of sulfur dioxide, 22.273 million tons of nitrogen oxides and 12.7814 million tons of smoke (powder) and dust. Of the 74 cities in the Beijing-Tianjin-Hebei region, the Yangtze River delta, the pearl River delta and other key regions, as well as municipalities directly under the central government, provincial capitals and cities city specifically designated in the state plan, 95.9% had air quality exceeding the standard. The proportion of cities exceeding air quality standard was 95.9%. The average number of haze days nationwide was 35.9 days, 18.3 days more than that in 2012 and the most since 1961. Fog and haze are frequent in the central and eastern regions, and the number of fog and haze days ranges from 50 to 100 in most areas from the central and southern parts of north China to the northern part of south China, and more than 100 days in some areas. In January and December 2013, two large-scale regional haze pollutions occurred in central and eastern China. Both processes of haze pollution show wide pollution scope, long duration, severe pollution degree and rapid accumulation of pollutant concentration, which is the highest in history and the world. PM2.5 "storm table" and "cough in Beijing" have aroused people's great concern about air pollution.

Soil Pollution Has a Wide and Far-Reaching Impact

Soil is the basic environmental element of ecological system, the material basis for human survival, and the indispensable important resource for economic and social development. The overall situation of soil environment in China is not optimistic. Some areas have heavy soil pollution, the quality of soil environment in cultivated land is worrying and the soil environment in abandoned industrial and mining areas is prominent. Due to human activities in industry, mining, agriculture and other reasons as well as the high background value of soil environment, the overall over-standard rate of soil was 16.1%, among which the proportions of slight, mild, moderate and severe pollution sites were 11.2, 2.3, 1.5 and 1.1%, respectively. From the perspective of land use type, the

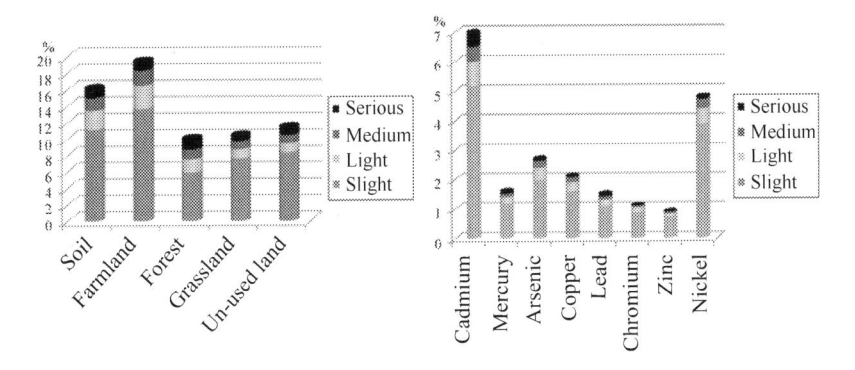

Fig. 5   Soil pollution in China

over-standard rate of cultivated land is 19.4%, woodland 10.0%, grass-land 10.4% and unused land 11.4% (see Fig. 5). In terms of the types of pollution, the majority were non-organic, accounting for 82.8% of the total. Cadmium, mercury, arsenic, copper, lead, chromium, zinc and nickel were found to have exceeded the standard by 7.0, 1.6, 2.7, 2.1, 1.5, 1.1, 0.9 and 4.8%, respectively (see Fig. 5). The point overrun rates of organic pollutants including BHC, DDT and PAHs were 0.5, 1.9 and 1.4%, respectively. Heavy and moderate soil pollution poses a serious threat to the quality and health of agricultural products. The pollution of heavy metals on soil is basically an irreversible process, and the pollution of many organic chemicals also takes a long time to degrade, which is very difficult to control.

1.3   Ecological Constraints

The Overall Trend of Ecological Environment Deterioration Has Not Been Fundamentally Curbed
In 2008, China's total ecological footprint reached 2.9 billion hectares worldwide, the largest of any country in the world. The per capita ecological footprint is 2.1 hectares, lower than the global average per capita ecological footprint (2.7 hectares), 80% of the world average, ranking 74th in the world. However, China's per capita biological carrying capacity is 0.87 hectares, which is nearly 2.5 times of its per capita biological carrying capacity. China ecological footprint report 2012.

China's per capita water consumption footprint is less than half the global average, yet China has a large population and correspondingly less water per capita. Therefore, China faces greater pressure and challenges in water resources. In 2009, the water resource pressure of large cities and the northern region dominated by agricultural economy in China was under severe pressure, while the water resource pressure of the lower reaches of the Yellow River and the Yangtze River in north and central China was high to severe pressure, and the water resource pressure in most regions gradually increased, showing a trend of extending from the north to the south.

Biodiversity Is Still Declining
China is one of the most bio-diverse countries in the world, and one of the areas where species are most threatened and where biodiversity is declining at an alarming rate. In the past 50 years, about 200 species of plants have become extinct in China, and as many as 4000–5000 species of wild higher plants are endangered or threatened, accounting for 15–20% of the total species, and gymnosperms and orchids are up to 40%; China's endangered animals and wild animals are increasingly endangered, 233 vertebrates are facing extinction and about 44% of the wild animal population is on the decline (see Table 1).

Soil Erosion Is Still Very Serious
According to the first national water conservancy survey, the total area of soil erosion in China was 2.9491 million square kilometers, accounting for 30.72% of the country's total land area. Among them, the hydraulic erosion was 1.2932 million square kilometers, and the wind erosion was 1.6559 million square kilometers. The total area of desertification was 2.6237 million square kilometers, accounting for 27.33% of China's total

Table 1 Endangered animals in China

Animals	Family	Genus	Species	Proportion of animal species (%)	Endemic to China
Fish	24	78	92	11.7	66
Mammals	35	91	133	22.9	26
Amphibians	3	13	31	10.6	17
Reptiles	20	54	96	24.3	30

land area. Desertification covers an area of 1,731,100 square kilometers, accounting for 18.03% of China's total land area. State Forestry Administration: *Bulletin on Desertification and Desertification in China*, 2011. China has 395 million hectares of natural grassland, accounting for 41.15% of the country's total land area. However, due to long-term overgrazing, excessive digging and cutting, 90% of available grasslands have been degraded to varying degrees. Especially in the north, the degradation area was about 51% at the beginning of 1990s, and it developed to about 52% at the end of 1990s. The degradation rate was quite fast, and the production capacity of grassland decreased and the grass yield decreased. China's forest coverage rate is 22.6%, and the world's forest coverage rate is 31%. Primitive natural forests have decreased from about 4% of the total land area in 1949 to 1.2% today. This is worrying.

2 External International Pressure on China's Green Transformation and Development

From a global perspective, with the rise of emerging economies such as China and India, the pattern of world resources and environment has also changed, and resource and environment issues have become the focus of international attention.

2.1 International Environmental Friction

In the era of globalization, when ecological and environmental systems are being destroyed and energy and resources are increasingly scarce, the world's resource and environmental problems are evolving into comprehensive and complex problems involving resources and environment, politics, economy, diplomacy and other aspects. In order to gain more power and resources in the world, all countries have the initiative and the right to speak on ecological and environmental issues.

The economic development of all countries are seeking international environmental cooperation ways, making the international environmental laws and regulations, fulfill the international environmental conventions and agreements, international environmental disputes and the surrounding resources and processing of foreign territory, the territorial disputes environment, take the initiative and control on environmental issues, secure in its voice in the international environment problem, which results in the friction of international environment. China's extensive mode of development promotes rapid economic development, but at the expense of the ecological environment. In 2011, China's GDP accounted for 7.6% of the world's total. The share of major resource consumption and pollutant emissions in the world is much higher than the share of GDP. Primary energy consumption accounts for 21.4% of the world, and finished steel consumption accounts for 45.1% of the world. A considerable proportion of resources, such as oil, iron ore, copper, aluminum and potash, are obtained by imports. China's air pollution level is worsening, has formed a cross-administrative complex pollution pattern. The water resources pollution develops into the regional pollution, and the shortage degree is aggravating; China faces deforestation, grassland degradation, soil desertification, soil erosion, loss of biodiversity and extreme climate change, among other environmental problems. It not only threatens the survival and development of the country, but also causes international environmental friction.

Western countries have been creating the "China threat theory" and attacking China for it, calling China "one of the biggest polluters in the world", one of the biggest demander of energy and resources, advocating "China's ecological environment threat theory", "China's ecological environment responsibility theory", "China's energy crisis theory", etc. (see Table 2). China is blamed for global air and water pollution, low resource and energy efficiency, and negative response to greenhouse gas emission reduction. They complicate China's ecological problems and put pressure on China. One is the internationalization of China's environmental problems, they provoke the relationship between China and foreign countries, such as the use of the Songhua River pollution problems to alienate the relationship between China and Russia, make the use of coal-fired power plants such as acid rain, soil pollution problem to alienate the relationship between China and South Korea and other countries, and so on, which has caused China environmental disputes with its neighbors. Second, China's environmental problems have been infiltrated into international trade to curb China's development. For example, through carbon emission restrictions, carbon tariffs, carbon labels and other green barriers, the responsibility and cost of ecological and environmental governance will be transferred to China and other foreign trade powers, in order to weaken the market competitiveness of China and other developing countries, causing environmental friction in international trade. The third is to infiltrate environmental issues into the diplomatic field. Fourth, China's environmental problems

Table 2 Various "China threat theories" in the world

Traditional	China's political threat theory	"China's political threat theory" means that China's political system and values are incompatible with the west, and China is a "totalitarian state"
	China economic threat theory	"China economic threat theory" refers to that China will retaliate against the west if it becomes economically powerful, China is a competitor in the international market
	China's military threat theory	"China's military threat theory" means that China's military is opaque, a strong China will expand and China will challenge US hegemony
Unconventional	China's civilization threat theory	"China's civilization threat theory" means that there will be a clash of civilizations between the Western world and the non-Western world, and the combination of the Chinese civilization and the Islamic civilization will threaten the Western civilization
	China's energy threat theory	"China's energy threat theory" means that China is the "predator" of international energy, and its large import of energy leads to the increase of energy prices
	China's environmental threat theory (China's climate threat theory)	China's massive consumption of resources and energy damages the global environment and threatens human survival (China's massive emission of greenhouse gases and failure to commit to emission reduction obligations threaten human development)

have been infiltrated into the field of human rights. The pattern of overseas investment, development and mergers and acquisitions led by stateowned enterprises is causing "alarm" and "fear" in some countries about China's rise.

2.2   *International Trade Frictions*

With the development of global economic integration, the scale of international trade is expanding, and the problem of resources and environment is becoming more and more prominent. *Agenda 21*, adopted by the United Nations conference on environment and development in 1992, points out that the relationship between man and nature must be coordinated along the path of sustainable development. It is urgent for all countries to resolve the contradiction between coordinated development and environmental protection. In this context, the green wave swept across the world, the concept of green people, green economy has become the mainstream of global economic development, hence green trade came into being. In order to develop green trade, all countries in the world, especially developed countries, have formulated the green trade system one after another. The WTO/GATT has also included environmental protection into the multilateral trade system, such as the "right of exception for environmental protection" stipulated in the GATT, since all countries adopt environmental standards based on protecting their own environment and promoting their own level of economic development when formulating their own laws and regulations related to green trade. Therefore, different standards set by different countries lead to different standards for measuring the same product, which limits international trade to a certain extent and leads to green trade barriers. The main forms of green trade barriers are: technical regulations and standards system, green tariffs and market access, environmental labeling system, green packaging system, green health inspection and quarantine system, green subsidy system, etc. Green trade barriers affect a wide range of products from food and clothing to digital mechanical and electrical, and can be set up barriers by green trade barriers. Through the Uruguay round negotiations, green barriers to trade have permeated services, intellectual property and investment.

Export is one of the three engines driving China's economic growth, which has effectively promoted China's economic and social development. In 2013, China's imports and exports of goods totaled us \$4.16 trillion, ranking first in the world. However, in the structure of China's export trade, high pollution and resource-intensive industries account for a large proportion in the traditional export industries, such as textiles, leather and products, chemicals, food and agricultural products, cement and building materials, coke and steel. In the international industrial division of labor system, China is located in the low-end industry supply chain, more than 55% of exports from the processing trade, 90% of the high-tech products in the form of processing trade exports; China's exports of services are lower than those of goods. As a result, Chinese products are greatly impacted by green trade barriers in the international market and frequently encounter various forms of trade restrictions such as anti-dumping, countervailing, safeguard measures, special safeguard measures, product recall or notification. In the first three quarters of 2013, a total of 63 relief investigations were launched by 17 countries (regions) against China's export products, an increase of 10.5% year-on-year, involving many large leading enterprises in China's strategic emerging industries. In the first three quarters of 2014, a total of 75 relief investigations were launched by 21 countries (regions) against China's export products, up 17% year-on-year. Many of these frictions are aimed at China's strategic emerging industries and involve large amounts of money. Green trade barriers have affected the development of China's foreign trade, almost all areas of China's foreign trade exports.

On the one hand, China's environmental standards are relatively low and poorly implemented. One is accepting the transfer of pollution from developed countries to China. Developed countries transfer a large number of resource-intensive and labor-intensive industries from developed countries to China through investment, trade and other means. Many environmentally harmful technologies, processes and equipment that have been eliminated or will be eliminated in developed countries have been transferred to China in the form of trade. China has become the world's processing plant and importer of pollution. Second, many domestic enterprises are weak in environmental protection awareness and weak in green technology innovation. As a result, the products made in China fail to meet international standards and are frequently rejected in export, exposing a huge "made in China" crisis. On the other hand, China's foreign trade powers are the European Union, the United States, Japan and other countries, which have accumulated high environmental awareness and advanced technological advantages, and are the leading framers of green trade standards and systems. China is a passive recipient of the green trade system. Strict technical standards and strict environmental protection laws and regulations, quarantine system, certification system and so on set up numerous barriers for Chinese products, and many Chinese export products are excluded from the international market because they cannot meet their green standards. The "301" investigation and the "Anti-dumping and anti-subsidy investigations" investigation carried out by the United States on Chinese clean energy enterprises, the European Union's levy of carbon emission tax on aviation, etc., various green trade barriers have a particularly obvious impact on China's export, which has formed an impact on China's foreign trade transformation and upgrading, and the foreign trade situation is grim.

In the face of green barriers and severe trade frictions, developing green economy and cultivating new competitive advantages in foreign trade are the key points to promote the healthy development of China's foreign trade.

2.3   International Image Contest

International image is the international community's cognition of a country. International image is also an important part of national interests. All countries in the world hope to establish a good national image. With the development of global environmental issues, environmental issues have become a major issue affecting a country's international image, and resource and environmental governance has become an important factor to consider a country's international image. Environmental issues can affect China's national image in terms of ideology, system, policy, diplomacy, culture and morality. China is actively participating in international environmental governance. China has been involved in climate negotiations since 1990, when the 45th session of the United Nations general assembly adopted resolution 212, setting in motion international negotiations on climate change. In 2009, on the eve of the Copenhagen climate change conference, the executive meeting of the state council proposed to reduce carbon dioxide emissions per unit of GDP (GDP) by 40 to 45% by 2020 compared with that in 2005, and incorporate it into the medium- and long-term plan for national economic and social development as a binding target. In 2011, the *Outline of the 12th Five-Year Plan for National Economic and Social Development of the People's Republic of China* refined these binding targets. It stipulates that by 2015, carbon dioxide emissions per unit of GDP will be 17% lower than 2010, energy consumption per unit of GDP will be 16% lower than 2010, and non-petrochemical energy will account for 11.4% of primary energy consumption. At the APEC meeting in 2014, China pledged to increase the share of non-fossil energy in primary energy consumption from 15% in 2015 to about 20% by 2030.

China has established the national leading group on climate change and relevant working bodies, and actively and constructively participated in international negotiations. It has formulated and implemented *China's National Program on Climate Change*, the 12th Five-Year Plan for Controlling Greenhouse Gas Emissions and the *National Strategy for Adapting to Climate Change*. China has signed more than 50 international environmental conventions.

China has made remarkable achievements in energy conservation and emission reduction. In 2013, China's carbon dioxide emissions per unit of GDP were 28.5% lower than in 2005, and the share of non-fossil energy in primary energy rose to 9.8%. The installed capacity of hydropower, wind power, nuclear power, solar water heaters and rural biogas users all rank first in the world. The forest coverage rate increased from 18.21% in 2005 to 21.6% in 2013. Our capacity to adapt to climate change in key areas such as water resources, agriculture and forestry, and disaster prevention and reduction has increased.

Ecological and environmental problems affect China's international image. After more than 30 years of rapid development, China's overall image has been increasingly recognized by the international community. In 2014, the majority of overseas people believed that China's economy developed rapidly, people's living standards were high and its technological innovation ability was enhanced. They recognized the international influence of China's economy and believed that China's economy promoted the global economic development. Severe environmental pollution and eco-system degradation, such as the trans-boundary pollution of the Songhua River, the cyanobacteria incident in west lake, the PX incident in Xiamen, cadmium rice and Beijing cough, have affected China's international image. There is overseas public distrust of China's quality and food safety concerns, as well as the perception that Chinese enterprises' entry is a threat to local ecological environment, energy/resource plunder and destruction.

In the face of the international ecological environment and other issues to curb China's development, China on the one hand has to face up to the ecological environment; on the other hand, adjust the traditional way of development, promote green development, solve domestic environmental pollution problems with a positive attitude, take an active part in global environmental governance activities, eliminate the negative impact of the "China environmental threat theory" and other arguments in the international community, and construct a harmonious international environment for China's development.

3   Subjective Pressure from Chinese Citizens and Government

China's traditional development mode, while facing the above objective pressures at home and abroad, also faces increasing subjective pressure from two aspects: One is the growing pressure on China's citizens to become more environmentally aware and the second is the pressure to commit to construct a "responsible" good government.

3.1   Increasing Pressure on Chinese Citizens' Environmental Awareness

Pressure of Open and Transparent Environmental Information
The Chinese government's disclosure of information on environment, ecology, food regulation, water, atmosphere and soil, as well as the disclosure of ecological environment by newspapers, radio, television, Internet and other media, have enabled citizens to obtain more and more information and pay more and more attention to ecological environment.

Frequent Environmental Events and Their Impact
The impact of environmental pollution on health has aroused the improvement of environmental awareness of citizens, and mass incidents of environmental protection have occurred continuously, promoting green transformation and development. China's traditional development mode causes resource depletion, environmental pollution and ecological damage. The water pollution is serious, and the water quality standard rate in the water function area is only 46%. The air quality is not good. Of the 74 cities in the Beijing–Tianjin–Hebei region, the Yangtze River delta, the Pearl River delta and other municipalities directly under the central government, as well as provincial capitals and cities specifically designated in the state plan, 95.9% exceeded the air quality standards. The average number of haze days nationwide is 35.9 days, more than 100 days in some regions, and acid rain occurs frequently in some regions. The discharge of waste water, waste gas and solid waste continues to increase, and the discharge areas spread from cities to rural areas, and rural pollution spreads rapidly. The state of the soil environment is grim, with 16.1% of the soil area contaminated, a wide range of heavy metals exceeding the standard, and 30.72% of the soil subject to wind

and water erosion. Water pollution, air pollution (haze) and soil pollution all cause serious harm to the public health, from food safety and water pollution to air pollution (haze) and soil pollution. "Melamine", "arsenic poison", "blood lead", "chromium water", "cadmium rice" and other teratogenic, carcinogenic, mutagenicity phenomenon occur frequently, which have an impact on the environmental awareness of citizens, arousing the environmental awareness of citizens. The environmental awareness of the public is increasing and the attention paid to the ecological environment and food which are closely related to their own life is increasing; the demand for fairness, justice, environmental protection and security is also increasingly high; the willingness to participate in national public affairs is increasingly strong; the demand for environmental rights and the right to health is also increasingly high; various types of environmental letters and visits, environmental mass incidents, etc., continue to occur, prompting the green transformation and development of the government (see Table 3).

Environmental Quality Becomes an Element of People's Quality of Life
Citizens' living standards have improved and increased green consumption demand "forced" green transformation and development. In 2011, China's per capita GDP reached 5432 US dollars, surpassing the 5000 US dollars for the first time. In 2013, China's per capita GDP reached 6807 US dollars, making it a middle-income country. With the development of national economy and the improvement of per capita income, people's life will be transformed from subsistence to comfort, and their needs will be transformed from survival level to safety and other higher levels. They will pursue the improvement of life quality and quality of life, especially the higher requirements on environmental quality. People are able to bear the additional costs of green development based on their own income and cost estimates and trade-offs. And the way people live is changing in terms of diet; people choose pollution-free organic food and green food; choose public transportation, bike or walk when travel; construct and use energy-efficient and environmentally friendly buildings; adopt clean energy sources such as wind, solar and bio-energy; advocate clear plate campaign, etc. The increasing public demand for green consumption, to some extent, "forces" the greening of the supply of goods and services, puts forward higher and higher requirements for the government's market regulation and promotes the green transformation of the production and service industries.

Table 3 Environmental mass incidents in China in recent years

Time	Place	Design project	Environment impact of the project (possible)	Time of intervention
June 2007	Xiamen, Fujian	PX chemical project	Located too close to the residential area, carcinogenic pollution	Before pollution
January 2008	Shanghai	Maglev project	Electromagnetic radiation and noise pollution	Before pollution
August 2008	Lijiang, Yunnan	Cement shaft kiln production line	Water pollution	After pollution
November 2009	Guangdong Panyu	Waste incineration plant	Toxic gas emissions	Before pollution
May 2011	Tin Linguo Lemeng, Inner Mongolia	Mineral resources development	Malignant criminal cases	After the case
September 2011	Zhejiang Haining	Jinko Solar Company	Water pollution, dead fish pollution	After pollution
July 2012	Sichuan Shifang	Molybdenum copper project	Groundwater and surface water pollution	Before pollution
July 2012	Jiangsu Qidong	Papermaking discharge project	Sewage discharge	Before pollution
October 2012	Zhejiang Ningbo	Sinopec PX project	Carcinogen pollution	Before pollution
July 2013	Guangdong Jiangmen	Nuclear fuel processing base	Nuclear radiation pollution	Before pollution

Source Strategic research group on sustainable development, Chinese academy of sciences. *2014 China Sustainable Development Strategy Report—Ecological Civilization Road in the Next 10 Years.* Beijing: Science Press, 2014

3.2   Pressure to Build a Responsible and Good Government

Over the past 30-plus years of reform and opening up, driven by the dividends of economic restructuring, China has made tremendous achievements in production, development and prosperity. China's economic strength and overall national strength have increased significantly, its economic and social structure has improved significantly, its people are leading a moderately prosperous life, and its international influence has increased significantly. In 2013, China had become the world's second largest economy, with a per capita GDP of US $6807, an urbanization rate of over 52%. The market economy has basically taken shape and, on the whole, it has entered the upper middle-income countries. Under the new normal of economic development, the Chinese government is also under pressure from economic growth, social stability and harmony, ecological environment and international climate change.

Pressure to Sustain Economic Growth
The global financial crisis has not only engulfed the Western countries, but also many emerging economies and developing countries, causing a sharp downturn in the world economy. To weather the crisis, many economies have rolled out fiscal stimulus packages and counter-measures in the hope of an early recovery. Unlike in the past, this financial crisis and global climate change are intertwined, creating a double global crisis. Although the economy of the United States and other countries has begun to recover, the prospects for recovery are not clear and the industrial recovery is not stable. With the withdrawal of the next round of stimulus policy and the tightening of monetary policy, the possibility of turbulence still exists and it is still difficult to predict the long-term sustainable growth.

China has also been severely affected by the global financial crisis. The government has implemented a number of measures, including the economic stimulus plan, the ten-industry revitalization plan and the vigorous development of new energy industry, to achieve the goal of maintaining economic growth. However, due to the focus of economic stimulus on traditional industries and large state-owned enterprises, the development of strategic emerging industries is still faced with problems such as insufficient funds, small scale, weak ability of independent innovation and so on. Small- and medium-sized enterprises are beset with difficulties and various structural problems still exist. The short-term economic stimulus has led to the excessive development of traditional industries with high energy consumption, high pollution and high emissions, and the heavy industry has continued. Insufficient attention has been paid to energy conservation, emission reduction and ecological improvement, and the ecological and environmental effects of economic development have gradually begun to be released, leading to ecological crisis. In addition, the government also needs to address the impact of the financial crisis covered by the rise in production costs, insufficient innovation capacity, the extension of the growth model is difficult to maintain. In the period of shifting economic growth speed, painful structural adjustment and digestion of early stimulus policies, the government is faced with opportunities and challenges of green development mode transformation.

Pressure to Build a Harmonious Society
China still has a large number of poor people. According to 2011 standards, there are still 26.88 million people living in poverty. According to the poverty level raised in 2011, there are still 128 million poor people. Problems such as relative poverty and urban poverty have become increasingly prominent, and the phenomenon of returning to poverty has occurred from time to time, which has become a difficulty in building a harmonious society and realizing the goal of building a moderately prosperous society in all respects. With the development of the economy, the contradiction between the total supply and demand of China's labor force and the structural contradiction have emerged. In the next 10 years, about 10 million new urban jobs will be created every year. The vocational skills of the labor force do not adapt to the job demand, and problems such as transitional employment, youth employment and rural labor force transfer employment are becoming increasingly prominent. Therefore, it is urgent to implement more active employment policies. There is a large gap between urban and rural areas and between regions. Problems affecting the vital interests of the people, such as education, medical care and social security, are prominent. The fight against bureaucracy and anti-corruption is in a grim situation. Social crises caused by ecological and environmental problems occur frequently, and food safety is a concern. The government is faced with a huge problem of social governance.

Pressure for Resource Environment Governance

On the one hand, China faces serious resource security problems. First, as a large developing country, the most serious crisis facing China's sustainable development is the deepening domestic resource and environmental problems. In the face of rapid economic growth and upgrading of consumption structure in the heavy chemical industry stage, China's strategic resources and energy, especially high-quality energy and China's strategic mineral resources such as iron, copper, aluminum and uranium, will remain in a state of supply and demand tension for a long time, with a high degree of external dependence, threatening China's resources and energy security. Second is the deterioration of the ecological environment. China's ecological and environmental problems have undergone profound changes and are facing increasingly complex and diverse pollution patterns and extensive ecological degradation pressures. Driven by development interests, insufficient detection capability and lagging supervision capability, the overall trend of environmental pollution in China has not been comprehensively curbed, and has developed into regional air pollution, water pollution and soil pollution across departments and regions. Although China has carried out large-scale ecological construction projects since 1998 and achieved certain results, with the rise of central China and the implementation of the Western development, the ecosystems in the central and Western regions and some vulnerable areas will face new and broader ecological pressure.

On the other hand, China also faces severe environmental security problems. At present, the relationship between the Chinese people and nature is highly strained. There is a shortage of strategic mineral resources and energy, serious pollution of the atmosphere, water and soil, and worsening damage and degradation of the ecosystem. The situation of greenhouse gas emission reduction is grim, and resource and environmental challenges are becoming more and more comprehensive issues concerning economic development and social stability. The construction of ecological civilization reflects the major transformation of the party and the government's governing philosophy. We should change the old mindset of only depending on growth rate and GDP, adopt a comprehensive approach of promoting "five-in-one" development from the height of building ecological civilization, give priority to environmental protection and make use of the system to protect the environment and rebalance the relationship between "environment and development". Looking ahead, it is reasonable to believe that with the major changes in the institutional framework and governance model of China's ecological civilization, sustainable development will gain new momentum.

In the face of international and domestic development and environmental challenges, China needs to become a responsible major country, actively promote green transformation and development, foster green industries, increase green employment, improve green competitiveness and realize green rise.

CHAPTER 4

The Driving Force of Green Transformation and Development

1 The Subject of Green Development

In the process of economic and social development, China pays attention to the protection of ecological environment and puts forward the concept of ecological civilization construction. But resources are scarce, and the trend of environmental pollution and ecological deterioration has not been reversed. At the macro-level, China's various resource, environmental and ecological problems not only affect the sustainability of economic growth and development, but also lead to social problems, affect social stability and China's image in the international community, and even affect China's rise. At the micro-level, it will affect the local environment and the life and health of residents. In the final analysis, all environmental problems are determined by the current development model-extensive development with high consumption, high emission and high pollution. Both macro- and micro-levels need to adjust the current development model and implement green transformation development. Green transformation and development is the way to achieve the harmony between man and nature, and the only way for the rise of China The government, enterprises and the public are the "troika" driving the green transformation and development.

The central government is the leader, facilitator and promoter of green development. The central government should play a key role in green transformation. It can promote green transformation not only

© The Author(s) 2019
S. Gu et al., *Green Transformation and Development*,
The Great Transformation of China,
https://doi.org/10.1007/978-981-32-9495-0_4

through legislative, administrative and judicial means, but also through economic means. The central government mainly formulates and improves various laws and policies on green development from the national perspective, including laws and policies on resource conservation, environmental protection, ecological conservation, green science and technology innovation, and formulation of green development strategy planning. First is to cultivate the growth of environmental protection industry and the ecological concept of citizens, balance the public interests, ecological interests, economic interests, social interests and environmental interests, and pay attention to the harmonious development of society, human and nature, which is the most important subject of green development and plays a leading role. Second, promote and guide local governments and enterprises to establish the concept of development, green transformation of development mode, and promote the gradual transformation of China's economic development to the direction of resource conservation and environmental friendliness. The third is to guide the public to establish the concept of consumption and advocate green lifestyle. Local governments are the promoters, regulators and guides of green development in the region. As the entrusted agent of the central government, local governments exercise the responsibility of green development management of the central government. Local governments, as regional administrative managers, formulate strategic plans for green development in their regions and local regulations and policies to promote green development, and guide and encourage enterprises to innovate in green science and technology and transform their modes of production into green ones. As supervisors of the implementation of green development, local governments are responsible for environmental supervision, administrative examination and approval, environmental protection law enforcement and social publicity, etc., to restrain enterprises' illegal behaviors and ensure the smooth progress of green development.

Enterprises are the implementers of green development. In the face of the government's guidance and promotion, industry competition pressure, consumer green demand and public opinion pressure from the public, media, etc., on the one hand, enterprises must not only pay attention to economic interests, more should pay attention to resource benefit, ecological benefit and environment benefit, to perform on the natural ecological environment of the market, the public consumption of ecological responsibility, to carry out the whole process from product design, production to product recycling green development concept, to protect the environment, saving resources, change the economic development model. On the other hand, it is also the focus of enterprises to find new opportunities and realize green development transformation. Enterprises are not only the subject of green development, but also the object of green development, playing a key role.

The public is the most fundamental and important driving force for green transformation, and the implementers, supervisors and beneficiaries of green development. With the continuous development of economy and society, people's pursuit of material life and spiritual life has been constantly improved, and the concept of green has been constantly promoted. Green consumption and green travel are advocated and put into practice to become the implementer of green development. With the improvement of the awareness of green development, the public also pays more and more attention to the ecological environment and ecological rights and interests. By participating in environmental assessment, the public can participate in the green development through complaints, reports and other channels. The public is the most extensive and fundamental stakeholder in green development, and the most direct beneficiary of the elimination of outdated production capacity, upgrading of industrial structure and green economic transformation.

2 THE DRIVING FORCE FOR CHINA'S GREEN DEVELOPMENT

2.1 The Driving Force for National Governance

Green development has become a trend in today's international community. All countries have raised the banner of green new policies to get out of the economic crisis and achieve good governance.

The overall goal of comprehensively deepening reform set out in the third plenary session of the 18th CPC central committee is to improve and develop the socialist system with Chinese characteristics and modernize the country's governance system and capacity.

The national governance system is the institutional system for managing the country under the leadership of the party, including institutional mechanisms, laws and regulations in the fields of economy, politics, culture, society, ecological civilization and party building; National governance capacity refers to the ability to manage all aspects of social affairs with the use of the state system, including reform, development and stability, domestic and foreign affairs and national defense, and the ability to run the party, state and army.

The Problem of Resource Ecology Caused by the Extensive Development Model Has Become a Major Pass Challenging the Modernization of National Governance System and Governance Capacity

Since reform and opening up, China has made remarkable achievements in economic and social development. Its economic aggregate has risen from the 10th place to the second place in the world. China's overall national strength and people's living standards have improved significantly. In terms of the mode of economic growth, there are problems of "high input, high consumption, high emission, uncoordinated, difficult circulation and low efficiency". Resources and environment have paid a heavy price for the rapid economic development. China's per capita possession of important resources is far below the world average, and its per capita possession of arable land and fresh water is only 43 and 28% of the world average; The external dependence of strategic resources, such as oil and natural gas, has continued to rise, reaching 59.5 and 31% in 2014. In particular, the mode of development is still relatively extensive, which further aggravates resource constraints. China's energy consumption per unit of GDP is twice the world average. Haze weather occurred frequently in 2014, only 8 out of 74 key cities met the air quality standards; 150 million mu of arable land was polluted and more than 40% of it was degraded. The proportion of heavily polluted inferior class V water body is about 10%. The area of soil erosion accounts for nearly one-third of the total land area. The ecological systems of forests and grasslands are severely degraded, and land desertification and rocky desertification still threaten the safety of people's lives and property. The problem of resources and environment has become the most pressing constraint and shortcoming in achieving the goal of completing the building of a moderately prosperous society in all respects. It is an urgent problem that cannot be avoided, get around or retreated. In particular, China's environmental carrying capacity has reached or nearly reached the upper limit, posing major challenges to the country's governance capacity and becoming the biggest bottleneck in the modernization of the country's governance system and governance capacity. If we continue the development model of the past, it will be hard to return.

Green Transformation and Development Is the Internal
Urgent Requirement for the Modernization of National
Governance System and Governance Capacity
China's sustained rapid economic growth and structural changes in
the economy and society have inevitably produced a series of serious
socio-economic problems, such as the problems of ecology, resources
and environment, the widening gap between urban and rural areas and
regional economies, the widening gap between the rich and the poor,
the large floating population and land-lost farmers caused by urbanization, and the social problems caused by the lagging of social security system and redistribution policy. As an extensive mode of development with
high investment, high energy consumption and high pollution, the phenomenon of diminishing marginal effect has emerged, which has been
the end of the road and to the point where absence of transformation
will make it unsustainable. It is in urgent need of green transformation
and development, so that economic growth will be driven by consumption, investment and export instead of investment and export, shift from
relying mainly on the development of the secondary industrial belt to
relying on the synergy of the primary, secondary and tertiary industries
and shift from relying mainly on increasing material resource consumption to relying mainly on scientific and technological progress, improving the quality of workers and making innovations in management.
Economic and social development should be built on the basis that
resources can support it, the environment can accommodate it and the
ecology can be protected. We will keep green hills, clear water and fresh
air, and that the people live and work in a sound ecological environment.

2.2 Improve the International Image of China as a Responsible Major Country

To properly handle the relationship between economic development,
social progress and energy, resources, ecological environment and climate change is a common challenge faced by all countries in the world.
It is also an important criterion to measure a country's international
image in the international community. China is the largest developing
country in the world, and it is also a country with greater environmental impact. The handling of the relationship between environment and
development is not only related to the solution of domestic environmental and development problems, but also affects China's economic and

social development process as well as the construction model of socialism with Chinese characteristics, as well as China's international image and reputation. As the world pays increasing attention to China's development model, China's role in global environmental affairs will be closely watched.

Resource and environment issues have become a point of confrontation between China and other countries and are the important issues affecting national security and international image. As an emerging economic power, China's green economic development will have a profound impact on its future economic prosperity and even the global economic development. Since the reform and opening up, China has made remarkable achievements in economic and social development. The proportion of China's GDP in the world rose from 1.7% in 1978 to 12.34% in 2013. China's economy grew from the 10th largest in the world to the second largest in the world. The output of steel, cement, electricity, coal and cotton cloth ranks first in the world, and the output of crude oil ranks fourth in the world. China's overall national strength and people's living standards have improved significantly. But rapid economic growth comes at the expense of resources and the ecological environment. China is the world's largest energy consumer and carbon dioxide emitter. China's energy consumption per unit of GDP is 1.6 times that of the United States, 1.5 times that of South Korea and 2.2 times that of Japan. Carbon dioxide emissions per unit of GDP are 5.3 times that of the US, 8.2 times that of Germany and 12.3 times that of France. In 2013, the world produced 36 billion tons of carbon dioxide from fossil fuels. China accounts for about 27% of global carbon dioxide emissions, ranking first in the world. The consumption of energy and resources ranks first in the world. China's resources, environment and ecological problems have become an excuse for Western countries to accuse China. Moreover, in the global climate political negotiations, the United States withdrew from the Kyoto protocol in 2001 on the grounds that China and other developing countries did not undertake quantitative emission reduction obligations, and again refused to sign the Kyoto protocol in 2005. Western countries spread the "China resource threat theory", "China environmental threat theory" and other theories, causing some countries to be vigilant and panic about China's rise, damaging China's international image, setting up green trade barriers in international trade and hindering China's economic development.

The international community also has increasingly high expectations for China, hoping that China will assume responsibilities and obligations commensurate with its capabilities and become an important participant in international energy and environmental issues. At the Copenhagen climate conference in 2002, China made a voluntary commitment to reduce carbon dioxide emissions per unit of GDP by 40–45% by 2020 compared with 2005, highlighting its image as a responsible major country. In the 2014 *Sino-Us Joint Statement on Climate Change*, China set a goal to peak its carbon dioxide emissions by around 2030 and increase the share of non-fossil energy in primary energy consumption to about 20% by 2030. Reducing carbon emissions is conducive to mitigating climate change and improving the living environment of human beings. China has pledged to peak carbon dioxide emissions by around 2030, highlighting its responsibility as the world's second largest economy.

Promoting green transformation and development is the best way to alleviate and improve the increasingly serious environmental problems in today's world. As a big developing country, China should follow the trend of The Times and actively deal with a series of problems caused by climate change. On the one hand, China can fulfill its international commitment to emission reduction and respond to the threat theory related to China. On the other hand, it can provide useful experience for other developing countries and lead the global green transition.

On the international stage, China should not only assume the responsibility of being an economic power of a developing country, but also bravely assume the responsibility of being an environmental power of a developing country, fulfill its international environmental obligations and make contributions to the green development of the world.

China needs to change its extensive economic and trade growth model, develop a green economy and improve its image and status in international economic, environmental and political relations.

2.3   Continuously Improve National Competitiveness

With the deepening of economic globalization, the countries in the world are more closely connected and the international competition is more and more fierce. Under the dual pressure of global resources and environment problems and global economic crisis, the wave of green change has swept the world, and green development has become an important part of improving national competitiveness of all countries in the world. The strategies of major countries to improve their competitiveness are shown in Table 1.

From the perspective of the new demand for global economic growth and the basic direction that the plight of human survival requires to break through, we should firmly grasp the green trend that dominates the world, and the green transformation and development has become a significant historical opportunity for China not to be expelled from the "Earth's nationality" in the reshuffle of international competition.

The main driving force of China's economic growth is cheap resources and low cost factors, which tend to lead to a long-term unbalanced industrial structure, and the service industry plays a small role in promoting economic growth, while the chemical industry accounts for a large proportion, often resulting in irreversible environmental pollution and resource waste. From the perspective of independent innovation ability, Chinese enterprises are short of core technology and weak in scientific and technological innovation ability. The growth of enterprises is mainly driven by the expansion of scale and input of natural resources, human resources, capital and other factors, and lack of core competitiveness. Only by promoting green transformation and development, supported by green science and technology, through circular and low-carbon development, building a resource-conserving and environment-friendly society, and taking intensive development as a new growth point, can China occupy an advantageous position in global competition.

A series of new concepts of the Chinese government, including new industrialization, modernization of agriculture and animal husbandry, new urbanization, informatization and greening put forward in 2015, circular economy, resource-conserving, environment-friendly society, harmonious society, energy conservation and emission reduction, innovative society, ecological civilization, etc., many of these concepts are synchronized with or even lead the world. It has a place in world economic development in terms of energy conservation and emission reduction, elimination of outdated production capacity, clean industrial structure transformation, green innovation capacity, technology demonstration level and development of green and low-carbon industries. Practice has proved that green transformation and development can improve China's international competitiveness.

Table 1 Strategies for major countries to improve their competitiveness

Country	National competitiveness strategy	Specific measures
The United States	Leads the world in innovation	First, by substantially increasing funding for basic research; second, research and experiment on making tax deduction and exemption permanent; third, strengthening mathematics and the science education, the reform of labor force training system
Japan	The revitalization of the Japanese economy The six strategies	Promote technological innovation, with an emphasis on supporting research and development in the fields of environment, energy, IT broadband communications, biotechnology, nanotechnology and materials technology. To develop the "safe and secure" food and food material industry and create potential market demand for improving living environment and quality of life
UK	The low-carbon national strategy	Takes the low-carbon economy as an important breakthrough for economic recovery, seizes the commanding heights of new growth areas in the twenty-first century and builds the core competitiveness of the UK's country and enterprises
Brazil	World bioenergy Major-country strategy	To diversify the sources of clean energy, with hydropower, nuclear power, wind, solar and bioenergy going hand in hand. Bioenergy will be the main energy source for Brazil, which aims to become the world's leading exporter of bioenergy
German	National high technology Development strategy	Ensures a leading position in 17 professional fields, including life medicine, energy technology, space technology and material technology

3   The Driving Force for Green Development of Local Governments

3.1   Green Development Will Help Enhance the Region's Overall Competitiveness

Green productivity is directly related to the overall competitiveness of a region. For a long time, in order to achieve rapid economic development and create more GDP, local governments have followed the traditional extensive economic development model. In the process of industrial development, local governments have encouraged and supported any industry that can bring a large amount of investment, generate GDP and increase taxes, regardless of its adverse impact on the ecological environment. This has resulted in high consumption of resources and energy, frequent pollution problems, serious ecological damage and even environmental accidents, affecting local social image and affecting the promotion of local leaders. Non-compliance with clean production causes high carbon dioxide emissions and great pressure to save energy and reduce emissions. This is reflected in the energy-saving barometer issued by the state. The occurrence of environmental accidents, etc., calls into question the local ecological environment. Products lack of competitiveness in the domestic market and encounter green barriers to trade in foreign trade, which weakens the comprehensive competitiveness of the local government.

Green development is not only conducive to transforming local development mode, adjusting industrial structure and protecting ecological environment; more conducive to the development of low carbon products, scientific and technological innovation, enhance the comprehensive competitiveness of local government. In order to improve their comprehensive competitiveness, local governments must transform to green development, take green economy as a new growth point of local economy and green technology as the support of local development, develop green industries and produce green products, so as to seize the domestic and even the global green market. Only by protecting the ecological environment can we win a good reputation and be praised by the people.

3.2   Increase the Green Performance of Local Governments

In the past, local governments were judged on their performance based on GDP growth rate and total GDP. In order to increase GDP and obtain good performance, local governments paid insufficient attention to social development, improvement of people's livelihood and environmental protection. In some localities, violations of scientific development still occur from time to time. Some localities have a strong interest in "short, adaptable and fast" performance projects and borrow heavily to engage in "performance projects". Some have achieved economic growth at the expense of the environment, while others still have a "new blueprint". The economy has reached a state where resources are hard to support, the environment is hard to accommodate and the ecology is hard to recover, and sustained economic growth is hard to achieve.

In 2013, the Organization Department of the CPC Central Committee issued the *Notice on Improving the Performance Assessment of Local Party and Government Leading Bodies and Leading Cadres,* and in 2015, the *Opinions of the CPC Central Committee and the State Council on Accelerating the Construction of Ecological Civilization,* which stipulates the goal system, assessment methods, reward and punishment mechanism of performance assessment. On the performance appraisal of local party and government leading bodies and leading cadres, the "four Nos" are proposed: The GDP and growth rate should not be used as the main indicators of performance evaluation. No ranking of GDP and growth rates. The development effect of each province (autonomous region, municipality directly under the central government) cannot be measured solely by GDP and growth rate; the GDP of areas in which development is restricted and of ecologically fragile key counties in the country's poverty alleviation and development work will not be assessed. Indicators such as resource consumption, environmental damage and ecological benefits will be incorporated into the comprehensive evaluation system for economic and social development, strengthen the assessment of index constraints and increase the weight of indicators such as resource consumption, environmental protection, digestion of overcapacity and production safety. In this way, the performance of local governments will be measured in terms of their performance in development.

The new assessment standards will guide local governments in their green transformation and development. The *Notice on Improving the Performance Appraisal of Local Party and Government Leading Bodies and Leading Cadres* can not only evaluate the work of leading cadres more objectively and fairly, but also free leading cadres from the pressure of simply pursuing economic growth and focus on the overall development of the region. According to the actual situation of this region, we should rationally seek the development mode of this region and change the past development mode of exchanging high investment, high emission and high pollution for economic growth rate. By developing green economy, innovating green technology, cultivating green industries and increasing green employment, we will ensure that economic and social development is supported by resources, accommodated by the environment and protected by ecology. We will integrate economic development into the harmonious coexistence of society and nature, and truly blaze a trail of individualized and characteristic green development.

3.3   The Lifelong Accountability System Constrains the Extensive Development of Local Governments and Encourages Green Transformation and Development

The state has formulated a system of lifelong accountability, which will put on record leading officials who violate the requirements of scientific development and cause serious damage to resources, environment and ecology, and impose lifelong accountability. Those who make decisions blindly regardless of resources or the ecological environment, thus causing serious consequences, should be held seriously accountable for their leadership. In case of making a mess of a place's ecological environment, one cannot just walk away and become an official in another city. The behavior mechanism of ecological environment destruction should be investigated, the behavior of ecological environment protection should be praised and the green transformation and development of local governments should be encouraged.

Local governments formulate development plans and promote development modes, taking into account the actual situation of local resources, environment and ecology, and building on the capacity of resources and environment. Local development can only abandon the development model of temporary economic prosperity at the expense of resources and environment, transform the mode of economic development, optimize the mode of economic development and achieve the goals of industrialization and urbanization through green development, by building green industries, buildings and transportation systems; we will coordinate economic development with population, resources and the environment, adhere to the path of civilized development featuring production development, affluent life and sound ecology, achieve economic revitalization and sustainable development, and ensure sustained development from generation to generation.

4   THE DRIVING FORCE FOR GREEN DEVELOPMENT OF ENTERPRISES

4.1   *The National Policy of Green Development Guides Enterprises in Green Development*

China has deepened reform and opening up, reformed its economic system, adjusted its economic structure, built an ecological civilization, promoted green development, circular development and low-carbon development, and built a resource-conserving and environment-friendly society in an all-round way. By changing the concept of development, innovating the mode of development and improving the quality of development, the government has formed a unique path of China's economic development, guided enterprises to develop in the direction of economy and environmental protection, and achieved sound development of ecological civilization, economic construction, political construction, cultural construction and social construction. The state has invested a large amount of money in environmental pollution control, ecological restoration, energy conservation and emission reduction. In 2013, 951.65 billion Yuan was spent on environmental pollution control, accounting for 1.67% of GDP. In response to the severe smog, the central government allocated 5 billion Yuan to clean up the air in the Beijing-Tianjin-Hebei region and surrounding areas. The central government will liquidate incentive funds in accordance with the assessment of the effectiveness of air pollution prevention and control in various regions, so as to highlight the performance-oriented role and add impetus to the implementation of enterprises' green development strategy. The government's strengthened supervision, the enhanced authority of environmental protection departments, the enhanced punishment of environmental accidents, the strengthened environmental litigation and the use of resource and energy price leverage will all push enterprises to make green transformation.

Under the background of global low-carbon development and the policy of the Chinese government vigorously promoting ecological civilization, energy conservation and emission reduction, it is inevitable for enterprises to cope with the dual challenges of resource scarcity and environmental protection and take the road of sustainable and green development.

4.2   Green Development Will Enhance the International Competitiveness of Enterprises

In the field of international trade, the addition of ecological label, energy efficiency label and the latest carbon label has gradually become a practice in international trade and evolved into a new trade barrier. China's manufacturing industry is mostly at the middle and low ends of the industrial chain, and it is a manufacturing link that wastes resources, damages the environment and relies on cheap labor. It is weak in independent innovation, lacks core technologies and independent brands, and its environmental standards and technologies are far from those of developed countries, including pesticide residues in food, lead content in ceramic products, leather of PCP residues, organic chlorine content in tobacco, safety index of the mechanical and electronic products and toys, lead content of gasoline, car exhaust emission standards, packaging recyclability index, textile dyes, protection of the ozone layer of controlled substances, and so on. All export industries such as China's traditional industries and strategic emerging industries suffer from green barriers and are in a passive position in international competition.

Countries around the world are boosting their economies through a green economy. Green development becomes the focus of enterprise competition, and green trade barriers become the means to protect the development of local enterprises. Under the background of more and more stringent environmental standards in various countries and the continuous improvement and deepening of people's awareness of sustainable development, it requires Chinese enterprises to meet the standards and requirements of low-carbon, green and environmental protection. The enterprise implements green design and adopts advanced green technology and green technology with less waste and no waste to strictly control the production process and service process of products, realize the effect of resource consumption minimization, waste emission reduction, recycling and resource utilization, produce green products and establish the enterprise green brand. It can not only reduce the production cost of enterprises, but also enable enterprises to pass the green trade barriers and enter the world market.

4.3 Green Development Sets Up a Good Image for Enterprises

China's extensive industrial production model of treatment after pollution has made industrial pollution the culprit of environmental pollution. In 2013, industrial SO_2 emissions accounted for 89.79% of SO_2 emissions, and industrial nitrogen oxides emissions accounted for 69.4% of nitrogen oxides emissions. The comprehensive utilization rate of industrial solid waste was 62.3%. About 36.3% of the land used for ferrous metals, nonferrous metals, leather products, papermaking, petroleum, coal, chemicals and pharmaceuticals, chemical fiber, rubber and plastics, mineral products, metal products and electric power industries was contaminated. Environmental pollution caused by the discharge of various pollutants pollutes rivers, groundwater, air and soil, and even leads to the epidemic of some diseases and the extinction of some species and other environmental disasters. Among most of the pollution, 70% comes from industrial pollution, as well as the over-exploitation and exploitation of mineral, forest, land, fresh water and other resources, which leads to the destruction of the ecology and the ecological crisis caused by it from time to time troubling people. More and more enterprises are polluting the environment. From 2009 to 2013, there were 2634 environmental emergencies, 14 major environmental incidents and 17 major environmental incidents in the past three years. Environmental pollution and ecological destruction have seriously affected the normal life and health of local people, and have also caused adverse impacts on the international community.

Corporate image is the intangible wealth of an enterprise. The development of green economy makes the environmental behavior of enterprises become the most basic element in the new competition structure. Thus, the shaping of enterprise green culture and the implementation of green strategy are conducive to the establishment of a good green image in the public mind of enterprises, thus greatly enhancing the credibility of enterprises and the soft power of sustainable development.

4.4 Green Development Creates New Development Opportunities for Enterprises

With the increasing pressure on resources, environment and ecology, the traditional development model relies heavily on the exploitation and utilization of natural resources, especially those non-renewable mineral resources, which will inevitably lead to the continuous reduction in the number of these resources and eventually exhaustion, making the development process unsustainable. The main theme of the twenty-first-century economy is green economy, including green products, green production, green consumption, green market, green industry and other contents, which are the specific requirements of the concept of sustainable development for economic life. Green development is an ongoing process in the world. There is no mature experience or model. It is in the exploration from theory to practice. Whoever adopts the green strategy in advance will be able to take the initiative in the future competition pattern. All countries in the world are promoting the green development from the aspects of strategy, system and policy in order to gain the opportunity of a new round of development. All industries are actively exploring green development models and seeking new opportunities for development. Therefore, no matter in green technology innovation, green industry development and other aspects, or green packaging, green services, as long as it stays ahead, it will win the high point of green development.

5   THE DRIVING FORCE FOR PUBLIC GREEN DEVELOPMENT

5.1   *The State Grants the Public the Right to Participate in Green Development*

Public participation in environmental decision-making is also stipulated in international conventions. The *Rio Declaration* defines the basic principles of public participation in environmental protection decision-making, access to information and recourse to law. The *Bali Guidelines* have provisions for information disclosure and public participation. In the *Environmental Impact Assessment Law of the People's Republic of China* (2003), *Administrative Licensing Law of the People's Republic of China* (2004), *Interim Measures for Public Participation in Environmental Impact Assessment* (2006), the *Government Information Disclosure Regulations of the People's Republic of China* (2008), the *Environmental Information Disclosure Measures (Trial)* (2008), *Guidelines for the Disclosure of Government Information on Environmental Impact Assessment of Construction Projects (Trial)* (2014), the *Guidelines on Promoting Public Participation in Environmental Protection* (2014), the *Environmental Protection Law of the People's Republic of China* (2015) and other laws and regulations, there are provisions for public participation in environmental protection. The public can participate in environmental protection through hearings, questionnaires, expert consultation and lectures. This shows that while China attaches great importance to environmental protection, it also pays more attention to the power of public participation and the public's right to know, supervise and participate in environmental protection.

Although the state grants citizens the right to environmental protection, due to incomplete information disclosure in China and the lack of effective channels for the public to participate in environmental decision-making, some environmental accidents have caused concern and dissatisfaction. Mass incidents caused by environmental problems are increasing by nearly 30% every year. It not only undermines social cohesion and affects social stability, but also drives decision makers to reflect on unsustainable development decisions and promote green transformation and development.

Public participation depends on better ways to disseminate and communicate information about resources and the environment, including disclosure of all pollution sources, law enforcement information, corporate emissions information, environmental impact assessments, approvals and corrective actions. It also depends on the environmental awareness of the whole society (including the environmental science literacy and environmental education level of officials, enterprises and the public) and the public participation ability. Information disclosure and communication is the key to public participation.

5.2 Improve the Production and Living Environment and Maintain Life and Health

Nature is the carrier on which human beings live and develop. Environmental problems such as ecological imbalance, environmental degradation, resource waste and exhaustion threaten the survival and safety of human beings, prompting them to deeply reflect on their own way of life and arouse their green consciousness. The starting point and goal of pollution control and environmental protection are to restore the public's blue sky, green land and clear water, to safeguard the public's ecological well-being and to benefit the public the most. In order to effectively save resources, protect the environment and maintain health, the public should first of all start from their own, advocate green consumption, abandon excessive consumption, luxury consumption, advocate simple life, and force the government and enterprises to implement green transformation and development. Second, we paid close attention to food safety, river pollution, water pollution, toxic milk powder and harmful vegetables, and urged the government and enterprises to pursue green development. Only when the public actively participates in green development and monitors adverse events will the whole society have a healthy green development mechanism. The social consciousness of green economy needs the pressure of social masses.

5.3   It Is Urgent to Establish and Improve the Endogenous Driving Force for Green Development

Green development requires the joint efforts of the government, enterprises and the public. The government's driving force will promote enterprises to implement green transformation and guide the public to form a green lifestyle. The public's motivation will push the government to strengthen the green economic policy and form the social pressure of green transformation of enterprises. The motivation of enterprises will push the government to innovate green system, meet the green demand of the public and promote the green development of the whole society. To effectively promote green development, we need to establish a green development mechanism that connects the government, enterprises and the public. Information disclosure is the key to the establishment of linkage mechanism. Only through information disclosure can the public participate in green transformation and environmental protection and form social impetus. Only then will the enterprise restrain the negative externality behavior, transform economy development way and forms the green development main force. Only by taking responsibility for unsustainable decisions can the government make scientific decisions and become the leading force for green development. Secondly, it is the establishment of green assessment mechanism, the scientific assessment of local government and enterprise development performance, incentives and guidance of local and enterprise green transformation and development. Finally, forming green consciousness in whole society, and regarding greenery as the conscious choice of government, enterprise and public.

CHAPTER 5

The Resistance of Green Transformation and Development

1 THE BACKWARD AND LAGGING BEHIND CONCEPT OF DEVELOPMENT

The concept of development also has a significant impact on the formation and transformation of the mode of economic development. The traditional development concept maintains the traditional development mode, and once formed, it will also generate inertia, which is difficult to eliminate in the short term and is not conducive to the transformation of the development mode. For China, the concept of green development is an imported product. When developed countries issued policies and regulations to support green development, regulated the activities of enterprises and vigorously promoted green development, the concept of green development in China was still weak and had not been widely spread in the whole society.

1.1 Focus on GDP Growth

The reform and opening up established the guiding ideology of taking economic construction as the center, further strengthened the guiding ideology of economic development oriented by GDP goals, determined the GDP growth as the indicator to measure the achievements of economic and social development and evaluate the performance of cadres, and led to the blind worship of GDP by governments and officials

95
S. Gu et al., *Green Transformation and Development*,
The Great Transformation of China,
https://doi.org/10.1007/978-981-32-9495-0_5

at all levels from the central government to the local government. The national economic accounting system, which takes GDP as the main index, only reflects the total amount of national economic income. It does not reflect the contribution of natural resources to economic development and the huge economic value of ecological resources. It does not reflect the economic losses caused by the deterioration of the ecological environment, nor the depletion and depreciation of natural resources. The cost of environmental improvement invested by various departments is included in the total output value and added value of the department, and the input for disaster repair is also included in the GDP, which leads to a certain degree of false growth. In 2004, the cost of environmental degradation nationwide reached 511.8 billion Yuan, accounting for 3.05% of GDP. The cost of natural resource depletion and environmental degradation led to a 1.8% reduction in the original GDP in 2004. Taking this as the assessment index, it is easy to have the tendency of one-sided pursuit of development speed and neglect of development benefit, one-sided pursuit of natural output and neglect of environmental return, which is not conducive to changing the development mode and improving the quality and efficiency of economic development.

The negative effects of blindly pursuing GDP have gone beyond the capacity of the environment and society. The answer is already given in the form of smog, heavily polluted rivers and groundwater, and the depletion of vast amounts of resources, straining the relationship between population and resources.

1.2   Pure Focus on Heavy Investment Promotion and Capital Introduction

In order to meet the needs of performance evaluation and personal promotion, some local officials at all levels have formulated preferential policies, including free or low-cost use of land, water and electricity, to attract a large amount of investment in industrial projects, especially large-scale industrial projects with huge amount of investment. The launch of such projects has a significant impact on local GDP growth. Therefore, many local governments constantly increase investment, carry out redundant construction, and expand the heavy industry and chemical industry that consume high energy and pollute a lot of land in order to set up cities and set up projects through industry. It only focuses on attracting investment but ignores the negative impact on local environment caused by the new pollution sources caused by many imported construction projects.

1.3 Pure Focus on the Fiscal Revenue

Since the implementation of the tax sharing system in 1994, the fiscal revenue of local governments has decreased significantly, resulting in the mismatch between the administrative and financial powers of local governments, especially in the fields of environmental protection, medical and health care, basic education, social security and other public services. In order to increase local fiscal revenue and achieve higher GDP, local governments often shelter local large taxpayers and polluting enterprises in the pillar industries of local fiscal revenue, ignoring the inefficient abuse and waste of resources and the serious consequences to the environment. In some cases, they even offer listing protection for enterprises by not allowing environmental law enforcement personnel to investigate and punish them, and openly restrict environmental law enforcement departments from administrating according to law. As a result, some "special" large polluters cannot get effective environmental supervision for a long time.

Through extensive economic development mode, it creates GDP achievements and pursues rapid GDP growth through a large amount of material input. It ignores the quality of GDP, human environment and resource and environment indicators, and takes resource and environment as the price to blindly obtain from nature, causing serious ecological and environmental problems.

1.4 The Concept of Green Consumption Is Relatively Weak

China's awareness of ecological environment is generally low, making it difficult for the concept of resource conservation and environmental protection to penetrate into the conscious actions and behaviors of governments at all levels, production enterprises and the public. The consumption psychology of conformity, comparison and vanity leads to the increasingly prevalent unsustainable consumption behaviors such as premature consumption, over-consumption and luxury consumption.

First, the government's green consumption concept is missing. For the sake of economic development, the government has carried out super-standard construction in the process of urbanization, carried out image projects and landmark buildings, and "sought for novelty, sought for greatness, sought for foreign style and sought for novelty" in architectural style. This not only causes unnecessary waste, but also affects the production field and technological innovation direction. The construction of the new city area is in full bloom, and the urban construction has become a phenomenon of "spreading the big pancake". Large squares, wide roads, spacious office buildings and numerous buildings have occupied a large amount of high-quality farmland and forest resources in the suburbs.

Second, social public consumerism is increasingly prevalent. The public take consuming more material goods and occupying more social wealth as the label of success and the symbol of happiness in life, and spend freely and without restraint in life practice to show their identity and social status by pursuing new, unique and special consumption behaviors. He Xiaoqing. *Research on Consumer Ethics.* Shanghai Sanlian Bookstore, 2007, page. 72. There are forms of spendthrift consumption, extravagant consumption, advanced consumption, ostentatious consumption of high consumption. Disposable products are springing up like mushrooms, and even many durable consumer goods, such as refrigerators, cameras, mobile phones, cars and so on, are being updated quickly. As soon as new products with more functions and novel styles come into the market, old consumer goods are quickly discarded. The pursuit of famous brands, luxury packaging, disposable or quasi-disposable, throw-away items are more and more, which not only greatly increased the consumption of resources, but also caused a large number of household garbage, so that human life in a "garbage world".

Third, enterprises cater to the consumer's "consumerism" demand. With the basic characteristics of "more consumption, less accumulation", consumerism has rapidly spread to developing countries and China after the prevalence of capitalist countries. In modern society, the business philosophy of the customer is god seemingly is to give consumers a noble status, but in fact is the pronoun of consumer supremacy. In order to make profits, enterprises constantly create hot consumption spots and produce a large number of products to meet consumers' consumption desire.

This mode of mass production-mass consumption-mass discarding intensifies the contradiction between the infinity of consumption desire and the limitation of resources. Not paying attention to the environmental problems caused by consumption will inevitably cause greater problems to the environment, imbalance between man and nature, and lead to ecological crisis.

2 OBSOLESCENCE AND FETTERS OF THE OLD GOVERNANCE SYSTEM

2.1 The Ecological Environment Management System Has Not Been Rationalized

China's multi-sector management of ecological environment is characterized by decentralization, departmentalization and fragmented supervision. In the field of ecological and environmental protection, a multi-department and multi-level management system combining unified management and classification is implemented, which involves environmental protection, land, forestry, agriculture, water conservancy and other departments, with repeated and overlapping functions. For example, the functions of pollution prevention and control are scattered in the departments of ocean, fishery, public security and transportation, the functions of resource protection are scattered in the departments of mineral resources, forestry, agriculture and water conservancy, and the functions of comprehensive regulation and management are scattered in the departments of national development and reform commission, finance and land and resources. This system of overlapping functions and multiple governance needs multiple departments, with the various aspects to achieve the management of the ecological environment. However, driven by the interests of departments and regions, the phenomenon of buck-passing and avoiding responsibilities often occurs. That is to say, when something beneficial happens to us, we will rush in for more benefits. When something bad happens or a thankless labor occurs, everybody is passive antagonism even argues back and forth over trifles and mutually makes excuses. Therefore, it is imperative to establish a unified ecological environment management department.

2.2 Uncoordinated Planning

According to relevant statistics, there are a total of 72 laws in effect in China's legal system covering various types of planning, and 113 types of planning are stipulated, respectively, including special plans for national economic and social development, urban and rural planning, land use planning, ecological and environmental protection planning, energy development planning, electric power planning and power grid planning. These plans belong to different administrative departments, with various types, complex system structure, various special plans isolated from each other, and it is also very difficult to coordinate in actual operation, which consumes a lot of time and technical costs, resulting in the reduction of planning timeliness and the excessive deviation between the actual implementation and planning.

2.3   Weak Public Participation

The public is an important force of ecological environmental protection and ecological environmental supervision. Although China has made obvious progress in public participation and government information disclosure, relevant laws, regulations and systems have been formulated to provide legal basis for public participation. But the scope and model of public participation remain limited. Influenced by China's top-down decision-making model, public participation in legislation and technical operation to be improved, public participation is limited to petitions and environmental impact assessment hearings, the release of information through the mass media and the Internet, and the involvement of environmental NGO and experts in government policies and decisions. The public participation level is not high and the participation ability is insufficient. Due to the influence of factors such as the lack of information disclosure, the public's insufficient understanding of some issues, and the information asymmetry they have mastered, the public is unable to put forward constructive opinions. Even when the public makes constructive suggestions, they sometimes get no response or attention. As a result, the public believes that their own opinions are insignificant to the decision-making of environmental governance, and their participation enthusiasm is not high, which is a mere formality, and the depth and breadth of participation is not enough to supervise and restrict the decision-making behavior of the government and affect the implementation effect and efficiency of decision-making.

To realize the modernization of natural resources and ecological environment governance, it is urgent to improve the public participation mechanism and protect the right of public participation.

2.4   The Work of Amending Laws and Regulations Lags Behind

Although China has basically established laws and regulations on ecological and environmental protection, there are still some problems that need to be further improved.

First, there is a lack of coordination and cooperation between laws. The incompatibility between China's laws, regulations and rules on environmental protection, the basic law and the separate law, the separate law and the detailed rules for its implementation, the national law and the local law, and the environmental law and other relevant laws are quite prominent, with overlapping, disconnection, contradictions and conflicts. For example, the *Water Pollution Prevention and Control Law of the People's Republic of China* and the *Water Law of the People's Republic of China* have contradictions and conflicts on the same issue, which directly affect the authority and effectiveness of the law. There is a lack of interaction and linkage mechanism among various economic means, such as fiscal, taxation, financial, price and compensation mechanism. As a result, it is difficult to form policy synergy, and the policy effect is limited.

Second, there are blank areas in the legislation of important ecological and environmental protection. China lacks special laws and regulations on energy conservation, water conservation, climate change, ecological compensation, wetland protection, biodiversity protection, soil and environmental protection, nuclear safety, desertification control, wildlife protection, toxic chemicals management and ozone layer protection.

Third is the lack of procedural law provisions and operability. Environmental protection laws and regulations have all legal abstraction, which leads to poor operability and inflexible application. Problems such as law enforcement responsibility is not clear, if problems arise, which department and who is responsible for, what to do, the consequences of such action are unclear; environmental laws and regulations in the field of services and consumption is not perfect or standard. Producer responsibility system needs to be included into the environmental legal system.

Fourth is poor cohesion between administrative law enforcement and the judicial system with contradiction and fault. The natural resources of our country property right ownership is not clear, which makes issues about the construction of ecological civilization like real estate registration, be lost in the endless wrangling and conflict.

Fifth is some laws and regulations already cannot adapt to the development of the real need. The legal system of ecological environment protection and resource management needs to improve such as the *Land Administration Law of the People's Republic of China*, the *Law of the People's Republic of China on the Prevention and Control of Atmospheric Pollution, the Water Pollution Prevention Law of the People's Republic of China, The Energy Conservation Law of the People's Republic of China* (hereinafter referred to as the *Energy Conservation Law*), *Circular Economy Promotion Law of the People's Republic of China* (hereinafter referred to as the *Circular Economy Promotion Law*), *the Mineral Resources Law of the People's Republic of China, the Forest Law of the People's Republic of China, the Grassland of the People's Republic of China* and *Wildlife Protection Law of the People's Republic of China*. Some supporting reform policies have not been introduced, the relevant supporting policies and measures of laws such as *Clean Production Promotion Law of the People's Republic of China, The Energy Conservation Law, the Circular Economy Promotion Law, The Renewable Energy Law of the People's Republic of China (hereinafter referred to as the Renewable Energy Law)* are not timely followed up, which results in that the implementation effect remains to be verified.

It is urgent to revise relevant laws, regulations, policies and standards to provide a basis for green development.

3   THE LACK AND DEFECT OF GOVERNANCE MECHANISM

3.1   Lack of Market Trading Mechanism

First is the property rights trading mechanism has not yet been established. Energy saving, carbon emission rights, emission and water rights trading system are not perfect and even missing. It is difficult to give play to the decisive role of the market allocation of resources.

Secondly, the mechanism of effective competition has not yet been established. Oil, gas, electricity and other industries are monopolized. Sales price mechanism of effective competition has not yet been established. Market transactions between power enterprises and users are limited. Energy saving, high efficiency and environmental protection units cannot be fully utilized; there is phenomenon of giving up hydro-energy, wind energy and optical energy from time to time; redundant power and power shortage coexist in some regions.

3.2   Resource Price Mechanism Is not Sound

Price is the basis of market resources; resources are important material foundation to the survival of human society. The formation mechanism of resource price plays an important role in regulating the distribution and use of natural resources.

The prices of natural resources and their products are unreasonable. The per capita possession of most resources in China is far lower than the world average level, but its price is lower than the international average level, failing to reflect the scarcity of China's natural resources, market supply and demand, resource scarcity degree, cost of ecological environment damage and repair efficiency, production safety cost and so on. Due to the low price of natural resources and their products, they cannot play a leverage role in the development and utilization of natural resources. As a result, in order to achieve rapid development and political achievements, some local governments tend to attract investment with low-priced natural resources. Enterprises make more profits, rely too much on energy-intensive industries, and accelerate the consumption of resources; Energy-intensive industries are accompanied by high emissions and high pollution, which aggravate environmental pollution and ecological damage, are not conducive to the improvement of resource utilization efficiency and economical use, and are not conducive to environmental protection and ecological conservation. At the same time, the low price of natural resources and their products increases the resistance to the adjustment of industrial structure, making the development cost of clean energy such as wind power generation and solar power generation and emerging industries appear relatively high, which is not conducive to the innovation of energy-saving and emission reduction technologies.

The price relation of natural resources and their products is not straightened out. The price comparison between China's resource products is unreasonable, the transmission between upstream and downstream is not smooth and the price comparison between coal, electricity, natural gas, crude oil and refined oil is not reasonable. In particular, conflicts and contradictions between coal prices and electricity prices have been accumulating for a long time, and the ex-factory price of natural gas is relatively low compared with the price of alternative energy. Coal and oil have been replaced by natural gas in many places, and strives for the processing projects that take natural gas as the raw material, leading to the prominent contradiction between natural gas supply and demand in some areas. The disconnection between the cost of electricity and the selling price and the disconnection between the transmission and distribution price and the feed-in price makes it difficult to optimize and adjust the energy structure and restricts the optimization of the industrial structure.

Market-oriented pricing mechanism has not yet been fully formed. China's oil, electricity, water, gas and other resources are still subject to the government pricing. The government has too much control over resource prices. The government still controls the prices of some resources that could have been determined by the market. Some areas where government regulation is needed are less well regulated. In the field of energy and resources, due to the insufficient energy monopoly operation system and regulatory mechanism, the government lacks the transparent cost of price in some energy fields.

3.3 The Absence of Ecological Compensation System

Weak Ecological Compensation

First, the compensation range is narrow. Whether the current ecological compensation is reasonable or not is mainly concentrated in the fields of forest, grassland and mineral resources development. The ecological compensation of river basin, wetland and ocean is still in the initial stage, and the ecological compensation of farmland and soil has not been included in the work scope.

Second, the compensation standard is unreasonable. Compensation standard is directly related to the success or failure of ecological compensation and ecological construction. Due to the immaturity of ecological environmental value assessment technology, many compensation standards lack objectivity, with the phenomenon of high protection costs and low compensation standards. The compensation standard is fixed and unchanged within a certain period of time, and has not been timely adjusted according to the economic development, the increase of residents' income level and the change of ecological protection cost. For example, as the price of beef and mutton goes up, the balanced subsidy of grass and livestock is not enough to cover the economic loss caused by the increase of production cost and the decrease of livestock. In addition, in some areas, the compensation standard is uniform, without adaptation to local conditions, and does not adapt to the actual situation of different ecological regions.

Third, the compensation fund source channel and the compensation way are single. Ecological compensation is mainly the vertical compensation from the central government to the local government. The funds mainly come from the financial transfer payment from the central government. The compensation input from the local government, enterprises and institutions is obviously insufficient. Social compensation models such as ecological environmental damage insurance, NGO participation compensation, social donation and ecological compensation public welfare fund are seriously missing. Market-oriented compensation models are still being explored, and the inter-regional ecological compensation system has not yet been established. In addition to financial subsidies, industrial support, technical assistance, talent support, employment training and other compensation methods have not received due attention.

Fourth, the ecological compensation policy is not sustainable. China's ecological compensation is mostly in the form of projects such as returning farmland to forests, returning grazing land to grass, protecting natural forests, and controlling sandstorms in Beijing and Tianjin, stone desertification control in southwest lava region, Qinghai Sanjiangyuan nature reserve, Gansu Gannan Yellow River important water supply area and other ecological construction projects. Compensation funds include not only relevant construction funds, but also compensation for the residents who suffer economic losses in the process of ecological protection. Moreover, different projects often have a compensation period, during which residents will limit their behavior because they can get compensation. However, when the compensation period is over, if the local economy still maintains the traditional development mode, some residents will destroy the ecological environment again in order to make a living.

Fifth, the compensation fund payment and the management method are imperfect. In some places, compensation funds have not been distributed in full and on time, and some have even been misused or misappropriated. In addition, the relationship between ecological construction, comprehensive environmental management and ecological compensation funds has not been clarified.

Lack of Basic System for Ecological Compensation
First, the property right system is not sound. China's property right system for natural resources is not sound, and the relationship among ownership, right of use and right of management has not been straightened out. The subject, object and service value of ecological compensation

must be defined on the premise of property right. If the property right is not clear enough, it will restrict the establishment of ecological compensation mechanism. For example, the reform of collective forest rights system needs to increase the rate of issuing certificates and the rate of household registration. There are still nearly a quarter of the country's un-contracted grasslands, the area of mobile grasslands is too large, the ownership of grasslands in the south and semi-agricultural and semi-pastoral areas is not clear, and there are many disputes over the ownership of grasslands and woodlands.

Second, the national ecological function zoning and function positioning are not synchronized. Part of the provincial main functional area planning has not yet been released, resulting in the planning for ecological environment functional area cannot be released. The regionalization and function orientation of the provincial ecological function have not been carried out, and the foundation of ecological compensation is not clear.

Third, basic work and technical support are not in place. The construction of China's ecological compensation standard system, ecological service value assessment and accounting system, and ecological environment monitoring and evaluation system lags behind. Relevant parties have not reached consensus on the measurement of ecosystem service value and ecological compensation standards, and there is a lack of unified and authoritative indicator system and measurement methods. There are still some blind spots in ecological environment monitoring. Monitoring and evaluation in key ecological areas are scattered in various departments, which are independent and have not yet realized information sharing, which cannot meet the needs of practical work.

The Construction of Relevant Policies and Regulations on Ecological Compensation Lags Behind
First, there is no special legislation on ecological compensation. China has actively explored the establishment of ecological compensation mechanisms in such areas as forests, grasslands, wetlands, river basins, water resources, mineral resources development, oceans and key ecological functional zones. But at present, there is no special legislation on ecological compensation, and the existing legal provisions concerning ecological compensation are scattered in many laws, such as *Environmental Protection Law of the People's Republic of China* (hereinafter referred to as *Environmental Protection Law*), *Grassland Law of the*

People's Republic of China, Forest Law of the People's Republic of China, Marine Environmental Protection Law of the People's Republic of China which are lack of systematicness and operability.

Second, existing policies and regulations are not authoritative and binding enough. In recent years, some policies and regulations on ecological compensation have been issued such as Measures for the *Administration of the Central Forest Ecological Efficiency Compensation Fund, Grassland Ecological Protection Subsidy and Reward Mechanism and Mine Environmental Management and Ecological Restoration,* its authority and binding force are insufficient.

Third, the existing policies and regulations also have the phenomenon of non-compliance with the law, lax law enforcement. As a result of relevant policies, laws are not sound, resulting in management confusion. In the ecological compensation management system, the government is both an athlete and a referee, lacking of performance evaluation and supervision mechanism. Moreover, in the operation of ecological compensation mechanism, stakeholder participation is not enough.

3.4   Lack of Supervision System

Lack of Unified Ecological and Environmental Supervision Authorities
At present, all pollutants discharged by all sources of pollution, including industrial point sources, non-point sources of agriculture and mobile sources of transportation, and all pollutant carrying media, including the atmosphere, soil, surface water, groundwater and the sea, are subject to supervision in different fields, departments and at different levels. The authoritativeness and effectiveness of this supervision system are not enough to carry out scientific and reasonable top-level design and overall deployment of ecological civilization construction, and difficult to form joint forces for ecological civilization construction.

The Supervision Functions of Ecological and Environmental Protection Are Decentralized, Making It Difficult to Form Joint Supervision
First, the functions of ecological and environmental protection departments at the national level are scattered and intersected. There are problems such as insufficient decentralization and inadequate supervision, which make it difficult to form a strong synergy of strict supervision. There is a mismatch between the functions and tasks assigned to

grassroots ecological and environmental protection departments. There is the phenomenon of "little horse pulling big cart".

Second, there is a lack of coordination mechanism among various ecological and environmental supervision departments. There are many phenomena, such as multi-headed law enforcement, multiple government departments, disjointed powers and responsibilities, decentralized supervision and construction funds. It is difficult to form a strong synergy of centralized use of funds and strict supervision.

Third, the overlapping responsibilities of various regulatory departments are prominent, the division of functions is not clear and the law enforcement is difficult, resulting in the prominent issue of striving for the benefits and buck-passing. To a great extent, it reduces the administrative efficiency.

Weak Ability to Supervise Ecological and Environmental Protection and Weak Law Enforcement and Supervision
First, there is a lack of functional allocation of environmental law enforcement supervision for local governments and relevant departments. There is a serious shortage of ecological and environmental supervision personnel, and it is difficult to put environmental supervision in place.

Second, it is difficult to form "rigid" constraints. Due to the imperfection of ecological environmental laws and regulations, the rigidity of law enforcement, the unitary means and the insufficient punishment of ecological environmental violations, the cost of violation is low and the deterrent effect of violation cannot be formed.

Third, some departments of the ecological environment at all levels lag behind in supervision capacity construction with low level of equipment. Management measures such as investigation and evidence collection, early warning of pollution accidents and emergency response have not yet been adapted to the requirements of administration according to law, which has restricted the smooth development of ecological and environmental supervision and watered down the policies and measures to solve prominent environmental problems.

Fourth is the weak pre-approval. Some new projects, in order to catch up with the progress of the project, have adopted the method of starting construction while doing environmental impact assessment (EIA) reports. It has lost the barrier of environmental assessment pre-approval.

Supervision is an effective means to fulfill the responsibility of green development. In-depth analysis of the lack of supervision mechanism is an effective way to implement the responsibility of green development.

3.5 Serious Lack of Investment and Financing Mechanism for Ecological Environment Construction

The Effectiveness of Government Financial Investment Is Insufficient
With the reform of the economic system, the investment and financing of China's resource development and utilization and ecological and environmental protection have introduced bank loans and foreign capital, which have gone through three phases, namely appropriation-loan-multiple channels coexistence, initially breaking the single channel of financial investment. Although eco-environment investment and financing have made great progress in terms of total volume channels and benefits, it still has the imprint of planned economy in terms of investment subject, decision-making mode, operation mechanism, operation management and capital operation. On the whole, investment and financing are still within the framework of the traditional system, with government financial investment as the main investment and financing activities. Because the total amount of government financial input is insufficient, the source of funds is unreasonable, the investment policy is vague or unsteady and the guiding force is not strong, so the effectiveness is insufficient.

Narrow Financing Channels and Single Methods
In terms of fund structure, financial funds have become the main source of funds in the field of ecological environment construction in western China. Most of the ecological environment construction projects in western China are funded by direct government investment and indirect financing (loan), and the proportion of direct financing is too low. The foreign capital utilization form is single, the scale is not big. At present, China's utilization of foreign capital for ecological environment mainly includes foreign government assistance, donations and loans from the World Bank and ADB, with less foreign direct investment.

The development of private capital market is insufficient. China's ecological environment construction has not fully utilized the domestic and foreign private capital, and the scale of investment and financing is small. There are still many obstacles in the market access, the information asymmetry is very serious and the state's capital input has not activated and attracted more social capital input.

The property rights of resources and environment are not clearly defined, and the government's financial input cannot drive the private capital, so it cannot play a leverage role, which is not suitable for the large amount of construction funds.

Lack of Investment and Financing Incentive Mechanism
Investment in ecological environment, including investment in the development and utilization of natural resources, investment in environmental governance, investment in ecological restoration, investment in major comprehensive ecological construction projects and other positive externalities, the incentive, security and guarantee mechanism for investment and financing in ecological environment construction are still seriously missing.

Lack of Security Mechanism for Investment and Financing
In terms of resource development and utilization and ecological environment construction, many construction projects are in a closed operation state and lack of open, fair and just market competition environment. In addition, the supervision mechanism and constraint mechanism in the process of project operation are not perfect enough, which makes no one assume the full responsibility of the investor. Project financing, construction, operation, debt repayment, capital recovery and other links are extremely easy to block, to a certain extent have affected the performance of investment benefits, and even brought risks. At the same time, due to the lack of market-oriented investment and operation mechanism and strong professional investment and financing institutions, the financing channels are not smooth, the use of funds is scattered and the fund management lacks the vitality and momentum of sustainable development.

Fiscal investment is insufficient, investment and financing incentive and security mechanism are seriously missing, which makes it difficult to adapt to the huge ecological environment investment demand. Therefore, the reform and improvement of ecological environment investment financing mechanism is inevitable.

4   THE LACK OF AND WEAK BASIC ABILITY

4.1   Weak Industrial System

Chinese traditional industries rely on the advantages of low labor cost and low resource price, so the industrial structure is unreasonable. In 2013, China's three industrial structures were 10:43.9:46.1; industry accounted for 37%; primary and secondary industries accounted for

53.1% of GDP, which is still a large proportion. Due to historical reasons, the heavy industrial structure has been a serious problem throughout China (see Fig. 1). In 2013, the proportion of heavy industry and light industry was 71.31 and 28.69%, respectively. Some traditional industries eliminated in eastern China have been transferred to western China. In addition, China's economic growth has been over-dependent on investment for a long time, so the capital-intensive industries such as petrochemical, steel, cement and other high-energy industries account for a high proportion in the industry. During the 12th five-year plan period, 26 provinces listed steel as a key industry and 25 listed petrochemical as a key industry.

Nonferrous metals are listed as key industry in 20 provinces, and their heavy industrial features will continue to be strengthened. Due to the imbalance of industrial structure and regional development in China, the typical duality of economic structure determines the existence of extensive growth mode with its inherent inevitability.

In the international competition, along with the aging of the population, resource shortage and environmental degradation, the labor cost and resource price are gradually rising, and the technical content of China's export products ranks 30th in the world.

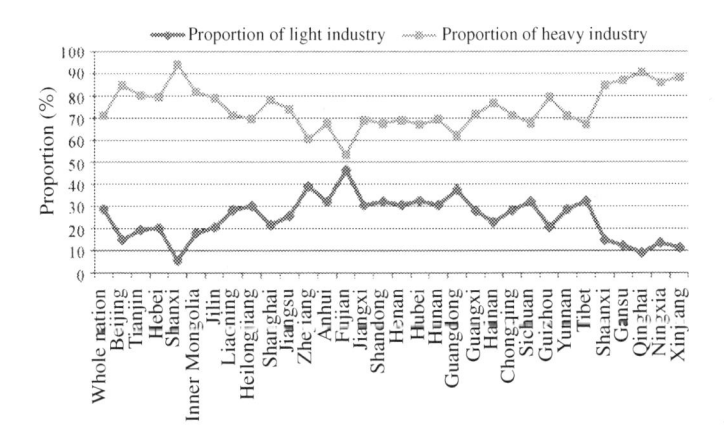

Fig. 1 Proportion of heavy industry and light industry in China's provinces (autonomous regions and municipalities directly under the central government) in 2013

4.2   Coal Is the Mainstay of Energy Production and Consumption

China's energy characteristics are "rich in coal, poor in oil and low in gas". In 2013, coal accounted for 66.0% of China's energy consumption, oil for 18.4%, natural gas for 5.8% and hydropower, nuclear power and wind power for 9.8%. In the world energy consumption structure, coal accounted for 30.1%, oil 32.9%, natural gas 23.7%, and hydropower, nuclear power and renewable energy 13.8% (see Figs. 2 and 3). The world's energy mix is moving toward efficient, clean, low-carbon or carbon-free natural gas, nuclear energy, solar energy, wind energy and biomass energy. China's coal-based energy mix is unlikely to change radically in the near term. The carbon emission of coal is 1.3 times that of oil and 1.7 times that of natural gas, causing serious pollution to the environment. Despite China's "west-east power transmission" project, the long distance, wide coverage and large network mode of supply pose great risks. Compared with distributed energy and smart grid, China's traditional energy supply mode relying on the huge energy power system is slow to respond, fragile and unable to give full play to the power capacity. Moreover, China's energy service industry is weak and difficult to operate. It is difficult to support green development.

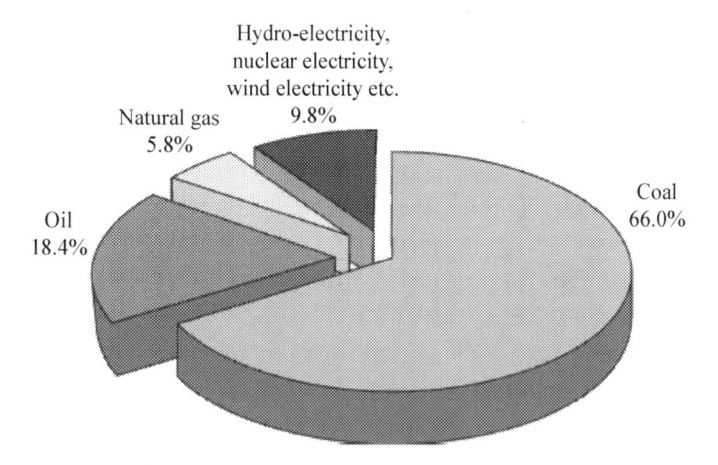

Fig. 2   Composition of China energy consumption in 2013

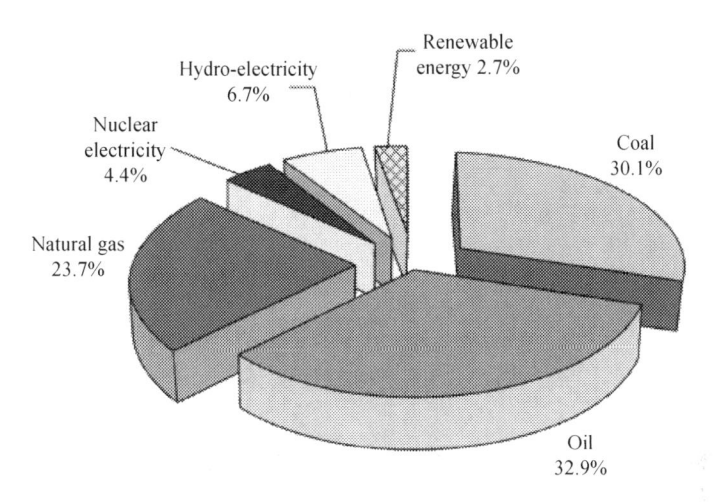

Fig. 3   Composition of world energy consumption in 2013

4.3   Weak Technical Support Capability

As a developing country, the biggest constraint for China's economic transformation from "black" to "green" is its relatively backward overall scientific and technological level and insufficient development and reserve of green technologies. Except for a few areas where China is at the forefront of science and technology in the world, most of them are in the catch-up stage. In the fields of energy production and utilization, industrial production and other fields, the technological development capacity and manufacturing capacity of key equipment are poor, the industrial system is weak and China lacks advanced and sophisticated technologies. Due to the blockade and restriction of Western countries, most of them cannot be imported, and the contribution rate of science and technology to economic growth is relatively low, making it difficult for China to adopt an intensive development mode. In some key industries in China, backward technology accounts for a higher proportion. The existence of a large number of backward technology and the absence of advanced technology make the traditional development of China fall into the "lock-in effect". In addition, China's overall investment in science and technology is low, and the process of scientific and technological innovation is relatively slow, which cannot effectively support the needs of green development.

4.4   Green Development Performance Has not Been Included in the Cadre Assessment System

First, the assessment of governance performance of leading cadres at all levels focuses on GDP, without including indicators such as resource consumption, environmental damage and ecological benefits as important indicators. The political performance view of GDP growth at the expense of blue sky, green mountains, clear water and other natural resources leads to the emphasis on development rather than protection.

Second, the audit system of leaving office of leading cadres for natural resources and assets and the lifelong accountability system for ecological and environmental damage have not been implemented, making it difficult to motivate and restrain leading cadres' behaviors. The audit system of leading cadres leaving office has been implemented for many years, but the audit mainly focuses on the economic responsibility of leading cadres leaving office. The audit of resource conservation and utilization, responsibility of environmental protection and whether the economic development is at the cost of sacrificing the environment has not been carried out yet. There is no corresponding system to restrain those who make blind decisions regardless of the ecological environment and cause serious consequences, especially those who endanger the physical and mental health of the people, harm their ecological interests and affect the stability of social order. There is no accountability or punishment. For those with good ecological environment management and having won the people's unanimous recognition, there is no corresponding system to give recognition and promotion.

4.5   Inertia of Traditional Development Path-Dependence of Traditional Development Path

Path dependence is similar to the "inertia" in physics. Once institutional change enters a certain path, it may be dependent on this path. After the reform and opening up, China's economy grew rapidly. Although many new ideas and thoughts appeared in the mode of economic growth, such as "exploring new ways" and "changing the development mode", the characteristics of growth can still be summarized as "three highs, three lows": That is, the traditional economic growth mode with high input and low output, high consumption and low return, high speed and low quality is a typical extensive economic growth mode.

*The Current Development Conditions Make It Difficult to Change
the Traditional Development Trajectory*
The condition of economic development is not only an important factor affecting economic development, but also an important factor determining the mode and type of economic development. For example, the transformation from extensive mode to intensive mode requires advanced technology, scientific management and high-quality labor force. Otherwise, this transformation cannot be realized. Although the conditions for economic development have improved since the reform and opening up, they still fall far short of the world's advanced level. This is an important reason why it is difficult for China to fundamentally change its mode of economic development.

High-quality labor force and relatively scientific management are also important conditions for the fundamental transformation of development mode, and intensive mode is also based on high-quality labor force and scientific management. Since the reform and opening up, through the development of education, learning by doing in developing market economy practice and the introduction of foreign advanced management tools and methods, China's labor force quality and management level have been greatly improved, but the labor force quality and management level is still not very high, which also restricts the fundamental change in the mode of economic development.

*China's Energy and Resource Endowment Structure Allows
the Continuation of the Traditional Development Path*
The coal-based energy structure restricts the transition to green development. China is endowed with rich coal, poor oil and little gas resources. It is rich in coal resources, accounting for 13% of global coal reserves. In terms of energy structure, China is one of the few coal-based countries in the world. Although the proportion of coal in China's energy consumption has decreased, it still accounted for 66.0% in 2013, compared with the world average of 30.1%. To ensure energy security, China's coal-based energy structure is unlikely to change fundamentally in the short term. With coal as the main source of economic growth, the six energy-consuming industries namely petroleum processing, coking and nuclear fuel processing industry, chemical raw materials and chemical products manufacturing industry, non-metallic mineral products industry, ferrous metal smelting and rolling industry, non-ferrous metal smelting and rolling industry and power and heat production and supply

industry, account for 3.66, 7.09, 5.32, 6.89, 4.26 and 5.17% of the main revenue of industrial enterprises, respectively. The problem of industry's high dependence on energy is acute.

China's Economic Development Stage Strengthens the Inertia of the Traditional Development Path

The stage of economic development is an important factor restricting the mode of economic development. Different stages of economic development have different goals and tasks, have different development conditions and have different characteristics of industrial structure, which will lead to different economic development modes.

China is still in the middle stage of industrialization and urbanization on the whole, and its strong demand for traditional industries will continue for another 15 to 20 years. In the future, China's urbanization will also grow at an average annual rate of about 1%. Under the condition that the extensive growth mode is difficult to change in the short term, the construction of urbanization infrastructure will drive the development of heavy chemical industry, increase the scale and intensity of the utilization of energy, water resources and land resources, and increase the difficulty of changing the pattern of complex regional air pollution and river basin water pollution.

China has just joined the ranks of middle-income countries and is moving toward high-income countries. The per capita living standard will also enter a stage of continuous transformation and upgrading. According to the experience of developed countries, this means that per capita resource consumption and pollutant emissions, especially per capita energy consumption, carbon dioxide emissions and solid waste production are rising, thus further aggravating the pressure on China's resources and environment. Coal consumption will peak at 4.7 billion tons in 2020, and emissions of major pollutants will peak in the next 10–30 years.

The Mindset of Putting More Emphasis on Speed Than Efficiency Slows Down the Pace of Change in the Mode of Growth

From the perspective of development goals and tasks, if people mainly pursue quantitative expansion and high-speed development, the development mode adopted will inevitably adapt to such requirements. If people pay more attention to quality improvement and efficiency improvement, they will adopt a development mode different from the pursuit of quantity and speed. In the early days of the founding of new China, it was the right decision to focus economic construction on the extensive mode of economic growth with the focus on accelerating the speed and expanding the scale in order to change the backward situation of China's economic situation as soon as possible and to establish a strong material foundation for the new-born socialism, which greatly promoted the economic development. However, the extensive economic growth mode is essentially at the cost of more resource consumption and environmental pollution. With the passage of time, resources are increasingly exhausted, environmental pollution is increasingly serious, and the contradiction with economic development is increasingly obvious. Since the twenty-first century, China has put forward the strategic concept of scientific development and started to attach importance to the transformation of economic growth mode. However, in the actual implementation process, due to the thinking pattern formed by history, governments at all levels pay insufficient attention to the transformation of economic growth mode. Constrained by traditional ideology and the old system, there is still a widespread tendency in various places to put more emphasis on input than output, quantity over quality, and speed over efficiency. Competition for investment, projects, the pursuit of output value and the speed emerged in an endless stream. This leads to repeated construction, repeated production and disorderly competition, resulting in waste of resources, increased investment costs, reduced investment returns and ultimately slowed down the pace of change in the growth pattern.

There Is an Urgent Need to Remove the Obstacles
to Green Transformation and Development
To meet the challenges of green development and follow the trend of international development, China must first adopt the concept of green development and improve its performance evaluation methods, promote the development of strategic emerging industries, encourage innovation in green science and technology, establish and improve institutions and mechanisms for promoting green development, accelerate green development and seize the commanding heights and development initiative of future international competition.

CHAPTER 6

Government Finance and Green Transformation and Development

1 The Meaning of Green Finance

The meaning of green finance can be understood from the following three aspects:

First, it is, conceptually, a new kind of finance. In other words, it is a kind of finance that introduces the concept of green environmental protection on the basis of the traditional public finance system, adapts finance to green transformation and development, and plays an active role in resource conservation and environmental protection. The development of economy cannot be separated from the exploitation and utilization of natural resources. The traditional public finance system fails to clearly include natural resources and ecological environment in the pursuit of goals. Therefore, while promoting economic development, it also brings destruction of natural resources and ecological environment. While pursuing economic and social development, the new finance also strives for the protection of resources and environment, and takes the protection of resources and environment as an important goal. Therefore, it is a new type of finance consistent with green transformation and development. Some scholars, such as Han Wenbo (2004), believe that green finance is to integrate "green elements" into the public finance system and integrate the extended concepts of low carbon,

© The Author(s) 2019   119
S. Gu et al., *Green Transformation and Development*,
The Great Transformation of China,
https://doi.org/10.1007/978-981-32-9495-0_6

health, environmental protection, safety, civilization and other economic development into the theory of the public finance system.

Second, it is formally a set of fiscal instruments. In other words, it is the "greening" of traditional financial tools, which integrates the concepts of economy, low carbon and environmental protection into various financial tools to achieve the effect of resource conservation and environmental protection while promoting economic and social development. Various financial instruments, such as taxation, subsidies, budgets, treasury bonds, government procurement, public investment and transfer payments, have regulatory and moderating effects on economic development. When the concept of finance becomes "green", the fiscal tools that play a role in operation and application are also "green" accordingly. Therefore, in the aspect of operation and application, green finance is a set of fiscal tools aimed at saving resources and protecting the environment. As defined by scholars such as Yang Tao (2006), green finance is to protect the environment, rationally develop and utilize resources, promote clean production and green consumption, and thus promote green economic growth.

Third, it is essentially an environmental protection means. That is, green finance is one of the environmental protection means. Together with many other environmental protection means, it achieves the purpose of promoting resource conservation and environmental protection by adjusting the distribution of economic interests and redistribution of national income in the process of economic and social development. There are many means of environmental policy, including legislative means, administrative means, economic means and technical means, and green finance is one of them. It corrects the negative environmental externalities of resource development and product use through green taxation, green procurement, green public investment and construction, and guides and promotes the development of green industry and accelerates the formation of a good ecological environment.

To sum up, green finance is a new type of finance that absorbs the concepts of resource conservation and environmental protection on the basis of the traditional public finance system, and makes the fiscal policy have the dual purposes of promoting economic and social development and resource and environmental protection by strengthening the green design of fiscal tools. In essence, it is a tool of environmental protection and plays a role mainly through the adjustment of economic interests and redistribution of social products.

2 THE MECHANISM OF GREEN FINANCE ON TRANSFORMATION AND DEVELOPMENT

2.1 The Mechanism of Green Fiscal Revenue

The revenue sources of the government's public finance mainly include tax revenue, income from state-owned assets, national debt revenue, fee revenue and other revenue. Among them, tax revenue is the main subject, which is the main source of government revenue (see Fig. 1). The income from state-owned assets is also an important source of fiscal revenue, especially in China, a socialist country dominated by public ownership. The amount of state-owned assets is huge, and the income from state-owned assets should be an important part of government fiscal revenue. It is mainly in the form of the operating profit of state-owned enterprises, the transfer or rental income of state-owned assets and the dividend income of state-owned assets. The national debt income is the compensatory income which the country obtains through the credit way, it is the government that raises the fund to society to make up the short-term fund insufficiency the important channel; fee income refers to the form of income in which the state government agencies or institutions

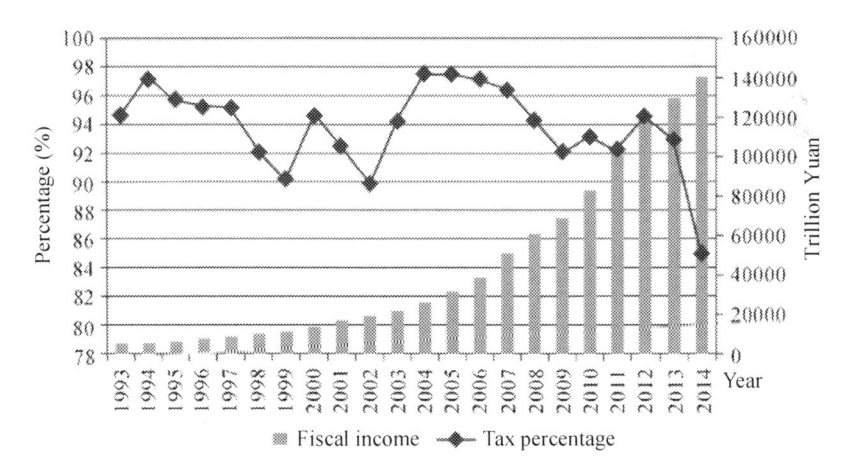

Fig. 1 Proportion of China's tax revenue in government revenue from 1993 to 2014 (*Data source* 1993–2013 data according to China statistical yearbook calculation, 2014 data provided by China news financial network)

charge certain fees to the beneficiaries when providing public services, implementing administrative management or providing the use of specific public facilities. It includes user fees and charges. The former refers to the fees charged by the government to the users of public facilities according to certain standards, while the latter refers to the fees charged by the government to citizens for providing specific services or specific administrative management. Other incomes include capital construction loan repayment income, capital construction income and donation income.

It is not difficult to see from the above that the main part of green fiscal revenue is green tax, followed by green state-owned asset income, green national debt and green government charges. The main principle of green taxation is to promote the formation of environment-friendly behaviors and industries through a good tax design and a guiding tax inclination mechanism, thus inhibiting the generation of environmental adverse behaviors or industries. The content of green state-owned assets income is quite rich. It can be the profit obtained by the green operation of state-owned enterprises, the green transfer fee obtained by the green transfer of state-owned assets and the green rent obtained by the green lease of state-owned assets. For example, in the process of transferring or leasing state-owned resource assets, the deduction of resource scarcity costs and environmental maintenance costs will result in green transfer fees or green rents, and dividends can be obtained by investing in environment-friendly enterprises and participating in their green management. In terms of green bonds, the central government can issue green bonds to raise funds at home and abroad to make up for the lack of funds in resource and environmental protection when the funds are insufficient. In terms of green government charges, the administrative cost can be reduced as far as possible through the electronic and low-carbon office, so as to reduce the revenue of fees and charges. At the same time, through the scientific research of people's behavior and the exquisite design of the fee standard, it induces people to form the behavior that is beneficial to resource conservation and environmental protection consciously when using public facilities.

2.2 The Mechanism of Green Fiscal Expenditure

With the exchange of goods and services as the criterion, fiscal expenditure can be divided into purchase expenditure and transfer expenditure.

The former is directly manifested as the government's purchase of goods and services, while the latter is manifested as the free and unilateral transfer of funds. Generally speaking, developing countries spend more on the former than on the latter, while developed countries spend less.

The purchasing expenditure of the government will have an important impact on green consumption and green production. First, the scale of government purchases will boost production of green goods. Since government procurement serves the whole society, it is difficult for private individuals to achieve the procurement volume. Especially in the early stage of economic development in the developing countries, due to the economic construction needs a large amount of infrastructure investment and the market economy development degree is not high, many economic activities have to be completed by the government directly involved. Therefore, the scale of government procurement directly affects the total scale of social commodity consumption. If the government orders a large number of green products, it will undoubtedly stimulate the production of green products in the whole society. Second, government purchasing expenditure legislation will promote green technology. In purchasing expenditure, the government is a special "private" consumer, who not only orders a large number of products with stable demand, but also may take measures such as punishment on the after-sales service experience of products. Manufacturers have to scramble to improve the product quality to win over such a special consumer. Therefore, if the government legislates to purchase green products with high quality and low price and adopts the way of public bidding and social supervision, it will stimulate many manufacturers to improve green production technology to gain competitive advantage, which will stimulate the progress of green production technology in the whole society. For example, the study of Xu Jinliang et al. (2014) shows that the procurement of new energy vehicles by the Beijing municipal government not only improves the air quality of Beijing, but also promotes the level of independent innovation of new energy vehicles and the transformation of scientific and technological achievements: Taking Foton Motor Company as an example, the government's procurement of new energy vehicles contributed as much as 86.16 and 56.25% to the increase of its development project expenditure and the number of patent approvals, respectively, and 17.89 and 74.24% to the increase of its main business income and profit margin, respectively. Third, the government's purchasing expenditure will produce the demonstration effect of green consumption and "soft force" effect. Government's purchasing expenditure includes consumption expenditure and investment expenditure, covering all areas of social consumption, especially the consumption expenditure of government departments, which will have a certain demonstration effect on the consumption of the public. Investment expenditure, to some extent, determines the behavior of the public and thus affects its green consumption. For example, many city residents with the awareness of environmental protection are willing to put some recyclable wastes into different categories, but they are troubled by the lack of convenient recycling facilities. For another example, in the process of urbanization, many local governments lack low-carbon and energy-saving planning for road traffic, so many citizens have to choose to buy private cars to travel.

Transfer spending also has a strong impact on green transformation and development. For example, the government's financial allocation for green technology research, economic subsidies for consumers to buy green products and producers to produce green products, discount support for green enterprise loans, etc., promote the development of green industry and green science and technology by directly adjusting the economic income distribution relationship. In addition, due to the existence of environmental externalities and environmental integrity, inter-governmental green transfer payment also plays an important role in green transformation and development. Green fiscal transfer payment includes vertical transfer payment between superior and subordinate governments and horizontal transfer payment between governments at the same levels. The green transfer payment from the central government to the local government will improve the enthusiasm of local governments in environmental governance, while the horizontal green transfer payment between regional governments will promote the cooperation and coordination of different regional governments in environmental governance. For example, economically underdeveloped regions are more dependent on the resource industry, and the development of resource industry not only destroys the ecological environment of the region, but also leads to the deterioration of the ecological environment of related and adjacent regions. The relevant and adjacent regions help the less developed regions through horizontal financial transfer payment, thus weakening the dependence of the less developed regions on the resource industry, and thus maintaining the ecological environment quality of the relevant and adjacent regions.

2.3   The Mechanism of Green Finance

Green finance operation includes several basic links, such as green finance legislation, green finance organization, green finance implementation, green finance supervision and green finance evaluation. These links affect each other and jointly affect green finance.

Green fiscal legislation is the foundation. It sets out the basic rules for the operation of green finance, involving green taxation, green procurement and green budget. The green transformation of finance needs to start from legislation, to force the green transformation of finance from laws and regulations and to strengthen its feasibility by formulating specific rules.

Green finance organization is the core. It involves the division and coordination of financial and administrative power between the central government and local government in the financial system and affects the enthusiasm of local governments in the practice of green finance. Due to the externality of environmental problems, improper financial division of labor aggravates the emergence of environmental problems and delays the governance of environmental problems. For example, in China's tax distribution system, local governments have to bear the basic costs of local economic and social development. Therefore, local governments in less developed areas often neglect environmental protection and indulge the development of polluting industries to a certain extent when they are unable to introduce high-tech industries with less pollution. For another example, due to the high concentration of tax power in the central government, local governments are unable to levy or regulate some green taxes according to local specific conditions, which makes some green taxes formulated by the central government very inefficient or even completely invalid in local practices.

Green finance implementation is the key. It determines whether green finance can be put into practice in the end, and it is also the fundamental way for finance to promote green transformation and development. Different from the previous financial system, green finance has a high degree of scientific and technical requirements. It not only needs to identify which substances are harmful to the environment, but also needs to design the tax system according to the user's behavior, so as to inhibit harmful production and consumption, and stimulate environmental protection behavior. The fundamental reason why many green taxes fail to play a role in promoting green transformation is that they are poorly understood and poorly designed.

Green fiscal supervision is promoting. As green finance is a kind of fiscal promoting the transformation and development, it is inevitable to encounter many obstacles in its operation. It not only needs to be enforced by legislation, but also needs to strengthen supervision to promote its thorough implementation, avoid deformation or distortion and find problems in operation.

Green finance evaluation is strengthening. The purpose of green finance evaluation is to evaluate the "green" degree of finance in practice through the establishment of green finance evaluation objectives and evaluation criteria in order to analyze its practical effect and existing problems, point out the direction and key points for the next step of green finance, so as to further strengthen the degree of "green development" of finance. The evaluation index can consider the energy consumption ratio of ten thousand Yuan of fiscal revenue, the proportion of total revenue of specialized green taxes in total tax revenue, the proportion of green fiscal expenditure in total fiscal expenditure, the ratio of total revenue of specialized green taxes to environmental governance expenses, and so on.

3   GREEN FINANCE PRACTICES ABROAD

3.1   Green Taxation

EU Countries

In general, the green tax system of EU countries has the following characteristics: Firstly, the establishment of the green tax system is quite early. Some countries are the earliest in the world in setting up green taxes. For example, Sweden is the first country in the world to levy environmental tax, and the Netherlands is one of the first countries to levy garbage tax. Secondly, with energy tax as the core, control over energy consumption can be strengthened by setting up a number of energy-related taxes, such as carbon dioxide tax and sulfur tax when general taxes are imposed on oil and natural gas. Thirdly, the system of levy is meticulous and perfect with gradation adjustment, emphasizing practicality and motivation. Fourth, the overall transformation of the tax system, from the original emphasis on the introduction of special green taxes to the later control not only from the source of consumption but also through the garbage tax or charges to promote the use of resources, recycling. Fifth, tax suppression and tax incentive should be combined to strengthen the taxation of environmental harmful products and their behaviors, and at the same time to improve people's enthusiasm for reducing consumption and environmental protection management through tax reduction and exemption. Here are a few examples of green tax systems in typical EU countries.

Sweden

Sweden is the world's first country to levy environmental taxes and promulgated the world's first environmental tax adjustment act in 1991. Its green tax revenue is large, accounting for about 13% of GDP, and its annual green tax revenue accounts for about 15% of the total tax revenue. Its green tax content includes two aspects: First, a sound energy tax system should be established, such as general energy tax, carbon dioxide tax, sulfur tax, gasoline and methanol tax, mileage tax and motor vehicle tax. The second is to achieve a green tax transition, with a focus on increasing taxes on environmentally damaging activities and reducing taxes on labor employment and income, such as those on fertilizers, pesticides and batteries.

Sweden's energy tax, a combination of specific taxes on fossil fuels, thermal power and greenhouse gas emissions, is at the core of its green tax. By levying general energy tax on fuel and various special energy taxes related to fuel, the energy consumption level can be controlled, so as to not only curb the excessive consumption of natural resources and achieve the goal of environmental protection, but also to raise funds for environmental protection. The energy tax is as follows: (1) The general energy tax on fuel. Oil, coal and natural gas are the targets. The taxpayer is the person who produces the taxable product in Sweden or uses the product to produce the corresponding product and imports the taxable product. (2) Value-added tax on energy. Introduced in March 1990, the tax is 25% of the energy price, which includes excise tax. (3) Carbon dioxide tax. A carbon dioxide tax is a tax on oil, coal, natural gas, liquefied petroleum gas, gasoline and domestic aviation fuels. It's a tax on fossil fuels that contain a certain percentage of carbon or on businesses or individuals that directly emit carbon dioxide. The tax base is based on the average carbon content and calorific value of various fuels at a rate of 0.25 Swedish krona per kilogram of carbon dioxide. Different fuels have different tax rates because of their emissions. (4) Sulfur taxes. The tax is on the sulfur content of oil and coal. (5) Gasoline and methanol tax, mileage tax, motor vehicle tax, etc. Gasoline is taxed according to the size of the lead content, the tax rate is Swedish krona 2.37 per kilogram of unleaded gasoline and Swedish krona 2.68 per kilogram of unleaded gasoline. Methanol is taxed at 0.8 Swedish kronor per kilogram. A mileage tax is levied on diesel vehicles, depending on the type and weight of the vehicle.

Sweden has taxed the use of fertilizers and pesticides since 1984, and the green tax transition began in 2000. To reduce carbon dioxide emissions from the air and encourage green production and consumption, Sweden recognized the need for a change in the tax system, reforming the existing tax structure to meet the needs of environmental developments, and shifting the focus of taxation to industries with high energy consumption and high pollutant emissions to control carbon dioxide emissions from related enterprises and individuals at the source. In order to control environmental pollution at source, Sweden imposes a tax on fertilizers, pesticides and batteries. The tax standard is as follows: fertilizer, 0.6 Swedish krona per kilogram of nitrogen, 12 Swedish krona per kilogram of phosphorus; pesticides, 20 Swedish krona per kilogram; batteries, including those containing alkali and mercury, 23 Swedish krona per kilogram, and nickel and tin batteries 13 Swedish krona per kilogram. The tax revenue is mainly used for environmental research, agricultural consultation and soil salinization treatment. To curb industries with high emissions and pollution, in 2006 the Swedish government decided to raise taxes on the petroleum-intensive transport sector and on commercial electricity users. Sweden has raised taxes on key energy users such as vehicles, residents and the service sector. It has eliminated tax breaks for traditional users, such as electricity and natural gas, and introduced new taxes under new EU rules.

In addition to establishing a relatively complete energy tax system and realizing the green tax transformation, the Swedish government also stimulates the enthusiasm of enterprises and the public to reduce energy consumption and protect the environment through appropriate tax reduction and exemption policies.

The Netherlands

As early as 1960, the Netherlands introduced green tax into the tax system, which is one of the earliest countries in the world to levy garbage tax. Green tax revenue in the Netherlands accounts for about 14% of total tax revenue and 3.2% of GDP. Its green taxes include fuel tax, carbon dioxide tax, energy regulation tax, water tax, garbage tax, surplus manure tax and noise tax, up to more than 10 kinds, the following are the main types: (1) Fuel tax. Fuel tax is a tax levied by the government on major fuels such as gasoline, diesel and natural gas to raise funds for environmental protection. The taxpayer is the producer and importer of fuel. It has a flat rate, which is set annually by the Swedish government based on the amount of money needed to meet environmental targets set by the environment ministry. (2) Carbon dioxide tax. The carbon tax was introduced in 1990 and changed to a 50% energy/carbon tax in 1992. A carbon tax applies to all energy sources. Electricity is indirectly taxed through a tax on the use of fuel. Part of the energy tax is exempt for some energy-intensive sectors (big gas consumers), and part of the carbon tax is not. (3) Energy regulatory tax. The subject of tax payment shall be enterprises engaged in energy. Household users and small commercial enterprises that substitute mineral oil (gasoline, diesel, etc.) for natural gas have also been subject to tax since 1996. (4) Water. The water tax consists of two parts: One is a water pollution tax, which is levied on the pollution of water resources. The tax will be levied according to the amount of oxygen and heavy metals emitted, and different tax rates will be applied to different water resource reserves. The other is a tax on the exploitation and use of water resources called a groundwater tax. (5) Garbage tax. The main purpose of the garbage tax is to raise funds for garbage collection and disposal. At first, every family was listed as the target of garbage tax, and families with small population could get certain tax deduction. However, this method does not take into account the amount of waste discharged by different households and fails to better reflect the fairness of tax and the incentive of tax to green development. To this end, the government later introduced a garbage collection tax, in the garbage collection tax, according to the number of each household bin and the number of units of each bin to collect, and local governments are free to choose between the two. (6) Surplus manure tax. The surplus manure tax is a national levy imposed by the Dutch central government on farms that produce manure since 1987. The rate is based on the weight of phosphorus produced per hectare of farmland. (7) Noise taxes. A noise tax is a tax levied on the use of civil aircraft, mainly by airlines, to produce noise in a particular area (a noise-affected area, mainly around an airport). Its tax base is the amount of noise produced. The main purpose of the levy is to raise funds for the government to install sound insulation near the airport and relocate residents.

The Dutch government not only collects taxes on environmentally unfriendly materials and their consumption behaviors, but also provides incentives through tax differentiation and tax deduction. For example, in the energy regulatory tax, there is no tax on fuel for transportation and natural gas for greenhouse and horticultural sectors, as well as natural gas for non-fuel use and power generation; specify the types of projects enjoying preferential energy tax policies; use tax law provisions to promote the development and utilization of cleaner production technologies. For enterprises adopting innovative cleaner production or pollution control technologies, their investment can be depreciated at 1 year (the depreciation period of other investments is usually 10 years).

Denmark

Denmark's green tax system is somewhat similar to that of Sweden, with energy tax as the main target, and "environmental tax" is introduced to help curb the occurrence of harmful environmental behaviors and reduce the scale of resource consumption to accelerate the green tax transformation. Conventional taxes are levied on traditional fossil fuels such as coal, oil and natural gas, including gasoline and diesel engine oils. In 1992, the tax on carbon dioxide was introduced, and in 1996, the tax on sulfur dioxide was increased. Green owner's tax is levied on conventional car owners based on the fuel consumption of cars. The basis of the tax is the fuel consumption of cars. Environmental taxes have also been levied on water, waste water, garbage, disposable tableware, plastic bags and pesticides. There are 16 in all.

Denmark's green taxes have paid off. In the past 30 years, Denmark's GDP has increased by 50%, while its carbon dioxide emissions have decreased by 13.9%, forming the "Danish model" of "coexistence of emission reduction and economic prosperity".

Germany

On April 1, 1999, Germany launched the green tax reform for the first time. Germany's green tax reform mainly includes increasing the tax on mineral oil, improving the water pollution tax and environmentally friendly tax breaks. For example, in Germany, a water pollution tax has been levied since 1981. The taxation system for water pollution is relatively complete. Based on the "pollution unit" of waste water (equivalent to one resident's annual pollution load), the unified national tax rate is implemented. All the taxes collected are used to improve the water quality of the region, and obvious ecological and social benefits have been achieved. For another example, products that eliminate or reduce environmental hazards can be exempted from sales tax and only need to pay income tax. Exemption of electricity tax on electricity generated directly from renewable energy sources such as electric energy, solar energy, biological energy and water energy; In the financial year of purchase or construction, the environmental protection facilities of the enterprise can be depreciated by 60%, after that, it will be depreciated by 10% of the cost every year.

Germany's green tax reform has achieved remarkable results. Since the reform, carbon monoxide and sulfur oxide emissions have been greatly reduced, and nitrogen oxide emissions have also been significantly reduced.

Other EU Countries

Finland has imposed a gas tax on cars since 1990. Finland uses different tax rates for vehicles with and without exhaust conversion devices and applies differential GST rates to petrol and diesel vehicles. Since 1993, a preferential tax rate has been applied to sulfur-free diesel and refined petrol.

British businesses can sign up for energy efficiency targets and carbon-dioxide reduction targets with the government. Companies that meet their targets can get a 20% energy tax cut. Tax breaks are given to solar, wind and other new energy sources for generating electricity.

The United States

The green tax in the United States has the characteristics of wide coverage and flexible preference. Both the federal and state governments have introduced environmental taxes of varying degrees, covering a wide range of categories, including energy, consumer goods and consumer behavior. Its fundamental purpose is to reduce the emission of harmful substances to the environment and provide funds for environmental governance and residents' health care. Its green tax is reflected in the following aspects:

Taxes on fuel: (1) Taxes on gasoline and diesel. The federal gasoline and diesel taxes are 18.4 cents and 24.4 cents per gallon, respectively. Tax rates vary from state to state. Rates vary from about 8 cents per gallon to about 30 cents per gallon. (2) High gas consumption vehicle tax. The tax is a federal excise tax on inefficient fuels that do not meet minimum combustion targets. (3) The formation of underground storage tank leakage fund tax. The tax, which comes from excise tax on gasoline, diesel, jet fuel and other fuels, is 0.1 cents per gallon.

Energy taxes: (1) Coal taxes. The tax is a special federal domestic tax on coal used to provide social security funds for "coal lung" patients. Open-pit mining is taxed at 55 cents a ton, while underground mining is taxed at 1.1 dollars a ton. (2) Mining tax. The tax is a consumption tax on the exploitation of natural resources, mainly oil and gas, in order to protect the natural environment by influencing the rate of extraction.

Taxes levied on urban environment and living environment pollution: (1) one-time razor and old tire tax. The environmental protection tax is levied on disposable razors, while the old tire tax is levied on production or import. (2) Garbage control tax and garbage tax. The garbage control tax is a service tax levied on products that become garbage after all business activities, such as production, wholesale and retail. The tax rate is 0.15‰ of the total income or value. In addition, about 3400 local communities in 37 states levy a tax on household waste, charging about $1–$1.50 per 30-gallon bag. (3) CFCS tax. The tax is based on the quantity of chlorofluorocarbons produced and imported. The rate was $5.35 per pound of Freon in 1995 and has increased by 45 cents a year since. The duty rate of CFCS is determined as the basic duty rate. Other ozone-depleting substances are classified according to their ozone-depleting potential. The duty rate is the product of the basic duty rate and ozone-depleting potential.

Favorable tax incentives and tax breaks for the environment. American tax incentives mainly include tax credits for clean fuels; reduce or exempt energy taxes on alternative fuels and renewable fuels; use accelerated depreciation in particular for investments in certain pollution control technologies; grant enterprises the preferential treatment of reducing or exempting income tax for research and development of new pollution control technologies and production of pollution substitutes; and grant preferential treatment of reduction or exemption of income tax on the income derived from comprehensive utilization of resources by enterprises. Tax credit and deduction for cyclic investment; The purchase of recycling equipment is exempt from sales tax. For example, under the *American Recovery and Reinvestment Act*, taxpayers can receive a $1500 tax credit for purchases of energy-efficient refrigeration and heating equipment, insulation and other products. A tax credit of up to $7500 will be given to buyers of more fuel-efficient plug-in hybrids. Another example is the use of solar and geothermal energy equipment; 10% of the equipment investment can be exempted from tax. A tax credit of $1.5 cents per kilowatt for generating electricity from renewable resources and from biomass; for owners use clean fuels such as natural gas, oil, liquefied natural gas and electricity, for ethanol fuel with an alcohol content of more than 85%, fuel costs are deducted from the total proceeds, etc.

America's green tax has three obvious advantages: First, it is targeted. Because the United States has a large area with few people and a long commute distance, automobile consumption is indispensable. If there is automobile consumption, there will be gasoline consumption. Therefore, the green tax in the United States strengthens the tax on fuel and gas-guzzling cars. Second is flexibility. The United States should give full play to the green tax initiative of the federal and state governments, and allow the states to develop their own tax systems according to their own situations on the premise of not violating the federal principles. For example, in California, the tax deduction for energy-efficient dishwashers, washing machines and water heaters ranges from $50 to $200; Arizona offers a 10% sales tax rebate to businesses that pay in installments for equipment that recycles renewable resources and controls pollution; Connecticut gives preferential loans to businesses that process renewable resources and waives state income taxes, equipment sales taxes and property taxes. Third is specificity. The green tax revenue of the United States is not only used for environmental governance, but also for the protection of residents' health. Therefore, it not only constructs a strict collection and management system, but also is strictly implemented in practice. For example, green tax is usually collected uniformly by the taxation department first and then transferred to the ministry of finance, which classifies them into general fund budget and trust fund (and then transferred to the subordinate super fund with special content of environmental protection). Superfunds are centrally managed by their competent authorities, and their management practices are highly modernized and incorporated into the federal budget. These green tax revenues have the characteristics of special fund and operation increment, because they are managed in classified management and effective operation value-added, so as to guarantee the capital demand for recovery of various environmental and health damages.

Russia

In 2001, Russia carried out a comprehensive tax reform, established a new natural resources tax system and strengthened the regulation of taxation in the exploitation and use of mineral resources and water resources.

Since January 1, 2002, the mineral resource exploitation tax has replaced the three existing taxes, namely the exploitation fee of mineral resources, the reproduction royalty of mineral raw material base and the consumption tax of petroleum and natural gas, while it has also stipulated the distribution method of tax revenue from oil and natural gas exploitation.

In order to effectively regulate the use and distribution of water resources, Russia has introduced a water resource tax and designed four taxes. The four taxes are: (1) tax on the use of groundwater resources. Taxpayers are all legal persons and natural persons who seek, explore and exploit groundwater in Russia. The maximum tax rate for the exploitation of fresh underground water is 8% of the value of the raw materials collected, and the tax for the use of groundwater resources is included in 40% of the federal budget and 60% of the main federal budget, respectively. (2) Reproduction tax on mineral raw material base for groundwater exploitation. The basis of taxation is the value of primary products obtained and sold from the actual exploitation of groundwater. (3) Industrial enterprises draw water tax from water conservancy system. The taxpayer of this tax is an industrial enterprise, which should pay taxes not only on water used for production but also on water used for other purposes. (4) Pollutant emission tax on water resources facilities. The tax is levied on the discharge of sewage containing hazardous substances exceeding the standards to water resources facilities and the discharge of sewage meeting the standards in excess of the quota. The tax rate is fixed according to the standards and discharge amount of sewage. It can be seen from the above that Russia attaches great importance to the protection of water resources and is also very careful in the design of taxes. There is a tax on groundwater resources, emphasizing the protection of groundwater; there is water collection tax to promote resource utilization of industrial enterprises; and there is water resources pollutant emission tax to prevent the deterioration of water quality, which are very worthy of China to learn with per capita water shortage.

Japan

Japan began to implement the environmental tax policy in 2007. The main goal of the environmental tax is to play the role of price guidance, publicity and financial resources. The basic approach is to implement various policies with macro-scopical and forward-looking nature by clearly stipulating in the law that power should be reasonably divided among all levels and departments, optimize the investment and consumption structure, stimulate the potential of the domestic environmental protection industry, improve its international competitiveness and strengthen the publicity to improve the national concept of green finance and taxation and environmental awareness, in order to cooperate with the national environmental protection work.

Japan's green tax is more scientific and sophisticated in tax design. For example, in order to control automobile exhaust emissions, Japan implements a "green tax system" for all types of cars and sets differential tax standards according to their fuel consumption, so as to promote consumers to actively buy cars with low fuel consumption.

Japan's green tax system attaches great importance to stimulating and guiding the development of environmental protection industry through tax reduction and exemption policies. For example, for units that reach the standard of energy conservation, the government will grant tax reduction or exemption in a certain period of time, special depreciation and tax reduction or exemption for listed energy-saving equipment, preferential treatment to the purchase of environment-friendly cars in the purchase tax. In the year of use, special tax refund will be given for the waste plastic products recycling treatment equipment at 14% of the obtained price in addition to the ordinary tax refund. The fixed assets tax will be refunded for 3 years for equipment such as waste paper deinking treatment unit, glass debris and inclusion removal, empty bottle cleaning and aluminum recycling manufacturing. Tax on fixed assets shall be reduced or exempted for public nuisance prevention facilities. In addition, there are special financial funds to guide and support the research and development of new energy technologies.

As can be seen from the above, Japan's green tax has two prominent characteristics: First, it is scientific and feasible to strengthen the tax collection link, such as determining the tax rate standard according to the level of automobile fuel consumption. The second is to strengthen the cultivation of green and environmental protection industry. For example, a detailed list of various environmental protection industry projects is listed in the tax deduction and exemption, which provides the operating basis for the implementation of tax deduction and exemption. Japan emphasizes the scientific nature and feasibility of green taxation, which is worth learning in China.

3.2   Government Green Procurement

Government procurement is also called unified government procurement or public procurement. It refers to the use of financial funds by state organs, institutions and organizations at all levels to purchase goods, projects and services from the domestic and foreign markets within the catalogue of centralized procurement formulated according to law or above the standard of procurement quota by means of public bidding for the needs of daily administrative activities. Government green procurement means that the government considers the environmental protection effects of procurement comprehensively from the perspective of social and public environmental interests. By introducing environmental standards, assessment methods and implementation procedures into the existing government procurement system, relevant policies and measures such as preferential procurement and prohibition procurement are formulated to affect social investment, enterprise production, public consumption and other activities, so as to achieve the purpose of energy conservation, emission reduction and environmental protection. Generally speaking, the scale of government procurement is huge and plays a leading and guiding role in consumption and production, while the green procurement of the government can also play a leading role in green consumption and stimulate green production, which is conducive to promoting green growth. Internationally, one of the major trends in the changes in fiscal structure in recent years is that social expenditure and environmental protection expenditure account for an increasing proportion of fiscal expenditure, accounting for 50~60% or even more than 70% in many countries. The green procurement of the EU accounts for 19% of its public procurement share. Among its member states, the green procurement of Sweden accounts for 50% of its public procurement, Denmark accounts for 40%, Germany accounts for 30% and Britain accounts for 23%. The UNSTAT survey showed 84% of the Dutch, 89% of Americans and 90% of Germans would consider environmentally friendly products on shopping. At present, more than 50 countries in the world have actively promoted green procurement, and green procurement has become a worldwide trend. Below, a few government green procurement more perfect countries are introduced.

Green Procurement Practices of Governments
The United States
The United States is the first country in the world to embark on the path of government green procurement. The green procurement system is relatively perfect, and the federal decree and presidential executive order are the legal bases for promoting government procurement. In 1991, the United States issued a presidential decree stipulating that green products should be given priority in procurement. Then, a series of green procurement plans were successively formulated and implemented, including the plan for purchasing renewable products, the "energy star" plan, the eco-agricultural products act and the procurement plan for environment-friendly products. For example, in March 1992, the Office of Federal Procurement Policy (OFPP), the Office of the President and the Office of Budget Management jointly issued a policy paper on procurement of products and services that meet environmental and energy efficiency requirements. In 1993, President Clinton signed a presidential decree stipulating that the federal government must purchase products with the "energy star" logo, which made the "energy star" logo more recognized by enterprises and promoted its development, making it an international energy standard. In 1998, the US government issued executive order No. 13101, namely *Greening the Government Through Waste Prevention, Recycling and Federal Procurement*, requiring administrative agencies to integrate waste prevention and recycling into their daily operations while requiring agencies to increase and expand the market for these products by increasing the priority and demand for recycled substances. In 1999, the *Environmental Friendly Product Procurement Guide* was published. In 2000, the executive order *Greening the Government through Leadership in Environmental Management* was issued, requiring administrative agencies to integrate the environmental management system into their daily decision-making and long-term planning processes. The number of renewable products purchased by the government increased to 54. The United States also further developed government green procurement promotion measures, such as the proposed procurement price incentives, the price of green products can be $5 \sim 15\%$ higher than the same function of non-renewable products. Put forward the

annual procurement proportion and made it clear that the proportion of green products to be purchased every year was 50%. In addition, the US government green procurement system also attaches great importance to information disclosure. For example, product catalogs designated by the environmental protection agency (EPA) are made public and frequently updated to facilitate government and public purchase and facilitate public supervision. Strengthening training is also one of its promotion measures. For example, through classroom teaching, training, seminars and publications, the United States often conducts green procurement education and training for federal procurement policy makers and executives.

To sum up, the green procurement system of the US government has the following characteristics: First, it has relatively perfect laws and regulations as the guarantee; second, there is a detailed "green product list" to facilitate the implementation; third, there is a corresponding agency responsible for management—the us environmental protection agency (EPA) assumes the three responsibilities of management, supervision and evaluation. Fourth, there is a positive policy to promote. Fifth, the disclosure and timely update of green purchasing information. Sixth, strengthening guidance and training for government procurement personnel.

Canada

Green procurement by the Canadian government is part of the federal government's "government green initiative", which is led by the federal environment ministry and began to develop many implementation guidelines for various departments after 1992. The environmental management guidelines of the Canadian government set out policies for sustainable development in all sectors and measures to be implemented. The government's "green operation" practice will be whether the procurement of environmental signs included in the assessment object in order to guide departments on how to adopt best practices for seven projects to achieve environmental objectives, including green procurement, waste management, water resource use, building energy use, official vehicle use, land use management and human resource management. In 1995, the Canadian government issued the *Green Government Guide*, requiring each government department to develop its own sustainable development strategy and specific plans, and incorporate them into the daily affairs and decision-making of the government, including government procurement. In addition, the "environmental specifications for office furniture" drawn up by the ministry of the environment lists in detail the items to be assessed by procurement personnel in each life cycle stage, such as bidding qualification, product design, product materials, manufacturing process, product packaging and marketing, product use and product waste disposal.

Germany

Germany is the first country in the world to carry out environmental label certification and also the first country to carry out green procurement. In 1979, the green label system was introduced, mainly represented by the "Blue Angle Mark" system. It stipulated that government agencies should give priority to the procurement of green label products and explicitly prohibited waste. The products must be durable, recyclable, maintainable and easily disposed of. Chapter 37 of the *Circular Economy Act*, adopted on 27 September 1994, sets out the principles for government procurement of circular economy products and clearly stipulates that the relevant agencies of the federal government should formulate work plans for the procurement and use of relevant goods, draw up the construction plan, purchase and use environment-friendly products and services that meet the requirements of durability, maintenance guarantee and reusability.

The green procurement of the German government has played a leading and exemplary role in the purchase of green products by consumers, improved the public's awareness of environmental protection, promoted voluntary adjustment of product structure by enterprises and increased the share of production and consumption of green products. By the end of 1999, the categories of products with environmental mark certification had reached 100, covering motor vehicles, building materials, interior decoration, IT technology, office supplies, horticulture and other fields. By 2005, there were more than 7500 environmental labeling products in Germany, accounting for 30% of the total number of goods sold in the country.

Britain

In its 1990 white paper, the British government required all government departments to complete the implementation of good management practices (GH) by the end of 1992, including environmental planning in green procurement, energy efficiency, waste management and other aspects. The UK government drives procurement primarily through the department for environment, transport and regional affairs (DETR). The DETR is responsible for providing green sourcing guidance to purchasers and suppliers, setting procurement requirements for each product and providing environmentally superior information products. The guidelines also remind government procurement personnel to pay attention to the green product bidding process and require government agencies to formulate corresponding green procurement policies and formulate specific procurement plans. In the implementation of the procurement policy, the lowest price or the bidder who can provide the most economic benefits shall be given according to the provisions of the British government procurement law. The purchasing unit can make the final decision by taking into account the factors of product quality, technical superiority and price. The government procurement law also provides some examples, such as emphasizing its concern on the environmental advantages of products purchased from the perspective of product life cycle environmental cost and requiring enterprises to provide explanations in bidding documents for the reference and decision of procurement personnel.

Japan

In 1994, Shiga prefecture of Japan took the lead in formulating the green procurement policy and started the organized green procurement activities in Japan, which was also regarded as the landmark event of the Japanese government's green procurement. In 1995, Japan formulated and implemented the first "government-operated green action plan", which set out the goal of green procurement and required it to be completed by the year 2000. In February 1996, the Japanese government and various industrial groups jointly established the green procurement network (GPN), which formulated a series of systems for government green procurement, including the guiding principles of green procurement, procurement guidelines, the establishment of product database, the provision of procurement center information, certification and the issuance of "green procurement certificate", etc., which indicates that the Japanese government's independent green procurement activities are carried out nationwide. GPN, a green purchasing group and alliance jointly formed by government departments, enterprises and social organizations, is different from the procurement of governments in the United States, Canada, Britain and other countries. However, it plays a very good role in promoting the concept of green purchasing among governments, enterprises and consumers, providing green purchasing information and exchanging information among members. By 2000, the Japanese government had made green procurement more standardized and promulgated the *Green Procurement Law* and the *Law on Promoting the Purchase of Recycled Products*. The *Green Purchasing Law* came into full force on April 1, 2001. The law stipulates that government agencies must take the lead in purchasing products with low environmental load. Government agencies can adopt the third-party certification system or the green product information system as the reference criterion for purchasing green products; draw up the annual green procurement plan, report regularly the actual procurement situation and its implementation results, and will encourage local governments and civil society to take an active part in green procurement. The *Procurement for Recycled Products Act* promotes the active purchase of environmentally friendly recycled products by international agencies and local authorities, while maximizing green procurement information.

Now the Japanese administrative organs have developed the green procurement policy, there are 166 kinds of items identified as the government's priority purchase items, among which the raw material is 100% waste paper and copy paper with less than 70% whiteness identified as the most priority purchase items. In 2001, the proportion of government purchases of specific goods has reached 92.6%. The proportion of recycled copy paper in the whole specific purchase has increased from 11.6% in 2000 to 23% in 2001. 6%. In 2005, all the central government departments in Japan implemented green procurement, 100% of 47 local governments and 12 designated cities implemented green procurement, and 68% of the 700 cities also implemented green procurement systematically (Cheng Yongming 2013).

Australia

A conference on green procurement was also held in Australia in November 2004. One of the most notable was the announcement of the ecological procurement plan for Victoria. The scheme has been a great success in attracting local governments to participate, greatly increasing the procurement of recycled and environmentally friendly products. On the basis of this plan, Australia will develop membership and establish a national green procurement network. Membership of the network requires the signing of a memorandum, the appointment of a responsible person as a liaison with the association, the establishment of a green procurement working group, the formulation of green procurement policies, the formulation of implementation plans, the continued promotion of green procurement and the submission of an annual green procurement report each year.

Inspiration from Green Procurement of Governments
(1) Improve green government procurement legislation. For example, the *Green Procurement Act* promulgated by the Japanese government and the presidential decree signed by the US government. (2) Develop detailed procurement guidelines. Governments such as the United States have developed detailed environmental friendly product procurement guidelines, including product catalogs. (3) Strengthen the assessment and training of government green procurement personnel. The government has not only formulated green product procurement guidelines, but also strengthened the assessment and training of green procurement management personnel, among which the governments of the United States and Canada are the representatives. (4) Strengthen product environmental labeling certification. For example, the "energy star" logo of the United States, the "blue angel" environmental protection logo of Germany, and the "ecological logo" of the Japanese government. (5) Communication with industry (enterprises). For example, Japan has strengthened ties with various industrial groups to establish green procurement network organizations.

3.3   The Green Budget System

Green Fiscal Expenditure Practices Abroad
The United States
Environmental finance is part of the US budget system. The budget system of the United States includes three links, namely budget formulation, implementation and review. In the budget-making process, the department budget prepared by the US Federal Environmental Protection Agency (EPA) needs to be submitted to the Office of Budget and Management directly under the President, and the Audit Department is responsible for the audit. The budget is then submitted to the Congressional Budget Committee for review, which, if approved, would authorize funding for the EPA as required. Finally, after the budget is completed, the agency is subject to a review by the General

Accounting Office to see if the agency's financial activities are limited to those approved by congress. The budget system of the United States is highly transparent and quite strict. The budget needs to be detailed into the expenditure of each project and released to the public in a certain way. Any expenditure on environmental protection must be carried out in strict accordance with the requirements of the budget. Financial expenditure on environmental protection mainly includes five areas: Clean air and global climate change, clean and safe water, land conservation and restoration, healthy biological communities and ecosystems, and related service functions and environmental benefits (see Table 1).

The fiscal expenditure on environmental protection in the United States is not generated consciously, but gradually increases its share with the continuous occurrence and increasingly serious environmental problems and finally forms the current result. The first large-scale environmental spending occurred in the early twentieth century to restore

Table 1 Structure of federal environmental finance expenditure in the United States

Objectives	Clean air and global climate change	Clean water and safe water	Soil conservation and restoration	Healthy biocenose and ecosystem	Relevant service functions and environmental benefits
Content	• Healthy outdoor air • Healthy indoor air • Protect ozone layer • Reduce radiation • Reduce Greenhouse gas emission • Strengthen scientific research	• Protect human health • Protect water quality • Strengthen scientific research	• Protect land • Restoration of land • Strengthen scientific research	• The harm of chemicals and pesticides to communities • Restoration and protection of endangered ecosystems • Strengthen scientific research	• Achieve environmental protection objectives by strengthening compliance with environmental regulations • Improving environmental performance by preventing pollution and encouraging innovation • Improving Indian health and the environment • Improve the capacity of sustainable society through scientific research

Sources Wu Jiang, Jia Lei, Shi Lei, et al. The Development Process of Environmental Finance in the United States and its Enlightenment to China. *Environmental Protection*, 2012 (20): 74–76

natural resources. The second, in the 1930s, was designed to take the last environmental movement further. The third was in the 1970s, when special investments in environmental protection appeared in the US budget. According to the statistics released by the environmental protection agency of the United States, in the 1972 budget of the United States, the investment in pollution control and environmental control was 26 billion dollars, accounting for 1% of the gross national product. In 1989, special budget expenditures for environmental protection reached 120 billion US dollars, accounting for 2.8% of the GDP. Between 1972 and 1994, except for the first three years, from 1975 to 1994, the GDP of environmental expenditure in the United States stabilized at 1.7~1.8%. Since then, the United States has continued to invest in environmental projects. As stated in the US environmental finance budget system, these funds are strictly used for environmental pollution control and to encourage the development of environmental technologies. For example, in the resource protection plan of the United States, in order to protect the environment in the ecologically fragile areas, the United States plans to invest 1.5 billion dollars every year to encourage the landholders in these areas to transfer their production activities, build vegetation in the transferred areas and restore the ecological balance. In addition, in the annual budget, the US government sets up a large amount of special funds for environmental protection projects. For example, $490 million annually is earmarked to encourage the export of clean energy and promote the development of clean energy programs worldwide. A $1.6 billion budget was used to develop low-carbon energy to reduce greenhouse gas emissions and prevent climate change. In the 2001 budget, $85 million was spent to create a new clean air partnership fund to help pay for air pollution and greenhouse gases. The US government also invests a lot of money in the green high-tech industry, usually through direct investment in research and development, which accounts for almost half of the US government's investment in scientific research.

Japan

Due to geographical factors and the lack of resources, Japan has always attached great importance to environmental protection, and its financial input has always been great. In the decade of the 1970s alone, Japanese government spending on environmental protection soared from 0.62% of GDP in 1970 to 1.65%. By the 1990s, it was over 1.8%.

Japan's budget expenditures on environmental protection mainly focus on strengthening environmental protection inspection, investment in public hazard prevention and control projects, relevant public utilities, victim protection and other environmental protection expenditures. At the same time, Japan attaches great importance to the financial input of energy conservation. In 1994 alone, the financial investment related to energy increased by 390 billion Yen compared with that in 1993.

The European Union
European Union countries spend a lot on environmental protection, and Switzerland's public finance accounts for 2% of its total fiscal expenditure on environmental protection. Finland's central government's environmental budget reached 2% in 2000. Under the ten-year transport plan, the government has invested 180 billion in modernizing transport, doubled spending on energy efficiency in 2002–2003 and spent 1 billion on home efficiency programs.

Inspiration from Foreign Green Fiscal Expenditure Practices
First, we will strengthen green fiscal spending and budget legislation.

The fund demand of environmental protection investment management is big but the effect is slow, is easy to be marginalized in the financial expenditure. Therefore, in the fiscal budget expenditure, we should make clear its position, subject, responsibility, scope and proportion.

Second, establish a strict management system. According to the major environmental problems of people's livelihood that need to be solved in each period, the scope and contents of key environmental finance expenditures in each period are clearly listed, and a set of environmental finance expenditure system consisting of budget, audit, publication, implementation, supervision and audit is established to ensure that every sum of money is really and effectively used for the governance or protection of environmental resources.

Third, ensure stable and high investment in environmental protection. The governance and protection of environment and resources requires long-term efforts and capital investment, so it is necessary to ensure stable and relatively high investment in environmental protection. In many countries, when preparing budgets, environmental protection expenditure is included in the budget. Generally, the proportion of public finance expenditure is set at 2%, and the mechanism for stable growth of government investment in environmental protection is determined.

In view of China's future haze and other environmental problems will continue for a long time, environmental protection investment should also be stable in 2 ~ 3% of the proportion of public financial expenditure.

4   CHINA'S GREEN FINANCE PRACTICES AND PROBLEMS

4.1   Green Tax Practice and Problems

Taxes

At present, China's tax categories directly related to resources and environment, such as resource tax, fuel oil tax, farmland occupation tax, land use tax, deed tax, vehicle and ship use tax and so on, play a direct role in reducing resource consumption and protecting resources to a certain extent, but due to the lack of system, the protection ability is relatively weak. However, the indirectly related VAT, enterprise income tax, export tax rebate and other design is not reasonable, there are a lot of "green" potential to dig. To sum up, China's green tax system mainly has the following problems:

First, the green tax system has yet to be formally legalized. At present, the effectiveness of green tax documents is too low. For example, tax breaks or other preferential policies that stimulate green production or consumption are almost all issued by the state council or its functional departments in the form of documents, which are somewhat arbitrary. This is contrary to the principle of tax legality and high seriousness, and cannot well play the incentive role of green tax system. From the perspective of strengthening national ecological civilization construction and legal system construction, the green tax system should be clearly confirmed by relevant laws, and be specialized, systematized, standardized and institutionalized in the form of special legal documents to improve its authority and influence.

Second, the green tax system lacks a holistic design. From the perspective of tax structure, green tax system cannot rely on a single tax, but should be targeted at all fields that need to curb consumption and protect resources and environment. Everything involved in the tax should be a comprehensive "green" treatment and a large and systematic system of green tax system. From the perspective of tax design, it is not only for the production link, but also for the consumption link, but also for the disposal link after use, such as the collection of waste and sewage treatment fees, the collection of cigarettes and other health care fees that can produce harmful gases. From the point of view of tax design, it not only emphasizes increasing the intensity of tax collection and restraining consumption, but also studies how to carry out scientific design and carry out effective regulation. From the perspective of tax revenue management, although it has been incorporated into the unified management of public finance, it lays more emphasis on the management of special accounts and special use. However, the current tax system still lacks the design of this overall concept, which is reflected in the following aspects.

One is that the scope of the current tax on environmental protection is too narrow, which does not really play a role in protecting the environment. Apart from the fact that there is no comprehensive "greening" of value-added tax and enterprise income tax, the resource tax directly levied on natural resources is limited to some mineral resources and does not include water, forest, grassland and other resources that have been seriously damaged. Consumption tax is also the same; the main role of consumption tax is to guide consumers to green consumption, but the scope of the current levy of consumption tax is too narrow. At present, it mainly includes tobacco, wine, cosmetics, ornaments, jewelry, jade, firecrackers, fireworks, gasoline, diesel, motorcycles, cars, batteries, paint, etc., and it does not completely cover biological products with high pollution, high energy consumption and great damage to the ecological environment in the development. Some rare traditional Chinese medicine products, such as saussurea involucrate and cordyceps sinensis, are scarce in quantity at present. However, large quantities of them have damaged the ecological environment and aggravated the extinction of species. A strict protection system should be established to impose heavy taxes on these rare products.

Second, the design of levy basis is extensive and unscientific, which cannot play the role of effective punishment and policy guidance. For example, the current resource tax is linked to the price of resources after several reforms. Although it has the advantages of convenience and easy operation for the collection of resource tax, it is not related to the mining behavior. In fact, the recovery rate of resources is closely related to the degree of resource waste. "Urban mineral resources" is conducive to the recovery and utilization of mineral resources and can greatly reduce the depletion of resource reserves and environmental damage caused by the primary development of non-renewable resources, but

China's resource tax has not been involved in this area. If subsidies are effectively used, such as "negative resource tax" and other preferential tax policies, they can promote the reuse of recyclable metal minerals in cities and reduce urban environmental pollution.

Third, the lack of resources after the use of waste management taxes cannot use these taxes for effective special environmental governance. For example, although the emission of municipal solid waste is increasing and some cities cannot find suitable landfill sites, the garbage tax has not been launched yet, let alone the special environmental governance with the garbage tax revenue.

Third, green tax management means are relatively backward. There are many defects in the current preferential tax policies on environmental protection, which have not played their due role in promoting environmental protection. Under the existing tax system, the tax incentives related to environmental protection are mainly reflected in the VAT and enterprise income tax preferences. The preferential means are direct tax reduction or exemption, which is less targeted and flexible than the internationally popular preferential means such as accelerated depreciation, reinvestment tax rebate and deferred tax payment. One of the problems reflected in this is that the research and design of green tax in China lags behind as a whole, leading to the fact that green tax preferential means are still very simple and there are few effective promotion measures.

Fourth, green tax collection and management and income distribution are not reasonable. There are two purposes for green tax collection. First, through taxation, resource development and resource consumption are inhibited, so as to achieve the purpose of resource protection and environmental pollution reduction. The second is to raise funds to fund the government's resource and environmental governance. The problem of resource and environment is an external one with strong spatial and temporal transference. Therefore, the collection and management of green tax and income distribution is a problem that needs to be jointly negotiated and solved by relevant stakeholders. However, the local management of resource and environment tax in China is quite serious, and there is no special management and reasonable distribution of income, which makes the environmental governance in large regions that need joint improvement, lack of strong subject and sufficient capital guarantee. In view of the particularity of the subject of resource and environment problems, the commonality of interests and the far-reaching influence, the collection and management and income distribution of green tax should be deeply reformed in the future, and the collection and management power and tax income of related subjects should be reasonably distributed.

Fees and Charges

China's pollution charging system began in 1979, when the *Environmental Protection Law of the People's Republic of China* (trial) stipulated the principle of charging for excessive pollution. In 1982, the state council formulated the *Interim Measures on the Collection of Pollutant Discharge Fees*, which stipulates the purpose, scope, standards, conditions for surcharge and reduction, fee management and methods of use for the collection of pollutant discharge fees, which has started to charge industrial enterprises for discharging wastewater, waste gas and waste residues that exceed standards. In January 2003, the state council promulgated the *Regulations on the Administration of the Collection and Use of Pollutant Discharge Fees*. In 2003, the State Planning Commission, the Ministry of Finance, the State Environmental Protection Administration and the State Economic and Trade Commission jointly promulgated the *Standard Administrative Measures on the Collection of Pollutant Discharge Fees*, which greatly reformed the pollutant discharge fee system.

The main changes of this reform are: (1) The expansion of the object of levy. The scope of the levy will be extended from enterprises and institutions to all units and individual businesses that discharge pollutants directly into the environment. (2) Strengthen the charging standard. The charge standard is changed from the original out of limits charge to pollutant discharge charge and out of limits charge in parallel; out of limits single factor charges will be changed to total multi-factor charges. (3) Special financial management of sewage discharge fees. In respect of the management and use of sewage fees, the *Regulations on the Administration of the Collection and Use of Sewage Fees* stipulates that all sewage fees shall be used exclusively for the prevention and control of environmental pollution, and no unit or individual may intercept, occupy or divert them for other purposes. The pollutant discharge fees must be incorporated into the financial budget and included in the special funds for environmental protection for administration, and shall be mainly used for the prevention and control of major pollution sources, regional pollution prevention and control, the development, demonstration and application of new technologies and techniques for pollution prevention and control, and other pollution prevention and control projects as stipulated by the state council, as appropriation subsidies or discount interest loans. This is more specific and targeted than "The environmental protection subsidy funds shall be jointly arranged and used by the environmental protection department and the ministry of finance". The subsidy funds for environmental protection shall be mainly used for subsidizing key units that discharge pollutants to control pollution sources and for comprehensive measures to control environmental pollution" stipulated in the *Interim Measures on the Collection of Pollutant Discharge Fees*. At the same time, according to the *Interim Measures on the Collection of Pollutant Discharge Fees*, the environmental protection subsidy funds may be used to subsidize the purchase of monitoring instruments and equipment by environmental protection departments, but may not be used for the administrative expenses of environmental protection departments themselves, as well as non-operational expenses such as the construction of office buildings and dormitories. The *Regulations on the Administration of the Collection and Use of Sewage Charges* stipulates that the collection and use of sewage charges must strictly follow the "two lines of revenue and expenditure". The fees collected shall be turned over to the finance department, and the funds needed for environmental protection and law enforcement shall be included in the budget of the department, which shall be guaranteed by the finance department at the corresponding level.

At present, the main problems of sewage discharge fees are as follows:

First, the low charging standard makes it difficult to effectively curb pollution emissions. According to Pigou tax theory, the collection of sewage charges can effectively curb pollution and provide funds for pollution control. However, from the perspective of China's practice, the effect of pollutant discharge fees in restraining pollution emission is low, which is also insignificant compared with the pollution control fund. Although China has strengthened the collection of pollutant discharge fees since 2003, the discharge of industrial waste water and industrial sulfur dioxide did not decrease significantly, and only after 2011 did they show a strong downward trend (see Fig. 2). This shows that only by charging the sewage charge itself the effect of its emission reduction effect is weak. The main reason is that the charging standard of China's sewage charge is low, and enterprises prefer to choose pollution rather than invest in pollution control. According to calculations, China's

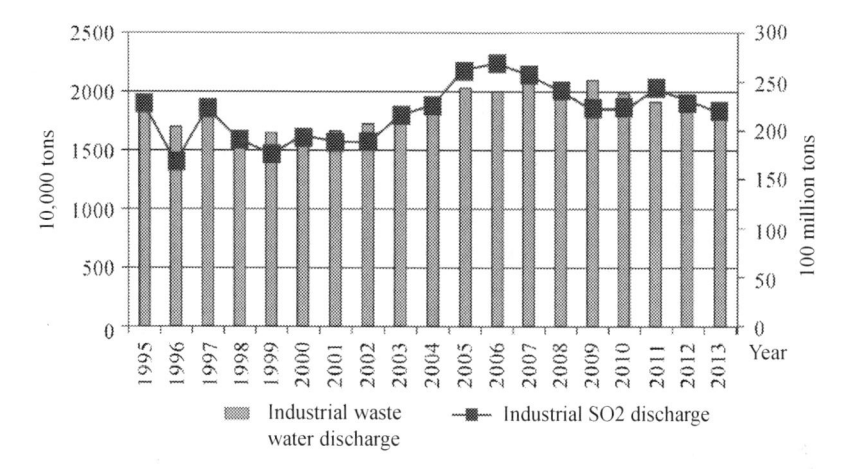

Fig. 2   Emission of industrial sulfur dioxide and industrial waste water in China from 1995 to 2013 (*Data source* National environmental statistics bulletin 1995–2013)

current standards for the collection of sewage charges are much lower than the current pollution control costs, only about 50% of the operating costs of pollution control facilities, and some projects even less than 10% of the cost of pollution control. A typical example is: At present, China's sulfur dioxide emissions charging standard is 0.63 Yuan/kg, and the average cost of thermal power plant flue gas desulfurization treatment is 4~6 Yuan/kg. Therefore, enterprises prefer to choose pollution rather than investment funds for pollution control, and pollution control enthusiasm is not high. The proportion of investment in pollution control in GDP is very low. From 2001 to 2013, the average investment in pollution control was only 1.39% of GDP (see Fig. 3).

Second, the pollution collection coverage is narrow, and the pollution control fund gap is huge. Although the total amount of sewage charges collected and paid in China has increased to a certain extent since 2003 (see Fig. 4), the gap is still large compared with the demand for pollution control funds. Since 2007, the proportion of pollutant discharge fees in the fiscal expenditure on environmental protection has become lower and lower, accounting for 6.00% in 2013 (see Fig. 5). The main reason for this is that the scope of pollutant discharge fee levy in China is

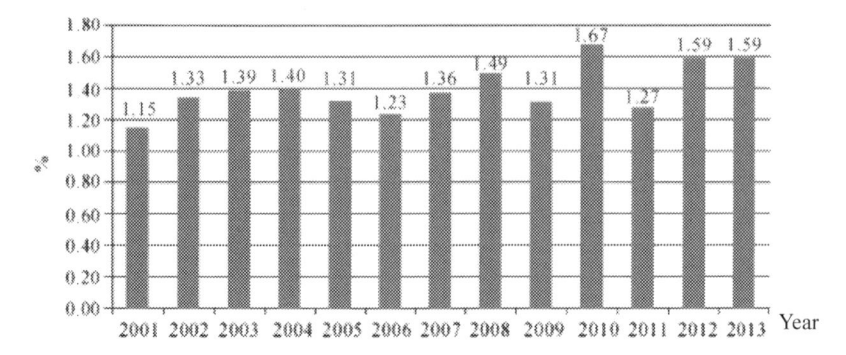

Fig. 3 Proportion of total investment in pollution control in China's GDP from 2001 to 2013 (*Data source* National environmental statistics bulletin 2001–2013)

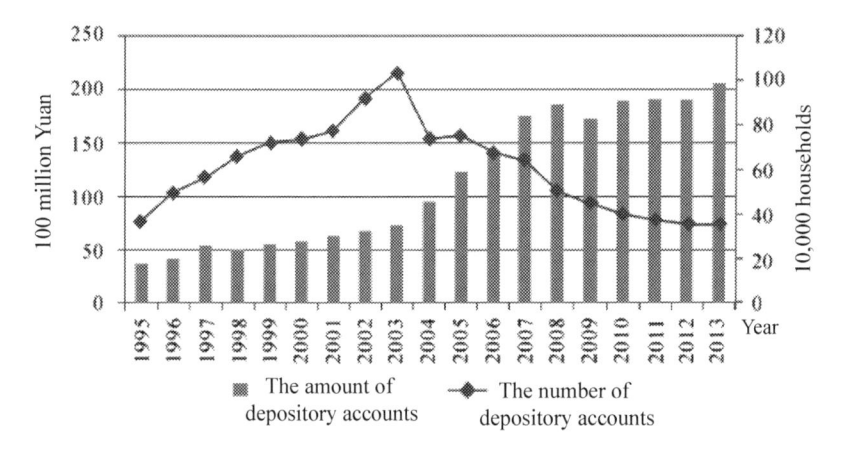

Fig. 4 Number and total amount of the pollutant discharge fee paid in deposits from 1995 to 2013 (*Data source* National environmental statistics bulletin 1995–2013; *Note* In 2003, the number of depository accounts was calculated by adding the first half and the second half of the year, which may be overlapped and tends to be high)

too narrow, which is reflected in the following aspects: (1) The pollutant discharge fee is mainly levied on the production field, while the levy is very weak on the consumption field, especially the consumption of ordinary residents. (2) Sewage charges are mainly collected by enterprises in

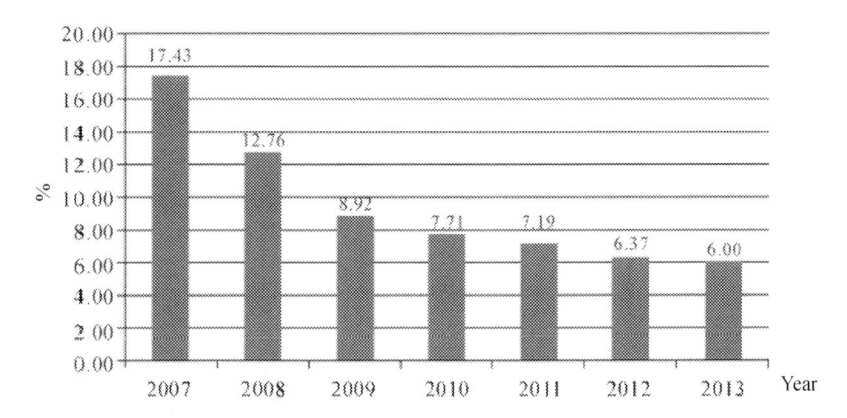

Fig. 5 Proportion of China's sewage discharge fees in financial environmental protection expenditure from 2007 to 2013 (*Data source* National environmental statistics bulletin 2007–2013)

large- and medium-sized cities, while charges for the tertiary industry, township and street enterprises are only implemented in some regions. (3) The pollutant discharge fee is only levied on some pollution items and does not include carbon monoxide, carbon dioxide, Freon, radioactive materials and other pollutants. For this reason, with the closure of some high-polluting enterprises, the number of deposit accounts in China has been greatly reduced in recent years (see Fig. 4).

Third, the current sewage charges belong to local administrative charges and are not rigid enough. First, this is reflected in the arbitrariness of the declaration. The calculation basis of the pollutant discharge fee collection amount is reported by the enterprise itself and approved by the environmental protection department. This may be due to "rent-seeking" and "bribery" and make the enterprise declare less and pay less. Second, regulatory capacity varies. Regulation relies on the establishment of systems and equipment, both of which are related to the level of local economic development. Due to the great difference in regional economy, the regulatory capacity is uneven. Third, the phenomenon of fund misappropriation, taking up and occupation is serious. At present, sewage discharge fees are collected by local governments and incorporated into local finance, but their use is not open to the public. They are not transparent and dedicated, and misappropriation, taking up and occupation occur from time to time.

4.2   Government Green Procurement Practices and Problems

Government Green Procurement Practices

Although China's government green procurement started late, it has developed rapidly in recent years, and a series of rules and regulations related to government green procurement have been formulated. The *Government Procurement Law of the People's Republic of China* (hereinafter referred to as the government procurement law), which came into effect in 2003, stipulates that government procurement shall protect the environment. In 2004, the ministry of finance and the national development and reform commission jointly issued China's first specific policy on promoting energy conservation and environmental protection through government procurement, namely the *Implementation Opinions on Government Procurement of Energy Saving Products*. In 2006, EPA and the Ministry of Finance jointly issued the *Opinions on the Implementation of Government Procurement of Environment-Labeled Products* and the first batch of *Government Procurement List of Environment-Labeled Products*, which requires state organs, institutions and organizations at all levels to give priority to the procurement of environment-labeled products and products listed in the procurement list and will be fully implemented from January 1, 2008. On July 30, 2007, the General Office of the State Council issued the *Notice of the General Office of the State Council on Establishing the System of Mandatory Government Procurement of Energy Saving Products*. This is China's first mandatory policy on government green procurement. In December 2007, China submitted an application to the WTO to formally start the negotiations on joining the *Agreement on Government Procurement* (GPA). In 2011, China's 12th five-year plan was included government green procurement in the country's medium-and long-term development plan for the first time, which clearly proposes to improve the compulsory procurement system, gradually increase the proportion of energy-saving and water-saving products and renewable products, so that it becomes one of the important means to build a resource-conserving and environment-friendly society. On August 21, 2012, the General Office of the State Council issued the *National Environmental Protection* 12th *Five-Year Plan> Key Work Division Plan*, which proposes to promote green government procurement, gradually increase the proportion of green products and study the implementation of green government procurement services. Since March 1, 2015, the *Regulations on the Implementation of the Government Procurement Law of the People's Republic of China* (hereinafter referred to as the *Regulations on the Implementation of the Government Procurement Law*) has been officially implemented. Article 6 of the *Regulations on the Implementation of the Government Procurement Law* provides that: "The financial department of the state council shall, in accordance with the state's policies on economic and social development, formulate policies on government procurement jointly with relevant departments of the state council. Through the formulation of procurement demand standards, reserve procurement shares, price review preferences, priority procurement measures, it shall achieve energy conservation, environmental protection, support for underdeveloped areas and ethnic minority areas, promote the development of small and medium-sized enterprises and other goals." It puts forward the energy conservation and environmental protection requirements for government procurement, and legally confirms the principle requirements for government green procurement. The *Opinions on the Implementation of Government Procurement of Environment-Labeled Products*, which has been implemented nationwide since January 1, 2008, has promoted the production of green products. In the past eight years, the Ministry of Environmental Protection and the Ministry of Finance have issued 14 copies of the *Government Procurement List of Environmental Labeled Products*. The product category increased from the original 14 categories to 42 categories. The number of enterprises increased from 81 to more than 1318. The number of product models also increased from more than 800 to more than 86,628.

Problems in Government Green Procurement
Laws and regulations need to be improved. The *Government Procurement Law*, which came into effect in 2003, the *Regulations on the Implementation of the Government Procurement Law*, which came into effect in 2015, and other systems mention that government procurement should be conducive to resource conservation and environmental protection. However, so far, there has not been a systematic and specialized legal document on government green procurement, which makes many problems in the actual operation quite vague and is not conducive to the real implementation of government green procurement.

For example, how to favor environment-friendly enterprises in government procurement, how to clarify the responsibilities of procurement supervision departments and procurement agencies, how to unify and standardize procurement methods and procedures, and how procurement personnel deal with some special problems have not been specifically involved, so green procurement is not standardized in practical operation.

Green procurement is smaller. According to statistics, the scale of government procurement reached 1.40 trillion Yuan in 2012, but the scale only accounted for 2.7% of the national GDP of 51.93 trillion Yuan and 11.11% of the national public finance expenditure of 12.60 trillion Yuan. In Western countries, where the government procurement system is relatively complete, the scale of government procurement is generally 10% of GDP or about 30% of fiscal expenditure. It can be seen that China's actual government procurement scale is still small. However, due to imperfect system, limited binding force and smaller procurement scale, China's government green procurement plays a limited role in promoting green consumption and green production. In the future, the proportion of green procurement must be increased as much as possible on the basis of regulating government procurement.

Green procurement standards are low. Since January 1, 2007, the *Opinions on the Implementation of Government Procurement of Environmental Labeled Products* has been officially implemented in the central and provincial budget units (including city specifically designated in the state plan), and has been fully implemented nationwide since January 1, 2008. The *List of Government Procurement of Environmental Labeled Products* shall be formulated by the Ministry of Finance and the Ministry of Environmental Protection. Products entering the list shall meet the following conditions: (1) the product belongs to the product category listed in the environmental protection list; (2) the product belongs to the environmental labeled product certified by the national environmental labeled product certification authority and has the valid environmental labeled product certification certificate, and the time of obtaining the certificate conforms to the regulations; (3) the product manufacturer shall submit relevant materials as required by the public notice; (4) product manufacturers shall meet the requirements of government procurement legal system for government procurement suppliers. Compared with other countries where the government green procurement system is relatively complete, China's green procurement standard is relatively low, making it difficult to play a positive role in green procurement (see Table 2). For example, the selection method of green environmental protection products in the United States is the

Table 2 Comparison of public green procurement standards of major countries in the world

	Green environmental protection product selection of methods	Adoption of standards	Ease of implementation	Professional requirement of environmental protection on procurement personnel
America	EPP principles + tools + database + successful cases		★★★★★	Very high
European Union	GPP standard	GPP standard		Higher
Japan	Green purchase law specific procurement items	Green purchase law specific procurement items	★★☆	Medium
South Korea	Follows the requirements of the green purchasing law	Environmental label certified product or equivalent/good recycling of green certified products or equivalent/other products conforming to MOE standards	★★	General
China	Environmental labeling certification products	Environmental labeling standards	★	Low

Source Liu Juan, Chen Yiqun, Zhang Xiaodan. Comparative Study on Government Green Purchasing Standards at Home and Abroad. *Environment and Sustainable Development*, 2014 (6): 87–90

principle of EPP (buy environment-first products) + tools + database + successful cases. It requires a high degree of professional environmental protection for purchasing personnel, and it is also difficult to implement. But our country request is very low. It only requires compliance with environmental labeling standards and access to the environmental protection list range.

Green purchasing information is not developed. Before making a green purchasing decision, the government must obtain detailed information about green products available in the market and make evaluation and comparison. Detailed information must be collected on the environmental impacts of different product and service life cycles, the environmental performance of different products and services, and the environmental costs of different products and services. And this massive information is usually dispersed in the hands of numerous suppliers, which requires the establishment of a perfect green product supply information platform. However, there are many irregularities in China's government procurement, not to mention the specialized green product supply information platform. This makes it impossible for the government to truly achieve "good quality and low price" when purchasing green products and services, and is not conducive to stimulating the production of real green product suppliers. It may even lead to the "lemon market".

Green procurement supervision is not in place. Green procurement first requires standardized operating procedures, which depend on the improvement of the legal system, while green procurement also involves relevant technical confirmation issues. This requires the development of green purchasing standards for different products, engineering and services in different categories. The supervision of procurement personnel requires not only the warning and prevention of relevant systems in advance, but also the green procurement performance evaluation to check whether the procurement personnel are conscientious and how to improve relevant systems. However, China's green procurement is still in the "notification requirements", far from evaluation and accountability, with weak binding force.

4.3   Green Fiscal Expenditure

In terms of system construction, a special financial expenditure system for environmental protection has been preliminarily established. Before 2007, there was no "class" special expenditure on environmental protection in the classification of government revenue and expenditure, but only "section" related to environmental protection. Some financial expenditures related to environmental protection work were also scattered in other subjects, which indicated that at that time our government did not give enough attention to environmental protection and sufficient financial support. Until January 1, 2007, China began to fully implement the "2007 government revenue and expenditure classification subjects" published by the ministry of finance, in which the "environmental protection" category was newly established. Under the "environmental protection" category, there are 10 sections, including "environmental protection and management affairs, environmental monitoring and supervision, pollution prevention and control, natural ecological protection, natural forest protection, returning farmland to forests, desert management, returning grazing land to grassland, returning cultivated grassland to grassland and other environmental protection expenditures", including 46 items in total. Since then, the Chinese government has set up three levels of special expenditures for environmental protection, namely "category, section and item", so as to ensure the financial security for environmental protection. Later, some subjects were added and simplified according to actual needs.

In terms of expenditure, the input increased year by year, but the proportion of expenditure is still low. Since the special category of "environmental protection" was set up in China's fiscal expenditure in 2007, fiscal expenditure on environmental protection has increased year by year, but the proportion of total expenditure is still low (see Fig. 6).

From 2007 to 2013, China's total fiscal expenditure on environmental protection reached 1584.3 billion Yuan, but the proportion of annual fiscal expenditure was still not high, below 3.00%, among which the highest was 2.72% in 2010. In general, China's special fiscal expenditure system for environmental protection has not been established for a long time.

From the point of view of expenditure structure, expenditure is limited and competition among various items is fierce. In recent years, China's environmental expenditure mainly focuses on natural ecological protection, renewable energy development and energy conservation (see Fig. 7). From 2008 to 2013, the annual growth rates of "natural ecological protection", "renewable energy" and "energy conservation and utilization" ranked the top three, with 48.38, 37.88 and 37.84%,

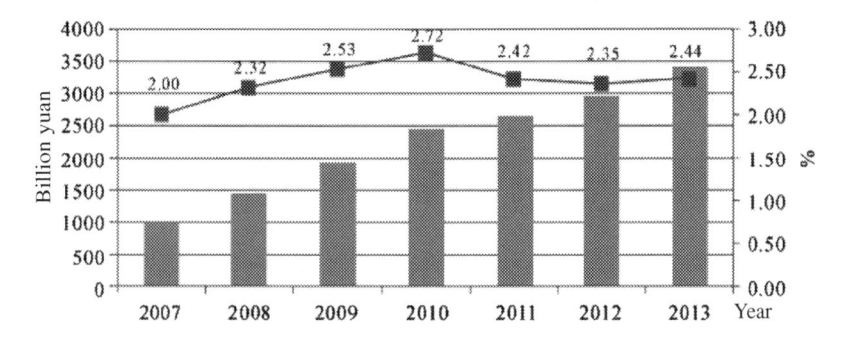

Fig. 6 Proportion of China's environmental protection expenditure in the total fiscal expenditure from 2007 to 2013 (*Data source* China statistical yearbook 2008–2014)

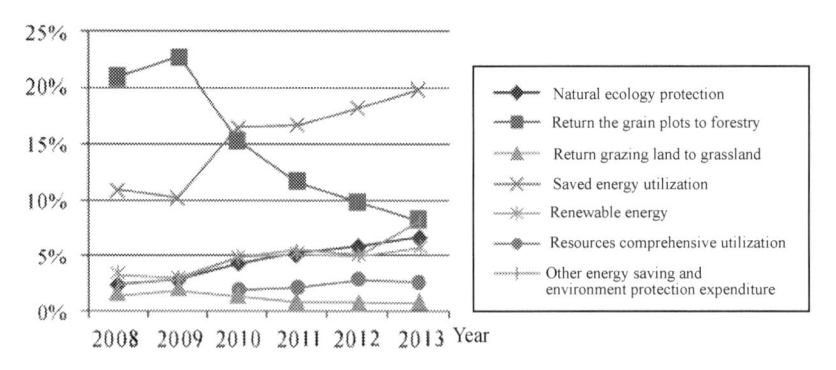

Fig. 7 Change of proportion of environmental protection expenditure from 2008 to 2013 (*Source* Wu Yang. Analysis on the changes of Environmental Protection Expenditure in the Classification of Government Revenue and Expenditure and Final Accounts. *Modern Economic Information*, 2014 [20])

respectively. At the same time, the expenditure of "returning farmland to forest" and "returning grazing land to grassland" decreased significantly, the former dropped from 21.14% in 2008 to 8.28% in 2013, and the latter also dropped from 1.35% in 2008 to 0.71% in 2013. On the one hand, it can be seen from this that ecological environmental protection, energy conservation and the development of new energy are increasingly urgent and need to continue to invest funds; On the other hand, it can also be seen that the financial fund for environmental protection in China is relatively tight, and the competition for various projects is very fierce. In the long run, if we want to improve the environment condition of our country continuously, we need to broaden the source of funds, increase the fiscal expenditure; if necessary, we should establish the minimum expenditure management system for some special important projects.

5 THE CONSTRUCTION OF GREEN FINANCE SYSTEM IN CHINA

5.1 Construction of Green Tax System

In order to better use the tax system to promote the construction of ecological civilization and green transformation and development in China, the tax reform in the new period can be summarized as the legalization of the effective status, the greenness of the overall design, the scientization of the regulation design, the advancement of the management means, the rationalization of the collection and management and the reform and evolution of the sewage charge.

Legalization of Status of Effectiveness
In view of the drawback of low overall effectiveness level of China's tax legal system, we should further accelerate the legislative process in China and improve the legislation of various taxes and explicitly include a series of goals related to green transformation and development, including resource conservation, pollution control, environmental governance and ecological civilization construction, into the relevant tax law. In the tax management system related to the above-related objectives, the management principles and methods should be clarified, so as to make green tax have laws to abide by and further improve its legal status.

Greening of Overall Design
It includes three aspects: The first is to strengthen the design of taxes directly related to resources and environment and further improve the design of existing green taxes. For example, resource tax should be extended to a wider range of natural resources. All natural resources that need to be protected and can be collected and managed should be included in the scope of tax and a reasonable tax rate should be set.

The same is true for consumption tax. Goods and services that are prone to environmental pollution and those that need to be restricted in order to protect resources and the environment are subject to consumption tax as far as possible. Second, strengthen the "green" design of other related taxes and strengthen the overall promotion function of taxation. For example, in the aspect of value-added tax, the major energy-saving and environmental protection equipment and products should be included in the scope of the reduction and exemption of value-added tax, the tax deduction should be made for the units or individuals who buy environmental protection equipment, and the conditions for the deduction of input tax for waste and used materials business units should be relaxed to encourage the reuse of waste and used materials. In terms of income tax, the preferential scope of enterprise income tax will be extended to all environmental protection industries, including environmental protection equipment manufacturing, environmental protection engineering, environmental protection technology and other fields. Special preferential tax policies will be set for industries that develop new energy and new technologies that are conducive to environmental protection. In terms of export tax rebate and tariff, we should adjust import and export tax policy and implement green tariff. Third, introduce new environmental taxes. For example, in view of China's large resource consumption, low resource utilization rate, waste disposal difficulties and other problems, it can accelerate the research and design of urban waste tax, and introduce and implement it in a timely manner.

Scientific Design of Regulation and Control
Green taxes are different from traditional taxes, which are mainly levied on wealth, while green taxes are mainly levied on behavior. Therefore, the scientific regulation of behavior determines the effectiveness of tax design. Since green tax is a new type of tax that regulates people's behavior, it needs to strengthen the research on people's behavior and the interaction between people's behavior and the environment, which requires high scientific, technical and specialized levels. In the future, it is necessary to study the interaction mechanism between human behavior and the environment around several key issues of resource and environmental governance, such as resource conservation and protection in mineral development, energy consumption and harmful gas emission control, so as to lay a foundation for the scientific design of green tax in China.

Advanced Management Methods

With the green transformation of the traditional tax system and the increasing influence of green tax, the traditional tax management means also need to keep pace with The Times and be updated in a timely manner. In this regard, some green tax developed countries, such as Sweden, Denmark, Finland and other EU countries, as well as the United States and Japan, have relatively advanced management methods and relevant experience and practices, with a high degree of modernization and information management. In the future, China should make full use of the green tax management experience of these countries to improve the management efficiency, reduce the management cost and increase the feasibility of green tax.

Rationalization of Collection and Management Distribution

The most important of these is the "three distributions": First, the distribution of the power of collection and management; second, the distribution of tax revenue; and third, the distribution of governance responsibilities. From China's current situation, in the collection of administrative power distribution, it is necessary to emphasize centralization and authority of the central government, to fully mobilize local initiative and creativity and to consider the participation and cooperation of relevant regions. The exact allocation of power will also depend on the environment and the extent of its impact. In terms of tax revenue distribution and governance responsibility distribution, according to the principle of the equivalence of financial power and administrative power, the distribution of the two among related subjects should be reasonably divided. From China's situation, sharing tax is one of the major trends. In a word, since the boundary of environmental problems is not clear and the overall responsibility is relatively vague, the collection, management and distribution of green tax should be the result of consultation, collaboration and coordination, rather than the traditional tax mainly determined by the regional boundary and the relationship between the upper and lower levels.

Evolution of Sewage Charge Reform

A progressive and selective fee-to-tax reform. Although there is a strong call for the sewage fee to be changed into a sewage tax, there is no unified form of sewage fee or sewage tax. In practice, it is generally determined according to the characteristics of the levy object, the difficulty of levy management and the ability of the levy unit. In view of the fact that the current sewage charge in China is a local administrative charge with low legal effect and the effect of pollution control and emission reduction will be weakened due to various interference in the implementation process, it is suggested to adopt the form of gradual reform. That is to say, for the pollution sources with large emission, relatively standard collection and low cost; first of all, it is changed into pollutant discharge tax, which is levied and distributed according to unified standards. For locally distributed pollution sources or those with a smaller amount of pollution, the pollutant discharge fee will be temporarily adopted, and will be changed into the pollutant discharge tax when conditions are mature.

We will appropriately expand the scope of collection of pollutant discharge taxes (fees). In view of the current narrow scope of pollutant discharge fee collection, the scope of pollutant discharge fee collection should be appropriately expanded, mainly as follows: Increase the emission levy in the consumption field; increase the tax collection of towns and rural areas; expand the collection of hazardous substances other than conventional hazardous substances, such as carbon tax, according to actual needs.

5.2   Construction of Green Government Procurement System

Improve Government Green Procurement Regulations
Amend the *Law of the People's Republic of China on Government Procurement* and the *Regulations for the Implementation of the Law of the People's Republic of China on Government Procurement*, clarify the status and principles of green procurement and stipulate that the government must fulfill the obligation of priority procurement of environmentally friendly products. On this basis, a more systematic and perfect government green procurement law is formulated to further clarify various specific issues in practical operation, such as standardized green procurement procedures, green procurement standards and procurement proportion of all kinds of products, the responsibility and authority of procurement personnel, green procurement supervision mechanism and evaluation system.

Standardize Government Green Procurement Procedures
In order to improve the performance of government green procurement, ensure the performance of government procurement personnel and stimulate the enthusiasm of enterprises for green products, a

relatively standard government green procurement procedure should be established. Such as the the government releases green product demand information—qualified enterprises respond to bidding-comprehensive evaluation of third-party green products (performance, price, etc.)—consultation between the two sides of supply and demand-information release of the winning bid- supervision by all parties in society-contract signing between the two side of supply and demand—tracking evaluation and information release of product use-rewards and penalties for suppliers and procurement personnel, etc. The whole green procurement process of the government is subject to social supervision, and all eligible enterprises participate in fair competition. Follow-up evaluation of products and purchasing personnel and corresponding rewards and penalties will be carried out to promote the standardization, efficiency and transparency of the whole green procurement process of the government.

Promulgate Green Purchasing Standards
In order to facilitate the procurement personnel and promote the scientific and technological progress of the industry, procurement standards for different items should be formulated according to the characteristics of different procurement items and the characteristics of the items themselves. In terms of environmental protection objectives, they are mainly conducive to energy conservation, emission reduction and comprehensive utilization of resources, as well as waste reduction, resource recovery and innocuity. In terms of technology, it mainly considers the most advanced technical progress and development trend at home and abroad in various industries, and dynamically adjusts technical standards to be among the same advanced level in the same industry in the same period. And, without affecting national economic development and impeding national security, appropriately raise technical standards, exert pressure and promote rapid technological progress in different industries in the country. In terms of standard mark certification, we will provide the support of people, finance and materials, reduce the cost of certification and management, and make more enterprises willing to improve standards and join the certification.

Establish Green Purchasing Network
Two aspects of network construction are included: First is the supply information network of goods or services; second is the relations network of the government agencies-suppliers-trade associations-social public. In terms of the supply network of goods or services, it is mainly to establish a

nationwide information network for the supply of goods or services. The central government and local government release demand information on it, while supply enterprises release supply information on it. The two sides establish a smooth and transparent connection, and require national enterprises to compete fairly to prevent local protectionism and "black box operation" of some enterprises. As China joins the international government green procurement, in the aspect of procurement network information, the supply information in the international market should be appropriately increased without affecting the national economic development and national security, so as to create effective competitive pressure and promote the domestic technological progress. In terms of network construction, the government should keep close contact with enterprises, industries and the public, timely communicate information, and jointly promote the production and consumption of green goods and the progress of green technology.

Some new demand of the public is timely fed back to the government, and the government procurement information reflects this new demand of the public and transmits to the supplier through the green procurement information platform. Suppliers cooperate with industry associations to obtain new technical progress in line with the demand, develop new products and release new product supply information to the government, and then purchase the products for the public to use; the public will provide feedback of the product performance, use situation and technical innovation desire to the government. Through government green procurement, the whole society has formed a relatively close cooperation network of green product research and development, production and consumption with multi linkage in this cycle.

Formulate Green Purchasing Policies
The formulation of green purchasing policy refers to the formulation of policies that conform to the development law of green industry and contribute to the production of green products, for example, the price, give green products or services a better price and priority procurement. In terms of technical requirements, we should encourage innovation, especially the unique innovation of small- and medium-sized enterprises. In the purchase order, we not only give priority to purchase, but also give certain share guarantee; in fiscal, taxation and finance, green technology innovation-oriented enterprises can be appropriately exempted or deducted from taxes, and can obtain preferential loans such as low interest or interest-free loans.

5.3 Establishment of a Green Fiscal Budget System

Continue to Improve the Management of Environmental Protection
Subjects in the Preparation of Budget Expenditure
It is mainly the actual environmental protection needs and the amount of disposable financial environmental protection funds, timely improve and adjust related subjects, to ensure that some important environmental protection projects have capital investment. In view of tight financial resources and fierce competition among environmental protection projects, minimum investment standards and priority investment guarantee mechanism should be established for some special important projects to ensure the governance effect of these projects and the sustainability of the improvement of governance effect.

Clarify the Responsibility of Environmental Expenditure
of Governments at All Levels
The environmental protection responsibilities and financial rights of governments at all levels and regions should be reasonably defined. On this basis, the environmental protection expenditure responsibilities of governments at all levels and regions should be determined and their expenditure structure should be optimized. In view of the fact that most environmental protection affairs are affairs with strong externality and publicity, neither governments at any level nor governments in a certain region can solely and completely undertake them. Therefore, governments at all levels and regional governments must strengthen cooperation, share the benefits of environmental protection and share the responsibility of expenditure. According to the principle of "benefit and burden equivalence", environmental public goods are divided into three levels: The central government is responsible for providing environmental public goods that benefit the whole country; local governments at all levels mainly provide environmental public goods at the local level. As for the environmental public goods intersecting with the beneficiary regions, they should be negotiated by the relevant local governments or coordinated by the central government, jointly provided by the beneficiary regions or provided by the central government. At present, the power of environmental affairs between the central and local governments is not clear.

The central government has often invested heavily, while local governments have been less enthusiastic. Therefore, it is necessary to clarify the environmental benefit sharing and environmental expenditure responsibility of governments at all levels as soon as possible, and mobilize the enthusiasm of local governments to participate in ecological environmental protection and environmental pollution control. At the same time, the central government must strengthen the macro-control and transfer system of environmental protection. In terms of environmental protection cooperation in relevant ecological regions, it is necessary to strengthen regional ecological compensation legislation and formulate reasonable compensation standards and implementation systems, such as a standardized horizontal regional transfer payment system.

Strengthen the Management of Funds Invested in Environmental Protection
We will further clarify the responsibilities of the government and ensure that funds for environmental protection are truly used to fight pollution and protect the environment. In terms of the investment in environmental protection projects, we should pay attention to the tracking and management of the projects to ensure that the environmental protection funds are really invested in projects that are conducive to environmental protection. In the process of project construction, problems found should be dealt with in a timely manner. If any behavior that does not meet the requirements of environmental protection is found, it must be improved in a timely manner and the subsequent appropriation should be stopped when necessary. In addition, a transparent and fair project selection and management system should be established. We must analyze the costs and benefits of government-invested environmental protection projects, and select projects that are truly conducive to environmental protection. Projects that are not conducive to environmental protection will never be launched.

Establish a Performance Evaluation System for Environmental Expenditure
In order to strengthen the budget project performance management of environmental protection departments in China, it is necessary to construct the whole process financial expenditure performance evaluation system of environmental protection departments. First, improve the system of policies and regulations. It is suggested that according to the latest policies issued by the ministry of finance, the performance evaluation management measures of environmental protection departments should be promulgated as soon as possible. Second, improve the organizational management system. It is suggested to set up an independent

performance evaluation institution to undertake long-term performance evaluation, carry out long-term research on departmental budget projects, overall departmental expenditure, financial budget evaluation and special environmental protection projects, and be responsible for formulating performance evaluation policies and organizing performance evaluation. Third, improve the technical system of performance evaluation. It mainly includes three aspects: First, the scientific classification of departmental budget items. Second, China's financial expenditure project declaration level needs to be further improved. It is suggested that the project declaration should contain quantified and measurable long-term goals, annual performance goals and project output, and continuous projects should contain specific requirements for project monitoring and evaluation, arrange certain monitoring and evaluation budget, and ensure the smooth implementation of monitoring and evaluation. Third, further refine the performance evaluation index system. Based on the common indicators of project performance evaluation of the ministry of finance and the scientific classification of projects, the budget performance evaluation indicator systems of different types of environmental protection departments are formulated, including: the performance evaluation principles, performance evaluation indicators and explanations, the weight or percentage value of evaluation indicators, the scoring criteria of evaluation indicators, and the effect indicators combining quantitative and qualitative analysis reflect the actual effect of project implementation. Fourthly, combine the results of performance evaluation with the budget, optimize the allocation of resources and improve the efficiency of budget funds. Timely release of project performance evaluation results to increase public understanding and support for environmental protection.

References

Cheng Yongming. Green Procurement in Japan and Its Implications for China. *Japan Studies*, 2013, 27 (2): 45–50.

Han Wenbo. Setting Up the Concept of Green Finance and Promoting the Sustainable Development of Finance. *China Finance*, 2004 (2): 49–51.

Xu Jinliang, Yuan Tingting, Chang Liang. Empirical Study on Green Procurement by Beijing Municipal Government to Promote the Transformation of Scientific and Technological Achievements. *China Population (Resources and Environment)*, 2014, 24 (11): 161–167.

Yang Tao. Circular Economy Needs "Green Finance". 21st Century Economic Report, July 5, 2006.

CHAPTER 7

Finance and Green Transformation and Development

1 Meaning and Characteristics of Green Finance

1.1 The Meaning of Green Finance

Green finance was first proposed by the United States in the late 1990s. There is no unified definition of this concept at home and abroad. To sum up, there are five different definitions with different focuses.

The first one focuses on the role of green finance as an environmental tool or means. In this definition, "green finance" is directly defined as "environmental finance" or "sustainable finance", which is an environmental protection tool or means. For example, the *American Heritage Dictionary* (4th edition, 2000) defines green Finance as "Environmental Finance" or "Sustainable Financing". Its basic connotation is "how to use diversified financial instruments to protect the ecological environment and biological diversity". Pan Yue believes that green finance is a means of finance and capital market in environmental and economic policies, such as green credit and green insurance. Tang Bohong (2009) also pointed out that the essence of green finance is the macro-control policy required by the law of market economy with the construction of ecological civilization as the orientation, credit, insurance, securities, industrial funds and other financial derivatives as the means, the goal of promoting the coordinated development of energy

S. Gu et al., *Green Transformation and Development*,
The Great Transformation of China,
https://doi.org/10.1007/978-981-32-9495-0_7

conservation and emission reduction as well as economic resources and environment.

The second one focuses on the supporting effect of green finance on green industry. For example, He Xiuxing (1998) believes that green finance refers to the policy that the financial industry takes green industry as a key supporting project in terms of loan policies, loan objects, loan conditions, loan types and loan methods, and gives priority and preference to green industry in terms of credit supply, investment amount, term and interest rate.

The third one focusing on green finance is the scientific accounting of the value of resources and environment. For example, Qiao Haishu (1999) argued that "the core of green finance is to measure the natural resource depletion and environmental loss caused by natural resource stock or human economic activities and apply them in the field of financial resource allocation and financial activity evaluation by measuring the environmental value or economic value".

The fourth one focuses on the implementation and embodiment of the awareness of resource and environmental protection in the financial industry. This is the view of most scholars that green finance is the embodiment of resource and environmental awareness in the financial industry. Financial activities should reflect the protection of resources and environment, and give play to the role of financial instruments to promote sustainable development. For example, Gao Jianliang (1998) believes that green finance is a financial operation strategy in which the financial sector takes environmental protection as a basic national policy, embodies the "sustainable development strategy" through the operation of financial business, promotes the coordinated development of environmental resources protection and economy, and thus realizes the sustainable development of finance. For another example, Wang Junhua (2000) believes that green finance means that finance should reflect "green" in its business activities, that is, it should pay attention to the treatment of environmental pollution and the protection of ecological environment in its investment and financing activities, and promote the sustainable development of economy and the coordinated development of economy and ecology through its guiding role in social funds. For another example, Li Xinyin also believes that green finance means that the financial industry should reflect the awareness of environmental protection in its business activities. That is to pay attention to the protection of ecological environment and the treatment of environmental pollution in the investment and financing behavior, pay attention to the development of environmental protection industry and guide the role of promoting sustainable economic development and ecological coordination through the investment and financing behavior of social resources. Wen Tongai and Yue Yuxia also believe that green finance means that the green concept should be reflected in the daily business activities of the financial industry, which should take environmental protection as the basic policy, pay attention to the protection of ecological environment and pollution control in the investment and financing behavior of financial institutions, pay attention to the development of green industry and promote the sustainable development of economy and society and the coordinated development of ecology through the guidance of social resources.

The fifth one focuses on the role of green finance in ensuring the sustainable development of the financial industry. This view holds that green finance is not only a public need for resource and environmental protection, but also a need for the sustainable development of the banking industry. For example, Song Xiaoling (2013) believes that the green finance policy of the banking industry means that the banking industry takes environmental protection as a basic policy. In each link of business operation, we should fully consider and scientifically evaluate the possible environmental impact, pay attention to the protection of ecological environment and the treatment of environmental pollution. By establishing the incentive and restraint mechanism of financing environmental protection policies, it guides the allocation of social and economic resources and promotes the sustainable development of banks themselves, society and economy.

Three points can be seen from the above definitions: First, green finance plays an important role in sustainable development. Second, green finance is the implementation and embodiment of the awareness of resource and environmental protection in financial activities in the strategy of sustainable development. Third, green finance is not only to meet the public interest needs of resource conservation, but also the needs of the sustainable development of the banking industry. Given that the main body of financial activities is financial institutions, and the sustainable development strategy and ecological civilization construction is a public interest need to ensure the long-term quality of human survival, and financial activities are an important link between resources, environment and economy, which has an important impact on resources and environment, which is a double-edged sword, while based on the need of resource and environment protection, the government strengthens the regulation of resource and environment for economic activities and promotes the green transformation and development of economic activities. In this context, the financial industry consciously implementing the awareness of resource environmental protection is not only to meet the environmental protection needs of public interests, but also to avoid the risk of national environmental protection policies and actively share the investment opportunities of green development. Therefore, green finance is defined as follows: In the context of strengthening environmental regulation by the government, green finance means, based on the public responsibility awareness of resource and environmental protection and its own sustainable development needs, the financial industry consciously implements the sustainable development strategy of resource and environmental protection in financial activities, strengthens the innovation of financial instruments and makes use of abundant financial instruments to promote resource and environmental protection and ecological civilization construction.

1.2   Features of Green Finance

Compared with traditional finance, the most important feature of green finance is that the main investors in financial activities do not pursue the maximization of economic interests as their only goal, but take social responsibility and resource and environmental protection into

Table 1 Comparison between green finance and traditional finance

	Form the environment	Characteristics	Goal	Environmental influence
Green finance	Strong environmental awareness	Investors with social responsibility	When pursuing economic interests, conscious investors should take into account environmental protection, fairness and other social responsibilities	Good
Traditional finance	Environmental awareness is weak	Ordinary investors	Only pursue the maximization of their own economic interests	Bad

consideration. The comparison of the two is shown in Table 1. In green finance activities, investment and financing subjects not only pursue the realization of their own economic interests, but also give consideration to the fulfillment of social equity and environmental responsibility.

2   FORMATION MECHANISM AND ACTION MECHANISM OF GREEN FINANCE

2.1   *Formation Mechanism of Green Finance*

Marcel Jeucken, a Dutch scholar, has divided the development stage of green finance. He believes that the attitude of financial institutions towards sustainable development can be divided into four stages from low level to high level, namely defensive, preventive, offensive and sustainable. In fact, from the perspective of the development history of world finance, green finance is not formed automatically, but when the economic and social development reaches a certain stage and the sustainable development strategy becomes a consensus, the financial circle will transform its development orientation based on its own sense of social responsibility and the avoidance of investment risks and the search for new investment opportunities, and its formation has a complex dynamic mechanism. From the perspective of interest subjects, green finance involves multiple related subjects such as the government, financial institutions, enterprises and the public. It is based on their different responsibilities, obligations and interests that green finance is formed and developed. The following takes green credit of commercial banks as an example to discuss the formation mechanism of green finance.

Government Regulation on Resources and Environment
Under the framework of sustainable development strategy, the government has the responsibility to protect resources and environment and the obligation to promote the economic and social transformation and development. The most important manifestation of green transformation and development in economy is the transformation of industrial structure and the change of economic growth mode, while the development behavior of enterprises determines whether the industrial structure and growth mode can be changed smoothly. Capital is the blood of the enterprise; without the support of capital, many enterprises will

not be able to run until the final collapse. One of the most important reasons why many polluting, energy-consuming and overcapacity enterprises fail in industrial restructuring is that they are supported by bank funds. The bank itself is a profit-seeking social subject, and the pursuit of high economic returns is one of its most important operating forces. Without the mandatory constraint of relevant laws, it is difficult to curb the profit-seeking impulse of the bank solely based on its sense of social responsibility at this stage. This requires the government to make clear constraints on the operation and investment behaviors of banks. For example, banks are required to evaluate the environmental impact of the loan project and examine the environmental protection plan of the loan enterprise when lending to the enterprise, or they have the right to refuse the loan. If loan is granted, any loss caused by environmental protection shall be borne by the owner. In this way, banks are encouraged to consciously strengthen the environmental assessment, review and supervise the loan enterprises in terms of operation and investment, adjust the loan issuing direction based on their own investment interests and supervise the environmental protection behaviors of enterprises. In this way, from the perspective of the whole society, "two high and one overcapacity" enterprises should be unable to obtain relevant loans and gradually die out. However, enterprises that can survive are subject to environmental audit and supervision from banks. As a result, the environmental protection level is gradually improved, energy consumption and pollutant emission are gradually reduced, and the resource conservation and utilization of the whole society and the improvement of ecological environment are also promoted.

On the other hand, the government's financial support for environment-friendly industries has also improved the level of environmental protection technology in the whole society and greatly increased the proportion of green industry in the whole industrial structure. At the current stage of transformation and development, many environment-friendly industries are juvenile industries, which are faced with the dual constraints of imperfect technology and insufficient capital. If the government provides preferential loans through policy banks, it can solve the problem of capital shortage and optimize the allocation of other resources such as talents and equipment by alleviating the problem of capital dilemma, thus overcoming the technical problem. This has promoted the development of environment-friendly green industry and the progress of environmental protection technology, thus optimizing the industrial structure of the whole society and enhancing the strength of environmental protection technology.

Financial Institutions' Aversion to Investment Risks
For commercial banks, profit is the most important motive, while enterprises are the most important loan subjects and the most important customers. From the perspective of interest connection, banks and enterprises are community of interests. High and stable profit returns mean more profit sharing space and more stable returns for banks that lend to them. Conversely, the opposite is true. Based on this, when the country takes sustainable development, building ecological civilization and strengthening resource and environmental protection as the basic national policies, it is bound to compress the development space of polluting enterprises and require them to increase environmental protection expenditure and improve the level of environmental protection. This is bound to increase the environmental cost burden of enterprises, affect the rate of return on profits of enterprises, and thus increase the investment risk of the banking industry. For example, the "two high and one high overcapacity" enterprises with serious pollution may face the risk of going out of business for rectification, environmental punishment or even outright closure. Either treatment scheme will directly affect the normal production and profit return of the borrowing enterprise, and in turn affect the principal recovery and profit return of the lending banking industry. Once the borrowing enterprise declared bankruptcy means no interest or capital for the banking sector, which greatly increased the risk of banking operations. Today, with the increasingly high requirement of environmental protection, the cost of environmental protection expenditure of enterprises with general pollution severity cannot be ignored. The cost of environmental protection is bound to affect the rate of return on investment of enterprises, thus affecting the capital and interest of the banking industry. Moreover, for some enterprises in the resource extraction industry, high pollution not only makes them face the risk of being directly eliminated and closed, but also means that more resources are consumed and the period of resource exhaustion will come sooner. Once the resources are exhausted, resource-based enterprises will need to switch to production. Resource extraction industry itself is a capital and technology-intensive industry, which can be said to be

symbiotic relationship with the banking industry. Resource-based regions are generally a unique resource-based industry, while other industries are not very developed. The withdrawal or production transformation of resource-based enterprises has a predictable impact on the local banking industry. Therefore, the banking industry, which itself pursues high profit returns, cannot choose the loan subject without considering the impact of environmental risks on its profit margin. Green finance is a wise choice for it to avoid investment risks.

In turn, the financial industry provides financial support and guarantee for the green development of enterprises, which not only helps reduce the investment risk of the financial industry itself, but also opens up new areas for investment. First of all, environmental protection and energy saving is the general trend of the world's development, which is also in line with China's current sustainable development strategy. Since this investment direction is consistent with the country's strategic direction, it is easier to obtain policy support from the country and other relevant parties. Secondly, the direction of energy conservation and environmental protection is conducive to reducing the development cost of enterprises and improving the market share of products, which is conducive to the sustainable development of enterprises and the rate of return of capital, as well as the sustainable development of the financial industry with which they cooperate. For example, with the price reform of resource products, the price of resource products keeps climbing, and reducing the consumption of energy and other raw materials can not only directly reduce the cost of raw materials, but also help reduce the environmental protection expenditure of enterprises. In addition, the energy-saving and environment-friendly products produced due to the progress of energy-saving and environment-friendly technologies are more popular in the market, which is conducive to improving the market share, which is also a positive factor for enterprises. Thirdly, the environmental protection industry has become a rising sunrise industry, and the investment-oriented environmental protection industry is a profitable new industry and a new direction for the development of the traditional financial industry. In conclusion, it is a wise choice for the financial industry to avoid environmental risks and promote its sustainable development to pay attention to the environmental impact in investment, supervise enterprises' environmental protection behaviors and select promising environmental protection enterprises.

Public Supervision of Corporate Environmental Responsibility
In the case of environmental regulation by the government, the government generally grants the public with higher environmental rights, including the right to know and the right to supervise the environment. In addition to directly supervising enterprises' environmental behaviors, the public can also urge enterprises' environmental behaviors through green finance. For example, the majority of bank loans come from the savings of the public, while the development behavior of enterprises that are not environmentally responsible will directly affect the quality of life of the public. In addition to avoiding investment risks for themselves, banks also perform conditional (mainly environmental responsibility) loan qualification supervision obligations for the public and urge enterprises to fulfill their environmental responsibility. For another example, in green securities, enterprises' listed financing needs to report their own environmental protection behaviors and their effects, and enterprises that fail to meet the environmental protection standards are refused to go public. In a word, green finance provides an effective window for the public to supervise the environmental responsibility of enterprises.

Breakthrough of Enterprises in Traditional Development Mode
Under the condition that the government strengthens the environmental regulation and the financial institution carries on the environmental protection loan audit, the traditional extensive production mode which the enterprise disregards the resources environment influence faces the dilemma: On the one hand, it directly makes it difficult for enterprises to sustain their own development. For example, extensive production consumes a large amount of raw materials, increases the expenditure cost of raw materials for resource products and weakens the market competitiveness of products. Extensive production also increases waste emissions, increases the cost of environmental protection expenditure or even faces the risk of being ordered to close; Extensive production makes the product low in technology content and unpopular in the market, which affects the sales volume and the sustainable development of the enterprise. On the other hand, the traditional extensive production mode has worsened the external living environment of enterprises. For example, faced with the increasingly severe environmental protection policy pressure from the government, financial institutions are worried about the environmental protection risks of enterprises and are not willing to

provide loans or risk guarantees. The public complains or refuses to buy the products or stocks of the enterprises because of their pollution emission behaviors. However, if an enterprise carries out green transformation production, it is a path of virtuous cycle development. Although green transformation production will have some impact on the enterprise in the short term, in the long run, it will do more good than harm: Firstly, the cost of raw materials and environmental protection costs of enterprises directly decreased; secondly, it improves the social relations and living environment of enterprises. For example, there is less pressure from the government to protect the environment. Financial institutions are more confident to provide loans or risk guarantees for enterprises. The public recognizes their environmental behavior and prefers to buy their products or stocks; thirdly, it relies on the connotative development mode of technological progress to improve product quality and make it more competitive in the market. Therefore, the ultimate rational choice of enterprises is to embark on the green transformation development path, which in turn improves the survival environment of enterprises and forms a self-reinforcing virtuous circle of "green transformation and development- internal and external conditions improve-survival environment improved-green transformation and development". For the whole society, it promotes the greening of industrial structure and the intensification of economic growth model (see Fig. 1).

In Fig. 1, the first is the government's environmental regulation, which requires financial institutions to assume certain environmental responsibilities in investment and operation, which prompts financial institutions to strengthen the environmental audit of production enterprises. At the same time, the government also endows the public with certain power of environmental protection supervision, so that the public has the power and opportunity to supervise the environmental protection behavior of enterprises through certain channels. In environmental regulation, the government also requires enterprises to conduct green production and promote green transformation by means of law, economy, administration, science and technology and culture. In such an environment, enterprises have two choices: One is to continue the traditional high-pollution and extensive production mode, and the other is the environment-friendly and energy-saving green production mode. The former increases the cost of production and operation of enterprises, and worsens the relationship with government departments, financial institutions and the public, the development prospect of which

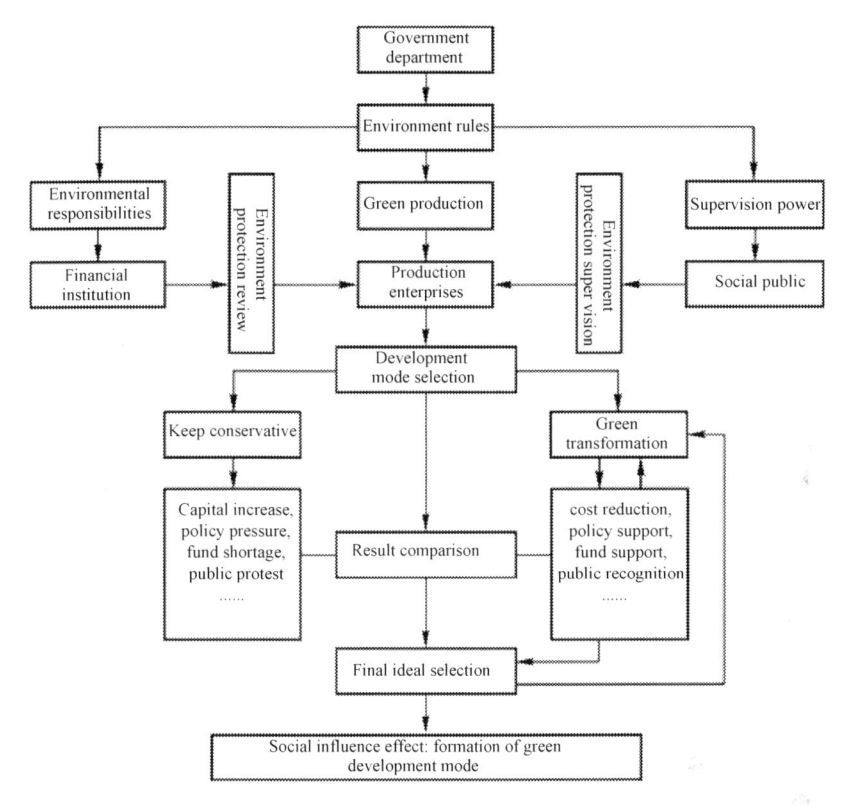

Fig. 1   Green credit formation mechanism of commercial banks

is worrying; After the short-term adjustment of the latter, the comprehensive cost of the enterprise decreases, the product competitiveness improves and the relationship with government departments, financial institutions and the public improves. The whole living environment tends to be better, and enterprises finally embark on the road of green development, and promote the optimization of the industrial structure of the whole society and the transformation of economic growth mode.

2.2   The Mechanism of Green Finance

Awareness of Environmental Protection and Correction of Market Failure
In the process of transformation and development, environmental governance will undoubtedly increase the burden on enterprises. For this reason, many enterprises try their best to avoid environmental protection. After the launch of the green finance system, due to loans, guarantees, listing and other financing needs, environmental audits are conducted and environmental certificates are provided. This makes many enterprises have to take the initiative to carry out environmental governance, so as to avoid the phenomenon of market failure in the production process, such as enterprise profiting, community suffering and government paying.

Technological Progress and Industrial Structure Optimization
The greening of the industrial structure requires a large number of advanced environmental protection technologies. Compared with traditional technologies, environmental protection technologies have the advantages of environmental protection, energy saving, emission reduction and low carbon. However, it is often a new technology that is not mature enough, which requires more research efforts and certain material support, among which capital is an indispensable element. The preference of green finance to green technology, green projects and green industry can accelerate the development of green industry and promote the technological upgrading of traditional industry, which is conducive to the greening of the entire industrial structure.

Internal Governance and Improvement of Governance Efficiency
Although the collection and payment of resource tax and sewage fee can restrain the resource consumption and pollution emission of enterprises to a certain extent, and promote the enterprises to control the environment. However, it belongs to external governance and has certain remedial nature. More often, it is difficult to effectively curb the pollution of enterprises due to asymmetric information, difficulty in accurate measurement of pollution emissions and design defects of green taxes and fees. However, due to the openness and externality of resource and environmental property right itself, its transaction cost is extremely high in the actual micro-individual behavior and cannot be effectively implemented in practice. Fundamentally speaking,

more effective environmental governance needs to be carried out from within the micro-economic subject first, and only by truly restraining the micro-economic subject's impulse of pollution emission from within can the pollution be rooted from the source. Green finance, on the one hand, through the financing of environmental audit, improves the consciousness of enterprise pollution control; on the other hand, financial support for energy conservation, pollution control, emission reduction and other environmental protection activities will help curb pollution at the source and improve the effectiveness of environmental governance.

Environmental Supervision and National Environmental Protection Culture

The investment assets of financial institutions mainly come from the savings or investment of social members, while financial institutions strengthen the environmental protection audit of enterprises in the investment behavior, which is actually responsible for the environmental welfare of social members. This is conducive to enhancing social members' sense of identity and cooperation with financial institutions and forming green residents' savings and green society investment fund. Germany's "eco-bank", Britain's "green choice account", Japan's green investment fund, etc., are green financial institutions formed by social members based on their willingness and pursuit of environmental protection. In addition, in the modern green financial system, many enterprises choose to regularly and actively announce their environmental governance reports to the society and accept the supervision of the public, which is conducive to stimulating the enthusiasm of the whole people for environmental protection and forming the social culture of the whole people actively participating in environmental protection. For example, the "socially responsible investment in Japan" advocated by the Japanese financial circle is the result of the nationwide environmental protection culture.

3   FOREIGN GREEN FINANCE PRACTICES

3.1   Germination and Development Process

The green financial system originates from the exploration of sustainable development and the reflection of the financial industry on its traditional development mode. In the 1970s, the large-scale financial crisis broke out in major Western developed countries, which prompted people to rethink the traditional development model of the financial industry and began to link finance with the environment. In 1987, the world commission on environment and development put forward the concept of "sustainable development" in its report *Our Common Future*, which inspired people to explore the path and implementation tools of sustainable development, including the innovation of financial system. In 1988, more than 1200 members of the green party of the federal republic of Germany invested in Frankfurt, the financial center of the federal republic of Germany, to establish the world's first ecological bank. The bank is also known as green bank because it is mainly engaged in credit business for nature and environmental protection. Its establishment plays a decisive and groundbreaking role in the global development of green finance system and is the first step taken by green finance system in the global development process. After the Rio conference in 1992, the green revolution swept the world. The United States first put forward the concept of "green finance" in the late 1990s and made pioneering efforts to combine environmental factors with financial innovation, to evaluate environmental risks in financial activities and to develop many successful environmental financial products. So far, green finance worldwide can be roughly divided into three stages according to its popularity:

The first stage is the rise and implementation of green finance system in a few developed countries. This stage was mainly in the 1980s and 1990s, and was characterized by the small distribution range of green finance, which only emerged and implemented in a few developed countries (regions) such as Europe, the United States and Japan. As mentioned above, the first green bank in the world was established by the federal republic of Germany in 1988. After 1993, the German government increased the fund year by year to support green industry. In the 1990s, the Japanese government strongly supported the development of green industry. The United States has increased the development of green agriculture and eco-industry; The EU actively supports the production of green products through green credit, green taxation and other policies.

The second stage is that green finance has been widely accepted by Western developed countries after its achievements. After the green finance in Europe, the United States, Japan and other countries achieved results, many developed countries followed suit and increased the research on the construction of green financial system and the development of green financial products. For example, in 2004, Japan policy investment bank, a large state-owned bank in Japan, launched the financing business of "promoting environment-friendly operation", which aims to promote the development of enterprises' environmental protection work. Through its "environment-friendly enterprise evaluation" system, on the basis of scoring the enterprise's environmental performance, provide special low-interest loans for environmental protection to enterprises with excellent performance in environmental protection, and support enterprises to increase their investment in environmental protection. In Europe, there are about 45 green venture capital institutions with a total investment of 100 million euros, investing in renewable energy, water and clean technology equipment.

The third stage is the universal implementation of green finance in developing countries (regions). The success of green finance system in developed countries and the borderless nature of ecological protection have led many developing countries (regions) to introduce green finance system one after another, and green finance system has been implemented on a global scale. In the "green economy initiative" launched by the United Nations environment program (UNEP) to reinvigorate global markets, a total of 50 countries, 14 of which are developing countries, have set renewable energy targets to mobilize investment in clean technology and natural infrastructure. These include: Mexico, Argentina, Brazil, Dominica, China, India, the Philippines, Iran, Morocco, Syria, Tunisia, Senegal, South Africa and Uganda. In October 2002, the international finance corporation (IFC), a subsidiary of the World Bank, and ABN, a Dutch bank, proposed a corporate lending standard at a conference of the world's leading commercial banks in London. The guidelines require financial institutions to make a comprehensive assessment of the possible environmental and social impacts of a project when investing in it, and to use financial leverage to promote the positive role of the project in environmental protection and harmonious social development. This principle became known as the "equator principle" and became widely accepted by the international financial industry (the original name of the "equatorial principles" was "Greenwich principles", the name came from the consideration that the meeting was held at Greenwich, the prime meridian around the earth). Since its inception, the equator principle has been accepted by an increasing number of financial institutions (see Table 2). As of 16 October 2012, 77 financial institutions from 32 countries had announced the implementation of the equator

Table 2   Banks adopting the equator principles (part)

Serial number	Bank	Serial number	Bank
1	ABN (the Netherlands)	31	HSBC group (UK)
2	ANZ (Australia)	32	Yubao Banking Group (Germany)
3	Banco Bradesco (Brazil)	33	ING Group (the Netherlands)
4	Banco do Brasil (Brazil)	34	Intesa Sanpaolo (Italy)
5	Bank of Galicia (Argentina)	35	JP Morgan chase (United States)
6	Mascot bank (Oman)	36	United financial group of Belgium (Belgium)
7	Bank of America (United States)	37	KFW Bank (Germany)
8	Republic Bank (Uruguay)	38	The Savings Banks (Spain)
9	Montreal Financial Group (Canada)	39	Lloyds TSB Bank (UK)
10	Bank of Tokyo-Mitsubishi (Japan)	40	Manulife Life Insurance (Canada)
11	Barclays Bank (UK)	41	Mondragon Union (Italy)
12	Foreign Bank of Bilbao Vizcaya (Spain)	42	Millennium Bank (Portugal)
13	Sheng Jing Banking Group (Portugal)	43	Mizuho Industrial Bank (Japan)
14	Bank of Navarre (Spain)	44	Nedbank Group (South Africa)
15	Calyon Bank (France)	45	Noble Bank (Denmark, Netherlands, Norway)
16	Canadian Imperial Bank of Commerce (Canada)	46	Rabobank Group (the Netherlands)
17	Infrastructure finance international corporation (United States)	47	Royal bank of Canada (Canada)
18	Citigroup (United States)	48	Bank of Nova Scotia (Canada)
19	Industrial Bank (Chile)	49	Nordea bank of Sweden (Sweden)
20	Credit Suisse Group (Switzerland)	50	Sumitomo Mitsui Bank (Japan)
21	Dexia Group (France, Belgium)	51	Societe Generale (France)
22	DnB Nor (Norway)	52	Standard Chartered Bank (UK)
23	Dresdner Bank (Germany)	53	Td Banking Group (Canada)
24	Export credit fund (Denmark)	54	Royal bank of Scotland (UK)
25	E Co(United States)	55	United Bank (Brazil)
26	Export Development Canada (Canada)	56	Wachovia (UK)
27	Financial Banking Corporation (Togo)	57	Wells Fargo (United States)
28	Dutch Development Finance Corporation (the Netherlands)	58	WESTLB (Germany)
29	Fortis Bank (Belgium)	59	Westpac Bank (Australia)
30	Halifax Bank of Scotland (UK)	60	China Industrial Bank

principles. By January 22, 2013, a total of 78 financial institutions around the world have incorporated the "equator principles", and their business scope has radiated to more than 100 countries (or regions) around the world. China's Industrial Bank also announced its acceptance of the "equator principle" in 2008.

3.2 Industry Standards and Practices

Industry Standards

According to the sorting out by Song Xiaoling (2013), the green finance policies of the Western banking industry mainly adopt IFC performance standards, equator principles, *Responsible Investment Principles, Manual on Pollution Prevention and Reduction* and other international standards. Each bank combines international standards with its own situation to formulate its financing environmental protection policies and guidelines.

(1) The United Nations *Principles on Responsible Investment.* Focusing on the environment and sustainable development, the UN has formulated such principles and provisions as the *UN Declaration on the Human Environment, the Rio Declaration, the Framework Convention on Climate Change, Agenda 21, the Kyoto Protocol, Johannesburg Sustainable Development, the Monterrey Consensus* and *the Principles of Responsible Investment.* The UNEP Financial Action Agency developed the *Principles for Responsible Investment* in early 2005 and issued and implemented the principles in April 2006. The six investment principles proposed in the *Principles of Responsible Investment* aim to standardize financial investment decisions and enable financial institutions to fully consider the social and environmental impact of project implementation when investing in corporate projects.

(2) World Bank handbook on *Pollution Prevention and Reduction.* The World Bank in 1975 published "project environment development guidelines", since 1984, successively promulgated and revised the relevant business manuals, instructions and business process, also for the first time in 1999 published the *Pollution Prevention and Reduction Manual* (hereinafter referred to as "the manual"), and in 2001 passed the new strategy of environmental protection, have continually revised and improved

its environment policy. The *Manual* has formulated pollution prevention guidelines for more than 40 industrial sectors, fully implemented the governance concepts of strengthening pollution prevention, promoting clean production, improving energy efficiency, reducing resource consumption and improving management, and put forward quantifiable pollution reduction targets and the maximum pollution emission standards. Currently, the manual is widely used by international financial institutions, multilateral development banks, export credit agencies, private financial institutions that have signed the equator principles, industry and consultants, governments and non-governmental organizations.

(3) IFC performance standards. The IFC, part of the World Bank, is increasingly the global standard setter for environmental and social development in financial markets and the private sector. The IFC sustainable development framework, which includes social and environmental sustainability policies, performance standards, and disclosure policies, was adopted on February 21, 2006, and became effective on April 30, 2006. Among them, there are 8 performance standards, which not only involve the comprehensive evaluation and management system in the original performance standards, but also include the requirements of labor rights, human rights, community health and safety, prevention and reduction of pollution, expansion of social investigation, expansion of community participation and new comprehensive methods to protect biological diversity. On January 1, 2012, the IFC updated the sustainable development framework to better reflect the evolution of sustainable development and risk reduction practices. The new framework addresses challenging issues including supply chain management, resource efficiency, addressing climate change and business and human rights that are increasingly important to the sustainable development of businesses. The performance standard has become an important standard for financial institutions to implement the environmental policy of project financing.

(4) The Equator Principles. The Equator Principles (EPs) are a set of voluntary guidelines established by the world's leading financial institutions under the IFC's social and environmental sustainability policies and performance standards to address social

and environmental issues related to development project financing. Drafted by financial institutions including Citibank, ABN, Barclays and WESTLB, it was first announced by 10 leading international banks in June 2003. The equatorial principles constantly revise and update their policies and standards in response to changing circumstances and practical needs. On July 6, 2006, the financial institutions under equator principles modified the old EPs and released a new version of EPs (EPs II), which was officially adopted in January 2007. EPs II has carried on the significant changes to the original equator principles, which has a great progress on the breadth and depth, expanded the scope of application, raised awareness of social issues and raised standards for social and environmental issues. Then it drafted the third version of the equator principles (EPs III) draft, and on October 12, 2012, consulted with stakeholders and the public opinion. The detailed classification of equator principles, specific measures and strong guidance and operability in practice (see Table 3) have

Table 3 Classification and measures of equatorial principles

Category	Definition	Preventive measures
Category A	Projects have serious negative social or environmental impacts that are diverse, irreversible or unprecedented	1. Social and environmental assessment report 2. Action plan 3. Public information disclosure 4. Complaint mechanism 5. Independent review report 6. Contract
Category B	Projects have a certain negative impact on society or environment, and the impact is small in scope, generally concentrated in a certain area, mostly reversible, and can be easily improved through mitigation measures	Essential measures 1. Social and environmental assessment report 2. Action plan 6. Contracts Non-essential measures (partial applicable measures): 3. Public information disclosure 4. Complaint mechanism 5. Independent review report
Category C	Projects have little or no adverse impact on society or the environment	N.A.

Table 4 Comparison of green financial policies of major Western banks

Bank name	The environmental protection regulations	Core system	Characteristics
Export-Import Bank of the United States	1. OECD *Common Methods* 2. The World Bank's *Pollution Prevention and Reduction Manual*	Environment assessment procedure and guidance	Focuses on medium- and long-term export credits for its environmental assessment procedures and guidelines A policy consistent with the *Common Method* format
HSBC (Hong Kong and Shanghai Banking Corporation)	1. "Environmental credit and ethical investment" guidelines 2. The equator principles 3. Sectoral guidelines	Environmental credit and ethical investment	1. Environmental protection "start from yourself" 2. Expand the concept of environmental protection and influence the market and customers 3. Labor standards, human rights and environmental responsibilities 4. Accreditation of international institutions
Citibank	1. The equator principles 2. IFC environmental and social risk standard	Environmental and social risk management mechanism	1. Forest protection 2. Independent investment center 3. EPs initiator and key core and leadership roles
Asian development bank	1. Environmental policy 2. Operation manual 3. Environmental assessment	Environmental policies	1. Integration of environmental protection and operation procedures 2. Make environmental sustainability a prerequisite for economic development 3. Based on poverty alleviation
Bank of America	1. Internal guidelines 2. World Bank *Manual on Pollution Prevention and Reduction* 3. Credit guidelines for developing countries 4. Equator principles	Core business environmental incentive mechanism	Especially formulated relevant financing policies and procedures for forest and climate change-related projects
Japan bank for international cooperation	1. New environmental and social guidelines 2. Guidance on international financial operations 3. Guidelines for the operation of overseas economic cooperation	New environmental and social guiding principles	Seven basic principles for environmental and social considerations

Source Song Xiaoling. Green Finance Policy of Western Banking Industry: Common Rules and Differential Practice. *Exploration of Economic Problems*, 2013 (1)

increasingly become the industry standards of the international financial industry. As of January 22, 2013, a total of 78 financial institutions around the world have accepted the "equator principles", and their business scope radiates to more than 100 countries (regions) in the world.

It is worth mentioning that financial institutions of various countries have formulated their financing environmental protection policies and guidelines according to their own situations and in combination with international financial industry standards (see Table 4).

Practical Development
Since the German eco-bank took the first step in global green finance, many international financial institutions have also penetrated the concept of green finance into their operation and management. In addition to the greening of traditional businesses such as credit, securities and insurance, green bonds have also developed rapidly in recent years.

In green credit, financial institutions, on the one hand, formulate corresponding management measures to strengthen the environmental management of loan projects. On the other hand, financial product innovation should be accelerated to induce and stimulate people's green consumption and other environmental protection behaviors (see Table 5). For example, Citibank in the United States has set up an internal environmental and social policy assessment committee and established a series of environmental management mechanisms, including environmental policy and process training mechanism, risk management mechanism for environmental and social issues, external public and private affairs cooperation mechanism and environmental protection business development mechanism. Barclays bank is committed to the promotion of sustainable development projects. At present, the projects have spread to more than 50 countries, and in the practice process, the bank has compiled a set of social and environmental credit guidelines, which have been issued to more than 170 financial institutions around the world. ABN bank has specially established the database of environmental factor analysis to study the impact of each industry on the environment and the existing environmental risks, and took the database as an important basis for evaluating and selecting loan customers and providing risk assessment. By installing wind power, water power, solar power and other

Table 5 Specific measures taken by international commercial banks to practice green finance

Banks	Concrete practice measures
Citibank	• Setting up the environmental affairs department to launch various green credit products and services • Announced $50 billion over 10 years to tackle climate change in 2007 • Established an environmental and social policy assessment committee and a risk management mechanism for environmental and social issues • Energy-saving mortgage products were launched for customers from middle and low-income families, and the energy-saving index was incorporated into the credit evaluation system of the lender • In 2008, together with Morgan Stanley, it announced guidelines for financing carbon emission projects
ABN (Algemene Bank Nederland)	• Providing green loan products involving socially responsible investment funds • Establish the environmental factor analysis database as an important basis for evaluating loan customers and risk assessment • Issue a climate credit card to calculate the customer's carbon dioxide emissions based on the consumption of the card as the emission reduction payment for the purchase of renewable energy • The index based on sample stocks of climate and water resources was designed, and corresponding financial products were launched
HSBC	• It has installed hydropower, wind and solar power generation equipment, clean air conditioning chillers and automatic ventilation equipment, becoming the first commercial bank in the world to achieve zero carbon dioxide emissions • Launch of the global climate change benchmark index fund • Through the guidelines of "environmental credit and ethical investment", refuse to invest and finance projects with potential environmental pollution
Barclays Bank	• Launch "green breathing card", and offer discounts to cardholders for purchasing green products • Launch the first global carbon index fund to track carbon credits in greenhouse gas emissions reduction trading

Source Zhang Ping. *Brief Analysis on Connotation, Function Mechanism and Practice of Green Finance.* Chengdu: Southwest University of Finance and Economics, 2013

power generation equipment, automatic ventilation system and clean air conditioning chillers, HSBC has realized an annual emission reduction of more than 1000 tons and become the first international commercial bank in the world to realize zero carbon dioxide emissions (Lin Xiao, 2011).

In terms of green financial product innovation, green credit products mainly include housing loans, auto loans, commercial buildings, transportation loans and green credit cards (see Table 6). For housing loans, giraffe currency launched a "carbon dioxide mortgage" with carbon emissions as part of the collateral, and participants can enjoy a discount of about 2% interest rate. The united financial services' "eco-home loan" incorporates household energy efficiency and carbon reduction indicators into the borrower's credit score system; Citigroup makes easy loans to homeowners who buy solar equipment. On the auto loan front, VanCity bank of Canada provides concessional rate loans to all low emission and clean energy vehicles. Australian MENU bank "Go Green car loan" program also requires lenders to plant trees to absorb the car emissions. In terms of commercial construction and transportation loans, financial institutions also encourage enterprises and individuals to support environmental protection by providing preferential loans and convenient loan services. In addition, some banks have launched green credit cards. Barclays bank has launched a "green breathing card", offering discounts for green products and services with low borrowing rates. RABOBANK has stipulated that users of its "climate credit card" will contribute a certain proportion to the world wildlife fund after purchasing energy-intensive products or services (Lin Xiao, 2011).

Table 6 List of green financial products of foreign financial institutions

Category	Specific case
Housing loans	• Giraffe currency's 'carbon dioxide mortgage'
	• United financial services 'eco-home loan'
	• Citigroup structured energy-saving mortgage products
Auto loan	• VanCity bank, Canada, "Clean air auto loan" auto loan
	• Australian MENU bank 'Go Green auto loan'
Commercial buildings	• Citigroup energy-saving building loan preference
	• New resources bank energy efficient building credit
Transportation loans	• Bank of America's 'quick loan for small business administration'
Green credit card	• Britain's Barclays Bank "green breathing card"
	• Rabobank "climate credit card"

Source Lin Xiao. *Research on the Development of Green Finance in China Under the Background of Low-Carbon Economy.* Guangzhou: Jinan University, 2011

In terms of green bonds, green bonds have become an important carrier of green finance in recent years, as they are more likely to be included in the investment portfolio of institutional investors (pension funds, insurance companies, etc.) as medium- and long-term financial products. Since the first "green bond" was issued by the European investment bank in 2007, the global green bond market has developed rapidly at a compound annual growth rate of more than 50%. At present, the balance of green bonds has exceeded 35 billion us dollars (Zhang Chenghui, Tian Hui, 2015). In one case, EDF's 1.9 billion green bond sale in November 2013 was twice oversubscribed. Just a day later, Bank of America issued $500m in green bonds to support its renewable energy and energy efficiency businesses. In March 2014, Unilever and Toyota issued 250 million euros and 1.75 billion dollars of green bonds, respectively. In May, Regency Centers, a real estate investment trust in Florida, issued a green bond of 250 million dollars, and Suez issued a green bond of 2.5 billion euros, breaking the record of 1.9 billion euros issued by EDF (Guo Peiyuan, Cai Yingcui, 2015).

3.3   Green Finance Practices in Typical Countries

The United States
The United States leads the world in the development of green finance, which has achieved remarkable results and has been widely imitated and accepted by other countries.

First of all, with legislative guarantee, relevant laws are improved, matched and coordinated. The United States is a country with a developed legal system, and its environmental and resource laws are no exception. Since the 1930s, a series of laws related to resources and environment have been formulated, especially in the 1970s, a large number of laws on resource and environment protection have emerged intensively (see Table 7), which has laid a good legal foundation for the development of green finance. The federal government's *Comprehensive Environmental Response, Compensation and Liability Act* of 1980, later known as the *Superfund Act*, which is the beginning of green finance in the United States. Under the bill, banks must take responsibility for environmental pollution caused by their customers and pay for repairs. It requires financial institutions to shoulder the responsibility of green society, bear the corresponding responsibility for the environmental

Table 7 Resource and environmental laws enacted in the United States

Year	Law	Year	Law
1936	*Bus Exhaust Control Act*	1976	*Federal Land Policy and*
1969	*National Environmental Policy Act*		*Management Act*
1970	*Environmental Quality*		*Resource Protection and Recovery*
	Improvement Act		*Act*
	American Environmental		*Toxic Substances Control Act*
	Education Act		
1972	*Coastal Zone Management Act*	1980	*Acid Rain Act*
	Marine Mammal Protection Act		*Motor Vehicle Fuel Efficiency Act*
	Marine Conservation Research and		*Biomass and Alcohol Fuel Act*
	Closed Fisheries Act		*Solid Waste Disposal Act*
	Federal Environmental Pesticide		*Superfund Act*
	Control Act		
	Noise Control Act		
1973	*Endangered Species Act*	1982	*Nuclear Waste Policy Act*
1974	*Safe Drinking Water Act*	1990	*Clean Air Act*
			Pollution Prevention Act
			Clean Air Act Amendments
1975	*The Toxic Substances Transport Act*	1992	*Energy Policy Act*

Notes According to Ni Yuxia's master's thesis *Research on Green Financial System in the United States* (Hunan Normal University, 2011), relevant materials were sorted out

pollution caused by it and urge banks to prevent and avoid all kinds of risks caused by potential environmental problems. In order to regulate the behavior of the government, enterprises and banks and adjust the relationship among the three, in addition to the *Comprehensive Environmental Response, Compensation and Liability Law*, which stipulates that banks must be responsible for environmental pollution caused by customers, there is also the *Resource Conservation and Recovery Act* for the prevention and disposal of pollution-related cleanup incidents and the *Energy Tax Act* to stimulate and promote the development of green finance industry.

Second, advanced means, the comprehensive use of economic, legal, scientific and technological means. After the 1990s, the green finance system of the US federal government was further improved, with a wider range of participants, more flexible and efficient means, and a comprehensive use of economic, legal, scientific and technological means to promote the benign mutual development of the environment and economy.

For example, the *Clean Air Act Amendment* provides for the emission trading system. The US environmental protection agency promotes the purchase and trading mechanism of emission credits for automobile engine manufacturers, advocates the improvement of product quality in the automobile industry, the development of public transportation and the use of economic leverage such as taxation to encourage the production of clean energy vehicles. The law has been effective. According to statistics, sulfur dioxide emissions in the United States in 1990 were 10 million tons lower than that in 1980. By 2000, the United States had established a relatively complete sulfur dioxide permit trading market, which saved the United States about $1 billion per year in reducing sulfur dioxide emissions and achieved the goal of creating certain economic value in pollution control (Ni Yuxia, 2011).

Thirdly, the system has been improved, and the fields of credit, securities and insurance are all green. Since the *Superfund Act* was enacted, its strict joint and several environmental liability system has spawned a series of relevant environmental management policies, such as "green credit policy" and "environmental liability insurance policy". American financial institutions have to strengthen the environmental risk management of financial activities and develop diversified green financial products to avoid the risk of environmental responsibility. For example, some export–import banks in the United States have established environmental assessment policies. Bank loans for various projects need to be evaluated for their environmental impact first, and decisions on whether to grant loans are made based on the assessment. According to the survey of 1741 member banks conducted by the American banking association in 1991, 62.5% of the banks have changed the traditional lending procedures to avoid potential environmental debts, and 45.2% of the banks have stopped lending due to the fear of environmental problems (Li Xi, 2011). In terms of green securities, in 1993, the US Securities and Exchange Commission required listed companies to make substantive reports on their environmental performance from the perspective of environmental accounting. In terms of green insurance, in order to ensure the implementation of judicial punishment, the United States has developed a sound environmental pollution liability insurance system, which mainly includes two aspects: The first is to clarify the liability of the insured for environmental damage caused by pollution of water, land or air. The second is to clearly own its own governance liability insurance, compulsory insurance will be enforced against liability for damages arising from the disposal of toxic substances and wastes. In addition, it has established a professional environmental pollution risk insurance company—environmental protection insurance company. It has provided lower premium and other preferential conditions for enterprises that attach importance to environmental responsibility risk management, and hired professional environmental experts to strengthen the prevention and control of environmental risks for the insured.

Finally, conditional construction that emphasizes environmental protection, economy, technology and other information sharing. In view of such problems as the difficulty in integrating environment and economy into green finance activities and the information asymmetry between banks and enterprises, American banks attach great importance to the improvement of their information technology systems and have established effective information communication mechanisms.

In short, the United States has established a complete set of green finance system and achieved good social and economic benefits in practice. The establishment of its green finance legal system provides legal guarantee for the development of green finance in the United States.

The UK

As an active advocate and practitioner of green finance, Britain, on the one hand, strengthens the construction of green finance system through legislation and other means, and strengthens the design of constraint mechanism and incentive mechanism. On the other hand, it actively develops green financial products and promote the penetration of green financial products in various fields.

Constraint mechanism: In 1997, the Chartered Institute of Certified Public Accountants issued the *Guidelines for the Preparation of Environmental and Energy Reports*, requiring environmental considerations in the audit of financial statements. In 2000, the government amended the pensions act to require pension trusts to consider the environment when making investment decisions. In 2002, British Prime Minister Tony Blair announced the sustainable development strategy of Britain—*London Principles for Sustainable Development*. The document calls for the full cooperation of all departments to promote the support and integration of financial markets for sustainable development strategies. It is suggested that the financial sector should make prudent decisions on the amount of financing in accordance with the principle of environmental protection and the comprehensive consideration of environmental cost and social risk cost, and that risk management products should reflect environmental and social risks. In response to this, National Westminster set up a department dedicated to environmental finance, which formulated guidelines on environmental finance for internal learning and instructed the bank to use the guidelines to effectively investigate and measure the environmental risks of loans. After years of research, the London center for financial innovation has put forward a set of innovative schemes for environmental risk rating of enterprises from the two dimensions of adverse degree to the environment and the ability to eliminate harmful factors.

Incentives: The UK has implemented a climate change tax, a climate change agreement and an emissions trading regime. The climate change tax will be levied at different rates depending on the type of energy used, but the government will return the proceeds from the tax to companies through "enhanced investment subsidies", such as encouraging them to invest in energy-efficient and environmentally friendly technologies or equipment, and setting up a carbon fund. Among them, carbon fund is an independent company between government and enterprise, which was invested by the government and operated according to the enterprise mode in 2001. The fund is mainly used for activities that can immediately produce emission reduction effects, the development of low-carbon technology and projects to help enterprises and public sectors improve their ability to cope with climate change.

Green financial products development: Green credit and green insurance development is better. Green credit is similar to giraffe money's green home loan and united financial services' eco-home loan (see related article). In addition, the British bank HSBC has set up a "green choice" account, in which customers will donate 5 pounds to the world wide fund for nature, earth watch and the climate group within a certain period of time. Its bills will be sent directly via e-mail instead of paper, to inspire and expand customer's green behavior. Green insurance has the "green car insurance" program launched by royal united insurance company, which aims to encourage more people to buy environment-friendly cars and provide insurance discounts for environment-friendly car owners. There is also the "green travel insurance" program launched by the UK climate safety travel insurance company. Under the premise that the travel company does not increase the insurance cost of passengers, it will invest part of its insurance premium into the company's environmental protection project.

The German

Green finance in Germany mainly aims at green transformation and development through sound environmental legislation, financial support from national policy banks and the development of green insurance.

Sound environmental legislation is the basis for the development of green finance in Germany. Since the *Waste Disposal Law* of the federal republic of Germany was promulgated in 1972, Germany has enacted a series of laws on environmental protection and development of circular economy, making Germany one of the countries with the most perfect green finance legislation in the world. These include the *Energy Conservation Act*, the *Waste Water Tax Act*, the *Circular Economy and Waste Materials Act*, and the *Renewable Energy Act*, which have played their respective environmental roles in various fields (see Table 8). Between 1999 and 2006, the German government also promulgated the *Law on the Introduction of Ecological Tax Reform* (1999), the *Law on the Further Development of Ecological Tax Reform* (2003) and the *Biofuel Quota Law* (2006). The implementation and promulgations of these three laws have reduced the energy consumed by the company and enterprises in their production activities, promoted the company and enterprises to invest in new energy, reduced the emission of pollutants, and protected the ecological balance (Mei Yan, 2013).

National policy banks have played the role of green financial leverage and demonstration. In addition to the ecological bank mentioned above,

Table 8 Environmental legislation and its role in Germany

Law	Function
Waste Disposal Act	At the beginning of the legislation, the main emphasis was on the end disposal of wastes. After the amendment in 1986, the focus shifted to reducing the waste generated in production and life
Energy Conservation Act	It sets energy conservation standards for new buildings and reduces energy consumption
Wastewater Tax Law	It stipulates that companies and enterprises shall pay taxes when discharging wastewater into water
Circular Economy and Waste Law	It systematically expounds the idea of circular economy and clarifies new measures in waste management
Renewable Energy Act	It increases the share of renewable energy in the electricity supply

Source Mei Yan. *On the Legal Regulation of Green Finance in China*. Changchun: Jilin University of Finance and Economics, 2013

Germany's national policy bank-KFW bank also actively promotes green transformation and development through green credit. For example, the discount interest loan for energy saving buildings includes two aspects: first, the energy conservation of existing buildings; second, discount loans for new ecological buildings. For projects with good performance in environmental protection and energy conservation, a preferential credit policy with a loan interest rate of less than 1% can be granted for 10 years, and the central government will subsidize the interest rate difference. In addition, KFW also actively innovates green financial products and discloses environmental information. Led by the bank, other financial institutions have also strengthened environmental risk management in financial activities. Since 2001, 30 German financial companies, including banks, savings offices and insurance companies, have published public environmental reports and continuously reported on environmental affairs, following the practice of the industry.

Green insurance strengthens the responsibility of environmental risk management. The *Environmental Responsibility Law* promulgated in 1990, based on the consideration of ensuring that the environmental tort victims can be compensated and the infringer can fulfill the obligation of compensation, Article 19 specifically stipulates that the owners of facilities must take certain preventive measures to guarantee the performance of obligations in advance. The scope of compensation of the insurance company only includes the liability caused by the accident of the production and operation of the enterprise. And the victim must put forward a claim for compensation, to those who knowingly do not comply with the relevant laws and regulations, resulting in environmental damage that is not within the scope of compensation. Germany's green insurance law specifically stipulates in the environmental liability insurance clauses that the loss found within 3 years after the termination of the policy is still responsible by the original policy unit, which is conducive to the repair and treatment of those deep and difficult to be found major environmental pollution accidents.

Japan

Japan's green finance mainly promotes green transformation and development by formulating comprehensive green finance laws, increasing investment in environmental protection industry and advocating socially responsible investment.

Comprehensive green finance legislation. Japan's rapid economic development after the war led to a serious ecological crisis. In face of this reality, the Japanese government promulgated the *Basic Law on Environment*, which stipulates the responsibilities of companies and enterprises, and provides a legal basis for future laws related to green finance. Since then, Japan has continuously formulated and improved other relevant laws to ensure sustainable development, thus becoming the country with the most comprehensive green finance legislation in the world. Japan's green finance legislation can be divided into three parts: first, on the basis of the *Basic Law of the Environment*, the *Basic Law of Promoting the Formation of a Recycling Society* has been promulgated. Secondly, the Japanese government promulgated two comprehensive laws. Through the promulgation of the *Law on the Promotion of Effective Use of Resources* and the *Law on Solid Waste Management and Public Cleaning*, the responsibilities and obligations of companies, organizations, social citizens and the government are clarified, and the evaluation objects and standards of the law are determined. Thirdly, the Japanese government has promulgated six separate laws (see Table 9), which enable the Japanese government to comprehensively regulate the development of green finance from the aspects of society, companies, associations and individuals, and point out the way for the further development of green finance (Mei Yan, 2013).

Strong support for the development of the environmental protection industry. In 1993, in order to further promote the development

Table 9 Green finance legislation and its role in Japan

Law	Function
Law on Classified Recovery and Recycling of Packaging	It establishes a system of classified recovery of packaging and containers
Law on the Recovery of Household Electrical Appliances	It stipulates the legal responsibilities of natural persons
Law on the Recovery of Construction and Materials	It stipulates the legal responsibilities of the company and the society, and promotes the recovery and utilization of various construction wastes
Food Recovery Act	It details the responsibilities of governments, companies and consumers
Green Procurement Act	Through government influence demonstration, it affects the production and sales of green products, thus promoting the development of green finance
Law on the Recycling of Scrapped Automobiles	It will properly and reasonably recycle scrapped automobiles to reduce the waste of resources

Source Mei Yan. *On the Legal Regulation of Green Finance in China*. Changchun: Jilin University of Finance and Economics, 2013

of energy-saving technologies and increase the financial investment and loans related to energy and environment, the total amount increased from 560 billion yen in 1992 to 970 billion yen. In order to support the reduction of environmental pressure and better promote enterprises' investment in environmental protection, Japan policy investment bank carried out "promoting environment-friendly operation financing business" for large state-owned banks in 2004 and provided special low-interest loans for enterprises with outstanding performance in environmental protection to encourage enterprises to invest in environmental protection.

Socially responsible investing. Japan attaches great importance to the social responsibility in investment, especially the responsibility of public environmental protection. Policy banks, commercial banks and private investment funds emphasize the environmental protection in investment. From 2006 to 2007, Japan policy investment bank introduced updated business contents on the basis of the original environment rating financing business and put forward relevant countermeasures to reduce carbon dioxide emissions so as to control the greenhouse effect. In early 2006, a new score was introduced to "promote the achievement of Kyoto protocol targets", and in 2007, with the strong support of the ministry of environment, Japan policy investment bank launched the environment rating discount loan business again. In addition, commercial banks can also make full and reasonable use of the environmental rating system of policy banks to evaluate and supervise various loan target enterprises, so as to avoid investment risks in a more practical way and improve investment efficiency. In terms of social investment funds, although Japan started relatively late, it developed rapidly. So far, Japan has 11 funds, including eight eco-funds (six domestic funds and two international funds) and three socially responsible investment funds (one domestic fund and two international funds), which hold about $100m.

South Korea

South Korea's green finance is mainly to formulate the strategy of transformation and development, support the development of green industry, participate in international financial cooperation and create conditions for the development of green finance.

It has implemented the new green policy to promote the country's green transformation and development. The Korean government attaches great importance to green transformation and development, and elevates the implementation of the "Green New Deal" to the national strategic wisdom, aiming to create jobs and enhance future growth momentum through the implementation of the "Green New Deal". It has basically established the low-carbon growth strategy and the green national image, and turned the financial crisis into an opportunity for development. Therefore, it has formulated a series of relevant policies and regulations to promote green transformation and development. For example, in 2008, the *Low-Carbon Green Growth Strategy* was introduced, providing a policy framework for green development. In 2009, through the "green project" plan, it is planned to invest about 38 billion US dollars in the construction of ecological infrastructure, low-carbon technology development and the creation of a green living and working environment in the next four years, so as to provide new growth momentum for the future development of South Korea. In 2010, the *Basic Law on Low-Carbon and Green Growth* was promulgated, which clarified the trading system of carbon emission rights and planned to reduce the greenhouse gas emissions to 30% of the "estimated greenhouse gas emissions (BAU)" by 2020. At the same time, it summarizes the green technology R&D of energy corresponding to climate change and the green land, city, building, transportation, green life and other green growth programs that provide policy support for the transformation of green industrial structure. South Korea has also set up a green growth council under its President. The green growth council and eight affiliated departments jointly published the *Low-Carbon and Green Life Implementation Development Plan*. The program invests in ecological infrastructure, low-carbon technology development and the creation of a green living and working environment to provide new growth drivers for South Korea's future development. The above national green development policies provide opportunities and guarantees for green finance.

Energy and environment in parallel, actively supporting the development of green industry. South Korea is a country short of energy. In the financial crisis, energy problem is not only a resource and environment problem, but also a security problem related to the stable development of its economy. Therefore, energy and environment become an important part of its "green New Deal", and the government actively promotes the development of green industry through green finance. To this end, the Republic of Korea government has invested nearly US $30 billion to support the development of green industries and give full play to the employment effect of green industries. In 2008, the South

Korean government formulated the *National Basic Energy Plan*, hoping to improve the deteriorating international balance of payments caused by excessive dependence on crude oil imports. It proposed to achieve the development goal of 11% of new and renewable energy, the highest level of energy technology in the world and 40% of oil and gas self-development rate by 2030. Since 2009, the South Korean government has invested about $38 billion to develop 36 ecological projects, which are planned to create 960,000 jobs in four years (Chen Tong, 2011). In addition, the financial industry has also adopted flexible and diversified support programs for green industry, such as green financial assistance policies and financial support programs for green industry. By April 2009, South Korea had 28 publicly listed environmental and social governance funds and environmental protection funds, with total assets under management of 619 billion won. In 2009, Korea Development Bank invested about 1 trillion won in environmental protection and supporting equipment business. In terms of carbon emission trading market, in 2007, Korea investment trust management company firstly established Korea carbon emission reduction fund and Korea carbon emission reduction credit fund (Zhang Zhenmin, 2013). In order to promote green credit, South Korea has formulated and introduced the green tax rate system, giving credit preferential treatment and credit preference to green enterprises. For the green industry export enterprises, on the one hand, it has increased the credit line; on the other hand, it has set up a 100 billion won carbon fund through the export–import bank.

To participate in international cooperation and promote green finance in Korea. South Korean financial institutions have actively participated in the international agreement on green finance to promote the green transformation and development of the country's financial industry and improve the management level of environmental risks. By 2009, 53 organizations had signed contracts with the global reporting initiative, 8 with the financial initiative of the UNEP, 14 with responsible investment principles of the United Nations, 169 with the United Nations global compact, and 16 with carbon emission disclosure projects (Li Ruihong, 2011).

Actively create conditions to support green financial development. Green finance is a new type of compound finance, which needs the support of technology, information and talents. In order to achieve a low-carbon society, fulfill South Korea's long-term plan of "low-carbon and green growth" and promote the development and popularization of green finance more quickly, the south Korean government actively creates the conditions needed for the development of green finance to support its rapid development. From 2009 to 2011, South Korea held hearings for experts, industry and NGOs in related fields, introduced the low-carbon commodity certification system for products and services at the earliest, actively trained green finance practitioners, and established green finance infrastructure such as environmental information database.

In addition to these typical countries, the Australian government has also taken active measures in green finance. For example, in 2001, the *Financial Services Reform Bill* (FSRB) was amended by the Australian Senate to explicitly require all financial institutions to take into account the labor standards of their customers, the environmental awareness of enterprises and the sense of social responsibility when making loans to their customers and reports to the Australian government on the extent and scope to which these environmental and social responsibility factors influence the choice, retention or investment of banks.

3.4 Foreign Green Finance Development Enlightenment

Attach Great Importance to the Role of the Government
In green finance, the role of government is multiple and indispensable. First, the government is the advocate of the green development model, and all the green finance practices in the above typical countries are the result of the government's promotion. It is under the promotion of the government that all sectors of society respond to promote the development of green finance. The most typical ones are South Korea and the UK. The former promoted green development as a national strategy and made green development a weapon to successfully resolve the financial crisis. The latter issued the *London Principles for Sustainable Development*, which requires financial markets to support and respond to the sustainable development strategy. Second, the government is the regulator of financial activities. Sustainable development requires certain regulatory means, and finance is one of the edge tools. Therefore, the government makes financial regulations for the financial industry and financing enterprises to promote sustainable development through environmental legislation, financial legislation, administrative management and other means. The United States, Germany and Japan have all been active in this regard. Third, the government is a supporter of green

industry development. In the process of green transformation and development, on the one hand, the government should restrict the development of those "two high and one overcapacity" enterprises, cultivate the development of green industry, and promote the comprehensive green transformation of industrial structure. Therefore, the government should restrict the development of "two high and one overcapacity" industries in finance, finance and technology. On the other hand, it needs to promote the development of green industry; Germany, Japan and other countries make use of policy banks to actively support the development of green industry by means of loan preference and environmental protection behavior. Fourth, the government is the condition creator of green finance development. Green finance is a new type of compound finance. Practitioners need not only knowledge of economics, but also knowledge of environmental technology such as environmental protection and energy saving. Financial institutions need not only economic data, but also environmental protection data related to enterprises. Therefore, the government must strengthen the training of green finance talents, the research on green technology and its evaluation, and the construction of green information and data sharing network among the government, financial institutions and enterprises. Fifth, the government is the overseer of green finance. Although regulations such as green and technology can play a preventive role, the government, as an administrator, must also strengthen the supervision of green finance practice. For example, whether banks really follow the rules, whether enterprises conceal environmental information, whether the public's right to environmental information is protected and whether members of the government are corrupt or derelict.

Strengthening Legislation on Resources and Environment
In green finance, resource and environment legislation must come first and complete laws should be made. This is because: On the one hand, the behavior of resource and environmental protection in individual profit-seeking behavior generally requires mandatory restraint. Whether it is a financing enterprise or an investment institution, as a rational "economic man" in economic activities, his main motivation is to pursue the maximization of economic interests. The externality and lag of environmental problems as well as the impact of environmental governance on their economic interests make individual rational "economic man" generally choose to avoid environmental governance, which requires

environmental legislation and financial legislation to clarify the environmental responsibility of investment and financing enterprises and force them to carry out environmental protection. On the other hand, green finance is based on sound environmental legislation. Effective green finance is based on a deep understanding and accurate grasp of the law of environmental protection behavior, and the environmental protection field involves all aspects, and the environmental protection control in all fields is based on a scientific understanding of its environmental protection law. Although with the development of green finance, finance and environmental protection overlap to a certain extent, they are always relatively independent fields. Comprehensive legislation in all walks of life in the environmental field is the basis for the development of green finance, especially the innovation and development of green financial products. This can be seen from the complete environmental legislations of United States, Germany, Japan and others and its role in promoting the development of green finance.

Enrich Financial Product Development
Environmental protection is a systematic project that requires the participation of all members of the society and a variety of constraints and incentives. The traditional green finance with green credit and green securities as the main content cannot meet this demand. First, green credit is mainly pre-prevention, and green securities play a major role in process supervision. The lagging nature of environmental outbreaks (which may occur decades or even centuries later) requires late compensation. This needs green insurance, which makes investment financing companies dare not conceal environmental protection information, shirk responsibility, undertake sufficient precaution and active management in advance and executive process, however; although serious problems are discovered later, the victim also can get sufficient compensation. Even when serious problems are discovered afterwards, victims are adequately compensated. America's *Superfund Act* and Germany's green insurance take the lead, so the development of financial products should be serialized, which can be determined according to the law of generation and governance of environmental problems. Secondly, the current development of green financial products is mainly based on the inducement mechanism of economic benefit distribution design. However, with the popularization and popularity of green culture, moral and cultural mechanisms are also important generation mechanisms of green finance.

Therefore, in the design of financial products, not only the economic interest induction mechanism is needed, but also the moral supervision mechanism and cultural identity mechanism should be considered. The "green choice" account at HSBC, a British bank, is worth referring to. In the future, with the popularization of the environmental protection movement, it is also an important marketing direction to develop green financial products according to the characteristics of different groups of social members, such as the consumption characteristics of women and the development of green financial products, the target pursuit of young people and the development of green financial products, and the consumption characteristics of the elderly and the development of green financial products. Third, the current development of green financial products is mainly targeted at financing enterprises. In fact, residents' consumption and government purchase are also very important components, and green financial products can be further developed for these subjects. For example, green consumer financial products (green car loans, energy-saving building loans, etc.) developed for residents' consumption in Britain and the United States are some examples.

Increase the Construction of Supporting Conditions
Green finance needs the support of culture, talents, science and technology, information and capital, among which talents, science and technology and information are "hardware requirements" and essential elements. However, the insufficient supply of these three elements directly restricts the development of green finance. For example, for practitioners in the traditional financial industry, green finance is a new "technical activity". Environmental impact assessment, environmental protection prevention programs, environmental risk management and environmental financial product development are all based on environmental protection science and technology. This is no doubt very difficult for the practitioners of economic professional background; financial institutions will also have concerns about the development of green finance due to the shortage of green finance talent supply. For another example, in the aspect of science and technology and information, science and technology need scientific assessment of environmental risks and effective management means to make it economically possible for financial institutions to assess and supervise the environmental protection of loan enterprises. In terms of information, financial institutions and financing

enterprises need environmental information sharing network to avoid information asymmetry. The sharing of environment, information and technology in green finance activities in the United States is worth learning, which is one of the important supporting conditions to promote the development of green finance.

Strengthen International Industrial Cooperation

Different from green finance, green consumption and green urbanization, green finance is a commercial activity with strong industry and originated from abroad. At present, the international experience and practices are generally more mature than China's, with a relatively mature evaluation and operation system. China should strengthen international cooperation in this regard. South Korea signed an international financial cooperation agreement, on the one hand, to make its banks enhance environmental awareness and develop green finance; on the other hand, through the cooperation with relevant international industry institutions, to greatly improve the level of green finance development of domestic financial institutions. In this regard, it is worth learning for China. Given the public nature of green finance and the fact that talent cultivation is a medium- and long-term strategic investment, it is suggested that commercial banks should pay full attention to the cultivation of green finance talents in international cooperation and exchange in the future.

Reverse the Concept of Green Finance

The development of green finance in Japan and Germany shows that green finance is a concept of transformation and development embedded with the concept of sustainable development. From the awareness of environmental protection in financial activities to the discovery of business opportunities in environmental activities, this process is gradually established, which also means the painful transformation and development of the financial industry to a certain extent. The government should support the green transformation of the financial industry through ideological propaganda, knowledge education, talent training, information assistance and financial support. Only by alleviating the degree of "pain" can financial institutions, as the main body of financial activities, completely reverse their "resistance" or "fear" of green finance to a certain extent and make green finance develop rapidly.

4   THE DEVELOPMENT STATUS AND EXISTING PROBLEMS OF GREEN FINANCE IN CHINA

4.1   Development Status of Green Finance

System Construction

Although the construction of China's green financial system started late, in recent years, with the emphasis on environmental protection, the implementation of sustainable development strategy and the promotion of ecological civilization construction, the pace of green financial system construction has been greatly accelerated and a series of systems have been formulated (see Table 10). In 1995, the *State Environmental Protection Administration issued the Notice on Using Credit Policies to Promote Environmental Protection*, requiring credit policies to promote environmental protection; In 2001, the State Environmental Protection Administration and China Securities Regulatory Commission jointly issued the *Announcement on Environmental Audit of Listed Companies*; In 2003, it also issued the *Announcement on Further Environmental Audit of Listed Companies or Stock Refinancing* and *Suggestions on Environmental Information Disclosure of Listed Companies* to implement the green securities system. In 2004, the China Banking Regulatory Commission (CBRC) issued a *Notice on Earnestly Implementing the National Macro-Control Policies and Further Strengthening Loan Risk Management*, requiring strict loan examination and approval system for industries with excess production capacity and "two high", and starting to use financial means to restrict the development of industries with "two high and one overcapacity". In 2007, when the green credit system was officially implemented, the General Office of the China Banking Regulatory Commission issued the *Notice on Preventing and Controlling Loan Risks in Highly Polluting Industries*. This marks the beginning of the formal implementation of green credit in China. In July of this year, the State Environmental Protection Administration, the People's Bank of China and the China Banking Regulatory Commission jointly issued the *Opinions on Implementing Environmental Protection Policies and Regulations and Preventing Credit Risks*. In November 2007, CBRC further issued the *Guideline on Credit Granting for Energy Conservation and Emission Reduction*. For example, in December 2007, the state environmental protection administration and the China insurance regulatory commission jointly issued the guideline on environmental

Table 10   China's Green Finance System Construction

Time	Green financial system
1981	The State Council promulgated the *Decision on Strengthening Environmental Protection Work in the Period of National Economic Adjustment*
1984	The State Council issued the *Notice on the Provisions on Funding Channels for Environmental Protection*
1995	The People's Bank of China issued the *Notice on the Implementation of Credit Policies and the Strengthening of Environmental Protection Work*
	The State Environmental Protection Administration issued the *Notice on the Use of Credit Policies to Promote Environmental Protection*
2001	The State Environmental Protection Administration and China Securities Regulatory Commission jointly issued the *Announcement on Environmental Audit of Listed Companies*
2003	The State Environmental Protection Administration and China Securities Regulatory Commission jointly issued *Announcement on Further Environmental Audit of Listed Companies or Stock Refinancing* and *Suggestions on Environmental Information Disclosure of Listed Companies*
2004	The National Development and Reform Commission, the People's Bank of China and the China Banking Regulatory Commission jointly issued the *Notice on Further Strengthening the Coordination and Cooperation of Industrial Policies and Credit Policies to Control Credit Risks*
	The China Banking Regulatory Commission (CBRC) has issued a *Notice on Earnestly Implementing the State's Macro-Control Policies and Further Strengthening Loan Risk Management*, calling for a strict loan examination and approval system for industries with excess production capacity and "two high levels"
2005	The State Council issued the *Decision on Implementing the Scientific Outlook on Development and Strengthening Environmental Protection*
May 2007	The National Development and Reform Commission and other eight ministries and commissions jointly implemented the *Notice of the State Council on Carrying Out Special Inspections for Industries with High Energy Consumption and High Pollution*
July 2007	The General Office of the China Banking Regulatory Commission issued the *Notice on Preventing and Controlling Loan Risks in Industries with High Energy Consumption and High Pollution*
	The State Environmental Protection Administration, the People's Bank of China and the China Banking Regulatory Commission jointly issued the *Opinions on Implementing Environmental Protection Policies and Regulations and Preventing Credit Risks*
November 2007	China Banking Regulatory Commission issued the *Guidance on Credit Granting for Energy Conservation and Emission Reduction*
December 2007	The State Environmental Protection Administration and the China Insurance Regulatory Commission jointly issued the *Guiding Opinions on the Work of Environmental Pollution Liability Insurance*

(continued)

Table 10   (continued)

Time	Green financial system
January 2008	The State Environmental Protection Administration and the World Bank International Finance Corporation jointly formulated the *Green Credit Environmental Protection Guide in Line with China's Situation*
February 2008	The State Environmental Protection Administration issued the *Guidance on Strengthening Environmental Supervision and Management of Listed Companies*
August 2008	*Circular Economy Promotion Law of the People's Republic of China* was promulgated
October 2008	The State Council issued a 4 trillion Yuan investment plan, of which about 210 billion Yuan was for ecological projects and energy conservation and emission reduction projects
2009	The People's Bank of China, the China Banking Regulatory Commission, the China Securities Regulatory Commission and the China Insurance Regulatory Commission jointly issued the *Guidance on Further Improving Financial Services to Support the Restructuring and Revitalization of Key Industries and Curb Overcapacity in Some Industries* China Banking Association issued *Corporate Social Responsibility Guidelines for Chinese Banking Financial Institutions*
2010	The State Council issued the *Notice on Opinions on Accelerating the Implementation of Contract Energy Management and Promoting the Development of Energy Conservation Service Industry* The People's Bank of China and the China Banking Regulatory Commission jointly issued the *Opinions on Further Doing A Good Job in Supporting Energy Conservation, Emission Reduction and Elimination of Backward Production Capacity Financial Services*
2011	The State Council issued the *Comprehensive Work Plan for Energy Conservation and Emission Reduction in the 12th Five-Year Plan*, and *Opinions on Strengthening Key Environmental Protection Work*
2012	The China Banking Regulatory Commission issued the *Green Credit Guidelines*
February 2013	The General Office of China Banking Regulatory Commission issued the *Notice on Doing A Good Job in Rural Financial Services in 2013*
July 2013	The China Banking Regulatory Commission and the State Forestry Administration jointly issued the *Opinions on the Implementation of Mortgage Loans for Forest Rights*
September 2013	China Banking Regulatory Commission issued the *Guidance on Further Improving the Financial Services of Small and Micro Enterprise*
2014	The General Office of China Banking Regulatory Commission issued the *Notice on the Issuance of Key Evaluation Indicators of Green Credit Implementation*
January 2015	The China Banking Regulatory Commission and the National Development and Reform Commission jointly issued the *Notice on the Issuance of Energy Efficiency Credit Guidelines*

pollution liability insurance, and the green insurance system began to sprout and establish. For example, in December 2007, the State Environmental Protection Administration and the China Insurance Regulatory Commission jointly issued the *Guideline on Environmental Pollution Liability Insurance*, and the green insurance system began to sprout and establish. In August 2008, the *Circular Economy Promotion Law of the People's Republic of China* was promulgated to provide legal guarantee for the development of circular economy and green finance; In 2009, the China banking association issued the *Guidelines on Corporate Social Responsibility of China's Banking Financial Institutions*, which required financial institutions to strengthen industry self-discipline and assume social responsibility. In 2010, the state council issued the *Notice on Opinions on Accelerating the Implementation of Contract Energy Management and Promoting the Development of Energy Conservation Service Industry*, which specifically issued opinions on promoting the development of contract energy management service industry. Since 2012, there have been more and more guiding documents with technical guidance and normative operation such as *Green Credit Guidelines* issued by China Banking Regulatory Commission in 2012, the *Notice on the Issuance of Key Evaluation Indicators of Green Credit Implementation* in 2014 issued by the General Office of China Banking Regulatory Commission, the *Notice on the Issuance of Energy Efficiency Credit Guidelines* jointly issued by the China Banking Regulatory Commission and the National Development and Reform Commission in January 2015. In short, in terms of institutional construction, China's green financial system is becoming more and more refined and improved, from the original rough outline to the current specific guidance in the key implementation steps or key control indicators, with significantly enhanced operability, which is conducive to the popularization and promotion. In addition, in terms of institutional construction subjects, there are not only traditional government institutions, but also institutions within industry associations, which reflect that the concept of green finance has received social response, with more and more participants and extensive social support.

Institutional Action
On the whole, the development of green finance in China lags behind, but some institutions started earlier, and in recent years, all institutions have carried out green finance activities to varying degrees.

Industrial Bank is the first financial institution in China to implement the green finance concept. In 2005, Industrial Bank began to cooperate with the IFC on energy efficiency financing projects, which was a prelude to Industrial Bank learning from advanced international models and integrating new green finance concepts with daily business operations of commercial banks. In October 2007, China and the United Nations Environment Programme (UNEP) signed the *Declaration on Environment and Sustainable Development by Financial Institutions,* which further strengthened the concept of environmental risk management. In October 2008, Industrial Bank publicly promised to adopt the equator principle and became the first equator bank in China.

In practice, Industrial Bank has established a relatively complete professional management system. Under the guidance of the equator principle, Industrial Bank gradually established a relatively complete green financial management system from the aspects of strengthening decision-making management, optimizing organizational structure and improving system construction: At the decision-making level, the board of directors and operation management of Industrial Bank established the leading group for social responsibility and the leading group for equatorial principles, and merged the two groups into the leading group for social responsibility in early 2013, which is fully involved in sustainable development and the implementation of the equatorial principles to ensure their full and thorough implementation. In terms of organizational structure, the energy efficiency financing professional team was established in 2005, and the sustainable finance center was established in 2009. In 2012, the sustainable finance center was upgraded to the sustainable finance department of the head office, gradually improving the organizational structure of sustainable development. At the institutional level, in accordance with the requirements of the equator principle and in combination with the relevant guidelines on energy conservation and emission reduction credit granting work of the China Banking Regulatory Commission, the green credit guidelines and the characteristics of the existing credit procedures of Industrial Bank, Industrial Bank has formulated a series of normative documents, including systems, supporting tools, model texts and relevant guidance, to form a complete system of "basic systems- management methods-operating procedures" like *Environmental and Social Risk Management Policy, Measures for the Administration of Project Financing Applicable to the Equator Principles, Guidelines on the Classification of Project Finance under the*

Equator Principles and Environmental and Social Risk Expert Assessment Standards. In terms of business process and management mechanism, Industrial Bank has established and improved the environmental and social risk management system and business process. While comprehensively sorting out and improving relevant business systems and strengthening hard institutional constraints, supporting investigation tools, analysis tools, risk monitoring tools and legal documents were introduced to comprehensively improve the level of project risk management. In terms of cultural implantation, we should integrate green business philosophy into corporate culture, actively integrate corporate culture, corporate social responsibility and green finance, deliver the concepts of green finance and corporate social responsibility internally, build green finance capacity, strive to reduce our own carbon emissions and promote green operation.

In practice, Industrial Bank has intensified the innovation of green financial products and services, mainly introducing three types of financial services: The first type is energy saving and emission reduction financing service; the second type is emission right trading service; and the third type is personal low-carbon financial service. In terms of financing services for energy conservation and emission reduction, the company cooperated with IFC to launch energy efficiency financing products for the first time in China in 2006, and then launched "8+1" financing service modes according to different demands and project types of customers for energy conservation and emission reduction. In the emission trading services, Industrial Bank has created products of pledge financing, platform construction, trading services and information consulting and a variety of service products and models that serve all aspects of emissions trading, which have developed special products and services for international carbon trading, domestic carbon trading pilots and emission rights trading pilots. In terms of personal low-carbon financial services, Industrial Bank launched China's low-carbon credit card nationwide in January 2010. Relying on the industry experience accumulated in green finance, green finance was extended from the enterprise project field to the personal consumption field, providing a feasible new way for individual customers to realize "carbon neutrality". By the end of December 2014, Industrial Bank had issued a total of 319,500 low-carbon credit cards and purchased 75,616 tons of voluntary carbon emission reduction, which was equivalent to neutralizing the carbon emissions generated by 544,000 people taking airplanes and flying for 1000 kilometers.

In addition to Industrial Bank, other banks have also actively carried out green finance activities. For example, in 2013, the former Wanjiali Road Sub-Branch of the Bank of Changsha was renamed as the Environmental Protection Sub-Branch, providing credit support for the energy conservation and environmental protection industry and promoting the environmental protection concept. Energy conservation and environmental protection projects can enjoy the green channel of preferential loans and moderately relaxing credit conditions in the bank, and the credit release in the "two high levels and one overcapacity" industry will be strictly controlled. Typical practice measures of green finance of various financial institutions in China are shown in Table 11.

Table 11 Typical practical measures for China's financial institutions to develop green finance

Financial institutions	Typical practical measures to develop green finance
China Development Bank	• Open Financial Cooperation Agreement signed with the Ministry of Environmental Protection • Develop the first Opinions on Development Review and Formulation of Solar Power Generation in the industry
Export–Import Bank of China	• Joint implementation of China energy efficiency financing project with World Bank
Industrial Bank	• China's first and only "equator bank", the first bank that promoted energy efficiency loan in China • Signing of the UNEP Statement on the Environment and Sustainable Development by Financial Institutions • Jointly released China's first low-carbon credit card with the Beijing Environment Exchange
Industrial and Commercial Bank of China	• Implemented credit classification and implement "one vote veto system for environmental protection" • Launched "Credit via Network", "Easy Financing" and other network financing green financial products
Agricultural Bank of China	• Launched China's first environmental protection theme credit card-Jinsui environmental protection card • Implemented the plan to build an energy-saving agricultural bank of China that will allow banks to operate without paper and save energy as much as possible
Bank of China	• Developed the clean development mechanism (CDM) project financing business and the green heart benefits through environmental protection deposit business

(continued)

Table 11   (continued)

Financial institutions	Typical practical measures to develop green finance
Bank of Communications	• Initiated the implementation of environmental management system for all credit customers and businesses
China Merchants Bank	• Participated in the second phase of China-France green credit project cooperation • Promulgated *Marketing Guidelines for Renewable Energy Industry* and *Green Finance Credit Policy*
China Minsheng Banking	• Set up its first green finance franchise in Beijing
China Everbright Bank	• Took the lead in the launch of sunshine financial low-carbon public welfare products and green zero-carbon credit card • Created "personal green file" in Beijing Environment Exchange
China Construction Bank	• Implemented the plan of "promoting the recycling of office supplies and reducing office energy consumption through various ways" • Issued the *Plan on Strengthening the Management of Emission Reduction and Credit Extension of China Construction Bank* • Issued the "Korean pine dragon card" credit card with the theme of nature conservation
Shanghai Pudong Development Bank	• Launched the *Green Credit Integrated Service Scheme* • Issued the *Building A Low-Carbon Bank Initiative* • Develop "Contract energy management future earnings right buyout factoring" products

Source Zhang Ping. *Connotation, Function Mechanism and Practice of Green Finance.* Chengdu: Southwest University of Finance and Economics, 2013

Effectiveness Prospects

On the whole, green credit business in China's green finance is developing well. According to the China banking regulatory commission, by the end of 2013, China's major banking institutions had outstanding loans of 5.2 trillion Yuan for green credit projects, accounting for 8.7% of all outstanding loans. In terms of energy conservation and emission reduction, the green credit projects supported by China's major banking institutions are expected to save 18.671 million tons of standard coal, 43.807 million tons of water and 47.902 million tons of carbon dioxide per year. By the end of June 2014, loans outstanding for energy conservation and environmental protection projects and services at 21 major banking institutions totaled 4.16 trillion Yuan, accounting for 6.43% of their loans, according to data released by the China Banking Regulatory Commission.

Individually, green finance such as Industrial Bank has achieved remarkable results. From 2007 to the end of 2012, Industrial Bank provided a total of nearly 200 billion Yuan of "green finance" financing for thousands of enterprises, among which the loan balance accounted for nearly 10% of the balance of public credit, and green finance developed on a large scale. By the end of 2012, the projects supported by Industrial Bank could save 255,790,600 tons of standard coal annually in China, has achieved an annual reduction of 66,834,700 tons of carbon dioxide, 886,500 tons of chemical oxygen demand (COD), 15,100 tons of ammonia nitrogen, 43,600 tons of sulfur dioxide, 6900 tons of nitrogen oxides, 15,012,900 tons of solid waste and 2,557,990,600 tons of water with significant environmental benefits.

On the other hand, enterprises are the main body of bank loans. With the promising development prospect of the environmental protection industry, the demand for green loans from banks will further increase, which in turn will stimulate the development of green finance business and form a benign pattern of mutually promoting the development of green industry and green finance. For example, in 2014, most of the 17

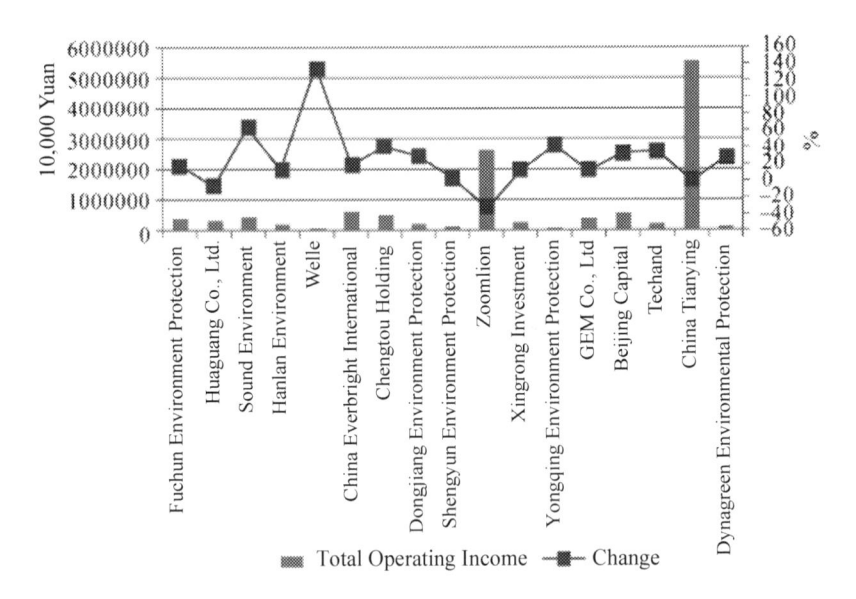

Fig. 2 Operating income of 17 listed waste treatment companies in China in 2014 and the increase or decrease range (*Data source* http://huanbao.bjx.com. cn/news/20150527/623308.shtml)

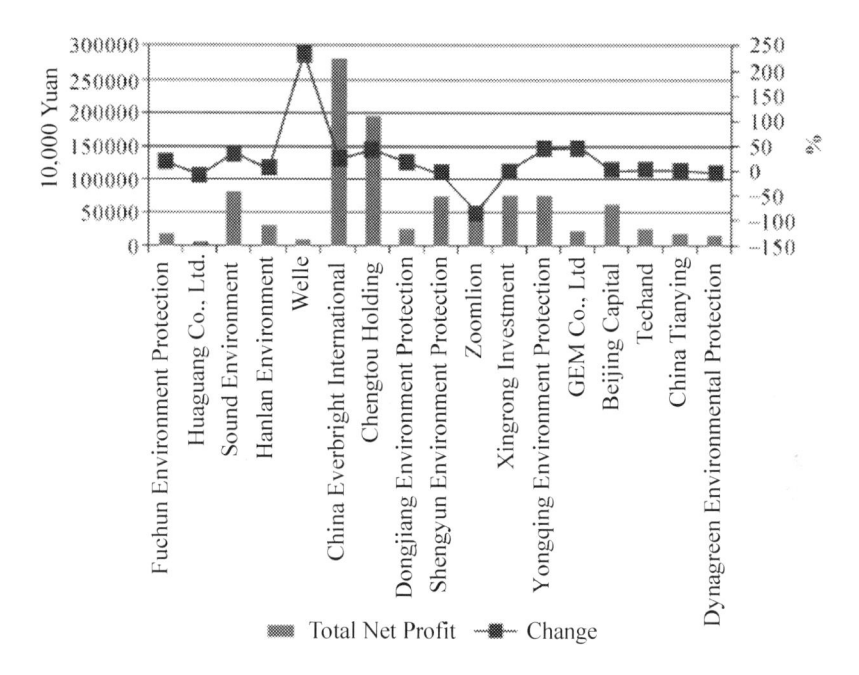

Fig. 3 Net profit of 17 listed waste treatment companies in China in 2014 and the increase or decrease range (*Data source* http://huanbao.bjx.com.cn/news/20150527/623308.shtml)

listed waste treatment companies or those concurrently engaged in waste treatment business achieved profitability in terms of operating revenue and net profit (see Figs. 2 and 3). This also means that in the future, enterprises will be more active in the development of green industry, and the demand for green loans from banks will be further increased. The development of green finance will have market momentum and have an expected prospect.

4.2   Existing Problems in Green Finance

The Scale Is Too Small to Meet the Demand
Data from several commercial banks surveyed show that the balance of green credit is small, accounting for less than 2%. The *2014 Annual Report on the Development of Low-Carbon Finance in China* shows that the green credit balance of the 18 major commercial banks ranked high in total

assets accounts for about 1.81% of the total assets, among which the green credit of Industrial Bank ranked first only accounts for 3.46%. According to the report, green financing demand is expected to reach 2.75 trillion Yuan in 2020. At present, green financing accounts for only about 1% of the assets of China's commercial banks, and the capital gap is as high as 20 times of the existing financing, far from meeting the actual needs.

Incomplete Environment and Lack of Coordination Conditions
Green finance is a systematic project. In the transition period, the development of green finance requires certain collaborative conditions as the environment for its development, including the environment of economic strategy, cultural concept, legal system and information construction. Although China has set resource conservation, environmental protection, transformation development and construction of ecological civilization as the basic strategic principles, there is still a lack of corresponding synergistic conditions in cultural concepts, legal systems, information construction and other aspects. For example, in terms of cultural concepts, local government officials who lead local economic development, employees of financial institutions engaged in investment and financing activities, and enterprise managers engaged in production, service and other industries still do not take environmental and social responsibilities in economic activities into consideration in their decision-making. In terms of legal system, although China now has resource and environmental regulations on financial activities, there is still a lack of top-level design, overall design and systematic design. Low-level legal effectiveness and fragmentation of management regulations can be seen everywhere. In terms of information construction, the information construction of government agencies, production enterprises and financial institutions is carried out independently. Information concealment and information asymmetry are very serious. In particular, due to the restrictions of management power and scope of knowledge, financial institutions have no direct grasp of enterprise environmental protection information.

Insufficient Talents and Limited Development Business
Green finance is an emerging and intersecting industry, which integrates economy, finance, environment, chemical industry, law, information, architecture and engineering. It is highly practical and skilled. Compared with traditional industries, the talent standard of green finance shows the characteristics of high quality and compound. Green finance started late

in China and professionals are scarce, which directly affects the development of green finance. Particularly in business product development, being failure to understand, be familiar with, or grasp the knowledge of energy saving, environmental protection, low carbon and other aspects of related industries, it dares not carry out or does not know how to carry out many green finance activities, it can only stay in the shallow level, or follow the footsteps of peers. The product development innovation ability is very limited and the effect is low.

5 China's Vision for the Development of Green Finance

5.1 Basic Thinking

From the current situation of China, the current economic transformation and development and industrial structure upgrade need green finance to promote. Although China's green finance has achieved good development in some financial institutions, its development level is still very low. The most important reason is that green finance is a comprehensive and systematic project, which needs all-round and multi-subject promotion. At present, green finance in China has gradually strengthened the regulatory role of the government, but the supporting and encouraging role still lags behind. Financial institutions have different degrees of sensitivity to green finance. Some of them consciously strengthen their awareness of environmental and social responsibility, and make full use of their business opportunities to actively develop financial products. And some are still in a state of resistance, passive acceptance of green finance government norms. The reason for this is the lack of necessary conditions to support the green transformation of traditional finance in addition to the current interest factors. If the development conditions can be fully cultivated and the transformation costs can be reduced, the development of green finance will be more dynamic. Therefore, the current promotion of green finance development is to construct the system engineering of green finance development, strengthen the role norms of each subject, establish an effective driving mechanism, accelerate the construction of supporting environment and formulate a number of effective policies.

5.2   Strengthen the Norms of the Main Roles

Government
In the green transformation process of traditional finance, the primary role of the government is regulation, followed by assistance, supervision and finally regulation. Regulation is to compulsorily promote the green transformation of traditional finance by means of law, administration, technology and so on. The support includes various forms, such as discount loan, tax reduction and exemption, information supply, talent training, entrepreneurial opportunities and other forms to support the development of green finance. Supervision mainly includes inspection, information release, reward and punishment on green finance of financial institutions and financing enterprises. Regulation mainly refers to the balance between the development of green financial products and supply, such as increasing the supply of green insurance products to meet the governance needs of different environmental problems.

Financial Institutions
In the green transformation process of traditional finance, the main task of financial institutions is to fulfill the social responsibility of environmental protection, consciously abide by the national laws and regulations on green finance, find and use the business opportunities of green finance, develop a variety of green financial products and realize the growth of their own economic benefits while meeting the green financing needs of enterprises and social and environmental protection.

Enterprises
Enterprises should conscientiously fulfill their environmental protection obligations, make use of relevant national policies to win the support of green finance for the transformation and development of enterprises or the cultivation of green industry and actively disclose the environmental protection status of enterprises to the public and the media, so as to build a responsible positive social image of enterprises and strive for the long-term sustainable development of enterprises.

Social Public
The public should actively exercise three rights in green finance: the right to know, the right to supervise and the right to choose. The right to know means that the public has the right to know and obtain information, including the environmental impact and risk in the process of

project implementation, the behavior of enterprises to eliminate or reduce environmental risks and their efforts. Supervision right mainly means that the public has the right to supervise whether enterprises fully fulfill their environmental protection obligations and actively take effective measures to reduce adverse effects. Options include two aspects: First, in terms of consumption, enterprises should choose the products or services they produce and resolutely refuse the products or services with negative environmental impacts, so as to encourage enterprises to provide environmentally friendly products or services. Second, in terms of production, financial institutions or production enterprises are selected through capital supply. For example, with the help of information disclosure by the government and social media organizations, people refused to take deposits and other obligations in banks with low awareness of environmental and social responsibility, so as to reduce their capital supply and refuse to buy shares of listed companies that are not environmentally responsible, which will affect their stock prices.

Media Organizations
In the green transformation process of traditional finance, media organizations should not only assume the basic responsibilities of traditional information dissemination and diffusion, but also the tasks of information bridge, public opinion guidance and popular science. To be specific, in addition to reporting the green finance policies of government institutions, it is also necessary to make use of the information gathering and diffusion advantages of the media to investigate the problems existing in the development of green finance, disclose relevant restrictive factors actively, and promote the participation of all parties, such as scientific research institutions, in the construction of green finance. To actively expose environmental dereliction of duty by government agencies, financial institutions or production enterprises, so as to urge them to perform their duties and assume environmental responsibility in corresponding positions; In view of the weak situation of green finance development in China at present, the experiences, models and measures of green finance abroad as well as the options and methods that can be improved in China are introduced.

Research Institutions
Scientific research institutions should serve and support green finance. To be specific, the government should provide effective and easy-to-operate key concise indicators and policy tools for green finance

regulation, supervision, regulation and other functions. Similarly, financial institutions should also provide convenient tools for auditing, evaluating, supervising and controlling enterprises' environmental behaviors. For production enterprises, scientific and technological research should be strengthened to provide scientific and technological support for effective environmental governance and cost reduction. To the public and media, should have the effect such as popular science, dispel suspicion. To the public and media, it should have the effect such as popularization of science and clearing up doubts.

5.3   Establish an Effective Driving Mechanism

Legal Regulation Mechanism
From the perspective of power source, in the transition period, the formation of green financial market mainly comes from the government's legal mandatory regulation and the stimulation of economic interests, among which legal regulation is the primary premise. From the perspective of the subject, legal regulation should at least make corresponding regulations for the following three related subjects: First, the social public is the consumer of products and services, and the green consumption of the public is the condition to promote the generation of green products and services; Second, the supply of products and services to enterprises, forcing these enterprises to green production and green services to effectively promote the green transformation of enterprises; Third, financial institutions are required to assume environmental responsibility in their financial activities so that financial institutions can consider environmental impact in their investment activities. Therefore, green finance should not only be regulated by relevant laws, but also be systematized and regulated in consumption, production, investment and financing activities. It is suggested to strengthen the legislation in the field of green consumption according to the current legal system in China, especially to regulate the environmental impact in the process of bulk procurement and consumption by the government and enterprises.

Economic Induction Mechanism
Both for consumers, production enterprises and financial institutions, green transformation needs to pay a certain cost and face some uncertain risks. Therefore, in the process of transformation, certain economic benefits need to be induced and stimulated and certain risk guarantee

conditions need to be provided to reduce the cost and risk loss of transformation. Price subsidies, low-interest loans and tax incentives may be provided to consumers. Although low-interest loans and tax incentives can also be adopted for production enterprises, they are different from individual consumers in that the transformation costs are high and the risk uncertainties are more. It is suggested that the government, in addition to low-interest loans and tax incentives, should take the forms of risk guarantee, conditions (talents, technology, information, etc.) support and product (service) procurement to make production enterprises more confident in transforming production. For financial institutions, the government can use direct tax relief to stimulate them, but more importantly, it should actively create conditions to greatly reduce the cost of transformation, such as green finance talent training and education, green finance network information construction, green finance supervision technology research and so on.

Information Disclosure Mechanism
The concealment, hysteresis and specialty of environmental problems need to strengthen information disclosure. This includes environmental information disclosure in the process of consumption, information disclosure in the process of production and information disclosure in the process of investment and financing. Information disclosure in the process of consumption makes consumers choose green products and reject products that are harmful to the ecological environment and their health. Information disclosure in the production process enables enterprises to consciously carry out green production and environmental protection in order to shape their own good image and improve the living environment. For example, the public can know the environmental protection behaviors and efforts of enterprises by regularly releasing the environmental audit announcements of enterprises, so as to make consumption or investment choices on the products, services and stocks of enterprises. Information disclosure in the process of investment and financing exposes the awareness of environmental responsibility of production enterprises and financial institutions to the public, and prevents them from colluding to cause moral failure. From the current situation of our country, we should strengthen the environmental audit information disclosure system of production enterprises and the green investment report disclosure system of financial institutions.

Cultural Construction Mechanism

Although legal regulation, economic inducement and information disclosure can promote or stimulate the development of green finance from the perspective of external motivation to varying degrees, the formation of green finance is more dependent on the internal consciousness of a kind of cultural consciousness. For example, the birth of the German eco-bank and the formation of the equatorial principle were initially based on the managers' internal awareness of environmental and social responsibility of financial institutions, which was the result of an internal cultural consciousness. Therefore, only a whole environmental protection cultural identity consciousness from the whole society can continue to promote the development of green finance. As previously analyzed, only the terminal green consumption demand from the market can make the production enterprises finally make up their minds to realize the transformation production. Only with a strong sense of internal environmental protection can financial institutions consciously strengthen environmental audit in the process of investment and strengthen the development of green financial products. Cultural construction is a prerequisite for the development of green finance and ultimately determines how far it can go.

5.4   Accelerating the Construction of Supporting Environment

Strengthen Legal Environment Construction

Improve legislation and formulate systematic laws to promote the development of green finance. There are two aspects: first, formulate the basic law of green finance; second, improve the relevant laws for green finance. In view of the drawbacks of low legal effectiveness, scattered legislation and weak professional regulation of green finance in China, it is imperative to formulate a green finance basic law that is more systematic and has stronger regulation effect. Among the related laws needed to form green finance, they mainly involve green production law, green consumption law, green transportation law and green waste disposal law. Due to the promulgation of *Environmental Protection Law, Circular Economy Promotion Law* and other relevant laws, laws on green production are relatively mature, while laws on green consumption law, green transportation law and green waste disposal law are relatively backward. Improving green legislation in these areas is one of the important conditions to promote the further development of green finance.

Strengthen the Construction of Information Environment

Information supply improves the basic environment of green finance development. Functionally, such information mainly includes information on industrial investment opportunities, information conducive to supervision and management, information on technological progress of enterprises, information on promoting rational choice of the public and information on international exchanges and cooperation. Information on industrial investment opportunities mainly refers to the green investment opportunities brought by the green transformation and development. In particular, because of the green investment opportunity information brought by the national green transformation and development strategy, profitable green investment information will attract more enterprises and financial institutions to join the green finance industry. Information conducive to supervision and management mainly refers to the current situation that the environmental information of the government, enterprises and financial institutions which are independent, non-sharing and asymmetric, etc. The information sharing network construction enables the information of the three parties to be networked and shared, which is accurate and transparent, so as to make the government and financial institutions more effective and efficient in environmental supervision of enterprises on the premise of ensuring the accuracy, effectiveness and consistency of basic information. Information about technological progress of enterprises refers to the fact that under the background of green finance, enterprises are also faced with unprecedented pressure of environmental protection. From the perspective of its internal motivation, seeking effective, simple and low-cost environmental protection technology is one of its basic needs. The information provided by the government is one of the necessary conditions to promote its green production transformation and realize green finance. Information on promoting the rational choice of the public mainly refers to the release of information on the environmental and health impacts of product consumption, the environmental governance of enterprises and the responsible investment of financial institutions. Information on international exchange and cooperation refers to the current situation that China's green finance industry is underdeveloped and backward in management. By releasing information on international exchange and cooperation, China's green finance industry will have the opportunity to learn foreign advanced management methods and experience, so as to improve the management level of China's green finance industry.

Strengthen the Construction of Cultural Environment
Cultural construction creates a green financial formation of the cultural environment. Fundamentally speaking, the construction of green cultural environment needs to "start from the baby", starting from the formal education in schools, and cultivate their cultural consciousness of protecting the environment, saving resources, green production and green consumption from childhood. In the transition period, apart from the development of green environmental education in schools, it is more important to cultivate people's awareness of green culture through mass media and community activities, so as to promote their green consumption, green savings and supervise the environmental protection behaviors of financial institutions and production enterprises. In view of the disadvantages of excessive commercialization and low awareness of public responsibility for environmental protection in China's current mass media fields such as TV, Internet and newspapers, it is suggested to introduce the promotion measures of green culture publicity and management for mass media, stipulate that mass media must produce and release a certain number of green culture creative promotion advertisements, so as to enhance the awareness of green culture identity of the whole society.

Strengthen External Environment Construction
International exchange improves the green finance industry management level. It must be admitted that the management level of China's green finance industry lags behind that of European and American capitalist countries. In view of this objective fact, it is suggested that the country strengthens international cooperation in this field, such as promoting the cooperation between domestic financial institutions and foreign financial institutions in investment and financing, and learning foreign experience in green financial management. In the fields of education and scientific research, special funds will be set up in the form of public and private investment, and domestic financial institutions will be encouraged to strengthen cooperation with international organizations in personnel training, technology research and development, and project management.

5.5   Some Specific Operational Suggestions

Set up a Special Green Bank
For example, a special green investment bank will be set up with the government's contribution and the participation of social capital. The bank mainly invests in large-scale projects related to environmental protection,

energy conservation, new energy, clean transportation and other environment-related projects. The government provides certain preferential policies and innovation incentives. For example, interest subsidy, tax exemption and deregulation, allowing them to issue green bonds for financing, developing green financial products independently and having certain green investment preference.

Formulate Green Loan Incentives
Set aside a certain amount of financial funds to set up special funds to subsidize green loans. For example, different discount rates are set according to the environmental contribution of energy-saving and emission-reduction renovation. The higher the environmental contribution, the higher the subsidy ratio will be.

Establish a Green Credit System
Banks are required to strengthen environmental risk control when lending, such as setting up internal environmental risk management institutions, formulating environmental risk assessment and control management methods, and regularly publicizing the implementation of green credit.

Improve Environmental Information Disclosure
It is mandatory for listed companies and enterprises issuing bonds to regularly issue social responsibility reports, disclose their environmental impact information, including environmental risk control information, environmental pollution control information, environmental impact information of product or service consumption, and accept public supervision and selection.

Promote Green Insurance System
A basic green insurance system should be established to encourage enterprises to develop green insurance products, and green insurance products should be purchased for potential consumers in projects with long-term environmental risks.

Establish an Information Sharing Network
An environmental information sharing network should be established among production enterprises, government departments and financial institutions to ensure the authenticity, accuracy and consistency of information, and provide data basis for the supervision, regulation and cooperation between government departments and financial institutions.

REFERENCES

Chen Tong. South Korea's Transformation Strategy and Enlightenment Under the International Financial Crisis. *Comprehensive Competitiveness*, 2011 (5): 64–69.

Gao Jianliang. "Green Finance" and Sustainable Financial Development. *Financial Theory and Teaching*, 1998, 34 (4): 13–17.

Guo Peiyuan, Cai Yingcui. The Development of Green Finance in Developed Countries and Its Enlightenment to China. *Environmental Protection*, 2015 (1): 44–47.

He Xiuxing. Implementing "Green Financial Policy" is a Strategic Choice for the Financial Industry Facing the 21st Century. *Journal of Nanjing Finance College*, 1998 (4): 22–25.

Li Ruihong. Green Finance: Global Trend, Korean Practice and Chinese Suggestions. *Theory and Contemporary*, 2011 (4): 18–21.

Li Xi. Foreign Green Finance Policies and Their References. *Journal of Suzhou University*, 2011 (6): 134–137.

Lin Xiao. *Research on the Development of Green Finance in China Under the Background of Low-Carbon Economy*. Guangzhou: Jinan University, 2011.

Mei Yan. *On the Legal Regulation of Green Finance in China*. Changchun: Jilin University of Finance and Economics, 2013.

Ni Yuxia. *Research on American Green Finance System*. Changsha: Hunan Normal University, 2011.

Qiao Haishu. Establishing Financial Ecological View. *Ecological Economy*, 1999 (5): 18–19.

Song Xiaoling. Green Financial Policy of Western Banking Industry: Common Rules and Differential Practice. *Exploration of Economic Problems*, 2013 (1): 170–174.

Tan Cheng. *Problems and Countermeasures of China's Green Consumption Legal System*. Guilin: Guangxi Normal University, 2014.

Wang Junhua. On the "Green Revolution" of the Financial Industry. *Ecological Economy*, 2000 (10): 45–48.

Zhang Chenghui, Tian Hui. Recent International Green Finance Development Trend and Enlightenment [EB/OL]. China Economic News Network. http://www.cet.com.cn/ycpd/sdyd/1474624.shtml. March 2, 2015.

Zhang Zhenmin. Comparative Study on Green Financial Systems in China, Japan and Korea. *Heilongjiang Social Science*, 2013 (6): 75–79.

CHAPTER 8

Consumption and Green Transformation and Development

1 CONNOTATION, CHARACTERISTICS AND CLASSIFICATION OF GREEN CONSUMPTION

1.1 Connotation of Green Consumption

In 1987, British scholars John Elkington and Julia Hailes published the book *Green Consumer Guide*, which first proposed the concept of green consumption. In this book, "green consumption" is defined as avoiding the consumption of the following products: (1) products that endanger the health of consumers and others; (2) products that obviously harm the environment in the process of production, use or abandonment; (3) products with excessive packaging, redundant features or products caused by unnecessary waste due to the short life of the product or other reasons; (4) products made from materials obtained from endangered species or environmental resources; (5) products that include the abuse of animals and unnecessary indiscriminate hunting; (6) products that adversely affect other countries, particularly developing countries. In addition, other scholars have also defined green consumption. For example, Chen Qijie defined green consumption as a rational consumption by consumers considering the protection of their own health and individual interests on the premise of paying attention to protecting the ecological environment, reducing resource waste, preventing pollution and assuming social responsibilities. According to Yin Shijie, green

© The Author(s) 2019
S. Gu et al., *Green Transformation and Development*,
The Great Transformation of China,
https://doi.org/10.1007/978-981-32-9495-0_8

consumption refers to the consumption of material consumer goods (including food, clothing, housing, use, transportation, etc.) in a certain ecological environment, which requires non-pollution, pollution-free, high-quality and healthy "green consumer goods". Si Linsheng believes that green consumption contains four meanings, namely economic consumption (the consumption of consumers is the least consumption of energy and resources), clean consumption (with minimal pollution and waste), safe consumption (with results that do not harm the health of consumers or others) and sustainable consumption (with results that do not threaten the needs of future generations); Kaisa and Minna believe that green consumption means to minimize the purchase frequency and choose durable, high-quality and recyclable products with ecological labels. Johanna believes that green consumption is a specific type of consumption behavior with social awareness and social responsibility. The China consumers' association defines green consumption as a way of consumption that not only meets the consumption needs of contemporary people and their safety and health, but also meets the consumption needs of future generations and their safety and health. The United Nations Environment Programme (UNEP) defines green consumption as a consumption of "In the whole life cycle of a product or service, it is necessary to minimize the use of toxic materials and natural resources and minimize the generation of wastes and pollutants, so as to meet people's demand for products and services and bring about a high-quality life without causing harm to the needs of future generations".

Any kind of consumption behavior contains several elements such as consumer, consumption object, consumption process and consumption result. Compared with traditional consumption behaviors, green consumers have a stronger sense of social responsibility and consider the impact of the products they consume on resources, environment, themselves and others; The object of consumption is characterized by less consumption of resources and materials, less emission of harmful substances, favorable to recycling and regeneration, health care and environmental protection. In the process of consumption, it will do not cause adverse effects to consumers and others and the surrounding environment. In the consumption result, it is beneficial to health and environmental protection, and produces less waste, which is easy to deal with and recycle. On the other hand, the realization of green consumption depends on the green design and green production of products or services, so green consumption is defined as follows: Based on a high sense of responsibility for the environment and society, consumers choose products or services with low material consumption, low environmental impact, and beneficial to their health, resources and environmental protection. In addition, in the process of consumption and waste disposal after consumption, consumers choose rational and fair consumption behaviors that do not adversely affect the environment, resources, themselves and the health of others.

1.2 Characteristics of Green Consumption

Green consumption originated from the environmental protection movement in the 1960s. As a response of the consumption field to the action of resource environmental protection, it has its own obvious characteristics compared with the traditional consumption mode (see Table 1).

First, consumers have a high sense of social responsibility. Considering the impact of personal consumption on the environment and others, individual consumption behavior becomes an effective way to fulfill social public responsibility and achieve sustainable development. Consumers' power of consumption choice was once regarded by some Western scholars as "a power more independent and freer than national sovereignty". But under the social responsibility consciousness, consumer spending

Table 1 Comparison of green consumption and traditional consumption

	Green consumption	Traditional consumption
Consumer awareness of social responsibility	High	Low
Resource consumption of products or services	Small	Much
Waste generation and emissions	Little	Much
Product quality and durability	High quality, durable	Poor durability, easy to damage
Purchase frequency	Low	High
For your health	Conducive to health	Bad for health
Environmental impact	Environment friendly	Harmful to the environment
Impact on the society	Promote fairness	Unfair
Impact on sustainable development	Support sustainable development	Harm sustainable development

power is restrained, consumers not only need to take into account the consumption of the utility itself, also need to consider to the external effect of personal consumption may be produced, and accept the relevant state laws and social public moral constraint, consumption is no longer merely a completely free and unfettered individual behavior choice, but an effective practice green development and completion of the civic duty of public goals.

Second, the product (or service) consumes less resources, with less waste generation and emissions and is durable and of high quality. Green consumption starts from the green design of products (or services) and relies on the green design of products (or services). These products have the characteristics of less resource consumption, less waste discharge, environmental friendliness and no harm to the health of consumers themselves and others in the society. Moreover, these products are of high quality and durable, which can effectively reduce the purchase frequency.

Third, consumption results are beneficial to the health of consumers themselves and can effectively overcome negative environmental externalities, promote social equity and support sustainable development. Green consumption must first satisfy consumers' pursuit of their own health and refuse to accept products or services that are harmful to their health. Green consumption must also be conducive to environmental protection and social equity, and overcome the heavy ecological and environmental burden of traditional consumption patterns. Meeting the needs of others and the next generation for their own health is an important goal of green consumption and the ultimate embodiment of the difference from the traditional consumption mode.

1.3   Classification of Green Consumption

According to the main categories of consumption, green consumption can be divided into government green consumption, institutional green consumption and private green consumption. Government green consumption generally refers to green government procurement, institutional green consumption refers to the green consumption of enterprises, institutions and social organizations, such as enterprises' green procurement, while private green consumption refers to the green consumption of individuals and families.

According to the purposes of consumption, green consumption can be divided into living green consumption and productive green consumption. Active green consumption mainly refers to the green consumption to meet the needs of daily life, while productive green consumption mainly refers to the consumer goods or services purchased for reproduction, such as various raw materials and services used by enterprises in the production process.

2 The Role and Action Mechanism of Green Consumption

2.1 *The Role of Green Consumption*

First, reduce the depletion of natural resources. The apparent characteristic of green consumption is abstemious, rational consumption. It requires the reduction of unnecessary consumption and the abandonment of luxury consumption, advocates the purchase of high-quality and durable goods so as to reduce the production times of goods, and requires that the discarded goods after use can also be recycled and recycled. Therefore, it helps to reduce the production of commodities, thus reducing the depletion of natural resources.

Second, reduce the emission of harmful substances. Green consumption advocates a kind of healthy and harmless consumption, which requires that the goods or services consumed are harmless to human health and ecological environment no matter in the manufacturing process, consumption and enjoyment process or in the waste disposal process after consumption. Therefore, it encourages producers to use green raw materials or provide services that do not harm health and ecological environment, which is conducive to reducing the emission of harmful substances.

Third, guide the transformation of the production sector. Nowadays, the consumption demand determines the production supply. The green consumption demand of consumers will stimulate the producers to increase the supply of green products, so as to guide the production of green goods and the formation of green industry. In particular, some consumers with social influence, such as government agencies, large enterprises and celebrities, have more demonstration effect and guiding effect on their green consumption, which can lead the whole society to conduct green consumption. Once consumers have the awareness of green consumption and the demand for green goods, it will promote the arrival of the green market in all directions-producers not only actively research and provide green goods, but also strengthen the awareness of "green" in the marketing process, such as green packaging, green logistics and green publicity. In short, consumers' green consumption will lead to green production and stimulate the formation of green market.

Fourth, strengthen the formation of green production. The green consumption demand of consumers naturally stimulates the green production in the production field. However, today's enterprise production is a social division of labor, and few enterprises complete the whole process in their own production workshops. This requires enterprises to conduct green product research and development and green product design, and put forward requirements on various suppliers in the upstream and downstream industrial chain, so that they can produce green products and provide green raw materials. Enterprises that do not meet the requirements of green production will be excluded from the industrial chain. In particular, some core enterprises in the industrial chain, its green production requirements will guide other enterprises in the industrial chain to follow the transformation, which plays a role in urging, promoting and self-organization, and is conducive to the arrival of the era of green production.

Fifth, accelerate the formation of a green society. Green consumption plays a very important role in green development. It not only directly reduces the consumption of natural resources and the emission of harmful substances, but also guides the green production in the production field. Moreover, due to the role of social division of labor, it will accelerate and strengthen the self-organization mode of green production, which is conducive to the whole green transition from production to consumption, and accelerate the formation of a green society.

2.2   The Mechanism of Green Consumption

Analysis of the Main Role of Green Consumption

Green consumption involves consumers, producers, regulators and intermediaries. Consumers include individuals, families, enterprises and governments, producers are mainly enterprises, regulators are mainly governments and intermediaries are mainly social media organizations.

These main bodies work together to promote the formation of green consumption and the arrival of green production. Among them, the role of the government is complicated: On the one hand, the government itself is a consumer, and a very influential consumer. On the other hand, the government is also the manager of green production, playing the role of guidance, management and supervision. It has the obligation to guide enterprises' green production through fiscal, taxation and financial policies, and strengthen the management of green products and services through environmental labeling. At the same time, it also supervises green production through legal, administrative, scientific and technological means. Individual and family are the main bodies of green consumption, and its green consumption will affect the green production of producer directly. As a provider of goods and services, green production is not only a prerequisite for the provision of green goods, but also an effective means to improve competitiveness. In green production, it requires industrial chain suppliers to provide green raw materials and services, so as to help them reduce environmental management costs and ensure the completion of green production. In this process, it plays a very broad role in communication, organization and supervision. It urges relevant enterprises in the industrial chain to join the green production organization, thus strengthening the green production of the whole society. Social media organizations mainly play the role of communication and supervision. On the one hand, they provide timely information on the demand for green goods or services in the society, and at the same time help enterprises release information on the supply of green products and services. On the other hand, social media organizations also timely expose the green production status and product quality of enterprises, and supervise enterprises to carry out green production.

The Mechanism of Green Consumption
The role of green consumption is most obvious and concentrated in the leading enterprises in the industry. The following is an example of a core enterprise in an industrial chain to illustrate the specific mechanism of green consumption. As shown in Fig. 1, in the process of green development, enterprises are faced with the "five forces" environment, namely:

In terms of impetus, the green demand of the market constitutes a powerful driving force for the green development of enterprises. As a major supplier of products or services, green consumption by the government, families and individuals, especially the large green purchase demand of the government, has formed its huge green production power, which urges it to accelerate the research and development of green products and green design, so as to continuously gain advantages in the market competition.

In terms of pressure, the government's environmental regulation and daily administrative supervision as well as the supervision and report of

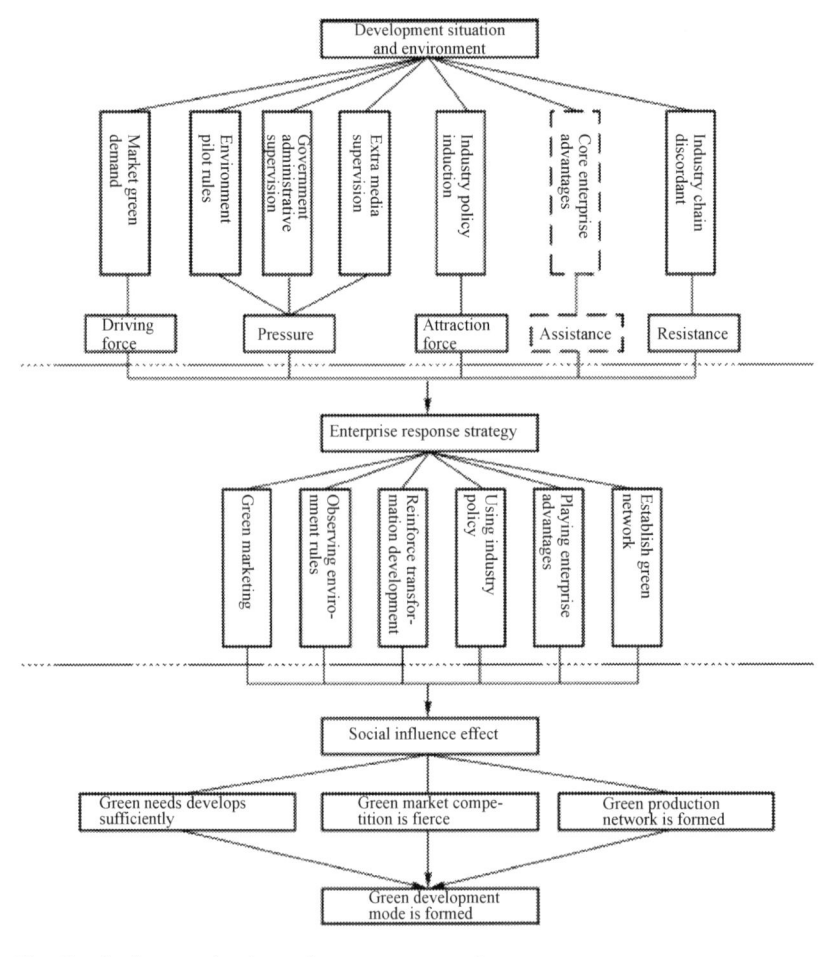

Fig. 1   Action mechanism of green consumption

social media will put pressure on the green production of enterprises. Since the government needs to comply with the demand of green consumption and guide the transformation of green production, it needs to regulate green consumption and green production in advance through laws and other means, and make clear which behaviors are not allowed in green development. For example, the government has set green production energy consumption standards for enterprises, and enterprises that do not meet the standards will be eliminated. At the same time, in addition to the advance regulation of the law, the government will also strengthen the regular supervision of enterprises' daily behavior. In addition, social media will also strengthen the reporting of enterprises' green behaviors, which virtually constitutes a kind of social supervision.

In terms of attraction, the green industrial policy guidance from the government to promote enterprises' green production transformation constitutes the attraction of enterprises' green production. Generally, in order to promote the transformation of green production, the government will guide and stimulate enterprises through fiscal, financial, tax and land supply. For example, land supply will be given priority to enterprises that meet energy consumption and pollution discharge standards, with tax and loan preferences will be given. In this way, enterprises will be constantly stimulated to carry out green production, otherwise they will face the restriction of industrial policy.

In terms of assistance, core enterprises in the industry are generally more likely to receive additional help from the government. For example, when the government intends to guide the transformation of green production, it will pay special attention to the progress of green key and core technologies of relevant enterprises in the industry, and as the leading benchmarking enterprise in the industry, it may obtain assistance from the government in technology research and development. At the same time, the government may also take the relevant technical standards of the enterprise as the green technology standards in the industry, so as to enhance the position of the enterprise in the industry and give the enterprise a technological edge in the competition.

In terms of resistance, the biggest resistance to the green development of enterprises is the unmatching and uncoordinated supply chain between industries. Although the key green technology innovation of the enterprise itself can gain a leading edge in the competition, the modern mode of large-scale production division of labor and the fierce requirements of enterprise competition efficiency do not allow the enterprise to complete all the details by itself; in fact, it is impossible to do this. Therefore, enterprises are required to conduct close collaboration between the industrial chains and stay invincible by giving play to their core competitive advantages. The uncoordinated and asynchronous development of the industrial supply chain is undoubtedly the biggest obstacle to the green development of core enterprises. In order to promote green development smoothly, core enterprises need to rely on industry influence to establish green supply chain in line with their own development.

In response, enterprises need to make rational choices according to the requirements of development environment and situation, make rational use of various forces in development and actively promote their own green transformation and development. For example, as a core enterprise in the industry, in order to meet the huge social green consumption demand for green transformation and development, it needs to strengthen communication and cooperation with social media, actively collect market green demand information and accelerate product research and development. Consciously, abide by the relevant environmental regulations of the government and make full use of various favorable industrial policies to accelerate the transformation of green development. In order to overcome the resistance of green production effectively, a green supply chain that meets the demand of green production should be established while strengthening its own core technology progress. It will continue to cooperate with suppliers that meet their green production requirements, exclude enterprises that do not meet their green production standards and gradually build a green supply network conducive to their own development. More and more enterprises are brought into the green supply chain. Through this self-strengthening green production self-organization mode, a strong and perfect green production network is built. The main obstacle of green consumption has been broken down, and with the increase of the supply of green products or services in the market, the competition becomes more and more fierce, and consumers become more and more picky and mature, and a new round of green market competition has begun. Finally, a green development model guided by green consumption is gradually taking shape.

The list above is the best in the industry. It's the same for the general enterprise, but a little weaker in terms of assistance. In a word, enterprises in green consumption, on the one hand, are strongly stimulated by green market demand; on the other hand, it faces the triple constraints of legal regulation, economic inducement and administrative supervision. The rational choice of enterprises is to follow the trend and to transform to green development, besides their own active efforts, seeking the support of partners in the industrial chain has become a prerequisite. Due to the mutual cooperation and supervision among enterprises, a comprehensive green production society has been gradually formed. In turn, comprehensive green production also stimulates green competition in the market, and thus continuously promotes the progress of green technology and the formation of a comprehensive green society.

3 FOREIGN EXPERIENCE IN GREEN CONSUMPTION DEVELOPMENT

3.1 Government Experience

Green consumption, in the long run, is mainly led by consumers themselves, but as a kind of transformation, the role of the government is indispensable, playing a role of rapid promotion. From the experience of foreign countries, the government mainly adopts legislative regulation, economic inducement, administrative supervision and other means in the consumption transformation, and attaches importance to the development of environmental education, so as to cultivate consumers' awareness of green consumption and fundamentally reverse the consumption concept. Since the government itself is also a consumer and can be a big to the extent of "big customer bullying shop" consumers, and has the function of public image, therefore, governments of all countries attach great importance to the role of developing green government procurement in promoting green consumption, so as to give full play to its role in stimulating domestic demand and social demonstration. The following is a list of typical green consumption experience in the United States, Germany, Japan and other countries.

United States
Legal Regulation
Although the United States does not have a national green consumption promotion regulation, its promotion of green consumption is reflected and regulated in different laws, and the laws and regulations enacted by

the federal government and various state governments also reflect the promotion of green consumption. For example, the *Pollution Prevention Act*, the *Resource Conservation and Recovery Act* (formerly known as the *Solid Waste Disposal Act* until 1976, when it was renamed) and other laws embody the requirements of the US government to develop a circular economy and advocate green consumption. Since the mid-1980s, Oregon, New Jersey, California, Wisconsin and other states have enacted laws and regulations to promote the recycling of resources. According to statistics, more than half of the states in the United States have enacted laws and regulations on resource recycling. The *Comprehensive Waste Management Act of California*, passed in 1989, requires glass containers to use 15–65% recycled materials and plastic garbage bags to use 30% recycled materials. Wisconsin requires plastic containers to be made from 10 to 25% recycled material. Although these laws are scattered, they outline the key areas of resource conservation and emission reduction, which is conducive to green consumption and effective conservation and emission reduction in key areas. Moreover, the decentralized legislation of local states, though not unified, has strong regional adaptability and is conducive to implementation.

The regulation of green consumption in American law emphasizes the responsibilities and obligations of each subject, and the relevant legal provisions clearly stipulate the responsibilities and obligations of each subject on environmental issues. For example, for the government, relevant laws stipulate that the government has the responsibility and obligation to manage the environment. The *National Environmental Policy Act* (NEPA) passed by the United States in 1969 is the representative of environmental legislation in the United States to clarify and strengthen the government's environmental responsibility. The act stipulates that "the federal government has the responsibility to coordinate and improve the programs, plans, resources and functions of the United States federal government in all ways that are coordinated and feasible with national policies". The act also stipulates methods to solve national environmental problems and promote green consumption. In addition to state control, effective federal scientific intervention and control is required. In this way, the government has legally confirmed its responsibility and obligation to manage ecological and environmental issues and promote green consumption, thus establishing its unique authority and obligatory obligation to manage national environmental issues. For manufacturers, the law also stipulates their responsibilities and obligations in green consumption. For example, the *National Energy Policy and Energy Reserve Act* promulgated by the United States in 1975 stipulates that some home appliance manufacturers must indicate the energy efficiency of the product and the energy consumption within one year on the product label, so that consumers can understand the environmental hazards in consumption. For consumers, relevant laws, such as the *Law on Resource Protection and Recycling*, also stipulate the environmental responsibility of consumers. When purchasing, consumers will generally look at the internal components and environmental impact marked on the package first. Goods with great harm to the environment will be excluded from the selection scope under the action of consumers' awareness of environmental responsibility. In this way, the environmental responsibilities of the government, manufacturers and consumers are clear and unified, which is conducive to the overall implementation of green consumption.

American laws on green consumption regulation are very clear, specific, rigorous, informative, with good feasibility and operability. Taking the *Resource Protection and Recovery Act* of the United States as an example, the act contains 8 chapters and 64 articles, which make detailed and specific provisions on solid waste from generation to disposal, who to dispose and how to dispose. The main contents can be summarized as the following 7 aspects: (1) determine the form of the existence of waste, caused by the waste of resources and the impact on the environment and citizen health and stipulate that state, regional and local authorities shall perform their duties in the effective collection and proper disposal of wastes. The federal government must take further steps to reduce the amount of waste and ensure environmentally safe disposal of unrecyclable waste; (2) the legislative purpose of this law is to protect the environment, safety and human health, and protect valuable energy and materials. The act provides for a number of specific measures: Provide a higher level of solid waste collection, classification and recycling methods and processing technology, provide financial assistance and technical support, provide financial support for vocational training in solid waste disposal and establish close partnerships between federal, state and local governments and businesses to better recycle valuable materials; (3) define the relevant terms; Article 1004 defines "hazardous materials", "resource protection", "recycling resources", "resource recovery system", etc. For example, "resource conservation" means to reduce the amount of solid waste, reduce the waste of various resources and make better use of recycling resources; (4) determine the organization, management and implementation of the law and their respective functions and powers, and set up a special departmental coordinating committee for resource conservation and recycling to manage and coordinate the various departments dealing with solid waste in accordance with the act; (5) stipulate the hazardous waste management system, including the identification standards and procedures for hazardous waste, the different standards applicable to producers and sellers, and the permit system applicable to owners and operators; (6) the determination of these management systems must follow legal procedures; state and regional regulations on solid waste programs; (7) set out the responsibilities of the department of commerce in resource recovery, such as setting accurate specifications for recycled materials, providing incentives for market development of recycled materials and providing BBS for recycling communication. In addition, the act clearly stipulates that the EPA should provide, assist and encourage the public to participate in the formulation, modification and implementation of laws and regulations, especially in the approval process of permits for the disposal and storage of waste business, so that the public can know the types and disposal methods of waste.

Economic Induction
The economic inducement of green consumption in the United States can be divided into two types: one is a direct economic inducement, with government incentives or subsidies. For example, in order to encourage farmers to produce green agricultural products, the US government gives various direct or indirect subsidies to agricultural production and trade. The other is indirect economic inducement, mainly for emission permit trading and green tax system design. Although the former is simple, convenient and easy to operate, it is difficult to distinguish the efforts of each subject in reducing consumption and emission, and it is also difficult to adapt to the specific technical requirements for reducing consumption and emission of different types of resources. Therefore, the emission permit trading system and green tax system are mainly adopted. In trading permits, polluters are incentivized to reduce emissions by converting their capacity to economic gain. In the green tax system, the range of tax objects and the design of tax rate play a role in guiding consumers' green consumption. The following examples are fuel tax, tax on gas-guzzling vehicles and mining tax to illustrate how green tax system induces green consumption.

In the fuel tax, because gasoline is a non-renewable resource, and the use of gasoline will cause carbon dioxide emissions and air pollution, so the tax on gasoline started very early, and is the top priority of the fuel tax. For example, as early as 1919, the Origen State Government was the first in the United States to impose the tax on automobile fuel. By 1929, all states in the United States completed the establishment of the tax system and put it into practice. In addition to the states, the Federal Government also imposes a uniform federal fuel tax. Federal gasoline is taxed at 18.4 cents per gallon, and aviation fuel and other energy products used for transportation are taxed at 19.4 cents per gallon. To encourage the use of clean fuels, users of clean fuels will receive tax incentives. For example, when a car owner USES liquefied petroleum gas (LPG), natural gas, hydrogen, electricity, or ethanol fuel with an alcohol content of more than 85% as the energy source of the car, he is allowed to deduct the fuel cost from the total income before calculating the tax payable. Owners who use an alcohol-gasoline blend will get a 5.4-cent-per-gallon exemption from the gasoline tax. Tax incentives for consumers who use clean fuels or alcohol-gasoline blends can encourage consumers to use clean energy and protect the environment. In addition to gasoline, the United States imposes a excise tax on some other fuels. General kerosene and other energy products for transportation are taxed at 24.4 cents per gallon, kerosene and other energy products for transportation for trains are taxed at 4.4 cents per gallon, and kerosene and other energy products for certain motor vehicles are taxed at 7.4 cents per gallon.

In the tax on gas-guzzling cars, energy consumption standards and tax design also guide consumers' choice of environment-friendly models. For example, the Federal Government has set fuel efficiency standards for cars, requiring them to travel no less than 12.5 miles per gallon. If they fail to meet that standard, owners will have to pay a $7500 gas-guzzling tax, which will help eliminate the gas-guzzling models and encourage consumers to choose the environmentally friendly ones.

In excise duties on ozone-damaging chemicals, a tax is imposed on chlorofluorocarbons (CFCs) to reduce the consumption of such products. The United States Federal Government began taxing ozone-damaging chlorofluorocarbons (CFCs) in January 1991, based on the amount of chlorofluorocarbons produced and imported. In terms of tax rates, the CFCS rate is set as the base rate, while other ozone-damaging chemicals are taxed as the product of their ozone-depleting potential and the base rate. Through this tax system, the United States reduced the consumption of CFCS products, effectively slowing the rate of destruction of the ozone layer.

In a mining tax, fossil fuel resources such as coal, oil and natural gas are taxed to keep the air clean. By imposing a mining tax, the United States has reduced carbon dioxide by 99% from the 1970s, carbon monoxide by 97% and particulate matter by 70% as car use has increased.

In the case of disposable razors and used tires, the United States levies a tax on the production and import of disposable razors and used tires. By levying taxes, the price of these two types of products will be raised, the purchase cost of consumers will be increased, and consumers will be restrained from purchasing these two types of products, so as to realize the effect of saving resources and energy.

Consumption Demonstration

The US government, fully aware of their own consumer identity by implementing green government procurement, set an example guiding green consumption. For example, since the early 1990s, the United States has successfully formulated and implemented a series of green procurement plans, such as the recycling product procurement plan, the "energy star" plan, the eco-farm product act and the environment-friendly product procurement plan. Chapter 23 of the *US Government Procurement Act* specifically provides for this. The chapter, titled "environmental, natural protection, labor safety and non-toxic workplaces", focuses on green procurement regulations. Paragraph 904 clearly states that "procurement of goods and services that have the least impact on people's health and the environment is a government procurement policy". Nearly all US states have preferential purchase policies for products made from recycled materials.

In addition, the US government has actively created conditions to promote the trade of used goods and the full use of resources. For example, the US government, realizing the diversification and convenience of consumption in the context of informatization, has set up a special website to provide consumers with a convenient trading platform for second-hand goods.

Educational Guidance

Environmental education legislation promotes green consumption and green production in the United States. The United States is the first country in the world to enact *Environmental Education Legislation.*

As early as 1970, the environmental education law was enacted and implemented in 1990 after many amendments. The law has reiterated the country environment education's responsibility and obligation to the public; it has confirmed the urgent need of the state to educate and cultivate high-quality citizens with knowledge and skills of environmental protection, a sense of responsibility for environmental protection and the ability to make correct environmental decisions; it has comprehensively standardized the organization team construction, project management, funds input, awards and other affairs of environmental education in the United States. The promulgation of this law has played an important role in improving the environmental ethics of the American public and promoting the coordinated development of economy and society. Especially in the aspect of green consumption, the multi-level, nationwide and open environmental education has cultivated the green consumption consciousness of American consumers. According to a 1994 Rodale Press survey, one in three Americans has changed their eating habits in the past few years. About 72% of Americans are willing to buy organically grown vegetables and fruits, 77% of Americans say a company's environmental credibility affects its purchasing decisions and 89% of Americans consider environmental standards for consumer products when they are on shopping. At present, almost all consumers in the United States when shopping for agricultural products in supermarkets will consider whether the product is "organic" and whether it is good for the environment and health. The increase of green consumption demand in the market stimulates more enterprises to produce green products, resulting in the market situation of flourishing supply and demand. In 1990, more than 6000 new green products were launched in the US, accounting for 10% of the total number of new products launched in the whole year, while the proportion in the world market was only 1% in the same period. Since the 1990s, organic food sales in the United States have grown at an average annual rate of 20%, reaching $7.7 billion in 2000, making it the world's largest organic food market. Currently, the United States exports a wide range of organic produce to the world.

The development mode of extensive social participation makes environmental education continuously develop and strengthen and virtuous circle. Different from the government-led system in other countries, in the environmental education system of the United States, the government does not directly interfere in environmental education with administrative power, but participates in it as a service provider and supervisor.

Non-profit organizations are the main force, and enterprises also actively participate in it. It is just this kind of development mode that makes environmental education develop continuously. Taking American farms as an example, community and NGO organizations are widely involved in environmental education for farmers, and the results of environmental education stimulate farmers themselves to participate in education: On the one hand, environmental education is directly beneficial to the production and sale of organic agricultural products. On the other hand, the demand of environmental education for practice sites also provides various sources of non-agricultural income for farmers, which greatly arouses the enthusiasm of farmers to participate in environmental education, and some of them provide financial help for environmental education.

The design of the tax exemption system has mobilized more social organizations to participate in environmental education. Non-profit organizations are the main force of environmental education in the United States, and the tax exemption in the United States tax law has undoubtedly aroused the enthusiasm of more social organizations to participate in environmental education. For example, paragraph 501 of Chapter 26 of the *Us Tax Code* is effectively a tax exemption provision, which outlines 25 types of non-profit organizations that qualify for tax exemption. Almost all nonprofits are exempt from state and local property and business taxes. At the same time, for a company that donates to a non-profit organization, if the donation does not exceed 3% of its total income, the donated income will be exempted from all taxes, while individual donations will also be exempted from income tax; In addition, US states have set up some preferential taxes for non-profit organizations. California's tax code, for example, exempts non-profits from the GST. The existence of non-profit organizations needs to be guaranteed by certain sources of funds, and the tax-free donation of enterprises and individuals to environmental education non-profit organizations encourages more social members and related organizations to provide survival conditions for environmental education non-profit organizations. In turn, it promotes the development of environmental education, which is also one of the successful experiences of the development of environmental education in the United States.

Germany

Germany is the first country in the world to propose the development of circular economy. As early as the 1870s, Germany began to explore how to develop circular economy and how to promote green consumption.

Its development thought has experienced the transformation from the end of environmental protection to the fundamental control from the source control and from only aiming at the production link to the integrated management of production and consumption. Therefore, green consumption plays a very important role in the idea of circular economy. Germany has established a complete legal system and an effective regulatory system to manage and promote it.

Legislative Regulation
The complete legislation of green consumption in Germany is not only reflected in the systematicness of laws, but also in the task differentiation of different consumption subjects. In addition to the restrictive nature of relevant laws, it also has the characteristics of both guidance and feasibility.

Germany's green consumption legal system is very complete, mainly reflected in the laws and regulations to promote the circular economy. Up to now, Germany has developed a set of well-structured legal system concerning circular economy and green consumption. It has enacted and promulgated laws, regulations and guidelines for the development of circular economy in different aspects such as Waste *Disposal Act, Packaging Waste Disposal Act, Circular Economy and Waste Disposal Act, Federal Soil* and *Water Conservation and Old Waste Act, Sustainable Eco-Tax Reform Act, Renewable Energy Act, Disposal of Motor Vehicles Ordinance, Technical Guidelines for Waste Management.* In addition, the EU Directive on recycling of waste oil, agricultural sewage, titanium oxide, batteries and batteries, packaging materials, sewage sludge and other materials also plays a guiding and constraining role in Germany's green consumption.

Like the United States, the legal system of green consumption in Germany also stipulates the environmental responsibility, basic rights and obligations of relevant subjects. For example, the *Circular Economy and Waste Disposal Law* promulgated and implemented in 1996 stipulates the relevant responsibilities and basic obligations of the state, the state government and the people responsible for waste. Legal provisions: (1) the German federal government is responsible for formulating the core principles, rules and regulations, as well as the implementation of the eu regulations, in accordance with the legislative process by the parliament to discuss and enact the implementation. For example, the basic waste classification standard in this law, the material recycling treatment method, the rights and obligations of the responsible person and the relevant penalty rules for violations. (2) The state governments shall be responsible for designating the competent authorities of their respective states to implement the law and shall be responsible for compiling the development plans of the recycling economy of their respective states, examining and approving the qualification certification of waste recovery and disposal, examining and verifying the professionals and management of the practitioners, and establishing the information base. (3) This paper makes a clear distinction and special provisions for the people responsible for waste management, mainly including producer responsibility, waste owner responsibility and reporting responsibility of the people responsible. Another example is the implementation of the environmental protection labeling system since 1979, which stipulates that government agencies shall give priority to the procurement of environmental protection labeling products and stipulates that the principles of green procurement include prohibition of waste, product durability, recyclability, maintainability and easy disposal.

Germany attaches equal importance to the guidance and feasibility of green consumption legislation, which is fully reflected in its *Circular Economy and Waste Disposal Law*. Its main contents are as follows: (1) It is clear that the legislative purpose of this law is to protect the natural environment, promote the development of circular economy, and ensure that waste is disposed in a way that is conducive to environmental protection. (2) It has stipulated the basic responsibilities and rights and obligations of waste producers and clarifies the principles of circular economy development. The first is to avoid waste generation, especially to reduce the amount of waste and its harm. Secondly, for the reuse of energy and materials, and the implementation and development of circular economy, it puts forward specific requirements and norms, established the basic principles of waste disposal; (3) It has made provisions on product liability, making it clear that manufacturers should follow the "3R" principle to produce and recycle products, and should try their best to avoid producing wastes in the production process to ensure proper disposal of wastes. (4) For the preparation of a circular economy plan, it has stipulated the responsibilities for waste management planning and the preparation of a circular economy, and pointed out that the operation of waste management facilities must be approved and subject to inspection by the relevant competent authorities. (5) It has clarified some incentive policies, emphasizes the guiding role of the government, and required government agencies to follow the principles of circular economy in their daily work to promote the development of circular economy market. (6) For regulations on promoting the information dissemination of circular economy, including the regulations on the information disclosure of relevant government units, it requires the explanation and comparison of waste recycling planning, which plays a role of publicity and education. (7) It has clarified the responsibility of waste disposal supervision and management, and stipulated the general supervision responsibility, supervision method and responsible person for waste reuse. (8) It has also stipulated punishment methods for violation of this law, coordination between this law and relevant EU laws and regulations, protection of intellectual property rights, etc.

Product Management

In order to promote green consumption and develop circular economy, Germany has strengthened the whole-process management of the whole life cycle of products and now has formed a set of relatively effective consumption management system, including green product liability system and green product quality standard system.

Green product liability system. The green product liability system involves the whole process of waste disposal from production to use, and the green packaging system and environmental protection waste disposal system are the most prominent ones. In the green packaging system, Germany has made clear requirements to restrict the external packaging of commodities, so as to achieve the goal of waste emission reduction. In the environmental waste disposal system, it combines garbage disposal and resource recycling to reduce the amount of landfill and make full use of resources. These systems have achieved good practical results. For example, through the development of product liability system and the promotion of marketization and industrialization of waste disposal, the recycling rate of packaging materials increased from 13.6% in 1990 to 91% in 2009. The recycling efficiency of glass packaging is up to 90%, while that of paper packaging is up to 60%. In addition, Germany has reduced the amount of household kitchen waste by about 65% through the return of deposits and collection of garbage disposal fees, further promoting the recycling of packaging materials.

Green product quality standard system. In order to ensure the quality of green products, Germany has a "blue angel" standard, where environmental labels are posted on all products that meet quality standards to prove that they are of acceptable quality and that they meet environmental requirements for manufacturing processes and waste disposal. In this way, citizens can feel completely at ease when buying green goods. At present, in Germany, the products with environmental protection marks have accounted for 30% of the country's products, and the varieties have reached more than 4000, which greatly promotes the promotion of green consumption mode.

Government Action

In the green consumption in Germany, the government attaches more importance to its own responsibilities and actions, such as the establishment of fiscal subsidy system and the establishment of green government procurement system.

Financial subsidy system. The purpose of the system is to promote energy conservation and environmental protection and encourage the consumption of new energy. Germany enacted the *Electricity Transmission Law* in 1990 and the *Renewable Energy Priority Law* in 2000, which stipulate that the government should give certain financial subsidies to power grid operators. Under the strong promotion of this policy, although Germany's wind power started late, but the development is very fast, Germany has become the world leader in wind power generation.

Green government procurement system. This system makes the government play a good role in guiding consumers in promoting green consumption. Germany lays down some basic principles for government procurement, which are not to be wasted, should be durable, recyclable and easy to handle. (See the chapter on *Finance and Green Transition Development*, which will not be repeated here.)

Education Promotion

Germany regards environmental education as a part of national development support system, and environmental policies should be changed according to the time. So far, it has gone through three stages. Since the education conference held in Kiel university in 1965, Germany has been the first country in the world to put forward the idea of vigorously developing environmental education. Its environmental education policy has gone through three stages: In the first stage, from the 1950s to the 1970s, Germany had realized that economic development could not take the way of "drain the pond to get all the fish and burn the forest and hunt", and the protection of natural resources was put on the agenda. In the second stage, from the 1970s to the 1990s, Germany, which had experienced a series of environmental disasters, began to comprehensively solve environmental problems, and its environmental education began to change from "natural protection education" to "environmental protection education". "Education for environmental protection" includes not only providing educates with information on current environmental hazards, but also, more importantly, disseminating knowledge of the interconnectedness and interdependence of natural systems, economic and technological developments and policy-making. In the third stage, from the 1990s to the present, the German environmental protection agency issued the first German sustainable development report in 1998, which pointed out that the earth summit embodied the new insight of human beings that all human activities should be guided by the principle of sustainable development. The federal-state education research and planning promotion commission of Germany implemented BLK "21" plan to carry out comprehensive sustainable development education in German schools, which means that the environmental education in Germany has been promoted from "environmental protection education" to "sustainable development education". The environmental education in Germany is a kind of real "education for all and learning for all", the subject of environmental education continues to expand, and government institutions also become the subject of environmental education. First of all, for formal education in schools, the scale of its educators and educates continues to expand. For example, BLK "21" plan, which was implemented in 1999, aims to promote sustainable development by advocating and practicing interdisciplinary and participatory environmental education and innovative modes of environmental education. The BLK 21 plan has a total budget of 13 million euros and involves about 1000 teachers and 65,000 students from 200 schools. In 2005, the Transfer "21" plan (i.e., to transform the unsatisfactory part of BLK "21" plan into a more sustainable education) was launched, and the number of participating schools increased to 4500. Primary education in Germany was included in the plan, and a training program for teachers was initiated. This means that German teachers have a dual role in environmental education. On the one hand, they undertake the task of environmental education; on the other hand, they must receive timely training so as to constantly update their knowledge and skills to adapt to the constantly developing process of environmental education. Secondly, adult environmental education is also increasing. According to statistics, in 1989, about 150,000 German adults participated in environmental education activities mainly carried out by night schools, churches and Chambers of commerce. Statistics show that this number has continued to increase over the past decades. Finally, German government institutions are also the subject of environmental education. NGOs in Germany have been instrumental in environmental education. They often establish long-term connections with German schools and communities, carry out non-profit environmental education activities among the public, become an important communication channel between the public and policy makers, and reflect the public's demands on the environment to the German government in different forms. In this sense, German government institutions are often the recipients of environmental education, and many good environmental policies benefit from this education.

Environmental education in Germany, on the one hand, directly promotes green consumption and environmental protection; on the other hand, it turns green consumption into a new industry and economic growth point. Most hotels in Germany, for example, have seen environmental groups take part in initiatives to "recycle towels" by putting cards inside their hotels to tell guests. If you don't change the recycling towels and sheets every day during your stay, you can contribute to saving resources and reducing pollution. The Naturschutzbund Deutschland (NABU), with more than 110 years of history and about 250,000 members, is powerful economically and politically, and has successfully saved large areas of forests and wetlands by purchasing lands of conservation value. The "educatee" status of German government institutions makes them pay more attention to the formulation and implementation of environmental protection policies. The German government vigorously promotes energy conservation and emission reduction and the development of circular economy at home, which not only promotes the conservation and utilization of resources, improves the utilization efficiency of resources and reduces pollution, but also promotes economic development and employment. Statistics for 2006 show that the annual turnover of waste treatment alone has exceeded 41 billion euros, with 1 million employees.

Japan
Comprehensive Legislation

Japan's laws on green consumption are well developed. This is reflected in the following aspects:

First, the legal system is three-dimensional and comprehensive. Japan's laws and regulations to promote green consumption and circular economy can be roughly divided into three levels: At the basic level, the *Basic Law on the Formation and Promotion of a Circular Society* is a basic law. At the main level, two laws, the *Solid Waste Management and Public Cleaning Law* and the *Law on Promoting the Effective Use of Resources*, were formulated as comprehensive laws. At the branch level, five specific laws and regulations have been formulated, namely *Promoting the Classification of Containers and Packages*, the *Law on the Recovery of Household Appliances*, the *Law on the Recovery of Buildings and Materials*, the *Law on the Recovery of Food* and *the Law on Green Purchasing*. In this way, Japan has constructed a three-dimensional and overlapping legal system from three levels, which has created a good social environment for promoting green consumption and circular economy. Japan has not only formulated a set of laws and regulations directly related to green consumption and circular economy, but also formulated other relevant laws and regulations to coordinate and unify them as a whole. For example, in 2000, the Japanese government enacted the *Green Procurement Law*, which requires the government, enterprises and individuals to protect the environment through consumption. In 2003, the *Law on the Promotion of Environmental Education* was enacted to incorporate environmental education into the law on compulsory education, so as to promote citizens' awareness of environmental protection.

Second, the law can be translated into concrete actions. Different from the "principle" legislation, "framework" legislation and "advocacy" legislation in some countries, Japan's green consumption and circular economy legislation is very detailed, with equal emphasis on guidance and compulsion, which can be translated into concrete actions in practice. Take the *Basic Law on the Formation and Promotion of a Circular Society* as an example. As mentioned above, this law is the basic law on the development of recycling economy and the promotion of green consumption in Japan. Compared with Germany's *Circular Economy and Waste Disposal Law*, it is more profound and richer in objectives and contents. Its purpose is to change the traditional social and economic development model and establish a "circular society". The *Basic Law on the Establishment of a Circular Society* consists of three chapters and 33 articles. The main contents are as follows: (1) Clearly put forward the establishment of a "recycling society" and defined it, that is, "recycling society" refers to the construction of a society that minimizes environmental load by recycling resources, inhibiting waste generation, ensuring reasonable disposal, controlling excessive consumption of natural resources and energy. (2) It defines the object of adjustment of the law, and defines the concepts of "recyclable resources" and "wastes". For example, "recyclable resources" refers to those things in the waste that still have use value. (3) It stipulates the legal order for the utilization and disposal of recyclable resources: (a) inhibit production; (b) reuse and recycling; (c) heat recovery; (d) reasonable disposal. That is to say, in the use and disposal of wastes and recyclable resources, raw materials and products should be controlled to become wastes in the process of production, circulation and consumption as far as possible. Secondly, resources that can be reused should be recycled to the maximum extent. Thirdly, materials that cannot be recycled should be burned to obtain heat energy. Finally, resources that cannot be disposed according to the first three requirements should be disposed harmlessly. (4) The responsibilities of the central government, local governments, enterprises and citizens are clearly defined, mainly expanding the responsibilities of producers and emitters. Producer responsibility means that after the product is consumed, the producer and the seller still have the responsibility to manage the product cycle. The responsibility of emitters means that the producers, sellers and consumers who discharge wastes should bear the first responsibility for material recycling. (5) The government is required to formulate the "basic plan for building a circular society" according to legal procedures, so as to better guide enterprises and citizens to conduct green consumption and develop a circular economy. (6) It specifies some basic policies, such as requiring the state to take the lead in promoting the use of renewable materials, carrying out pre-evaluation of enterprise products, and popularizing relevant knowledge by the government. As can be seen from the above, the *Basic Law on the Establishment of a Circular Society* has three characteristics: It covers a wide range of areas, including the recycling and reprocessing of waste garbage during and after consumption. Strong operability, such as the disposal of a variety of sequence and should follow the principles of the method are specified. The responsibilities are clear. The responsibilities of the government, enterprises and consumers are all assigned and defined in relevant laws and regulations.

Third, highlight the government's environmental responsibility. Although the responsibility of each subject is clearly defined in the laws related to green consumption and circular economy in Japan, Japan especially emphasizes the responsibility of government in environmental management, and writes the responsibility of government in environmental management into various laws to make the behavior of government management legalized and normalized. For example, with the formation of the public hazard law system, the Japanese government has established its environmental responsibility accordingly. The *Basic Law on Countermeasures against Public Hazards*, revised in 1970, specifies that the environmental responsibility that the government should assume is mainly reflected in the following aspects: The government has the obligation to set various environmental standards and to revise and improve them according to the continuous development of science and technology. Establish the basic measures to be taken by the government to prevent and control public hazards, including pollutant removal control, establishment of pollution prevention and control facilities, tracking and investigation of public hazards, etc.; Local governments should carry out appropriate measures to prevent and control public hazards. The government should establish the mechanism of handling public nuisance disputes and the system of victim relief. Establishing a financial system to assist in the prevention and control of public hazards; setting up a special administrative body to promote the prevention and control of public hazards. To further promote the government's environmental responsibility, Japan enacted the *Basic Law on the Environment* in 1993. The law advocates reducing environmental pollution (the so-called load on the environment) by itself and building a sustainable society, so as to promote international cooperation to preserve the earth's environment while leaving a good environment for future generations to inherit.

Economic Guidance
Green government procurement. The Japanese government directly stimulates the development of green industry through large-scale green government procurement. In 1994, Japan formulated the green government action plan, which laid down the basic principles of green procurement policy and encouraged all central and local governments' regulatory agencies to actively purchase green products. In May 2000, Japan promulgated the *Green Procurement Law*. The law has been in effect nationwide since April 2001. It requires national and local governments and public bodies to take the lead in purchasing environmentally friendly renewable products, promote the dissemination of information on green consumption, require all central governments and their agencies to implement annual green procurement plans, and submit green procurement reports to the Minister of the Environment on time.

The law focuses on promoting the green procurement of stationery, paper, household appliances, automobiles and other specific products, and defines the duties, rights and obligations of local government departments, local public organizations, companies and enterprises as well as citizens. According to the survey, Japan's public sector expenditure accounts for about $1/5$ of the total domestic expenditure, while the government's green procurement enhances entrepreneurs' enthusiasm for environmental protection and green product production, directly promoting the development of Japan's green industry.

Green tax system. The Japanese government guides people's consumption behavior mainly through tax suppression and tax reduction (exemption, low). Tax suppression is mainly reflected in fuel tax and consumption tax. The purpose of Japan's fuel tax is to protect the environment, guide consumption and obtain income. For example, the tax on fuel consumption will inevitably affect the behavior of car owners in purchasing and using fuel. This encourages fuel consumers to use fuel wisely and save energy, so fuel tax has a positive effect on green consumption. Japan's consumption tax on fuel is shared between central and local governments, which is divided into four sub-items: gasoline tax, diesel tax, natural gas tax and local road tax. They are all off price taxes with amount based on quantity. Gasoline taxes are measured in liters and are levied when gasoline is shipped from the warehouse. Diesel is also taxed on a "liter" basis, when consumers who use diesel buy it. As an extension and supplement of oil consumption tax, natural gas tax is levied on liquefied natural gas. The road use tax takes the gasoline leaving the factory as the tax object, which is levied in conjunction with a gasoline tax when gasoline is shipped from the warehouse. In addition, Japan has set fuel economy standards for motor vehicles to promote reforms in its manufacturing sector, encourage consumers to buy fuel-efficient cars and reduce the amount of energy wasted due to inefficient fuel use. In terms of tax reduction (exemption and low tax), it mainly applies to environmental protection industry or behavior. There are many preferential tax measures related to environmental protection in the Japanese tax law. For example, the special depreciation rate ranging from 14 to 20% should be increased on the basis of the original depreciation rate for environmental protection facilities. The *Basic Law on Measures against Public Hazards* stipulates that fixed asset tax can be reduced or exempted for public nuisance prevention and control facilities. According to the difference of facilities, the reduced or exempted tax rate is 40~70% of the original tax.

Green consumption incentives. Japan's Ministry of Environment has also set up a system of consumption points to promote green consumption through economic incentives. In other words, when consumers buy designated energy saving and environmental protection products, they can obtain corresponding "ecological points". To participate in the program, consumers must submit an application form and then redeem points with a shopping receipt and a warranty card. Each point is worth one yen and can be spent in department stores, electrical stores, post offices or on public transportation. At present, the selected products include more than 2000 kinds of home appliances.

Education Promotion

Japan regards environmental education as an indispensable force to ensure the sustainable development of the economy and society. The environmental education, which was originally a pure environmental crisis education, has become one of the important driving forces for the construction of ecological civilization society. From the Second World War to the early 1970s, this was the stage of public hazard education in Japan. Before the war, the ecological environment in Japan's industrialized big cities like Hanshin began to deteriorate. However, after the war, the large-scale industrialization led to frequent outbreaks of various environmental hazards such as minamata disease and itai-itai disease in the 1950s. The outbreak of environmental pollution and various occupational diseases make people reflect on the relationship between human beings and ecology, and schools begin to educate on environmental pollution prevention. For example, in 1967, Japan established the National Primary and Secondary School Pollution Education Countermeasures Research Institute, and the school began to educate students about environmental education. In 1968, the term "public hazard" was first used in the revision of the syllabus of *Social Science*. In 1970, the Ministry of Education decided to increase the content of public hazard learning in the "social science" of secondary schools and implement public hazard education. From the mid- and late 1970s to the early 1980s, public hazard education changed to environmental education. The rapid growth of economy has brought about abundant material supply, while the excessive production and consumption have directly or indirectly brought about various environmental problems. With the development of international environmental education, such as the publication of the famous *Belgrade Charter*, the purpose, objectives, objects and guiding principles of environmental education have had an important impact on Japan. For example, in 1975, the original National Primary and Secondary School Pollution Education Countermeasures Research Institute was renamed as the National Primary and Secondary School Environmental Education Research Institute. From 1977 to 1979, primary schools, junior high schools and senior high schools set up units related to environment in relevant teaching subjects and carried out environmental education practice activities. Since the late 1980s, it has been a period of establishment and comprehensive promotion of the concept of environmental education. During this period, with the influence of the international concept of sustainable development and the development of environmental education, Japan gradually established the concept of environmental education. For example, in 1986, the Japanese environment agency set up the "Environmental Education Talkfest". In 1988, the Office of the Environment published the *Report of the Environmental Education Talkfest*. In this report, environmental education is positioned to enable the public to take reasonable actions by deepening the public's comprehension and understanding of the relationship between human and environmental education. It also lists five aspects of environmental education and environmental learning. On the basis of environmental education policies, local governments and autonomous bodies have formulated basic environmental education policies and plans suited to local conditions and put them into practice. In 1989, the environment department established the regional environmental protection fund to support the development of regional environmental education. In the 1990s, environmental education was written into relevant laws and combined with social development as an important driving force for social development. For example, in 1993, Japan enacted the *Basic Law on the Environment*, which made relevant provisions on environmental education in article 25 of the law. Since then, environmental education has been recognized and guaranteed by law in Japan. In December 1994, Japan formulated and promulgated the *Basic Environmental Plan*, which is the embodiment of the basic environmental law and shows that environmental education has been integrated into its long-term social development plan and become one of the important guarantees for its construction of ecological society.

The innovation of environmental ethics makes people establish a good concept of the relationship between man and the environment, and lays an ideological foundation for the whole society to correctly handle the relationship between man and the environment. The basis of environmental ethics in Japan mainly includes: (1) The natural right to life. Not only human beings, but also biological species, ecosystems and landscapes have their own right to live. Therefore, human beings cannot deny them arbitrarily. (2) Generational ethical issues. The present generation is responsible for the viability of future generations. (3) Globalism. The earth's ecosystem is not an open universe, but a closed world. These ethical thoughts have far-reaching influence and wide social response, which is the ideological basis for them to call on the whole society to participate in environmental "preservation". Its idea of environmental "preservation" has a far-reaching influence. It makes members of the Japanese society, when using natural resources and environment, regard "nature" as an organic organism with equal status with human beings, and deal with it from the perspective of friendly attitude and careful relationship maintenance, thus avoiding the ecological crisis caused by the abuse of the environment.

Japan regards environmental education as the education related to individual life survival, lifelong learning and everyone's responsibility. In environmental education in Japan, the relationship between people and the surrounding environment is highlighted, and it requires people to know the surrounding environment in which they live, and become a person with practical ability to properly deal with the relationship with the surrounding environment. Geographical grounding is one of the distinctive features of environmental education. Environmental education in Japan requires lifelong learning and everyone's responsibility. Environmental education is not limited to students and schools. All members of society have the obligation to learn how to better preserve the environment. All relevant places can be used as places for environmental education and learning. For example, Paragraph 2 of Article 3, "basic concepts", of the *Environmental Education Promotion Act* stipulates that: In order to deepen the understanding of environmental protection through natural experience activities such as forests, fields, parks, rivers, lakes, coasts and oceans and other experience activities, efforts should be made to obtain the participation and cooperation of local residents and various subjects constituting the society. It can be seen that

Table 2   Contents and essentials of environmental education in Japanese primary schools

Viewpoint	Environment learning content	Discipline
Symbiosis	Relation to other regions	Social sciences
	The relationship between the activities of animals and plants and their growth and seasons	Science
	The relationship between family work and family	Family science
Ecology	The relationship between land environment and industry	Social sciences
	The relationship between living things and the environment	Science
	Family life and environment	Family science
Cycle	Waste disposal	Social sciences
	The relationship between the sun and the ground form	Science
	Appropriate shopping	Family science
Balance	The stability of national life	Social sciences
	The regularity of leverage	Science
	Coordinated diet	Family science
Limited	Guarantee of the electricity and gas	Social sciences
	The production and growth of animals	Science
	Appropriate shopping	Family science
Diversity	The function of agriculture, aquaculture and its relation with natural environment	Social sciences
	Conditions for the germination and growth of plants,	Science
	Way of living	Family science
Conservation	The relationship between cultural heritage, cultural property and self	Social sciences
	Formation and change of land,	Science
	Make something useful for life	Family science
Value/ethics	Make every effort to improve the quality of life of the local people	Social sciences
	The structure of the human and other animal bodies	Science
	Simple food cooking (safe use of utensils)	Family science

Source Song Shuang. *Environmental Education in Japan and Its Implications.* Dalian: Dalian University of Technology, 2007

environmental education in Japan is not limited to places and requires participation and collaboration of all members of society.

In the context of environmental education in Japan, consumption education is regarded as an important part. The content of environmental education in Japan can be roughly divided into the following eight aspects: living together, ecology, cycle, balance, limited, diversity, conservation and value/ethics. At the same time, these eight viewpoints are also the constitutive framework and prominent contents of the textbook content. For example, the environmental education in Japanese primary schools reflects these (see Table 2). As can be seen from Table 2, students should not only understand the environment and understand the relationship between human activities and the environment, but also establish correct environmental concepts and principles. For example, "living together", "cycle", "balance", "limited", "conservation", it is more important to form behavioral habits and abilities that are conducive to environmental protection, among which "appropriate shopping" appears repeatedly in "cycle" and "limited". This shows that Japan's environmental education attaches great importance to the status of consumer education, which is one of the ultimate major goals of its environmental education.

3.2   Experience in the Enterprise

Develop Environmental Education

Environmental problems are not only related to terminal consumption, but also to production design and manufacturing process. For example, most of the world-famous public hazards are the results of unreasonable production methods. Therefore, in this sense, enterprises are the indispensable subject of green consumption implementation. While enterprises carry out environmental education and promote green consumption, which not only directly saves the cost of materials and environmental treatment, but also sets up a good public image and cultivates many potential customers who love green consumption. For this reason, many large enterprises in the world carry out environmental education activities, and Japanese enterprises are very typical in this regard. The main ways for Japanese enterprises to develop the environment include: (1) Advocate "ecological design", from the design of products to take full account of environmental factors, from the source to reduce and control the production of pollutants, to provide low environmental load products for the society. (2) The use of recyclable materials in production can save resources and protect the environment. (3) Actively develop and promote environmental protection products, and guide the public to choose and use environmental protection products as far as possible. (4) To compile environmental reports and report their environmental management status to the society and consumers. (5) Carry out comprehensive environmental education within the enterprise, including business philosophy, corporate culture and staff lifestyle, encourage employees to actively participate in regional environmental activities, advocate green consumption, and change the original lifestyle in order to reduce environmental load. (6) Combine with social public relations, marketing promotion and other activities; carry out environmental education for the public; guide green consumption; and cultivate potential customers.

Among them, Panasonic and NEC are typical. The environmental headquarters of Japan's Panasonic corporation, in addition to undertaking activities to solve the earth's environmental problems, also recognized the need to change the values and lifestyles of citizens. Therefore, since February 1982, the "earth citizen campaign" has been implemented among employees and their families to encourage employees and their families to actively participate in regional environmental activities and change their original lifestyle in order to reduce environmental burden. Panasonic held a home energy conference to reduce consumption of water, electricity, gas and gasoline, which has achieved good results. In 2000, CO_2 emissions per household of Panasonic employees decreased by 1.5% on average (Fan Lianying, 2005). Panasonic also held an "eco-tote campaign" with shopping bags and no-disposable polythene bags and also solicited design and production proposals for eco-tote bags from employees and their families, which were well received. In addition, through television, brochures and other methods, Panasonic also publicized and introduced the activities and a variety of ecological life information in the company. In Japan, NEC adopts various production and operation plans to protect the environment under the basic policy of "realizing all-field environmental management with the participation of all employees". In addition to environmental protection in the development of environmental products, recycling of waste, zero waste and other aspects of production and operation, NEC has also carried out environmental education workshops, environmental action meetings and other environmental learning, and increased the green shopping, green consumption lifestyle education.

Implement Green Procurement
Many enterprises have realized that the modern large-scale production division system, the crisscross industrial chain relations and the competitive advantages of each have made it almost impossible for a

single enterprise to rely on its own green design and green production. Therefore, many enterprises, especially large enterprises with influence in the supply chain, have demanded the implementation of green procurement. Many enterprises not only carry out green design at the source, but also require participating suppliers to provide green raw materials, green technology or green services, which ensures the completion of its own green production, and monitors the green production of suppliers and cooperative enterprises, so as to promote the green production and green consumption of the whole society. Japan's large firms in electronics and electronics are typical in green procurement (see Table 3). The green procurement of these large enterprises virtually guides, guides, supervises and helps other enterprises in the supply chain to produce green products through the interest relationship of the supply chain.

Table 3 Green procurement practices of Japanese enterprises in the electronics and electrical industry

Enterprises	Main practices
SONY	Sets the "SONY Green Partner Standard", which purchases parts and materials only from suppliers that have earned the green partner designation, which is reviewed every two years
Panasonic	Issues "Green Procurement Standards" and "Chemical Substance Management Grading Standards", requiring suppliers to understand and comply with their environmental policies and activities and give priority to purchase from manufacturers who actively carry out various environmental protection activities
Canon	Actively carries out earth environmental protection activities, strives to work with suppliers to carry out environmental protection activities, and requires suppliers to meet their environmental management evaluation standards
Fujitsu	Has three "green procurement" requirements for suppliers: an environmental management system; compliance with restrictions on specified chemicals; establishing a chemical substance management system
Ricoh	Establishes the Environmental Management System Guide (EMS) and the Chemical Substance Management System Guide (CMS), as well as the green purchasing standard based on the former two, and requires suppliers to meet the above environmental management standards
Mitsubishi Electric	Establishes management standards for hazardous substances in products, requires suppliers to comply with them, and evaluates the supplier environmental protection system

Source Chen Sheng. Practices and Experience of Japanese Enterprises in Implementing Green Procurement Standardization. World Standard Information, 2007 (10): 51–54

It overcomes the disadvantages of relying on the high cost of the government and the "impotence" of the public supervision in the traditional supervision, and is a new type of supervision and restriction relationship, which deserves special attention in the green consumption.

4   THE STATUS QUO AND EXISTING PROBLEMS OF GREEN CONSUMPTION IN CHINA

4.1   Current Situation of Green Consumption in China

The Demand for Green Consumption Keeps Growing
China's repeated product quality and safety incidents have greatly increased Chinese consumers' green consumption based on product quality and safety. For example, after the melamine-tainted milk powder incident, Chinese consumers travelled overseas to buy safe milk powder, or at home, they only bought milk powder produced by foreign manufacturers. In the field of medicines and personal care products, there are also a large number of consumers who buy high-priced foreign products based on the consideration of quality, safety and health. In addition, the improvement of residents' income level also enables high-income groups to favor healthier and more secure green products and environment-friendly goods. For example, the green consumption survey conducted by Zhang Zhimin (2011) in 2010, taking Dongguan as a case study, shows that the higher income groups purchase green products more frequently (see Table 4). As can be seen from Table 4, residents who "never" buy green products are all middle- and low-income

Table 4   Green product purchases by different income groups

Monthly income	Always	Often (%)	Occasionally (%)	Never (%)
Below 2000 Yuan	9.6>	32.5	55.0	2.9
2001 ~ 4000 Yuan	8.4%	36.0	54.2	13
4001 ~ 6001 Yuan	21.6>	29.7	48.6	0
6001 ~ 10,000 Yuan	12.5%	56.3	31.3	0
10,001 ~ 20,000	20.0%	50.0	30.0	0
Over 20,000 Yuan	25.0%	75.0	0	0

Data source Zhang Zhimin. Survey and Analysis of Green Consumption of Dongguan Residents. *Journal of Dongguan University of Technology*, 2011, 18 (4)

groups with a monthly income of less than 4000 Yuan. Among the people whose monthly income is 4001–6000 Yuan, 51.3% have the habit of purchasing green products. Among the people with monthly income of 6001 ~ 10,000 Yuan, 68.8% have the habit of purchasing green products. People with monthly income of 10,001 ~ 20,000 Yuan, up to 70.0% have the habit of purchasing green products. With monthly income of 20,000 Yuan and above, 100% have the habit of buying green products.

The Market Supply of Green Products Has Been Greatly Increased
In line with the green consumption trend in the market, Chinese businesses are also vigorously developing green products, and the market supply of green products has greatly increased. For example, in recent years, the state has repeatedly adjusted the prices of water and energy resources to promote resource conservation. In order to save the cost of water, electricity and other resources, many families purchase household electronic products that save water and electricity, which leads to the mainstream of water and electricity saving, health and environmental protection, mini multi-purpose home appliance market design in recent years. For another example, in China's green food market, green food manufacturers and annual supply has also greatly increased. In 1997, China's domestic sales of green food reached 24 billion Yuan and its

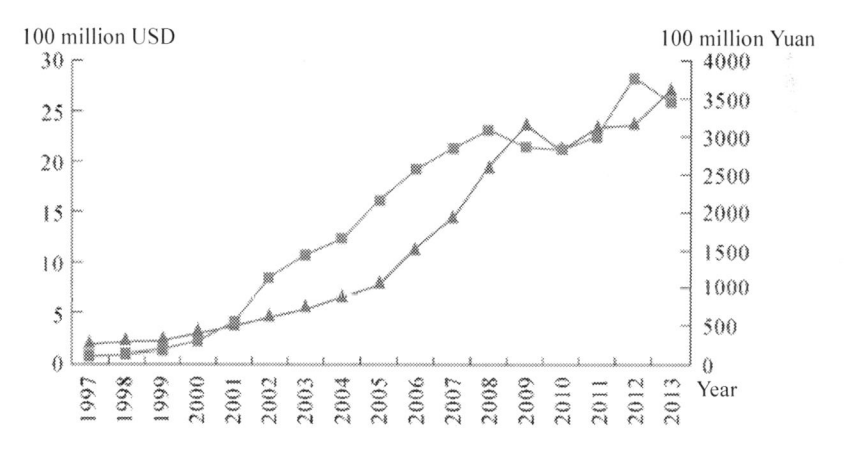

Fig. 2 Sales and exports of green food in China from 1997 to 2013 (*Data source* Du Haiyang, Liang Zhichao, Xiu Wenyan et al. Development Status and Prospect of Green Food in China. *Agricultural Prospect*, 2014 [10])

export value reached 70.5 million US dollars. In 2013, the domestic sales of green food increased by 14 times to 360 billion Yuan, and the export value of products also increased by 36 times to 2.6 billion US dollars (see Fig. 2).

The Government Management of Green Consumption Has Been Strengthened
In recent years, the Chinese government's management of green consumption is no longer limited to the quality and safety management from the perspective of health impact, but expands to resource conservation, environmental protection, social responsibility and so on. Management means are no longer purely economic penalties, but combined with legal norms, economic inducement, social demonstration and cultural construction. For example, in terms of legal norms, several laws related to green consumption have been enacted successively: The *Clean Production Promotion Law of the People's Republic of China* in 2002, the *Renewable Energy Law* in 2006, the *Energy Conservation Law* in 2008, the *Circular Economy Promotion Law* in 2009, etc. These laws and regulations have made relevant provisions on promoting green consumption at different levels, and the specific provisions are mainly reflected in the following provisions. For example, Article 10 of the *Circular Economy Promotion Law* points out that "citizens should enhance the awareness of environmental protection and resource conservation, make rational consumption and save resources". In addition to the above-mentioned laws, Article 9 of the *Government Procurement Law* also states that "government procurement shall contribute to the realization of the policy objectives of national economic and social development, including environmental protection". "Government procurement should give priority to the procurement of high-tech and environmental protection products to promote the development of environmental protection enterprises and ensure the sustainable development of the economy". The existence of these laws and regulations promotes the vigorous development of green consumption in China, and at the same time supervises the government's green procurement, which provides a clear legal basis for green consumption. In addition, China also has some relevant laws and regulations to promote green consumption. For example, in 2007, the general office of the state council issued the *Notice on Restricting the Production and Sale of Plastic Shopping Bags*, the *Regulations on Environmental Protection in Shenzhen Special Economic Zone*, *Regulations on the Construction of Circular Economy and Ecological City in Guiyang*

and other local government regulations. These legal systems and policies promote green consumption from different perspectives.

In terms of economic inducement, we have promoted the tiered pricing system for resource products, the green tax system and other relevant policies aimed at promoting green consumption. Since 2012, China has implemented tiered electricity price, tiered water price and tiered gas price in various regions. These tiered prices of resource products promote green consumption in the field of resource products in China. Local governments are also innovating to promote green consumption. For example, in Beijing, the lottery for buying a car has always been a difficult problem. In order to promote green consumption and solve the problem of air pollution such as haze, the government has promoted consumers' consumption of new energy vehicles through measures such as increasing the number of successful applicants for the lottery and unrestricted driving.

4.2   Problems in China's Green Consumption

Low Awareness of Social Responsibility of Green Consumption
Although Chinese consumers are also fond of "green consumption", they have low awareness of the social responsibility given by green consumption. At present, the basic motivation of green consumption of Chinese consumers lies in the beneficial "health and safety guarantee", "saving living expenses", "improving the quality of life", etc., but the awareness of social responsibility of green consumption is not well understood. For example, although many high-income people buy green food, they still eat rare animals and plants that are included in the scope of protection. They have little sense of social responsibility to protect rare animals and plants and biodiversity. For another example, many consumers purchase low-pollution environmental protection goods, but they have no idea about the impact of waste on the environment after the use of the goods. They seldom consider from the perspective of reducing the use and emission, but use as much as they want, and immediately replace the old with the new.

Higher Prices Restrain the Demand for Green Consumption
Although green products have been growing in China in recent years, the overall proportion is still not high. Just because the real green products are not enough, the price of green products is generally higher than

ordinary goods. For example, green organic river shrimp costs four times more than regular river shrimp; green pork is 50% higher than similar products. Although the variable frequency air conditioner is energy saving, the general price is hundreds or even thousands of Yuan higher than the ordinary air conditioner. Such a price puts off many consumers. Coupled with the imperfect management of the green product consumption market, the phenomenon of sailing under false colors and passing off fish eyes for pearls often occurs, which leads consumers to choose common products based on the consideration of product quality risk.

Low Recognition of Green Product Market Management
At present, China's green product market management system is not perfect, and the recognition degree of green product market is low, which affects green consumption. The "green degree" of products from all walks of life objectively requires certain evaluation standards and certification procedures. At present, except food, cosmetics, electronic products, building materials and other categories of green products in China are relatively perfect in the evaluation of green certification, the other products are not perfect in the evaluation and certification of "green degree". Moreover, due to bribery, rent-seeking, imperfect supervision and other factors, many products with the title or logo of green products are actually misnamed and have hidden dangers such as quality safety and health hazards, leading to general distrust of consumers and their reluctance to choose green products.

4.3   The Crux of China's Green Consumption Problem

Lack of Consumer Awareness of Social Responsibility
In China's consumer education, most of the education is still about "how to identify fake goods", "how to choose the right products", "how to save money and get a better deal", but little about the environmental impact, social effect and personal behavior regulation in consumption. This phenomenon leads to the low awareness of social responsibility of consumers when they consume, and the over-amplification of their own consumption demand while ignoring the social impact. Thus, the understanding of green consumption is only based on their own health and does not cover the health of social groups. From the perspective of

education, law and culture, we should strengthen the education of environmental knowledge and the consciousness of social responsibility in consumption.

The Effective Supply of Green Production Technology Is Insufficient

In a sense, the current high price of green products in China is due to the insufficient supply of green technology. Compared with traditional production technology, green technology is a "breakout", "breakthrough", so the cost of innovation is higher. In addition, the current green science and technology innovation organization system is not developed; many enterprises do their own research and development innovation, so the cost of innovation is high, and the cost of innovation is included in the production cost of enterprises, which naturally pushes up the price of green products produced by enterprises. On the other hand, it is the lack of similar green products in the market that makes manufacturers dare to sell their "green products" at a much higher price than ordinary products. Therefore, the high price of green products on the market reflects the undeveloped status of green production technology from another perspective.

The Green Consumption Management System Lags Behind

Compared with foreign green consumption management system, China's green consumption management system is still relatively backward. Foreign countries comprehensively use various systems to manage, like legal, economic, educational, scientific, cultural and social. As an important support for sustainable development, green consumption has penetrated into all aspects of social management system, and is very detailed and specific, involving deeper technical and knowledge issues. In contrast, China's green consumption management system, the legal provisions are still on the statement of principles, lacking detailed management of the environmental and resource issues that may arise in the consumption of various products. Moreover, the supporting implementation rules of management have not been established to improve and supplement it. The current management objects in the tax and price system are also limited to resource products such as energy, and they are mainly targeted at the links of consumption, but far from the links of production and waste disposal. In the education system, the slogan propaganda and the moral indoctrination are more than the scientific knowledge education and the management technology imparting. In the certification and supervision system, money can break through the strict technical standard threshold to some extent. All the above indicates that China's management of green consumption should be refined, perfected and rationalized in the future.

5   Ways to Promote Green Consumption in China

5.1   Environment Construction

Comprehensive use of education, law, culture and other factors to create a soft environment for green consumption. Consumption is divided into private consumption and public consumption, and the former accounts for the majority. Although the legal provisions can make all kinds of mandatory restrictions on residents' consumption, such restrictions are more rigid than flexible, and the cost of supervising the scattered private consumption subjects is too high. Therefore, green consumption must fundamentally improve consumers' awareness and initiative of green consumption, and the way to promote green consumption must fundamentally rely on education, especially environmental education related to green consumption. Although moralizing can temporarily urge consumers to choose green products, consumers are also strongly influenced by economic income level, personal feelings, likes and dislikes and other factors when choosing green products. Only when consumers have a strong awareness of the relationship between consumption and resources and environment, as well as the relationship between individual consumption behavior and social group life, can they improve their sense of social responsibility in consumption, consciously choose green products and form green consumption habits. In the future, China's education on green consumption should not be confined to simple preaching on the moral and emotional level, but should make use of all opportunities available for publicity and education to increase education on consumption behavior, environmental impact and action response, which enables consumers to rationally understand the relationship between consumption and environment from the perspective of knowledge and technology, so as to fundamentally establish the awareness of green consumption and develop green consumption habits. It is suggested to open more courses about ecological civilization and green consumption in formal school education, and to expand green consumption education in social education. For example, the use of television, the Internet, radio and other channels to increase public awareness of green consumption.

To give full play to the superiority of the legal system, we must strengthen the regulation and restriction in the key fields of green consumption. The legal system has the advantages of coerciveness, authoritativeness and seriousness, and the application of the legal system gives full play to the specialty of the legal system in the related fields where China must strengthen and promote green consumption. For example, China's current environmental degradation, basic subsistence resources (water, land, energy, etc.) are in short supply in many areas. Using legal system to regulate the green consumption of these basic survival resources can reduce consumption, reduce waste discharge and thus achieve the purpose of saving resources and protecting the environment. It is suggested to list the key areas and key lists of green consumption and formulate detailed green consumption management regulations on the basis of the investigation of the environmental impact of resources, environment, household income and waste discharge.

In terms of culture, the concept of green consumption is actively penetrated through advertising, film and television, conference and exhibition, celebrity and star activities and other Windows to promote green consumption culture. For example, international conferences, exhibitions, competition schedules and celebrity activities attracting worldwide attention should take advantage of this window to actively convey green consumption signals and establish a social culture advocating green consumption.

5.2   Incentives for Innovation

We will support innovation and development of green technologies. The underdevelopment of green technology is the fundamental reason for the limited supply and high price of green products. The government should encourage the innovation and development of green science and technology through various ways, such as providing financial support for green technology innovation of enterprises, preferential loans, tax breaks, capital subsidies and financing relaxation, etc. To provide human capital support for the green technology innovation of enterprises, such as providing opportunities for the scientific research personnel of enterprises to continue to study and further study, providing opportunities for the ordinary workers of enterprises to receive technical training, or directly providing certain economic subsidies to enterprises carrying out green technology training; The establishment of incentive system for green technology innovation, such as the establishment of a special patent protection system for green product enterprise innovation, and the granting of high rewards and other non-material rewards to enterprises that have achieved major technological innovation.

5.3   Organizational Strengthening

Establish a production organization system in line with the development of green enterprises. The production of green products is a collaborative process. Enterprises' fighting alone not only increases the innovation cost of enterprises, but also increases the risk of enterprises (industries) due to the too fragile production organization. Cultivating a strong and perfect green production organization system is one of the preconditions to promote green consumption. This requires: In terms of the upstream and downstream technology relationship chain of the industry, the industrial chain should be cultivated and improved according to the upstream and downstream cooperation relationship of the industrial chain. In terms of spatial layout and organization, regional agglomeration and park agglomeration should be appropriately promoted to promote the development of regional green production organizations and collaborative innovation. In terms of the relationship between enterprises, the leading role of enterprises, organizational role, internal self-supervision, industry standard formulation and implementation role should be played to encourage the formation of a sound supply chain organizational relationship.

5.4   Basic Guarantee

We will intensify reform of the asset management system in the resource sector. The green non-consumption behavior in China is related to the lag of the management system reform in the field of natural resources. For example, the one-sided understanding of the functional value of natural resources, the emphasis on economy over ecology, the emphasis on private use over public use, makes some of our country's natural resources that should be reserved for public use have also been developed and even completely exhausted. The state ownership income status is not implemented in place, leading to the sale of resources, which leads to the low price of resources and ultimately leads to the abuse, waste and other non-green consumption behavior. The unreasonable price comparison of various resources leads to the unreasonable consumption structure of resources and aggravates the further imbalance of China's resource structure. For example, the price ratio of primary resources and secondary resources is seriously unreasonable, which leads to the fact that people only pay attention to the exploitation of primary resources but neglect the recycling and reuse of recyclable resources, further aggravating the per capita shortage of resources and the pressure of waste disposal in China. In the future, we should further strengthen the reform of classified management of resource functional value, the reform of resource asset income and its distribution system, the reform of resource commodity price and fiscal and taxation system, so as to lay a foundation for green consumption in China.

5.5   *Management Improvement*

Actively improve the effectiveness of green consumption management: First, the extension of management objectives. It is no longer limited to the product quality management of private health impact, but expands to the social impact management and environmental impact management of private consumption. Second, the expansion of management means. Comprehensive use of a variety of means to manage, in addition to the traditional economic means and legal means, but also a comprehensive use of education and training, cultural communication and social demonstration means to promote green consumption. Third, expand the scope of management. No longer limited to the management of the consumption field, but the whole process of product consumption into the scope of green consumption management, from production to waste disposal to establish the product life cycle of green consumption management mode. Fourth, strengthen management. In particular, we should strengthen the green standard evaluation and certification system, production supervision system, market access and elimination system for various products and accelerate the circulation of high-quality green new products and the elimination of backward and fake green products. Fifth, improve management efficiency. In addition to the active participation of relevant government departments in management, relevant subjects in green consumption should be encouraged to participate in management to improve management efficiency. For example, consumers are the direct users of product quality and quality, and they are more concerned about product quality and safety than government personnel in some aspects. Therefore, consumers are encouraged to participate in the safety supervision of product quality and establish a product quality and safety supervision team including government departments, consumers, suppliers and social media.

5.6   Demonstration of Behavior

The government sets a good example by intensifying green purchasing. In terms of green consumption, apart from formulating various systems for effective standardized management, the government should also make use of its own identity as a consumer with huge influence to promote the development of green consumption by strengthening the procurement of green products and improving the government's green procurement system. The government may, on the basis of existing regulations, set technical standards, procurement proportion and procurement procedures for green procurement in various industries. Through competitive bidding, preferential procurement, long-term contract incentives and other forms, it encourages enterprises to increase the intensity of technological innovation, so that they become the top of the industry and compete for the government procurement suppliers, thus stimulating the innovation of green technology. In addition, the government should also strengthen the publicity of green procurement through various windows to demonstrate green consumption to the whole society.

REFERENCES

Fan Lianying. On the Construction of Recycling Society in Japan by Environmental Education. *Modern Japanese Economy*, 2005 (1): 61–64.
Zhang Zhimin. Investigation and Analysis of Green Consumption of Dongguan Residents. *Journal of Dongguan University of Technology*, 2011, 18 (4): 33–37.

CHAPTER 9

Science and Technology and Green Transformation and Development

1 Overview of Green Science and Technology

1.1 The Concept of Green Technology

In the face of global climate change, ozone layer problem, acid rain hazard, toxic and harmful chemical pollution and global ecological environment deterioration, the "green movement" since the 1970s, switching from the focus on resources, environment, ecology and other specific events, to focus on the way to solve the crisis, and the use of scientific and technological means to solve the crisis, has guided people to change the concept of resources, environment and ecology, promote the emergence and development of green technology. The idea of sustainable development put forward in *Agenda 21* formulated by the United Nations in 1992 laid the ideological foundation for the rise of "green technology".

Green technology is a production system and way of life that can promote human survival and development as well as corresponding science and technology. In essence, it is a scientific and technological system that can maintain the sustainable development of human society, emphasizing the rational development, comprehensive utilization, protection and proliferation of natural resources, the development of clean production technology and pollution-free green products, and advocating civilized, moderate consumption and lifestyle. Green technology is

© The Author(s) 2019
S. Gu et al., *Green Transformation and Development*,
The Great Transformation of China,
https://doi.org/10.1007/978-981-32-9495-0_9

the basic direction of the future of science and technology service for the society, also the inevitable choice of human toward sustainable development path. He Xiaoqing. *Research on Consumer Ethics.* Shanghai Sanlian Bookstore, 2007, page 72.

Green technology refers to technologies, products and services that can bring the same or greater benefits to users than conventional solutions. While reducing the negative impact on the natural environment, it can also maximize the efficient and sustainable use of energy, water and other natural resources. Green science and technology organization: *China Green Science and Technology Development Report 2013: China at the Crossroads.*

Green technology is the product of a new demand driven by the severe historical juncture of human survival and development. It is a new characteristic of contemporary science and technology development, reflects the theme of science and technology development, and is the key to achieve green development.

1.2   The Green Science and Technology Development

Technology develops with the exploitation and utilization of resources and the transformation of natural processes. Mankind's technological achievements in five key areas, including food production, metal extraction, smelting and forging, modes and means of transportation, modes and methods of energy production and use, and methods of communication and record keeping, occupy an important position in history. With the development of science and technology, the evolution of technology is becoming green (see Table 1).

Since the 1960s, with the increasingly serious environmental pollution and the emergence of environmental crisis, the rise of green tide, the improvement of people's environmental consciousness and the application of science and technology in environmental governance have promoted the innovation and development of environmental technology (see Table 2).

1.3   Composition of the Green Science and Technology System

The green science and technology system includes the green science and technology basic research system, the green science and technology application research system, the green science and technology

Table 1 Five important technology groups from 1750 to 2000

Type		1750–1820	1800–1870	1850–1940	1920–2000	Since 1980
Leading technology group	Energy	Water, wind, forage, wood	Wood, forage, coal	Coal	Oil, electricity	Gas, electricity
	Transportation	Communication toll road	Canal	Railway, ship, telegraph	Highway, telephone, radio, television	Highway, air transport
	Materials	Steel	Iron, puddle steel	Steel	Petrochemical products, plastics, steel	Aluminum alloy, special materials
	Industrial	Castings	Fixed steam engine, mechanized	Heavy machinery, chemicals, building materials	Flow factories, CNC machinery, consumer goods, pharmaceutical	Environmental technology, disassembly and recycling, consumer services
	Consumer goods	Textiles (wool, cotton, pottery) textiles	Textiles, pottery	Products diversification (import)	Durable goods, food industry, tourism customized products	Leisure vacation
Emerging technology group	Energy	Coal, coke	City gas	Oil, electricity	Gas, nuclear	Hydrogen energy (?)
	Transportation and communication	Canal	Mobile steam engine, telegraph	Highway and car, telephone, radio	Air transport, telecommunication, computer	Supersonic aircraft (?) high-speed train
	Materials	Steelmaking	Mass production of steel	Composite materials, aluminum	Custom materials, and composite	Recyclable and biodegradable materials
	Industry	Fixed steam engine propulsion plant, mechanical plant	Coal chemicals, dyes, building materials	Fine chemicals, pharmaceuticals, durables	Electronics, information technology	Services (software), biotechnology
	Consumer goods	Pottery and porcelain	Illuminators	Consumer durables, Refrigerator	Leisure and entertainment products, art	Integrated "package" (products and services)

Note The question mark indicates that this technology is emerging, but the trend is not yet fully clear
Source Sustainable Development Strategy Research Group, Chinese Academy of Sciences. 2010 China Sustainable Development Strategy Report: Green Development and Innovation Beijing: Science Press, 2010: 16

Table 2   Environmental technology innovation and development

Times	Innovation and development of environmental technology
1960	The end technologies characterized by the removal and resourcing of pollution
End of 1970s	A waste-free process characterized by rational utilization of resources
Mid-1980s	Waste reduction characterized by zero emissions
1990s	Clean technologies featured by energy saving, consumption reduction, pollutant discharge reduction and toxicity, and pollution prevention technologies featured by source reduction
Twenty-first century	A green technology system has been formed

Source Liu Ailing. Green Science and Technology and Sustainable Development. Beijing: Science Press, 2006

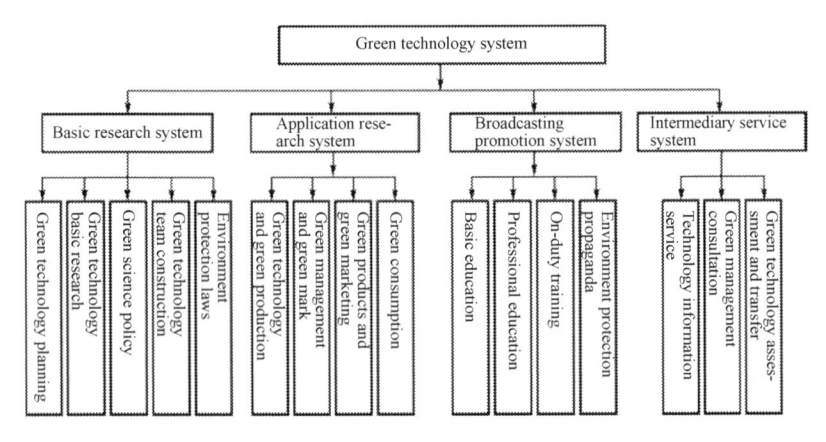

Fig. 1   Composition of green technology system

communication and promotion system and the green science and technology intermediary service system (see Fig. 1).

1.4   The Development of Green Science and Technology in China

Supported by the strategies of building a resource-conserving and environment-friendly society, saving energy and reducing emissions, and building an ecological civilization, China attaches great importance

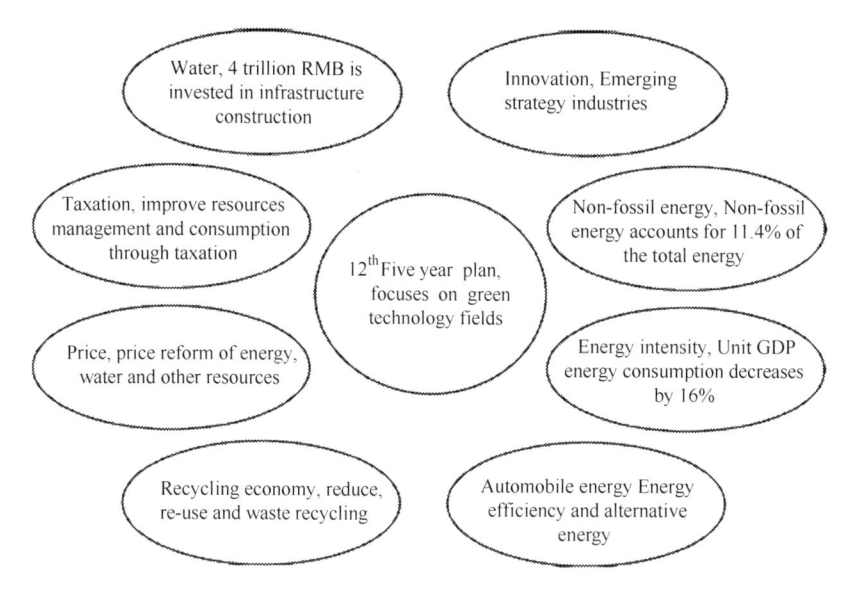

Fig. 2 Green science and technology fields in the 12th five-year plan for national economic and social development (*Source* China Green Technology. China Green Technology Report 2013-China at the Crossroads)

to the development of green science and technology. In the 12th five-year plan, China's major areas of concern include the development of non-fossil energy, technological innovation, the development of a circular economy, and the management of increasingly depleted natural resources (see Fig. 2).

China has increased investment in green science and technology. During the 11th five-year plan period, the national science and technology plan allocated more than 10 billion Yuan for research and development on energy conservation and emission reduction, allotted a total of 780 million Yuan to support scientific research in the public interest industry of environmental protection, and spent 11.266 billion Yuan on major science and technology projects for water pollution control and treatment. During the 12th five-year plan period, we increased fiscal investment in green science and technology. The central budget for investment in environmental protection was 22 billion Yuan, more than three times the 6 billion Yuan in the 11th five-year plan period. It plans to spend 34 million Yuan and 170 million Yuan annually on air pollution control between 2013 and 2017.

China has formulated strategies and plans in renewable energy, smart grid, strategic emerging industries, green buildings and new energy vehicles, effectively opened up the market for green technologies, promoted the development of green technologies and led the world in solar energy, wind energy, high-speed rail and other fields.

However, there is still a gap between China's overall level of green technology development and international development. According to the evaluation and ranking of China's technological level in major international reports, China's technological level is 68.4% of that of the United States, 9.5 years behind the international advanced level (see Table 3). Key technologies and integrated technologies for green development are still mainly imported, and their technological competitiveness is weak.

China is relatively under-invested in green technology. In 2013, the proportion of R&D expenditure in GDP was 2.08%, and the proportion of green technology expenditure in GDP was less than 0.7%, far lower than that of developed countries. Only 4.5% of enterprise infrastructure funds are used for green science and technology innovation. Some enterprises lack funds for innovation research, which hinders the development of green science and technology innovation.

The lack of effective green technology innovation mechanism. China lacks a green technology development strategy in terms of the green technology development system. The green innovation resources are scattered, the green standard and the sign system are imperfect, the green technology verification system is deficient, the green technology intellectual property rights protection system is imperfect and the green consumption incentive mechanism is imperfect and so on.

Table 3   Evaluation and ranking of China's technological level in major international reports

	National innovation index report	Global innovation index	The annual global competitiveness report	Global competitiveness report
Rating value	65.2	46. 57	73.26	4.89
Rank	19	29	23	28

2 THE DEVELOPMENT DIRECTION OF GREEN SCIENCE AND TECHNOLOGY

After more than 30 years of rapid development, China has achieved remarkable economic achievements and unprecedented prosperity. China has become the second largest economy in the world. Yet all this has come at great environmental cost. Over-reliance on coal means that increasingly affluent people are consuming more energy. The problems of air pollution, water pollution and soil pollution are becoming increasingly serious and resources are being exhausted. Based on the triple crisis of environmental pollution, resource shortage and ecological degradation, the ecological civilization formed by the reflection, sublation, adjustment and revision of the traditional civilization, especially the industrial civilization, is centered on resource conservation, environmental protection and ecological conservation.

2.1 Resource-Saving Green Technology

Resource conservation is the first way to break resource bottleneck and protect ecological environment. Water, land and mineral resources should be used economically and intensively.

"Water is the source of life, the basis of production and the basis of ecology". The per capita water resources in China are only 1/4 of the world average level, and more than 2/3 of the cities are seriously short of water, so saving water is an inevitable choice. It requires to develop and promote efficient water-saving technologies and technologies for recycling water resources.

Based on the strategic consideration of ensuring China's food security, protecting the precious cultivated land resources is related to both development and survival. Intensive land use technologies should be vigorously developed.

Energy conservation is not only a requirement for energy security, but also a requirement for reducing greenhouse gas emissions and improving air quality. It needs to promote research and development of major energy-saving technologies and equipment in high-energy-consuming industries such as electric power, iron and steel, building materials, nonferrous metals, chemicals and petrochemicals, and carry out research and development of technologies for the comprehensive utilization of energy at multiple levels.

Mineral conservation is the requirement of resource security. Research and development of efficient use of mineral resources technology, research and development of mineral resources to improve the recovery rate, mineral recovery and comprehensive utilization rate technology.

2.2 Environment-Friendly Green Technology

Environmental protection urgently needs to strengthen environmental protection and governance to significantly improve environmental quality. It is an inevitable choice for China to enter the ranks of middle-income countries, to adapt to the general improvement of "environmental consciousness" of Chinese citizens, to establish the image and status of China as a responsible major country, and to realize the peaceful rise of China. It needs to promote the development of biological resources and the production of gasoline, natural gas and hydrogen from biological resources, ecological fertilizers, and biological pesticides, and increase efforts to develop renewable and clean energy such as wind, solar, and nuclear energy.

2.3 Ecological Conservation Green Technology

Ecosystem is the foundation of human survival and development, and human is also an important part of the ecosystem. However, for a long time, the waste of resources, environmental pollution and ecological destruction have led to the decline of the structure, function and efficiency of forests, farmland, waters, towns and other ecological systems, which have seriously weakened the ecological system. Ecological conservation includes not only the protection of the ecosystem and its service capacity, but also the construction and cultivation of the ecosystem and its service capacity. We should promote research and development of technologies for reducing emissions in agricultural production, breeding and cultivation of high-yield and resilient crops, forest management, wetland protection and restoration, and desertification control, develop key technologies for restoring ecological functions and protecting rare and endangered species, and strengthen research on methodologies related to climate change in agriculture (forestry).

3 Key Areas of Green Science and Technology

3.1 Green Energy

Coal accounts for 66.0% of China's energy consumption, natural gas for 5.8%, and hydropower, nuclear power and wind power for 9.8%. In 2013, China's external dependence on oil and natural gas was 58.98 and 27.53%, respectively. Energy security is grim. According to the strategic action plan for energy development (2014–2020), energy development should adhere to the strategic principles of "saving, cleaning and safe" and accelerate the construction of a clean, efficient, safe and sustainable modern energy system. It requires to adhere to the four strategies of giving priority to conservation, based on domestic, green and low carbon, and innovation driven. By 2020, China will maintain its energy self-sufficiency at around 85%, with non-fossil energy accounting for 15% of primary energy consumption, natural gas accounting for more than 10%, and coal consumption within 62%. Energy technology mainly includes clean energy technology development and clean coal utilization technology (see Table 4).

3.2 Green Transportation

Transportation is a key area for energy conservation and emission reduction. By 2015, public service vehicles, railways and civil aviation must reduce energy consumption by 5% per kilometer and ships by 10%. Green transportation technologies mainly focus on improving the efficiency of fuel vehicles and developing non-fossil fuel ground transportation technologies and aviation technologies (see Table 5).

3.3 Green Buildings

In China, buildings account for more than 30% of total energy consumption. Heating and air conditioning systems with poor insulation, poor quality of building materials and high energy consumption are major contributors to low energy efficiency. So in the field of construction, we will give priority to research and development in technologies such as central heating, pipe network heat transfer, green buildings, flame-retardant and non-combustible energy-saving building materials, high-efficiency energy-saving doors and windows, clean stoves, green lighting,

Table 4 China's energy sector green science and technology development priorities

Key direction		Key green technology
Clean energy development technology	Nuclear power technology and fusion technology	Research and development of: the third- and fourth-generation emerging nuclear power technologies and nuclear waste disposal technologies, and continue to target the international cutting-edge nuclear fusion technologies
	Hydrogen utilization technology	Develop efficient, clean and low-cost hydrogen production technologies, high-capacity hydrogen storage technologies, low-cost and reliable fuel cell technologies, fuel cell power generation technologies, and fuel cell vehicle technologies
	The large-scale wind power generation and offshore wind power technology	Research and development of wind power control system, machine and blade design, new blade materials
	Solar thermal power generation technology	Solar thermal power generation mode mainly includes tower, groove and butterfly. Solar energy technology is mainly controlled by Germany, the United States, Spain and other countries; China is in the initial stage of research and development, in particular, needs to break through the Stirling system, low and medium temperature solar thermal function conversion technology, research and development of key equipment to reduce the cost of solar power generation technology
	Deep geothermal engineering	Technology research and development of large-scale enhanced geothermal systems (EGS) technology, breakthrough in deep geothermal resource definition and reserve assessment technology, development site selection technology, environmental assessment technology and mining technology, research and development of geothermal power generation cost reduction technology
	Second-generation bioenergy	Technology breakthrough in pilot plant, biological enzyme and catalyst technology, development of cost reduction and raw material supply technology
	Hydroelectric technology	Research and development of joint scheduling of water resources, ecological and environmental impact technology and research and development of cost reduction technology
	Smart grid, grid security and stability technology	Research and development of high-efficiency energy storage technology, sodium sulfur battery and liquid sulfur battery technology, breakthrough in superconductivity, flywheel and supercapacitor and other high technology

Key direction		Key green technology
Coal clean utilization technology	Ultra-supercritical power generation technology	Research and development of ultra-supercritical power generation technology including high-temperature materials and forging technology, research and development of ultra-supercritical power generation cost reduction technology
	The integrated gasification combined cycle power generation system (IGCC)	Research and development of integrated design regulation, large coal gasification and gas turbine technology
	Carbon dioxide capture and storage (CCS)	Research and development of carbon dioxide capture and storage technology, research and reduce the cost of using carbon dioxide capture and storage technology, etc. through carbon dioxide capture and storage (CCS) and international cooperation

Table 5   Priorities of green science and technology development in China's transportation sector

Key direction	Key green technology
Improve automobile fuel efficiency	Research and development and the introduction of engine technology, transmission system technology, vehicle light-weight technology and other traditional motor vehicle fuel saving and improve fuel efficiency
Hybrid vehicle technology	Research and development of strong mixing technology, energy recovery technology, matching and control technology, battery technology
Pure electric vehicle technology	Research and development of pure electric car battery, management system, integration technology, line transmission technology
New rail transit technology	Research and development of new linear motor rail transit technology and magnetic levitation train non-adhesive driving technology
Aviation technology	Research and development of aviation power integrated energy management, efficient general aircraft engines, aviation biofuels and other technologies
Marine traffic technology	Research and development of energy-saving ship technology

high-efficiency energy-saving air conditioners, and harmless disposal and resource utilization of sewage, sludge, household garbage and construction waste (see Table 6).

3.4   Green Manufacturing

Industry is by far China's biggest energy consumer. The six major energy-consuming industries include ferrous metal processing, nonferrous metal processing, petroleum, chemicals, electricity and building materials. In 2012, these six sectors accounted for 73.13% of total industrial primary energy consumption and 51.04% of China's total energy consumption. Priority will be given to the research, development, promotion and application of technologies for energy conservation and emission reduction, clean production and integrated utilization of solid waste in traditional industries such as iron and steel, nonferrous metals, cement and chemical industries (see Table 7).

Table 6 Priorities of green science and technology development in China's building sector

Key direction	Key green technology
The semiconductor lighting technology	Research and development of core technologies such as substrates and epitaxial production technologies and technologies that reduce drive costs
The building maintenance structure insulation technology	Research and development of various exterior wall and roof insulation technologies, technologies that reduce costs of external Windows and glass curtain walls
The regional cogeneration technology	Research and development of the technology of natural gas heating, electricity and cooling tri-generation, gas big power equipment with breakthroughs to improve the efficiency of power generation and reduce emissions, high density high conversion efficiency energy storage device and high efficiency of heat-driven air conditioning
The ground source heat pump technology	Research and development of ground source heat pump air conditioning system, etc.
The advanced ventilation and air conditioning technology	Research and development of Temperature and humidity independent control of air conditioning methods
The building energy management system	Research and development of intelligent, central management techniques for safety, air conditioning, lighting and ventilation, etc.

Table 7   Focus of green technology development in traditional manufacturing industry

Key direction	Key green technology
Iron and steel industry	Research and development of dry quenching technology, coal moisture control technology, residual heat and pressure recovery technology, gas-steam combined cycle power generation technology, new-generation coking technology, blast furnace waste plastic injection technology, melting reduction technology, direct steelmaking technology using microwave, arc and exothermic heating, advanced electric furnace, the third largest steelmaking technology
Cement industry	Research and development of new dry cement production process, waste substitutes for raw materials and fuels, new dry pure waste heat for power generation at low temperature, high efficiency grinding equipment and technology

4   GREEN SCIENCE AND TECHNOLOGY STIMULUS POLICY

Today, all countries in the world have taken green science and technology as the focus of scientific and technological development. In particular, the EU member states, the United States, Japan, the United Kingdom and other developed countries have formulated complete green science and technology systems and policies to promote the development of green science and technology.

4.1   The EU System and Policy on Green Science and Technology Development

The EU member states take measures from research and development to market, improve market environment, global action and future-oriented, establish rules and regulations to promote the development of green science and technology, and divide policies into four categories: command/control, information, market and hybrid, to strengthen the research and development, demonstration and promotion of environmental technologies (see Table 8).

4.2   Systems and Policies for the Development of Green Science and Technology in the United States

The United States has established a comprehensive system of systems and policies to promote the development of green technologies, including

Table 8 EU green technology system and policy

Field	Specific policy measure	Policy type
Research and development to the market	Strengthen environmental technology research, demonstration and promotion	Command/control type
	Establish a technical platform	Information type
	Establish a European network for environmental technology testing, performance certification and standardization	Information type
	To develop the EU environmental technology classification database and catalog	Information type
	Ensure that new standards and revision of standards take resource and environmental performance into account	Command/control type
Improve the market environment	Establish performance standards for key products, processes and services	Command/control type
	Use financial instruments to share investment risks in environmental technologies	Market type
	Public–private partnership	Market type
	Explore new business areas	Market type
	A policy tool for promoting the development of renewable energy and energy efficiency technologies	Mixed type
	Measures to support the development of ecological industries	Mixed type
	Promote socially and environmentally responsible investment	Market type
	The spread of the best practices of financial institutions	Market type
	Identify opportunities for integrating environmental technologies	Information type
	Examine the standards by which structured funds operate	Market type
	Review national aid guidelines	Command/control type
	Internalization of environmental costs through market tools	Market type
	Eliminate environmentally harmful subsidies	Market type
	Facilitate the purchase of environmental technologies	Market type
	Promote full life cycle cost and accounting	Information type
	Technology purchase survey	Information type
	Raise business and consumer environmental awareness	Information type
	Provide pertinent training	Information type
Global action	Help improve environmental technology in developing countries	Market type
	Promote responsible investment and use of environmental technologies in developing countries and countries with economies in transition	Market type
Future-oriented	Review the action plan regularly	Command/control type
	European commission for environmental technology	Information type
	Open coordination approach	Information type

Source Sustainable Development Strategy Research Group, Chinese Academy of Sciences. 2014 China Sustainable Development Strategy Report. Beijing: Science Press, 2014

Table 9 US green technology regulations and policies

Research and development	The EPA research and Development office	Supports all EPA projects in environmental technology
	Department of Energy: national laboratory	Laboratory system administered by the Department of Energy
	National research and development program	Technology incubator, national research and development investment fund, clean energy fund, technology certification for California public interest energy research program
Technical certification	Council on environmental quality	Technology platform, climate change technology platform, intelligent highway transportation partners, hydrogen fuel program
	Environmental protection bureau	Environmental technology verification project
Environmental performance standards and legislation	National regulations	Energy independence and security act, clean water act, clean air act, green jobs act, corporate average fuel economy regulations
	Environmental protection bureau	EPA national environmental performance tracking
	Energy policy regulations	Federal renewable fuel standards, home appliance/lighting minimum efficiency standards
	Voluntary criteria	Energy star, natural star
	Energy efficiency of Federal facility	Energy policy act, executive order No. 13423
Financing	Energy policy regulations	Energy policy act, renewable energy tax credits
	Biofuel	Bioethanol gasoline tax reduction and exemption
Marketing tool	Federal trading policy	Leaded gasoline emissions trading, sulfur emissions trading, water rights trading policy
	Subsidies	Subject to relevant WTO standards

Procurement	National procurement programs	Environmental responsibility procurement programs, vehicle and fuel standards
	Energy policy regulations	Federal agency energy consumption reduction goals, improving energy efficiency at federal facilities, and solar energy development
	Institutional projects for green innovation	National center for environmental innovation, environmental performance tracking
Improve the environment awareness and training	Environmental education	Environmental education programs implemented by the environmental protection agency, the North American association for environmental education
	Government departments: oceanic administration and environmental protection bureau	Coordinating international policies on environment and science
Global action	International development agency	Responsible for and implements international environmental projects
	Technical agreements	Asia-pacific partnership, methane marketization, futurism, global nuclear energy partnership, renewable energy and energy efficiency partnership

Source Sustainable Development Strategy Research Group, Chinese Academy of Sciences. 2014 China Sustainable Development Strategy Report. Beijing: Science Press, 2014 research and development, technology certification, environmental performance standards and legislation, financing, market tools, procurement, environmental awareness and training, and global action (see Table 9).

5   ESTABLISH AND IMPROVE THE INCENTIVE MECHANISM FOR R&D, PROMOTION AND APPLICATION OF GREEN TECHNOLOGY

5.1   Establish and Improve Green Standards and Labeling Systems

Guide all sectors of industry, universities and research institutes to jointly promote the study, formulation or update of important national green technology standards. Promote the internationalization of China's green technology standards and seize the right to speak on international green technology by setting internationally or domestically advanced standards. Promote the legalization of green label and energy efficiency standard procedures, improve the green label certification procedures and truly demonstrate the advantages of obtaining green label products and energy efficiency label products in environmental performance at all stages of the whole life cycle. Give preferential policies in finance, finance and taxation to enterprises with green marks and support the implementation of the green mark system.

5.2   Establish a Green Technology Verification System

The composition of the green technology verifier. The verification of green technology shall be carried out with the joint participation of the verification and evaluation institutions, expert groups, technology holders and other parties. The verification and evaluation institution shall be responsible for making verification plans, carrying out verification and preparing verification reports. The expert group shall be composed of industry experts corresponding to the verification technology and shall be responsible for reviewing technical documents and making suggestions; the technical holder shall submit the verification application and cooperate with the verification work.

Establish a technical verification center. According to the classification characteristics of green technologies, verification institutions of different types shall be established, including environmental protection technology verification center, energy conservation and emission reduction technology verification center and ecological conservation technology verification center. The environmental protection technology verification center conducts technical verification in clean production, pollutant monitoring, pollution control and other aspects, and the energy conservation and emission reduction verification center conducts technical verification in renewable energy, clean energy, energy conservation, low carbon and other fields.

Develop supporting green technology validation procedures. In order to ensure the scientific and standardized verification system, it is necessary to formulate supporting guidelines, procedures, standards and norms for green technology verification, and gradually integrate them with international standards.

5.3   Establish a System for Protecting Intellectual Property Rights in Green Technologies

Strengthening the protection of intellectual property rights is the basic institutional guarantee for promoting China's independent innovation in green technology and the creation, application, protection and management of independent intellectual property rights, and improving China's future competitiveness of green industry and developing rights and interests.

Establish the green technology patent classification number. With reference to the international patent green technology classification index of the world intellectual property office, China's green technology patent classification number is established in combination with China's green technology development priorities and actual conditions to guide innovation subjects to carry out green technology innovation. In the conditions of granting patent rights, the requirement of "greenness" should be added, and "greenness" should be taken as one of the conditions of patent authorization. At the same time, in some areas of technology that may have a significant impact on resources and environment, the "green standard" of technology is studied and established as a compulsory standard of patent authorization.

Build a green intellectual property public service platform and green technology patent database, provide international green technology patent dynamic information, and green key technology and product patent retrieval, analysis and early warning services to enable technology demand sides and the public to easily retrieve interested green technology patents from IP sites.

Focusing on the development needs of the industry, we will explore various ways to provide practical services, guide market players to strengthen the use of patent information and promote the transformation and application of patents.

5.4   Green Technology Preferential Tax Policies

Strengthen the exploration, improvement, promotion and implementation of tax incentives and management mechanisms for scientific research, such as pre-tax deductions and tax credits, so that research and development tax incentives become effective and universal incentives for enterprise innovation.

Timely adjust the incentive focus of preferential tax policies. It will focus on the production and sales of high-tech products in the tax incentives, and gradually shift to the development of tax incentives and intermediate experimental links; The incentive focus of preferential tax policies will be shifted from encouraging the introduction of foreign advanced technologies to enterprises' independent scientific and technological innovation, so as to reduce the risks and uncertainties of independent scientific and technological innovation and promote enterprises to form a sound scientific and technological innovation cycle mechanism.

Enterprises engaged in the research, promotion and application of green science and technology innovation shall be exempted from various taxes. The reduction and exemption of enterprise income tax for the research, promotion and application of green science and technology is mainly based on the reduction and exemption of tax, supplemented by the reduction and exemption of tax. As long as enterprises carry out green technology research, promotion and application activities, they can become the target of tax incentives. Tax relief is an ex-post facto preference, favoring the direct transfer of benefits. Encourage enterprises to research, promote and apply green science and technology, and gradually improve the competitiveness of Chinese enterprises in green science and technology. Accelerate depreciation of machinery and equipment for green technology research and development. Enterprises engaged in the research and development of green technology, or the key equipment purchased by enterprises for the implementation of green technology research and development, shall independently choose the depreciation period according to the nature of green technology projects. In order to speed up the green technology research equipment update and technological progress of enterprises, it is necessary to simplify procedures in the approval and practical operation of accelerated depreciation, shorten the depreciation period, increase the depreciation rate and reduce the capital cost.

The green technology innovation reserve is exempt from income tax. This allows enterprises to set up various green technology innovation reserves, such as risk reserves, technology development reserves, trial production reserves for new products and loss reserves, in proportion to their sales or operating income, which are used for research and development, technology update and other aspects, and these reserves are deducted before income tax, so as to stimulate enterprises' enthusiasm for green technology innovation.

Introduce preferential policies for the personal income tax of green science and technology personnel. First, the individual income tax is reduced or exempted for the green technology transfer fee and green technology patent fee. Second, the individual income tax will be exempted for all kinds of bonuses and special allowances obtained by researchers for their special achievements or contributions in green technology research and development activities. Third, the equity gains from green technology investment by R&D personnel, including dividends and transfer income, shall be exempted from individual income tax.

5.5 Establish a Green Technology Innovation Investment and Financing Mechanism

Financial input. The government provides financial support to policy-compliant green science and technology research, promotion and application projects through budget allocation, so as to enhance the initiative of green science and technology research, promotion and application.

Loan preference Policy-based financial institutions set up green science and technology loans to provide low interest and interest-free preferential loans for all links of green science and technology research, promotion and application, so as to solve the problem of insufficient funds for green science and technology activities.

Green tech venture capital. A large amount of decentralized funds in the society will be gathered to realize capitalization and provide financial support for green science and technology activities.

Government purchases. For green technologies and green products applicable to the public sector, the government will purchase them directly, apply them to social public undertakings, give full play to social benefits and promote the initiative of green science and technology innovation.

5.6   Establish a Procurement System for Green Scientific and Technological Achievements

Implement a government procurement system that promotes independent innovation in green technologies and includes energy saving and emission reduction products, low-carbon products and other green technology products in the list of products that the government is obliged to purchase under the *Government Procurement Law*. The connotation, implementation subjects, standards, lists and procedures of green technology products are be clearly defined at the legislative level, so as to ensure that the rights and obligations of all purchasing parties can be guaranteed and restrained by law. The legal system of government green procurement and formulate supporting implementation rules and specific measures should be built and improved, make it clear that the government procurement priority to choose domestic high-tech equipment and products with independent intellectual property rights, determine the proportion of green technological innovation products in government procurement and ensure the appropriate scale.

5.7   Set Up an Investment Fund for Green Technology Innovation

While the government provides subsidies and increases investment, it gathers social funds to participate in green technology innovation activities, reduces risks for research and development enterprises, improves capital allocation efficiency, speeds up the process of achievement transformation, and improves industrialization.

CHAPTER 10

New-Type Urbanization and Green Transformation and Development

1 The Unsustainability of the Traditional Urbanization Model

Urbanization refers to the development of industrialization accompanying the development of society. It is a historical process in which non-agricultural industries continue to cluster in cities and towns, rural population continues to transfer to non-agricultural industries and towns, rural areas transform into urban areas, the number and scale of cities and towns increase, and urban production and lifestyle and urban civilization continue to spread and spread to rural areas. Urbanization plays a positive role in economic and social development. In the process of urbanization, it has realized three structural changes. First, the industrial structure has been transformed economically. The primary industry with low efficiency is gradually replaced by the secondary industry and the tertiary industry with high efficiency. Secondly, the spatial structure of settlements has been transformed. The scattered and sparse rural village structure has been replaced by the concentrated and compact modern urban structure, greatly improving the land use level. Thirdly, with the transformation of social demographic structure, as a large number of rural population turns into urban population, the urban production and lifestyle and urban civilization gradually replace the traditional rural production and lifestyle and rural civilization. However, modern and contemporary world history shows that the process of urbanization is

S. Gu et al., *Green Transformation and Development*,
The Great Transformation of China,
https://doi.org/10.1007/978-981-32-9495-0_10

not always a civilized, beautiful and good process. Improper urbanization will also cause a series of problems in economy, society, resources and environment, among which the problems in resources and environment are particularly prominent, which is the fundamental reason for the unsustainable urbanization.

1.1   Main Features of the Traditional Urbanization Model

One-Sided Emphasis on Single Economic Growth
Sound urbanization development is the comprehensive development of economy, society and ecology. However, China's urbanization development over the past decades only emphasizes quantifiable and measurable economic growth. Under the GDP-oriented performance appraisal system and the local government-led urban development model, the development of a city is often simply and roughly understood as the city's economic aggregate, growth rate, non-agricultural industries and foreign investment. However, the development of population itself and the protection of resources and environment are understood as a kind of "ornament" existence, which is placed in an insignificant and dispensable awkward position. For example, the housing problem in China's big cities is a typical manifestation. The government relies on a large number of land sales and the development of real estate industry to maintain the rapid economic development of the city. But a large number of residents are burdened with the heavy pressure of mortgage and plagued by haze. Such a mode of urbanization development puts the cart before the horse for people. The graduates' escape from the big cities of "Beijing, Shanghai and Guangzhou" can be seen as a rejection of the development mode of putting the cart before the horse and a sign of the unsustainability of this development mode. Taking the green space in urban environmental construction as an example, although the urban green space area of China has increased somewhat (see Fig. 1), compared with developed countries, China still has a lot of gaps. The per capita green space area of many developed countries is in the range of 20~40 square meters, up to 60 or 70 square meters. For example, the per capita green space in Washington, United States and Stockholm, Sweden has reached 50 and 80 square meters, respectively, while the per capita green space in Chinese cities is only 12.2 square meters. In terms of urban green coverage rate, the green coverage rate of major cities in the United States

is about 60%, while the average green coverage rate of built-up areas in China was 39.6% in 2012. In 19 provinces (autonomous regions and municipalities directly under the central government), the green coverage rate is lower than the average, with the highest in Beijing (46.2%) and the lowest in Gansu (30.0%) (see Fig. 2). It can be seen that China's urban construction in the green construction debt is serious, it is urgent to make up lessons.

Extensive and Wasteful Urban Space Expansion
In the process of urbanization, the spatial expansion of a city is a natural process. Many foreign cities emphasize a compact and efficient spatial layout and smart and comfortable urban growth based on limited urban land and time and resource conservation. However, many cities in China have extensive management of urban land expansion and pursue a kind of "spreading the cake" type space expansion and spread, which not only causes waste and strain of precious urban land, but also brings trouble to people's green travel. It is reflected in: (1) there is a serious mismatch between urban land expansion and population growth, and land urbanization is much faster than population urbanization. Statistics show that in the 10 years from 1990 to 2000, the urbanization rate of land was 1.71 times faster than that of population, and from 2000 to 2010 it was 1.85 times faster than that of population, far higher than the normal 1.12 times. In 2000, the urban built-up area of China was

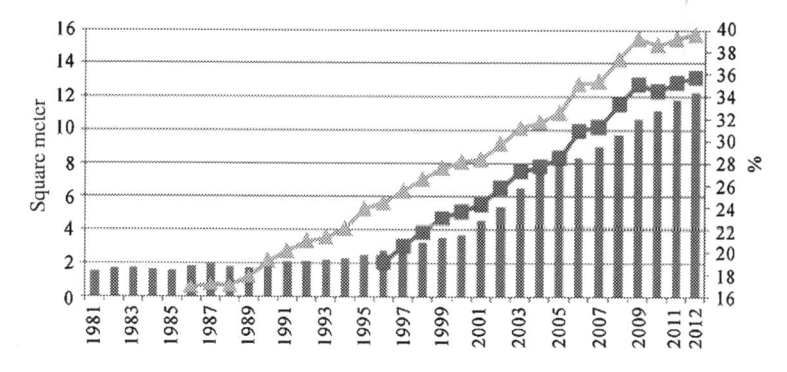

Fig. 1 Per capita green area of parks and green coverage rate of built-up areas in Chinese cities from 1981 to 2012 (*Data source* China urban construction statistical yearbook 2013)

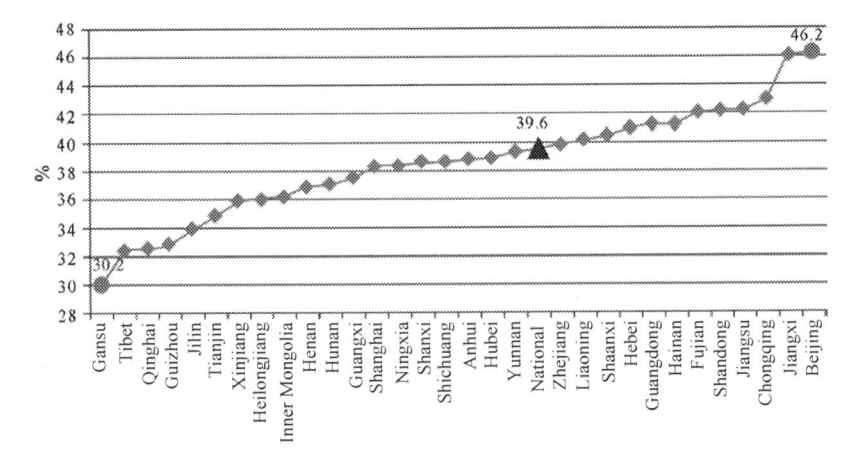

Fig. 2 Green coverage rate of built-up areas in all provinces (autonomous regions and municipalities directly under the central government) in 2012 (*Source* China regional economic statistics yearbook 2013)

22,439.28 square kilometers, which expanded to 38,107.30 square kilometers in 2009. From 2001 to 2009, the average annual growth rate was 7.76%, while the average annual growth rate of urban population was only 3.94%. (2) The average size of cities expands rapidly and grows extensively. From 1996 to 2008, the average built-up area of each city in China increased from 30.4 square kilometers to 55.4 square kilometers, and the average construction area of each city increased from 28.5 square kilometers to 59.8 square kilometers, an increase of 82.2 and 109.8%, respectively. (3) The one-sided emphasis on quantitative expansion in the development of new cities seems that the bigger the better. Many new areas in big cities cover hundreds of square kilometers, and some even cover thousands of square kilometers. It seems that the bigger the better, there is no smart growth concept. The same is true for all kinds of park construction. Under the background of accelerating catch-up and leapfrogging development, all levels of cities in our country, whether it is the construction of new industrial parks or the expansion of old industrial parks, are making efforts on the planning area, emphasizing on the of "number" and "size". Some are even as high as hundreds of square kilometers. There is little concept of resource conservation, especially land resource conservation. For example, in 2005, the planned area of various types of development zones in China reached 38,600 hectares, 1.5 times the area of urban built-up areas in China. After clearing and rectification, the total area is still over 10,000 hectares.

Extensive Growth with High Consumption and High Emission
Urbanization inevitably consumes resources, but China's urbanization is an extensive growth process, which is characterized by high resource consumption, high waste discharge and high environmental load. Since 1978, China's energy consumption has increased dramatically (see Fig. 3), and it has always accounted for a large proportion in the world.

In 2010, China's cement consumption nearly tripled to 1.851 billion tons in 2004, accounting for 56.2% of the global total. Steel consumption accounted for 44.9% of global consumption. In terms of energy consumption, China's primary energy consumption accounted for 19.5% of the global total in 2009, including 46.9% for coal and 10.4% for oil. China's energy intensity was three times that of the United States and five times that of Japan in 2010, according to data released by the China energy research association. On the other hand, high consumption of resources is accompanied by high discharge of pollution, garbage and harmful substances. In the process of urbanization in China, urban sewage and urban garbage grow rapidly (see Figs. 4 and 5), which far exceeds the load range of urban environment and leads to serious deterioration of urban ecological environment. China's carbon

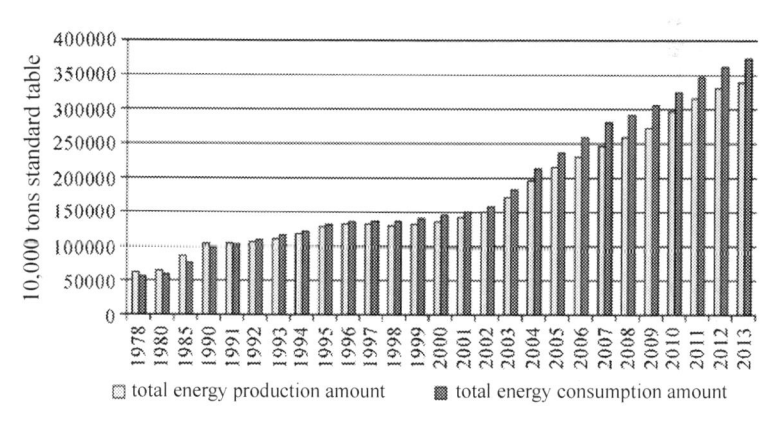

Fig. 3 Total energy production and consumption in China from 1978 to 2013 (*Source* China statistical yearbook 2014)

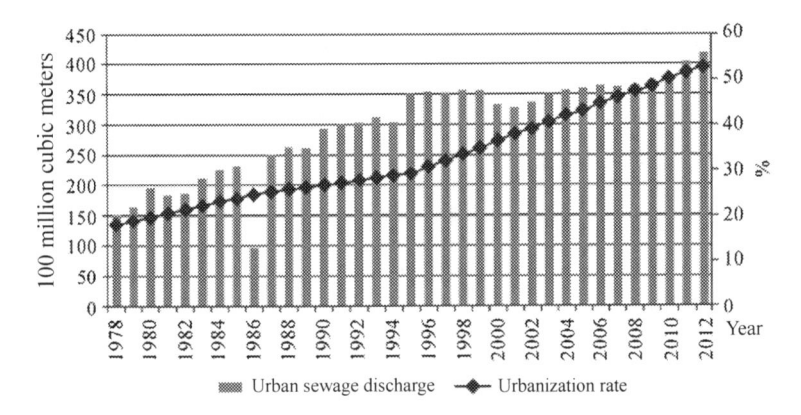

Fig. 4 China's urbanization and urban sewage discharge from 1978 to 2012 (*Data source* China urban construction statistical yearbook 2013)

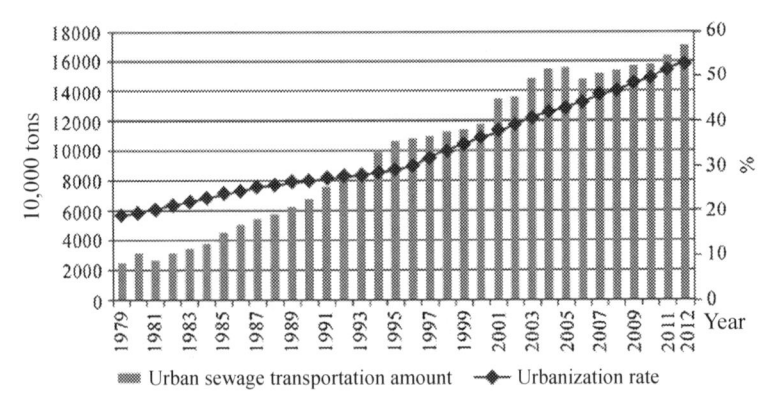

Fig. 5 China's urbanization and urban garbage clearance volume from 1979 to 2012 (*Data source* China urban construction statistical yearbook 2013)

dioxide emissions accounted for 21% of the world's total emissions in 2007, according to a report released by the international energy agency. Carbon dioxide emissions per unit of GDP were 3.16 times the world average and 5.37 times that of OECD countries. China's resources and energy consumption are mainly concentrated in urban areas. In 2009, among China's terminal energy consumption, public transportation industry and urban living consumption accounted for 85.2%. In the domestic energy consumption, urban areas accounted for 61%, and the per capita energy consumption in urban areas was 1.83 times that in rural areas. According to the data provided by the international energy agency (IEA), in 2005, 41% of the urban population in China generated 75% of the primary energy demand, which is in contrast to the developed countries. On the one hand, it reflects the huge gap between urban and rural areas in China. On the other hand, it also shows the extensive characteristics of high consumption and high emission in Chinese cities.

1.2 Resource and Environmental Crisis of Traditional Urbanization Mode

Increasing Resource and Environmental Constraints

The rapid urbanization in China is based on a large amount of consumption of land, water resources, energy, raw materials and other resources. As a result, the contradiction between supply and demand of resources is increasingly intensified, which has become a hard constraint for the development of urbanization. For example, China's total water consumption and per capita water consumption have remained high in recent years (see Fig. 6), and the domestic water consumption in cities is in a rigid demand state, but the total water supply and water supply capacity of cities are stagnant in terms of the supply of urban water resources (see Fig. 7). According to the statistics of water conservancy department, among more than 660 cities in China, there are more than 400 cities that are short of water, among which 114 are seriously short of water. There are 71 cities in the north and 43 in the south with severe water shortage. Even in the water-rich Yangtze River basin, there are 59 water-deficient cities and 155 water-deficient counties. There are only 10 provinces and cities in China that are not short of water, accounting for less than 16% of the country's land area. Severe and extreme water scarcity areas accounted for more than 60% of the country's land area. If divided by the number of cities, the number of cities lacking water accounted for 2/3 of the total number of cities in China, which restricts the sustainable development of Chinese cities. For another example, in terms of energy supply, China's energy gap continues to expand (see Fig. 8). In 2013, the gap between energy supply and demand reached 350 million tons of standard coal, and the energy abundance was −9.3%. As a result, China's energy external dependence continued to rise: In 2009, crude oil imports exceeded the 200 million tons mark, breaking

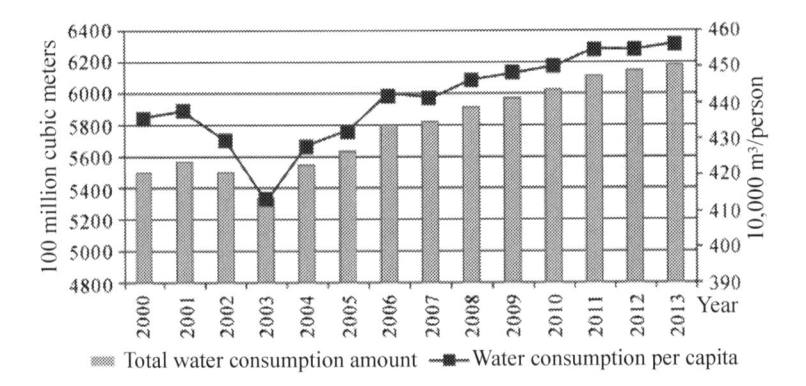

Fig. 6 Total and per capita water consumption in China from 2000 to 2013 (*Data source* China statistical yearbook of relevant years)

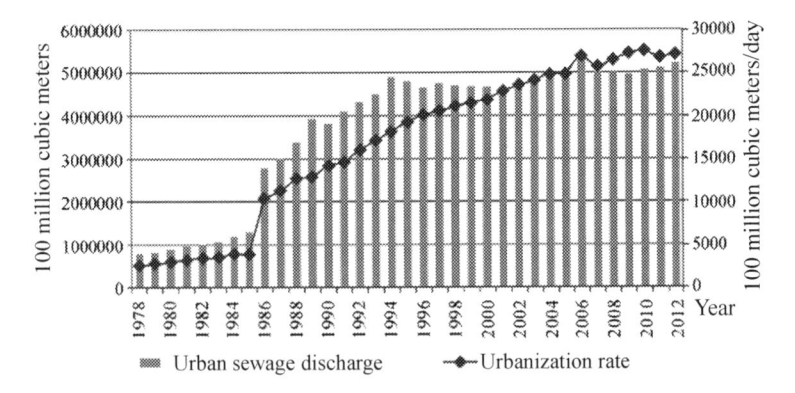

Fig. 7 Urban water supply in China from 1978 to 2012 (*Data source* China urban construction statistical yearbook 2013)

the 50% warning line for the first time. In 2011, it exceeded 250 million tons, but by 2013, it had exceeded 280 million tons, reaching 282 million tons, and its dependence on crude oil reached 58%. Not only that, it also paid a huge price in the economy, increased the cost of our country's development and weakened the international competitiveness of our industry. For example, China's crude oil import amount was less than 100 billion US dollars in 2009, rising to 196.66 billion US dollars in 2011, and reached 219.65 billion US dollars in 2013. There is also a crisis in the supply of urban land. Due to extensive land use, the quality of cultivated land in China has been sharply reduced, and the quality

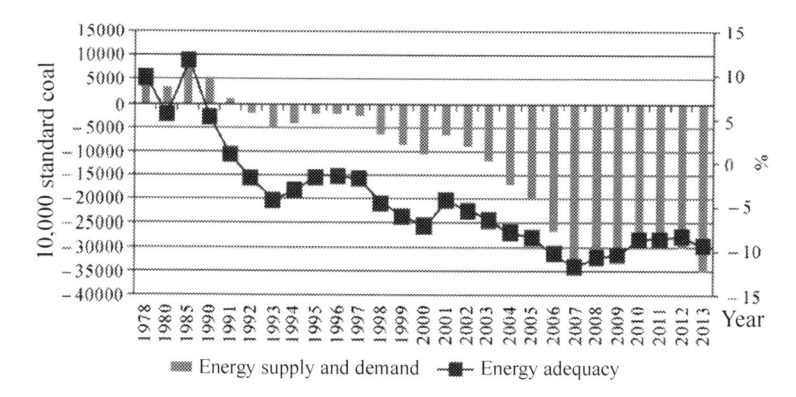

Fig. 8 China's energy supply and demand gap from 1978 to 2013 (*Data source* China statistical yearbook 1979–2014)

of cultivated land has been reduced. In order to ensure food security and other basic land needs, the supply of urban construction land has been limited. In short, extensive economic growth and irrational use of resources have wasted a large amount of precious natural resources, severely weakened China's ability to guarantee resources and environment for subsequent urbanization, and become an important prerequisite for the development of urbanization.

The Ecological Living Environment in Urban and Rural Areas Continues to Deteriorate

The traditional urbanization mode of extensive utilization of resources not only consumes a large amount of precious natural resources, but also produces a large amount of waste, pollutes the ecological environment and aggravates the deterioration of the ecological environment. It not only directly leads to the deterioration of urban ecological environment, but also damages the ecological environment of the vast rural areas with the increase and transfer of pollutants. The overall ecological and living environment in urban and rural areas continues to deteriorate, which is not optimistic. (1) The city is filled with a large amount of waste and harmful and toxic substances. In 2010, China's annual urban waste production reached 158 million tons, and the annual growth rate of 8~10%, per capita annual output reached 440~500 kg, some big cities increased by 15~20%. At present, China has accumulated nearly 8 billion tons of municipal solid waste, occupying 800,000 mu of land. About 2/3 of large and medium-sized cities in China are surrounded by garbage, and about 1/4 of them have developed into the predicament of no suitable place for stacking garbage. The "garbage siege" trend has become, and will become more and more intense. Urban air quality is poor, PM2.5 concentration is generally high, and haze weather is becoming more and more frequent. According to the newly revised *Environmental Air Quality Standards* in February 2012, two-thirds of the cities in China have substandard air quality. The pollution in big cities is worse than that in small cities. At the end of 2008, the country's 113 key environmental protection cities alone accounted for 59.3% of the country's wastewater emissions, 47.5% of chemical oxygen demand emissions, 49.4% of sulfur dioxide emissions, 55% of nitrogen oxide emissions and 44.8% of soot emissions. (2) The ecological regulation system of the city itself is constantly damaged. Wetlands and groundwater are important ecological regulation systems of cities, and they are the "immune system" to maintain the healthy development of urban resources and environment. However, China's urbanization does not pay much attention to the protection of these "immune systems". In the process of urbanization, the area of urban wetlands in China decreases sharply and the biodiversity continues to decrease. Especially, due to excessive artificial intervention, urban wetlands are often divided into small areas, broken habitats and isolated patches, and the wetland habitats are often damaged. However, due to the over-exploitation of urban groundwater, the ground subsidence accelerates, and the ground water level in many cities and towns in north China, northwest China and east China continues to decline. Some areas have already seen regional geological disasters such as ground subsidence, cracks and seawater intrusion and other ecological and environmental problems. More than 50 cities across China have suffered from land subsidence disasters (see Table 1), especially in the north China plain, with land subsidence exceeding 200 mm reaching 64,000 km^2, accounting for about 46% of the whole north China. On the other hand, the discharge of waste water also pollutes the groundwater and threatens the safety of drinking water. From 1991 to 2011, the discharge of urban sewage increased by 37.4%, while the discharge of county sewage increased by 84.1% from 2001 to 2011. At present, nearly 20% of urban sewage, 30% of county sewage, and most of the sewage in the established towns were not effectively treated and directly discharged into rivers, lakes and seas, resulting in serious water pollution and threats to the safety of urban drinking water. According to statistics, 54% of the water quality in functional areas nationwide is

Table 1 List of cities with serious land subsidence in China

City	Tianjin	Shanghai	Cangzhou	Suzhou	Changzhou	Wuxi	Tangshan	Jiaxing	Fuzhou	Ningbo	Zhanjiang	Nantong
Sedimentation/m	2.78	2.7	1.131	1.056	1.05	1.0	0.801	0.75	0.679	0.45	0.413	0.3
Area/km²	1300	850	–	150	200	100	1100	600	–	120	–	–

Source Fang Wujun, Ding Feng, Ge Pingtao, et al. Land Subsidence Caused by Groundwater Overdraft and Its Solution. *Science and Technology Information Development and Economy*, 2008, 18 (26): 205–206, 208

substandard, 90% of the groundwater is polluted, 64% is seriously polluted and 67.8% of the rivers are polluted, accounting for about two-thirds of the monitored river length. (3) Urban garbage and pollution tend to spread to the countryside. Taking urban solid waste as an example, data analysis shows that before the mid-1980s, the unit emission of urban solid waste in China was generally greater than 0.1 m^2/t. Since then, due to strict occupation of farmland and increased investment in comprehensive recycling and utilization, the area of waste per unit emission has been reduced to 0.09 m^2/t. In spite of this, the land occupation of solid waste in cities and towns still exceeds 60,000 hm^2. Most of these solid wastes are distributed around large- and medium-sized cities, which, together with other household wastes, continuously erode the farmland around the cities and threaten the local landscape ecology and water environment. (4) The health of urban and rural residents is seriously threatened. Severe weather such as smog aggravates the outbreak of lung cancer and other diseases in big cities. According to the monitoring data released by Beijing municipal health bureau in November 2012, the incidence of lung cancer in Beijing increased from 40.29 in 2001 to 62.68 in 2010, with an average annual growth rate of 2.4%. However, some small- and medium-sized cities, especially some industrial, mining and heavy industry cities, have neglected pollution control and environmental protection in the process of urbanization, leading to the emergence of "cancer villages" and other terrible phenomena in some towns and villages. It is estimated that there are about 459 "cancer villages" in China, and the phenomenon is gradually spreading to the Central and Western regions. In a word, the traditional urbanization model has produced various problems in terms of resources and environment. The next 20 to 30 years will be the period of rapid urbanization in China. If the urbanization model still follows the past thinking, it will bring more serious problems and the traditional urbanization model must be changed.

2   THE CONNOTATION OF GREEN DEVELOPMENT OF NEW-TYPE URBANIZATION

New-type urbanization is an open concept, which is defined differently by different scholars and research perspectives. However, no matter which definition is used, it is believed that the new urbanization is the reflection and transcendence of the traditional urbanization model, the overcoming of its various disadvantages and a relatively advanced urbanization model. In terms of resource and environmental protection, it is reflected in resource conservation, environmental friendliness, ecological civilization and the improvement of human survival and development environment. Because of this, the new urbanization is also a kind of green urbanization. For example, Chinese scholar Zhang Zhanbin believes that the connotation and characteristics of the new urbanization path are mainly summarized in four main aspects: First, industrialization, informatization, urbanization and agricultural modernization should coordinate and interact, promote the integration of industry and city through industrial development and scientific and technological progress, and realize the urban-rural development driven by green urbanization has the basic cities and towns as well as the urbanization of the continuation of rural civilization. Second, we should coordinate population, economy, resources and environment, advocate an intensive, smart, green and low-carbon development mode, build a beautiful China with ecological civilization and realize the sustainable urbanization of the Chinese nation. Third, build a city pattern that is closely connected with regional economic development and industrial layout. Take urban agglomeration as the main form, coordinate the development of large, medium and small cities and small towns, improve the carrying capacity of cities and show the urbanization of Chinese culture, civilization and confidence. Fourth, achieve all-round development of the people, build inclusive and harmonious cities and towns, reflect the orderly citizenization of the migrant agricultural population and the coordinated development of public services and commit to the urbanization of a harmonious society and a happy China. There are four aspects in the second aspect: First, the population, economy, resources and environment should be coordinated to highlight the overall and balanced development. Second, it needs to fully integrate the concept and principles of ecological civilization into the whole process of urbanization, highlight resource conservation and ecological environment friendliness, and demonstrate intensive, smart, green and low-carbon urbanization. Third, build a beautiful China with ecological civilization, realize the harmonious coexistence between man and nature, develop ecological economy and ecological products, and contribute to global ecological security. Fourth, achieve sustainable development of the Chinese nation, highlighting intergenerational equity and sustainable development. Green urbanization has the basic characteristics of low consumption, low emission, efficient and orderly. It is a new type of urbanization model that combines intensive urban development with green development, coordinates urban population, economy, resources and environment, saves resources, reduces carbon emissions, is environmentally friendly and is economically efficient, and embodies the scientific concept of comprehensive, coordinated and sustainable development.

The author believes that the green development of new-type urbanization is not only reflected in the above aspects, such as resource conservation, low-carbon emission reduction, environmental friendliness and economic efficiency, but also in the harmonious ecological livable environment and life support. To be specific, in terms of resource conservation, it is embodied in saving water, land and ore, etc. The use of resources no longer focuses on the quantity of input, but on the connotation and repeated use. In terms of low-carbon emission reduction, the city layout is compact, the energy structure is reasonable, environmental protection materials are widely used, and the emission of toxic and harmful substances is greatly reduced. In terms of environmental friendliness, the concept of environmental protection is prevalent, and the environmental protection industry is developed. Industrial development and human behavior reflect the protection of the environment. In terms of economic efficiency, resources can support economic and social development. However, resources are used to the best of their ability, which is reflected in less waste and more efficiency. In terms of ecological livability, urban construction is no longer targeted at GDP growth, but a people-centered urban construction mode with people's own development as the goal. In the urban construction, people's health, comfort, convenience, safety and other aspects are reflected everywhere. In terms of life support, people are not only regarded as the core and the main body, but also as a whole between people and various creatures in nature. Cities are not only regarded as an economic carrier, but also as an important organism of nature. We should actively open up various channels for communication and contact between cities and natural ecological organisms, build ecological cities, and turn cities into a new and important ecological organism.

3   FOREIGN PRACTICAL EXPERIENCE IN GREEN URBANIZATION

3.1   The Development Process of Green Urbanization in Foreign Countries

The international research on the development of green urbanization has a long history, which can be divided into three periods.

First, the green urbanization theory was in its infancy (before 1920s). As early as ancient Greece and Egypt, the important idea of urban construction is to consider the location, form and layout of a city according to its environmental factors. In 1898, the British scholar Ebenezer Howard proposed the idea of building Garden Cities in *Tomorrow: A Peaceful Path to Reform* and *Garden Cities of Tomorrow*. The core idea was: The layered design of the city, centered on the central park and supporting public buildings, radiates around and builds garden houses. The outermost part of the city is the industrial zone, which is separated by more than 1 m of avenue between the industrial zone and the residential zone to ensure the environmental quality of the residential zone. This idea of urban construction played an important enlightening role in the later ecological planning of urbanization, which can be regarded as the beginning of modern green urbanization. Later, Patrick Geddes developed Howard's idea in *Cities in Evolution* that urbanization should follow natural environmental conditions and plan and build cities according to ecological principles.

Second, the development and improvement period of green urbanization theory (1920s–1970s).

This period was characterized by the introduction of ecological thoughts into urbanization, the formation and development of urban ecological theories, and the widespread influence of urbanization. Under the influence of Howard's idyllic city thought, the urbanization development planning began to introduce ecological thought and gradually systematize it, and urban ecology was established and developed. In 1933, the *Outline of Urban Planning* (hereinafter referred to as the outline) formulated by the Congrès International d'Architecture Modern (CIAM), namely the Charter of Athens, began to introduce ecological thinking into the urbanization process. According to the outline, urban expansion devours the scenic green zones around it, alienates people from nature, further threatens public health and deprives people of the right to be nourished physically and mentally. Therefore, the primary responsibility of urban planning is to meet the most basic physiological and psychological needs of human beings. Starting from the four major activities of human's residence, leisure, work and transportation, "introducing nature into the city" should be considered in the overall influence of the city. Regional planning should replace simple administrative planning, and the boundary of urban aggregation should be determined by its economic influence scope. The *Outline* has a broad and far-reaching influence. It has not only achieved considerable development in research, but also reflected the importance and response to the ecological development of cities in many important documents. In terms of research, in 1952, R. E. Park, a representative of the Chicago school of human ecology, published city and human ecology, advocating the creation of urban ecology, studying urban environmental problems and improving the ideological system of city and human ecology. In 1977, American scholar B. J. L. Berry's "contemporary urban ecology" systematically discussed the origin, development and theoretical basis of urban ecology, and systematically analyzed the spatial structure, dynamic changes and formation mechanism of urban population in the process of urbanization, thus forming the ecological research foundation taking the city as the object. In terms of important documents, in 1971, the "Man and the Biosphere" (MAB) research plan formulated by UNESCO put forward 14 research projects, of which the 10th project was "the impact of engineering construction on man and his environment", and the 11th project was "ecological problems of urban systems focusing on energy utilization". This is a reflection of the research on urbanization from the perspective of ecology, and the direction of urbanization research is determined to be ecology. In 1972, the declaration of the United Nations conference on the human environment pointed out that human settlement and urbanization must be planned to avoid adverse effects on the environment, and to achieve the maximum benefits from the three aspects of society, economy and environment for everyone. It clearly expressed that the development of urbanization should deal with the relationship between the environment, economy and society. The above shows that the eco-city theory has achieved unprecedented development. Here, the city is considered as a part of the natural ecological green system, and urban planning should build the city itself as an important organic ecosystem.

Third, the comprehensive practice period of green urbanization theory (since 1980s).

During this period, the green ecological concept of urbanization was further developed from theory to practice, and the idea of green city construction penetrated into all aspects. Especially in the 1990s, green development became the mainstream. In the process of urbanization, green ideas were promoted in an all-round way, from focusing only on green planning to permeating into green production, green circulation, green consumption and green culture in an all-round way. In 1981, the Soviet union city ecologist O. Yanitsky proposed the ideal model of eco-city, in which technology and nature are fully integrated, human creativity and productivity are maximized, and residents' physical and mental health and environmental quality are protected to the maximum extent. Although the current reality is not very operable, this concept contains the yearning for a better city life and puts people-oriented and green development at the top of urban development. In 1987, Richard Register, an American ecologist, argued in *Ecocity Berkeley—Building Cities for a Healthier Future* that eco-city is a compact, energetic, energy saving and harmonious living place with nature, which reflects the idea of attaching importance to the harmony between environment, human and nature in the development of urbanization. In 1990, the urban ecology organization, which was organized and initiated by Richard Register, held the first international conference on ecological cities in Berkeley, putting forward the goal of reconstructing cities in ecological principles and improving the principles of ecological cities in 1996. These principles reflect the idea of emphasizing green and environmental protection. For example, the resource consumption and total amount of waste in cities should be much less than the current level of cities; choose green travel mode; give priority to the development of compact, green and safe mixed land use communities; advocate recycling, adopts new and excellent technology and resource protection technology; and reduce the discharge of pollutants and dangerous goods. In 1993, T. Domnski believed that the development of cities should follow the three-step pattern, that is, reduce, reuse and recycle. This is often referred to as the "three r's" principle, which embodies the green ideas in production, circulation and consumption. In 2002, the fifth international conference on eco-cities issued the *Shenzhen Declaration on Eco-City Construction*, which defined how to build an eco-city, including ecological security, ecological health, ecological industry metabolism and ecological landscape integration. These contents reflect that the urban construction reflects the concern for people everywhere, and puts green ecology at the center of urban construction, which greatly promotes the green construction of the city. This declaration has become a concrete action plan to guide countries to build eco-cities. In a word, the construction of eco-city in this period changed from idea to action and started comprehensive exploration and active practice.

3.2   The Practice Mode of Green Urbanization in Foreign Countries

From the practice of green urbanization in the world, the path of green urbanization development is not smooth. It can be said that it is to solve the problems of resources and environment in urbanization, and it is a reflection, inspection and transformation of the traditional urbanization model. For example, in the accelerated process of urbanization in the UK, serious air pollution incidents occurred in London and other places. The large-scale development of suburbs in the United States leads to the continuous expansion of urban land, resulting in traffic congestion, environmental damage, loss of traditional culture and a series of other problems. Due to water pollution, the United States once closed 11,270 lakes and beaches nationwide. In the process of rapid urbanization in Brazil, the construction of supporting facilities has not kept up with the rapid development, resulting in serious garbage siege and slum problems. In the course of Japan's urbanization, serious environmental pollution problems, such as mad hatter's village, minamata disease, itamata disease, asthma and nuclear pollution, which once shocked the world. In recent years, India's cities have been expanding rapidly. Due to the shortage of environmental infrastructure, serious "urban diseases" such as environmental pollution, environmental recession, slums and urban poverty have also been brought about. In this way, in order to cope with various environmental problems in the process of urbanization, many countries have begun to explore a new green urbanization model featuring green, low-carbon and sustainable development.

In the practice of green urbanization, all countries adopt corresponding models and practices according to their own characteristics and main problems (see Table 2). Among them, although the UK started to implement the idyllic city concept proposed by Howard as early as the beginning of the twentieth century, it was not until 2007 that the UK really started to build eco-town nationwide. It was initiated by British Prime Minister Gordon brown at that time. He attached great importance to promoting environment-friendly technologies to protect the environment and control carbon emissions and consider the use of public transportation and reduce the use of private cars in the stage of town planning; promote sustainable communities; focus on the storage, collection, treatment, classification and reuse of garbage; reasonable use of construction waste in the construction process, to achieve zero waste emissions in the construction process. The United States combined the pre-Second World War American urban design concept with modern environmental protection and energy-saving design principles, and promoted the new urbanism and "smart growth" model. It advocates the

Table 2 Foreign models of green urbanization development

Country	Model	Features	Major practices
UK	Ecological low-carbon green city Construction mode	(1) The concept of "garden city" and "idyllic city"; (2) long history of green buildings; (3) balance urban and rural regional development; (4) comprehensively promote the construction of ecological towns; (5) social equity and justice, and a sound social security system; (6) the treatment of "urban disease" is relatively successful; (7) planning and legislation to correctly guide the development of urbanization	(1) Simultaneous development of urbanization in the industrial revolution; (2) scientific planning and guidance for overall planning of urban construction; (3) strict control of carbon emission standards; (4) lay a solid foundation for agriculture and coordinate urban and rural development; (5) pay attention to rural industry and intensify the construction of urbanization; (6) develop green transportation and attach importance to urban green space management
United States	(1) Ecological sustainability and "smart growth" concept of cities; (2) compact mode of land use	(1) Modern environmental protection and energy-saving design, scientific management, the management idea and the mode are operable; (2) the large-scale expansion of suburbanization in the United States after World War II; (3) set up special ecological sustainable research institutions; (4) coordinate regional development and attach importance to coordination	(1) Build ecological towns with local characteristics; (2) to create a residential environment with humanistic care and intensive use of land suitable for walking; (3) improve the quality of life, pay attention to the short-term and long-term ecological integrity; (4) delimit "urban development" to curb excessive development; (5) advocate the mode of public transportation and walking; (6) emphasize ecological design in new urban construction and restoration; (7) promoting circular economy projects and resource recycling

(continued)

Table 2 (continued)

Country	Model	Features	Major practices
Australia	High public participation and the concept of eco-city community	(1) Attach importance to the construction of sustainable green transport and promote sustainable rural urbanization; (2) attach importance to investment in environmental protection and build a green and environment-friendly town; (3) Resource cycling use	(1) Strengthen the coordination and investment of public transportation construction; (2) through price reform, the urban construction increases the green space in a large number; (3) promoting renewable resources and energy, sustainable water use and sustainable building technologies; (4) formulated feasible environmental planning, urban planning, energy planning and climate protection planning
India	(1) Green revolution; (2) population explosion and central city agglomeration pattern	(1) The metropolitan and the neighborhood form lasting space gathering; (2) The economy, society and system all show characteristics of rural; (3) The transferring speed of rural population to the urban is slow in India; the level of urbanization is only 30%	(1) Supporting urban infrastructure to increase development momentum; (2) ensure the realization of "greening construction" requirements in urban planning; (3) implement strict pollution prevention and control policies; (4) give priority to the development of public transportation and the controlled use of motor vehicles; (5) focus on the development of large enterprises
Japan	"East Asian model" of centralized urbanization	(1) Export-oriented development strategy; (2) spatial agglomeration mode with big cities as the core; (3) low-carbon life; (4) merging of town and village	(1) Attach importance to the formulation of environmental strategies, and environmental protection is the forerunner of urbanization; (2) accelerate the construction of ecological industrial park; (3) low-carbon construction; (4) urban expansion and urban and rural population flow and transfer, timely merger of town (town) village

Source Dong Zhanfeng, Yang Chunyu, Wu Qiong, et al. Research on the Strategic Framework of China's New Green Urbanization. *Ecological Economy*, 2014, 30 (2): 79–82, 92 construction of a residential environment with humanistic care, intensive land use and walkability, and promotes the sense of local belonging.

Natural and cultural resources protection, community planning for equitable distribution of development costs and benefits, community design, community development and community revitalization. The United States attaches great importance to legislative norms, and has proposed 27 new urban development principles in the form of the charter, supplemented by the government's guidance to achieve green urbanization. Urbanization in Australia has strengthened urban green planning, increased green space, promoted renewable energy and promoted the reuse of resources. India, on the other hand, has adopted strict pollution control measures and green construction requirements in response to the random and disorderly development in the surrounding development of big cities, and has taken measures to control, reduce and eliminate pollution by prioritizing the development of public transportation and large enterprises and increasing supporting infrastructure in cities. Japan is vigorously promoting the construction of ecological cities and towns across the country, the main methods including advocate low carbon life concept, popularize low carbon technology, lead people to choose low carbon goods, such as the government introduced a policy of "green point", namely, when consumer is buying energy-efficient appliances can get a share of the green points, which can be used to buy other energy-saving appliances. Japan also vigorously promotes low-carbon construction technology to achieve low-carbon construction.

3.3 International Experience and Inspiration of Green Urbanization

The international experience of green urbanization can be summarized as follows: First, it is necessary to have clear problem orientation and feasible pursuit goals. Green urbanization is the substitution and transcendentation of the traditional urbanization model. As a transformation model of urbanization, it must clearly identify the problems to be solved, overcome the disadvantages of traditional urbanization and formulate feasible goals and implementation plans. Second, individuality, innovation and difference. Although the main problem to be solved by green urbanization is the construction of resource and environment problems and life support system in urbanization, the specific conditions of each city are different and the main problems to be solved are also different. Therefore, the path and content of green urbanization are also different. For example, for the same green transportation construction, some promote bicycles, some develop bus network system, some carry out equal planning and some focus on the development of big cities. Third, green urbanization is always combined with low-carbon environmental protection, resource conservation, circular economy and life support. Third, green urbanization is always combined with low-carbon environmental protection, resource conservation, circular economy and life support. Fourth, extensive public participation. Green urbanization is an activity that requires the participation of the whole society. No matter from the formulation of planning plans to the actual construction process, or the follow-up supervision and control; specific measures are required to ensure the broad participation and support of the public. Fifth, the perfect legal policy and the management system. Green urbanization not only needs to rely on sound laws and regulations to force the implementation, but also needs the support of science and technology to ensure its implementation in a sound management system.

4   PRACTICES AND OBSTACLES IN THE GREEN TRANSFORMATION AND DEVELOPMENT OF URBANIZATION IN CHINA

4.1   The Practice of Green Transformation and Development of Urbanization in China

The practice of green transformation development of urbanization in China started late, and it was not until the ninth five-year plan that it gradually received national attention. Although there is no systematic strategic consideration for green urbanization at the national level and relevant special policy documents are issued, a series of practices related to green urbanization have been carried out in a scattered way, aiming at preventing and controlling serious ecological and environmental problems in the process of urbanization. At the national level, the national development and reform commission, the ministry of housing and urban–rural development, the ministry of finance and the ministry of environmental protection have introduced a series of related policies, actively promoted green ecological construction, including supporting the construction of green ecological urban areas, subsidizing green buildings, promoting building energy conservation, carrying out urban pilot demonstration, issuing or updating the relevant norms and standards, etc. By carrying out some advanced benchmarking and demonstration activities for ecological environment construction, they promoted the pilot exploration of green urbanization in pilot areas to accumulate experience and give play to demonstration effect. For example, the ministry of housing and urban–rural development has cooperated with local governments to carry out pilot projects of low-carbon ecological provinces and cities. By April 20, 2012, a total of 83 cities in China had established national model cities for environmental protection. 15 provinces, including Hainan, Jilin, Heilongjiang and Fujian, have launched ecological province construction. More than 1000 counties (cities and districts) have built ecological counties, and 38 counties (cities and districts) have built state-level ecological counties. A total of 1559 towns and townships were built into state-level ecological towns and townships. The Ministry of Environmental Protection (MEP) has initiated pilot studies on overall urban environmental planning in Fuzhou, Jiaxing and other cities. In recent years, the spontaneous exploration of green urbanization in local areas has also been accelerated. Zhejiang province has put forward the strategy of building green cities and towns, focusing on developing green buildings, building low-carbon cities and towns and creating humanistic characteristics of cities. Guizhou province has issued the national first green small town construction evaluation standard *Green Small Town Construction Evaluation Standard of Guizhou Province*, which plans to build 30 provincial demonstration small towns and 70 city-level (autonomous prefecture) demonstration small towns through pilot projects. Hunan province put forward the idea of green development throughout the whole process of new-type urbanization construction to realize the green rise. In addition, many cities, such as Dalian, Beijing and Hangzhou, have begun to pay more attention to ecological and environmental protection in their overall urban planning. In general, China's green urbanization practice is currently mainly in the stage of "top-down" promotion of pilot demonstration and "bottom-up" spontaneous exploration. These practices and explorations have initially shown the concept of ecological civilization and provided good experience for the extensive promotion and implementation of green urbanization strategy.

4.2   Obstacles to the Green Transformation and Development of China's Urbanization

The Objective Existence of Regional Development Gap

The Environmental Kuznets Curve indicates that the economic development in urbanization has a regular relationship with material resource consumption at a certain stage (see Fig. 9). That is to say, in the early stage of urbanization, the economic development level is low and the environmental pollution is relatively light. Then with the accelerated development of urbanization, economic growth and development are accelerated, the intensity of environmental damage is also enhanced, and the environmental quality deteriorates to different degrees. However, after the economic development reaches a higher stage, the intensity of environmental damage declines, and the environmental quality tends to improve with the economic growth. In spite of this, different urbanization models have different resource consumption intensity, and the material consumption intensity of intensive development model is significantly lower than that of extensive and natural evolution model.

China's urbanization practice also shows that in recent years, with the economic strength of developed eastern coastal areas increasing, citizens' desire to pursue a good ecological living environment becomes more urgent. Local governments, on the other hand, "give in" to

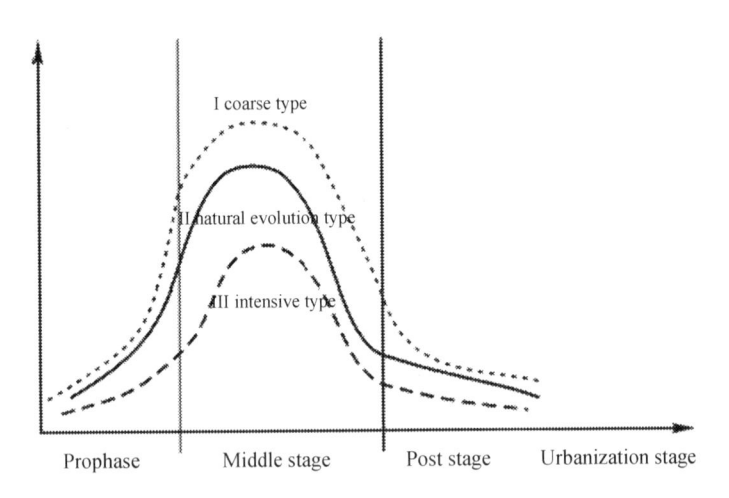

Fig. 9 Relationship between urbanization and material consumption intensity

citizens' pressure for environmental protection and "go with the flow". On the other hand, they have strong financial support from the government. Besides, promoting environmental governance can also give birth to environmental protection industry and cultivate new highlights of regional economy. Therefore, it is positive and effective in environmental governance, such as the environmental governance and environmental protection industry development around Taihu Lake in China. However, China's regional economic development is very uneven. There are still a large number of backward and poverty-stricken areas in the Central and Western regions, which are backward in economic and social development and have relatively low urbanization. In the future, the accelerated development of these areas is bound to increase environmental pressure, which is the objective resistance to the green transformation of urbanization.

The Reform of Resource and Asset Management Lags Behind
On the surface, the direct cause of the extensive use of resources in China is the low price of resources and resource products. But the fundamental reason is that the reform of China's resource asset management lags behind. The constitution stipulates that most natural resources belong to the state, and the state is the main owner of resource assets, while the state-owned natural resources adopt the principal-agent management mode. Some are delegated to corresponding ministries and commissions, while others are delegated to local governments, which in turn adopt a multi-level model of delegated and entrusted management. Thus, all natural resources of the state are managed separately by ministries and commissions and governments at all levels. More seriously, in the process of marketization, China's reform in the field of resources and assets lags behind, and is still affected by the past planned economic system. The ownership of resources is indistinguishable from the administrative right of resources and to some extent the executive power of resources wrongly replaces the ownership of resources. This leads to the sideline of the state as the owner of resources, the loss of the income of state-owned resource assets and the incomplete composition of the total cost of resources, which leads to the excessively low prices of resources and resource products in the market. Taking mineral resources assets as an example, China's mineral resources were allocated without compensation before the mid-1980s, but began to be used with compensation after the mid-1980s. The form of paid use is the collection

of resource compensation fees, resource taxes and paid mining rights in recent years. The compensation for resources is the state's past geological exploration input. In the resource market, the state should obtain the value-added income of capital input, and not just compensate for the past geological exploration input. Resource tax is a kind of tax, which is the income obtained by the government without compensation by virtue of administrative power, and it is not the income of the state as the owner of resource assets. In addition, these two charges are very low, the average rate of resource compensation is only 1.18%, and it has been canceled recently. The royalty rate of foreign countries equivalent to China's resource compensation is generally 2~8%, and that of the United States and other market economy countries is more than 12%. Compensation rates for some resources are even higher, ranging from 10 to 16% for petroleum, natural gas and mineral resources. Although the resource tax has been linked to the resource price after several reforms, it cannot reflect the purpose of the paid use of state-owned resources and the management of state-owned resource assets due to the weakness of the resource industry itself and the impact of the fluctuation of the market price of resource products. In terms of paid acquisition of mining rights, the proportion of paid acquisition through bidding, auction and listing is still relatively low. According to incomplete statistics, only 20,000 out of 150,000 mining enterprises have paid acquisition of mining rights through market mechanism, and the remaining 130,000 mining enterprises have paid acquisition of mining rights through administrative allocation. According to another survey, there are about 126,000 mining rights in China, and about 70,000, or 55.6%, of the state-funded mining rights are occupied free of charge. Therefore, the income status of the state as the owner of mineral resources assets is still not fully implemented. In addition, the environmental rights of Chinese citizens have not been clarified for a long time, and the environmental rights and interests violated in resource development have not been compensated. In this way, the total cost of resource production, which should be composed of the rent paid to the owner of the country, the compensation (governance) cost of resource development environment, the direct cost of resource production, the government fees and other parts, is saved from the rent paid to the owner of the country and the cost of resource development environment, which is the fundamental reason for the low price of resource products in China. Taking land resources as an example, China's constitution stipulates that urban land belongs to the state, and the state can expropriate collective owner's land for the need of public interest, while the state-owned land in each city is managed by the local government. Therefore, local governments have a lot of power to decide on the use of land. In pursuit of the total GDP, land management, real estate development and other utilitarian thinking, local governments tend to expand the scale of land, and have a very weak sense of land conservation. But the expropriated land is abused due to the low compensation of land. Therefore, in order to realize the green transformation of urbanization, China should not only reform the prices of resources and resource products, but also improve the resource property rights at the source and strengthen the management of resource assets.

The Subject of Urban Management Mode Is Single

The distribution of power in China's traditional society is "great officials, tiny people", and the power is highly concentrated in the government. Since the reform and opening up, local government is the leading force of regional economic development and the main body of urban management. Local governments manage cities with their own advantages and indispensable management power, but cities are an open ecosystem, and environmental problems have strong externalities. Therefore, the management of urban environment depends not only on the government, but also on the full cooperation of the general public. In the past urbanization development, local government officials were aware of the existence of environmental risks to varying degrees in their development decisions based on the GDP scale and their own pursuit of promotion, appointment and dismissal. However, from the perspective of interest distribution and risk bearing, it was a more rational choice for them to prioritize economic development. In this mode of urban management, it is not difficult to understand the development thinking of "economy before environment". It is precisely because the city management power is highly concentrated in the local government, even if there is a problem, it may escape the accountability due to the promotion or relocation of officials, so that the long-term environmental risks of urbanization show a state of accumulation or even continuous outbreak. Although the system of resource and environment audit and lifelong accountability for outgoing officials has been gradually implemented, it still remains a single subject of urban management. Governance is different from management, which is top-down and emphasizes authority and obedience, while governance is interaction, dialog and consultation, communication and cooperation between the top and the bottom. The practice of green city development abroad shows that the sustainable urban development mode is a kind of urban governance mode with the participation of multiple subjects, especially the citizens' economic participation. For example, in the preparation of the green infrastructure planning guidelines for the northwest region of the UK, it was realized at the beginning that the construction of environmental assets involves multiple interests and needs to fully mobilize the enthusiasm of all stakeholders. Therefore, the development partners were first identified to emphasize their coordination of the interests of the most important investors, and the local public interests were evaluated to maximize the public interests and reduce the implementation resistance. As a result, this green infrastructure planning and construction achieved great success. Another example is Portland, Oregon, which is a typical sustainable city in the United States. It was listed as the top 50 green cities in the United States by *Popular Science* magazine in 2008. Its green city planning and construction take from the citizen stratum, from bottom to top mode, citizen's active participation has played an important role. For example, let all citizens have the opportunity to participate in the process of traffic planning, express their interest demands and finally promote the formation of ecological traffic system planning and energy saving and efficiency of traffic. However, multi-subject participation in green city management itself is a gradually developing and mature democratic development process. For China, it is difficult to change the government-led, top-down and single-subject urban management mode in a short term. Without a good official assessment mechanism and performance evaluation system, resources and environmental protection will still be in a marginal position, which is also one of the difficulties in the green transformation and development of urbanization in China.

Support and Restriction of Green Science and Technology Strength
The development of green urbanization needs not only ideological renewal, but also solid scientific and technological strength. From the perspective of green city development abroad, green cities and towns need to make major breakthroughs in urban space planning, green transportation, green buildings, green energy, waste management and other key areas of green development and also need to make corresponding reserves in terms of talents, capital and materials. What's more, they need to constantly explore, practice and improve their management systems. However, the concept of green transformation and development has

not been popular in China for a long time. The development of green science and technology in energy, transportation, construction, waste disposal and other key fields is relatively backward. Many green management systems have just been established and are not mature and perfect, which restricts the development of green urbanization in China. Taking garbage treatment as an example, Japan, Germany, Denmark and other countries have improved garbage classification, recycling, and tax collection, while China's urban garbage classification management has not been thoroughly implemented even in economically developed big cities. Taking energy use as an example, China's energy structure is mainly based on coal, and the urban energy in the north is even more dependent on coal. However, China's coal cleaning is restricted by technology, cost, safety, economy and other aspects.

5 China's Urbanization Green Transformation Development Ideas

5.1 The Specific Legalization of the Concept of Green Development

In recent years, the construction of "ecological city", "green city", "low-carbon city", "livable city" these terms is frequently reported in the network, why not put into action? There are two key points: One is the lack of concrete operational research on how to implement it and the second is the lack of a mechanism to impose constraints on the key subjects of implementation. Then the future solution is also two aspects: First, strengthen research on key areas of green urbanization, especially on specific operational links. For example, to strengthen the study of various resource conservation standards, such as (energy saving, land saving, water saving, etc.), sewage standards (waste water, waste gas, waste residue, etc.), green standards (per capita park area, green coverage rate of built-up areas, etc.), standards for the use of materials and tools (green building materials, green furniture, green transportation tools, etc.), waste disposal standards (sanitary landfill, high-temperature composting, incineration). According to relevant laws and regulations, formulate operational standardization management system to make it real, concrete implementation. The second is to strengthen the key influential subject of a strong constraint. These main bodies mainly include government officials in charge of local urban construction departments (for example, urban construction department, resource department, environmental protection department, health department, etc.) and enterprises in related industries (such as real estate industry enterprises, energy industry enterprises, transportation industry enterprises, building materials industry enterprises, chemical industry enterprises and printing and dyeing industry enterprises, etc.), which are subject to strengthened constraints. Government departments mainly strengthen their sense of regulatory responsibility and supervision dereliction of duty accountability system. However, relevant enterprises need to combine the standard of "greening" of the industry with their actions to force some enterprises to update production technology or directly withdraw from the industry, so as to ensure the "green" support of green urbanization.

Although green urbanization can be made from green (space) planning, green energy, green transportation, green building, green coverage and other aspects, but the specific situation of each town is different, the focus of "greening" and the conditions available for "greening" are also different, so the choice of green path is also different. As a matter of fact, the international green city construction and management practice also shows that green urbanization is more of a way to break through than a comprehensive attack for each specific city. For China, a country with a vast territory, large differences in natural conditions between the south and the north, and large gaps in regional development between the east and the west, green urbanization should not only set basic baseline standards for green development, but also encourage differentiated and individual development. For example, for the regions in the eastern coastal region with a relatively high level of economic development, incentive policies should be formulated to encourage the development of their green industries. On the one hand, it should promote the industrial transformation and upgrading in a timely manner; on the other hand, it should provide technological progress and material support for the green transformation and development of other backward regions through the development of their green industries. The Central and Western regions, which need to accelerate urbanization and industrialization, are encouraged to upgrade traditional industries and pursue energy conservation and low-carbon development. Cities in the south, where the temperature is higher all year round and do not need to rely heavily on traditional fossil energy, are encouraged to change their lifestyles, make full use of renewable energy and optimize the energy structure. For the northern cities, clean and economical use of traditional fossil energy is encouraged to improve energy efficiency. In short, regional differentiation should be taken into consideration in green urbanization, and the exploration of green urbanization in various cities should be encouraged. Besides some mandatory green baseline standards, the choice and exploration of green development path should be respected.

5.2 Scientific and Systematic Management of Resources and Assets

First, implement classified management of resource assets. In view of the fact that the benefits of some natural resources are shared by all and should not be owned by individuals, the public welfare natural resources assets and operational natural resources assets should be strictly distinguished. The former is strictly prohibited from circulation in the private sector, ensuring that its public value (such as national security value, ecological value, genetic value, esthetic value, scientific research value, educational value) is shared by most people. For the latter, on the premise of not hindering its public value, it can enter the private circulation conditionally, but its negative effects should be strictly controlled through sound system. In new-type urbanization, the first step of urban planning is to identify and determine public welfare natural resource assets, carry out special protection for them and strictly limit their private interests such as operation and development.

Secondly, perfect the property right management of resource assets. At present, the ownership of state-owned natural resource assets is very clear, but the right of use and management need to be further set up scientifically. For example, the public welfare natural resource assets mentioned above need to clarify the right of use, supervision and management participation of the public, while the government needs to clarify the management obligation and the management power it can exercise. As for the state-owned operational resources and assets, the ownership is clearly owned by the state at present, but the rights of use, disposal and revenue need to be further clarified and improved. For example, state resources must be paid for, and must comply with the provisions on the protection of ownership. The power of local government and relevant ministries and commissions in resource and asset management should be clearly defined and standardized. The agent of the ownership of resource assets must faithfully fulfill the escrow obligation, and his behavior must not harm the interests of the state as the owner. For example, the state-owned resources and assets cannot be seized or sold cheaply, not to profit from rent seeking. The concentrated expression in the right of return is to improve the income system, fully implement the national owner's income and ensure that these benefits are owned by the state. In the new urbanization, the property right management of land resource assets, tourism development resource assets and mineral resource assets in resource-based cities should be strengthened.

Third, strengthen the price management of resource assets. In order to economize and optimize the utilization of precious natural resource assets, it is necessary to improve the socialist market economic system, further eliminate the influence of monopoly and planned regulation through reform and make the price of resource assets reflect the market supply and demand situation sensitively. In the process of new-type urbanization, it is particularly necessary to change people's extravagance and waste of water, energy, land and other natural resources through the transmission of market price signals, so as to promote the conservation and utilization of resources and the formation of intensive new-type urbanization. In addition, comprehensive use of tax, price subsidies and other means to adjust the price of resource products, promote the optimal use of resources. Many natural resources have similar uses, and they can replace each other to a certain extent. In the case of different degrees of resource scarcity and environmental impact, price reform of resource products can be adopted to promote the rational use of resources. For example, many non-renewable mineral resources in China are not fully utilized, resulting in excessive waste and serious environmental pollution. In the new urbanization, the development of waste disposal industry can be stimulated and the price of recycling resource products can be raised to curb the development of primary mineral resources.

5.3   Social Participation in Green City Management

Local governments are encouraged to mobilize the enthusiasm of the whole people and formulate the green city construction and management plan that all the people are enthusiastic to participate in, under the condition that the development of green urbanization path is differentiated and the choice is individualized. The local government should change the traditional top-down decision model, in the event of an important resource environmental impact on city development, such as a particular period of urban development strategy, urban space development planning, urban industrial layout planning, reconstruction of urban resource conservation projects, urban sewage management reform and reconstruction of the urban greening. We should fully assess its environmental impact and sort out the relevant stakeholders that may be involved, invite these stakeholders to participate in the joint decision-making of the project, optimize the design of the project implementation scheme, make the relevant stakeholders have the sense of equal participation in the decision-making and improve the consciousness of cooperation and promotion in the project implementation. In the east coast of China, where the economy is more developed, the public has more urgent requirements for a good ecological environment, and the decision-making participation degree is higher, the socialized participation mode experiment of green city management can be given priority to, and the basic path for the public to participate in green city management can be explored, so as to provide experience for the green urbanization in other regions in the future. It can also be classified by region to explore the social governance model of green urbanization in different regions.

5.4 Ensuring the Supply of Key Supporting Technologies

The key supporting technologies in green city construction include "hard technology" and "soft technology". The former mainly includes resource conservation and utilization, resource recycling and ecological environment pollution control, while the latter is mainly scientific and effective management in various fields of green city construction. In terms of resource conservation and utilization, key supporting technologies include land saving, energy saving, water saving, ore saving (non-energy mineral resources) and forest saving (forestry resources). The key supporting technologies of resource recycling technology are urban garbage treatment, resource recycling technology in factories and resource recycling design in households. In terms of environmental pollution control, the key supporting technologies include water control (urban sewage treatment), gas control (atmospheric environment control of cities and urban agglomerations), soil control (land pollution control of urban and rural suburbs and mining cities), etc. Soft science and technology, on the other hand, covers the management science knowledge of green city construction, especially the knowledge of humanities and social sciences, such as the formation, cultivation and application of urban green consumption culture, social participation design of green city construction, legal regulations of green city construction and so on. Priority should be given to these key support areas in the plan for tackling key scientific and technological problems, and special funds should be allocated to train and educate personnel and support scientific research. We will strengthen reform of the science and technology system and the financial management system, and encourage cities to formulate their own science and technology support plans for green cities in line with their own green city development plans. Through coordination and overall planning, the state shall conduct special research on key green supporting technologies with nationwide influence that are included in the national key science and technology program, and strengthen the sharing and promotion of research results. For the key supporting technologies with integrated ecological function, regional joint research is encouraged and necessary human, financial and institutional innovation support is provided by the state. As for the supporting technologies that are limited to the impact in individual cities, the state encourages local innovative research, and encourages research in the form of special funds, innovative selection, material awards and honorary titles.

5.5   Strengthening Practices in Key Influencing Areas

In terms of urban land use, it is necessary to adjust the structure of land use, increase the area and proportion of land used for public facilities, municipal facilities, external transportation and green space, and at the same time reduce the area and proportion of land used for living, industrial and especially heavy industry in the city. Improve land use efficiency and development intensity, adopt effective measures to coordinate land use, strictly prohibit land destruction and improve the utilization efficiency of existing urban land use and infrastructure utilization efficiency by improving plot ratio and population density; explore the internal potential of urban land, such as expanding urban space through old city reconstruction, strengthening the management of unused land and three-dimensional development of urban space; integrate planning of land use and transportation system; and promote the coordination of population, industry and transportation.

In the aspect of urban transportation construction, priority should be given to the development of public transportation system and the reduction of urban transportation energy consumption, such as the moderate construction and development of rail transit, the restriction of the use of cars, the emphasis on the development of slow traffic system (sidewalks, bicycle paths, etc.), the promotion of environment-friendly vehicles and the development of intelligent transportation system. In addition, it is necessary to strengthen the coordinated planning of land and transportation, attach importance to the ecological protection of transportation construction and to the participation of the public in urban transportation planning and construction.

In terms of green space system construction, we should build an urban ecological network system integrating urban and rural areas. We should not only pay attention to the green space construction in the urban area, but also the green space construction in the surrounding areas of the city, making urban construction a part of urban regional ecosystem; protect the restricted ecological land, prohibit the ecological sensitive areas, and ensure the realization of urban ecological public functions; adjust measures to local conditions, develop fully, reasonable arrangement of all kinds of urban green space; strengthen the renovation and renewal of the old green space ecosystem and call on the residents to participate in the construction of the green space system.

In terms of urban waste management, we should advocate green consumption and reduce the amount of waste at the source; improve the garbage classification collection management system and the development of resources recycling industry; strengthen science and technology, improve the garbage resources, harmless treatment technology; ensure the investment of management funds; increase the supply of garbage treatment infrastructure.

CHAPTER 11

Assessment and Green Development Transformation

1 WHY ASSESSMENT

Assessment, with the role of natural stimulation and incentive, has always been an important means of mobilizing people's subjective initiative toward the established goal of efforts and progress. Assessment plays an irreplaceable role in green development transformation. Especially in the early stage of green development transformation, the government often plays the role of an important advocate, promoter and organizer. At this time, the role of assessment is even more important and irreplaceable. This effect is mainly reflected in the following aspects:

First, assessment can mobilize the initiative and enthusiasm of green development subjects. Although green development has its inherent motivation, given the "positive externality" of green development, relevant subjects may not be able to actively promote green development. Therefore, in view of the overall situation of green development in a country or a region, it is necessary to establish and improve the assessment system aimed at mobilizing the initiative and enthusiasm of all green development subjects.

Second, the assessment can urge the behavior of the subject of green development. Green development is an ongoing process. The mobilization of green development subjects is just the beginning, and it needs to be constantly urged to keep forging ahead along the established track and goal of green development. Third, the assessment can correct the

S. Gu et al., *Green Transformation and Development*, The Great Transformation of China, https://doi.org/10.1007/978-981-32-9495-0_11

335

behavior deviation of green development subject. The assessment is helpful to find out the behavioral deviation of the subjects of green development and carry out necessary correction of the deviation through rewards and punishments, so as to help adhere to the direction of green development and achieve the goal.

Finally, the assessment can regulate the behavior of the subject of green development. Assessment helps to promote each behavior subject to constantly regulate their behavior according to assessment requirements (such as assessment methods), including behavior mode, behavior intensity, behavior progress, so as to help achieve the established green development goals or vision according to the overall deployment.

2   WHO WILL ASSESS

The question of who will assess is related to the various subjects of green development and their relations with each other. It is also highly relevant to the management system and legal system. Under China's current legal system and management system, the subjects of green development assessment can be divided into the following six categories: First, the upper level of government as the assessment subject. This kind of appraisal main subject arrangement is quite popular in our country at present, also often is most effective. The assessment of the superior government on the green transformation and development of the lower government is often more professional, systematic, targeted and operable, so it is easier to find the problems and the crux of the problems, and the efficiency of the assessment is often higher.

Second, the legislature at the same level as the assessment subject. As a legislative body, it naturally has the function and responsibility of supervision and accountability to the administrative body. It is an inevitable choice to accelerate China's green transformation and development to strengthen the supervision, inquiry and accountability of people's congresses at all levels over the implementation of green development by governments at the same level.

Third, the professional departments at the superior level shall be the subject of assessment. This also is more popular assessment subject arrangement in our country at present. Green development and its transformation involve many departments, including land, water conservancy, energy, environmental protection, forestry, development and reform, and industry and information technology. Each department has different responsibilities in green development and its transformation.

Strengthening the guidance and assessment of higher professional departments on lower professional departments can improve the capacity building of various professional systems on green development and transformation. In fact, the national development and reform commission, the ministry of environmental protection, the ministry of land and resources, the ministry of water resources, the ministry of industry and information technology, the ministry of finance and the state forestry administration all have assessment or evaluation methods for green development, which objectively play a positive role in the transformation of green development. In fact, the national development and reform commission, the ministry of environmental protection, the ministry of land and resources, the ministry of water resources, the ministry of industry and information technology, the ministry of finance and the state forestry administration all have assessment or evaluation methods for green development, which objectively play a positive role in the transformation of green development.

Fourth, independent third party as the assessment subject. Independent third parties should not only be the promoters and participants of green development, but also be the assessor of green development to assess and supervise the subjects and their behaviors. Independent third-party assessment boasts independence, objectivity, fairness, transparency and other natural characteristics or advantages. Of course, third-party supervision and assessment are still in their infancy in China, and they still face considerable obstacles and play a limited role. Fortunately, more and more independent third parties are deeply involved in the green development process, which has become an inevitable, good and irreversible trend.

Fifth, society as the main subject of assessment. As the assessment subject, society is a completely open assessment subject, that is, the progress and effect of green development will be evaluated and assessed by the whole society. This requires full disclosure of relevant information on green development and its progress, and the establishment and improvement of channels or platforms for social evaluation and assessment. In this regard, open evaluation or assessment platforms as well as objective, impartial and professional news media are necessary.

Finally, cadre is in charge of an organization to regard assessment as main subject. In China, cadres of party committees and governments at all levels are the key to the success or failure of almost all work, including green development and transformation. Strengthening the green development performance appraisal of party committees and government officials at all levels often gets twice the result with half the effort. Obviously, under the current management system and the cadre system, the cadre competent organs, namely the organizational departments and personnel departments of party committees at all levels, are often the most authoritative assessment subjects. In this sense, the inclusion of green development (transformation) into the cadre assessment system of the organization and personnel department is the concrete embodiment of the cadre competent authority as the assessment subject.

3   WHO WILL BE ASSESSED

The question of who will be assessed is related to the question of who will assess. At the same time, who will be assessed, fundamentally, depends on the green development of the main subject (structure) arrangement. The subject of green development is the object of green assessment. In this sense, the government, enterprises, institutions and so on are the objects of assessment. However, in view of the differences in responsibilities, rights, obligations and other aspects among subjects, the government is undoubtedly the key object of assessment, while various enterprises and institutions are the secondary objects of assessment.

The governmental assessment object is actually also quite complex. This involves the level of government, government departments, government and party committees and other key aspects or key issues. The first is the level of government. Our country has 5 levels of government, namely central, province (municipality, municipality directly under the central government), city (area, autonomous prefecture, league), county (city, district, banner) and town (town, street). Should we assess the central government's green transformation and development? There are different answers to this question, which are also related to the question of who will assess the actions of the central government. Obviously, the central government attaches great importance to green transformation and development, and its efforts in promoting green transformation and development are recognized by local governments at all levels. That, of course, is no reason to dismiss the central government. It is essential for the NPC and its standing committee to hold the central government accountable for green development and ecological progress. There is also plenty of room for improvement.

Second, is the government or related government departments to be assessed? In fact, this problem has been troubling us. For a long time, we only pay attention to the assessment of relevant government departments, but the effect is not ideal. For example, although it is reasonable to hold environmental protection departments accountable for environmental pollution, the causes of environmental pollution are various and complex, including the weak supervision by competent environmental authorities, the actions of resource development departments and the systematic thinking bias of the government that only focuses on economic growth. Obviously, relevant work, including green transformation and development, should not only pay attention to the assessment of government departments, but also pay attention to the systematic and comprehensive assessment of the government, that is to say, the assessment of the main government leaders.

Finally, the assessment relationship between the government and the party committee. Is government or party committee to be assessed? Together? This point, for a long time, has been only the assessment of the government, but the assessment effect is not ideal. Why is that? This is determined by the special national conditions of our country. All levels of government in China are governments under the leadership of party committees, including major decisions on economy, society, culture, resources and environment, which must be studied and decided by party committees at all levels and then referred to the government for specific implementation. This determines that the party committee has the final say or decision-making power in all kinds of major issues and important areas. From this, party committee should have the main subject responsibility that cannot shirk. The General Offices of the Central Committee of the Communist Party of China and the General Offices of the State Council issued in mid-august 2015 the *Measures for the Accountability of Leading Party and Government Officials for Ecological and Environmental Damage (Trial)*, which clearly states that "Local party committees and governments at all levels are generally responsible for the protection of the region's ecological environment and resources, and the leading members of the party committees and governments bear the main responsibility. This actually puts forward the same request to the party committee and the government main leadership and carries on the responsibility to investigate".

4   ASSESSMENT BASIS

To assess cadres, including leading officials of party committees and governments at all levels, concerns the immediate interests of cadres, the performance of party committees and governments at all levels, the implementation of major party policies and guidelines, and the building of the country's governance system and capacity. Therefore, the assessment should be extremely serious, extremely strict, extremely careful, the assessment should never be made without evidence and willfully. There are two main types of basis for such assessment:

First is to be assessed in accordance with the law. Assess the requirements of party committees, governments and their main leaders in accordance with party discipline and political law. Specifically, assessment should be conducted according to the relevant discipline regulations of the party such as *Civil Servant Law of the People's Republic of China*, *Land Management Law of the People's Republic of China*, *Water Law of the People's Republic of China*, *Environmental Protection Law*, *Energy Conservation Law*, *Circular Economy Promotion Law* and other relevant laws, as well as *Disciplinary Regulations of the Communist Party of China*.

The second is to assess according to regulations. There must be scientific, clear, fair and impartial assessment method. Absolutely avoid the arbitrariness and selective examination of "ad hominem" and "differential deliberation". We should set up the idea that everyone is equal before assessment, study and formulate scientific and standard assessment methods, make clear provisions on assessment objects, assessment contents, assessment methods, assessment time, assessment place, etc., and obtain the majority approval of assessment objects. If necessary, the assessment method shall be reported to the party committee or the government at the next higher level for the record.

5   What to Assess

What to assess depends on the understanding of the connotation of green development, on the main contradiction and the main aspects of the contradiction that affect green development, and on the main work deployment and target requirements of green development.

According to the main connotation of green development, especially according to the responsibilities that party committees and governments at all levels should perform in terms of green development or green transformation and development, party committees and governments at all levels should focus on the following aspects in terms of green transformation and development: (1) industrial optimization and upgrading performance appraisal. We will focus on assessing the adjustment of industrial structure, especially in encouraging the development of resource-conserving, environment-friendly and ecology-conserving industries. The core is to assess the changes in the proportion of modern service industry or tertiary industry. (2) Green finance assessment. We will focus on assessing the change in the total and proportion of fiscal input for resource conservation, environmental governance and ecological restoration, and encourage party committees and governments at all levels to put more emphasis on using fiscal funds for green development. (3) Financial greening assessment. It mainly assesses the government's efforts in promoting local financial institutions to focus on energy conservation and environmental protection, aiming to encourage and support the green development of finance and provide necessary financial support for enterprises committed to green development. (4) Assessment of work performance in resource conservation. We will focus on assessing the actual progress made in saving energy, water, land, grain and materials and the government's actions in this regard. (5) Actual effect of environmental protection and governance. We will focus on assessing environmental changes in the atmosphere, water and soil. (6) Actual effect of ecological protection and restoration. We will focus on assessing the delimitation and protection of red lines for resources, environment and ecology, and the core is to assess the protection effect of basic farmland, forests, grasslands and wetlands. (7) Assessment on the construction of green communities and green institutions. We will focus on evaluating the actions and effects of party committees and governments in promoting green communities, party and government organs, and green schools. (8) Check whether there are major events in resources, environment, ecology and production safety. (9) Other aspects to be included in the assessment according to the requirements of green transformation and development.

6 HOW TO ASSESS

Concerning how to assess, the first priority is to have an assessment method, including the assessment index system. There have been a lot of discussions and researches on the evaluation index system of green development or green transformation development, and the index system contains more or less indicators. The assessment index system of green development or green transition development is not discussed too much here; three points will be emphasized here. First, the indicators should be targeted to the problem or problem should be easy to appear in the assessment. These problems often include the insufficient attention paid to resource conservation, environmental protection and ecological conservation in the allocation and use of financial funds, resulting in a low proportion of such investment. In the process of industrial development, especially in the process of investment attraction, there is no threshold for non-green industries or the threshold is too low, which leads to the abnormal phenomenon of non-green industries increasing instead of decreasing. There are deficits in natural resource assets, including water, land, minerals, energy and biological resources, and the environmental quality of the atmosphere, water and soil. Party and government organs and public institutions have not played a leading and exemplary role in saving energy, water and land.

The second is to have a solid foundation of information and data. Both evaluation and assessment must be supported by data information. The assessment of green development or green transformation development, in particular, needs data information that can reflect the "green" aspects objectively, accurately and timely, that is to say, the data of changes in resources, environment and ecology are particularly needed. However, it is undeniable that the basic data information system related to green development, such as resources, environment and ecology, has not been completely established in China. There are many problems in the data of resources, environment and ecology. Inaccurate data cannot accurately reflect the changes in resources, environment and ecology. The problem that the data are not true and the false data information is not rare leads to the deviation of the ecological decision-making of resources and environment. Data information is not timely; this problem is more prominent, and as a result, the data cannot reflect the changes of resources and environment ecology in a timely manner, so it is impossible to judge, evaluate and assess the latest situation of green development. It is imperative and extremely urgent to establish and improve a comprehensive, systematic, accurate, real and timely data and information support system for resources, environment, ecology and other key issues.

Finally, a sound social evaluation and supervision system for green development should be established. Compared with the assessment of higher party committees and governments on lower party committees and governments, social evaluation and supervision can often play a more timely, more direct and more effective role. This needs to fully mobilize the enthusiasm of social supervision, but also to provide necessary data information and supervision channels for social supervision, but also to create a good atmosphere for social supervision. We must not retaliate against the supervisors of resources, environment and ecology (especially the whistleblowers), but must reward the supervisors and whistleblowers as necessary.

7   How to Use the Assessment Results

Whether the result of assessment is good or not depends on whether the result of assessment can be applied. Results not applied or not assessed are ineffective assessments and futile assessments. For this, want to examine and reward and punishment union to rise. For this, it is in need to combine assessment and rewards and punishments. In other words, the assessment results should be combined with rewards and punishments for cadres, including rewards and punishments for spiritual and material matters. Second, we should combine the assessment results with the appointment or removal of cadres for promotion, and practically take the assessment results as the basis for the appointment or removal of cadres. For this reason, the assessment of green development or green transformation and development must involve the cadre department in charge (party committee organization department and government personnel department) and the cadre discipline department (party committee discipline inspection department and government supervision department). Only in this way, the results of green assessment can be timely, accurately and effectively integrated into the cadre assessment system, and become an important factor affecting or even determining the appointment and removal of cadres, and the promotion and demotion of cadres.

8   Key Points for Strengthening Assessment in the Near Future

The assessment of green development or green transformation and development is a complex task with strong policy, scientific nature and systematic nature. It cannot be accomplished overnight. It needs to be pragmatic and gradual. From the perspective of the objectives and requirements of accelerating ecological civilization construction and economic transformation and upgrading, as well as the basis and capacity of green development assessment, the following tasks should be focused on in the near future: First is to strengthen the statistical work of resource environment ecology practically. Statistical work is the indispensable foundation of assessment; without statistics, there can be no assessment. To this end, it is necessary to further clarify the objectives and requirements of resource, environment and ecological statistics, adjust the indicator system of resource, environment and ecological statistics, clarify the responsibilities of relevant departments of resource, environment and ecological statistics, and ensure the authenticity, accuracy, credibility, timeliness and availability of resource, environment and ecological statistics. Second is to strengthen the monitoring of resources, environment and ecology. No supervising, no assessment. It is necessary to ensure the scientific, standardized, accurate and credible monitoring data of resources, environment and ecology. Human intervention and administrative tampering with resources, environment and ecological monitoring data shall be severely punished. The third is to speed up the resources and environment ecological information disclosure and data sharing. We will ensure that the people have a clear understanding of their surrounding ecological environment and the resource base on which they depend, so as to effectively supervise the resource, environment and ecological behavior of the party committee and the government. The fourth is to strengthen the evaluation of green development of cadres in office. Establish a scientific and effective assessment index system, highlighting resource conservation, environmental friendliness, ecological conservation and other aspects of the assessment indicators. The fifth is to strengthen the audit of leading cadres' leaving office. The audit will focus on changes in the quantity and quality of water, land, minerals, forests, grasslands and other important natural resources, as well as changes in the environmental quality of the atmosphere, water and soil during the term of office of leading cadres. Finally, it is necessary to strengthen the lifelong accountability of leading cadres for their behavior of resources, environment and ecology. We should never allow cadres to sacrifice resources, environment and ecology in exchange for promotion, putting an end to rash decisions, hasty promise and buck-passing.

Postscript

China's green development, or green transformation and development, is a gradual and long process, a complex and systematic project, a combination of theory and practice, and is not complete but ongoing, which determines that our understanding of this is constantly improving and deepening. Here, we try to systematize China's green development or green transformation development by combining the existing research results and literature analysis, policy analysis and case analysis. This book can only be regarded as a preliminary result or a periodical result of our review, and there must be some places that are not comprehensive, systematic, accurate or even fallacious. First, these problems depend on our self-renewal and correction in future research. Second, it depends on readers' correction and criticism. In any case, China's green development will be an important topic that we have been paying close attention to and studying. We also look forward to working with you to promote China's green development and make our due contribution to the early realization of the beautiful Chinese dream.

REFERENCES

An Wei. The Connotation, Mechanism and Practice of Green Finance. *Economic Review*, 2008 (5): 156–158.

Chen Ming, Zhang Jian-Zhi, Sun Dannian. Construction of Financial Expenditure Performance Evaluation System of Environmental Protection Department based on International Experience. *Environmental Protection*, 2013 (22): 68–70.

Chen Sheng. Practices and Experience of Japanese Enterprises in Implementing Green Procurement Standardization. *World Standard Information*, 2007 (10): 51–54.

Chen Tong. South Korea's Transformation Strategy and Enlightenment Under the International Financial Crisis. *Comprehensive Competitiveness*, 2011 (5): 64–69.

Cheng Yongming. Green Procurement in Japan and Its Implications for China. *Japan Studies*, 2013, 27 (2): 45–50.

Du Haiyang, Liang Zhichao, Xiu Wenyan et al. Development Status and Prospect of Green Food in China. *Agricultural Prospect*, 2014 (10): 44–47.

Fan Lianying. On the Construction of Recycling Society in Japan by Environmental Education. *Modern Japanese Economy*, 2005 (1): 61–64.

Gao Jianliang. "Green Finance" and Sustainable Financial Development. *Financial Theory and Teaching*, 1998, 34 (4): 13–17.

Guan Wanjie. *Research on Legal Issues of Green Consumption in China*. Harbin: Northeast Forestry University, 2014.

Guo Peiyuan, Cai Yingcui. The Development of Green Finance in Developed Countries and Its Enlightenment to China. *Environmental Protection*, 2015 (1): 44–47.

Han Wenbo. Public Finance Calls for "Green". China Financial News, November 1, 2005.

Han Wenbo. Setting Up the Concept of Green Finance and Promoting the Sustainable Development of Finance. *China Finance*, 2004 (2): 49–51.

Han Yanbin. Empirical Research on the Status Quo of Green Consumption in China. *Academic Circle*, 2006 (9): 50–51.

He Xiuxing. Implementing "Green Financial Policy" is a Strategic Choice for the Financial Industry Facing the 21st Century. *Journal of Nanjing Finance College*, 1998 (4): 22–25.

Huang Na. *On the Improvement of China's Legal System Related to Green Consumption*. Taiyuan: Shanxi University of Finance and Economics, 2014.

Li Ruihong. Green Finance: Global Trend, Korean Practice and Chinese Suggestions. *Theory and Contemporary*, 2011 (4): 18–21.

Li Xi. Foreign Green Finance Policies and Their References. *Journal of Suzhou University*, 2011 (6): 134–137.

Lin Xiao. *Research on the Development of Green Finance in China Under the Background of Low-Carbon Economy*. Guangzhou: Jinan University, 2011.

Liu Juan, Chen Yiqun, Zhang Xiaodan. Comparative Study on Green Procurement Standards of Domestic and Foreign Governments. *Environment and Sustainable Development*, 2014 (6): 87–90.

Liu Wei. *Research on Several Legal Issues of Green Consumption Promotion*. Kunming: Kunming University of Science and Technology, 2011.

Mei Yan. *On the Legal Regulation of Green Finance in China*. Changchun: Jilin University of Finance and Economics, 2013.

Ni Yuxia. *Research on American Green Finance System*. Changsha: Hunan Normal University, 2011.

Qiao Haishu. Establishing Financial Ecological View. *Ecological Economy*, 1999 (5): 18–19.

Qiu Han. *Research on the Legal System of Green Consumption Promotion*. Nanchang: Jiangxi University of Finance and Economics, 2012.

Ren Guorong, Huo Jinxin, Zhao Hongjie, et al. Investigation and Analysis of Green Consumption Status of Residents in Shijiazhuang. *Environmental Education*, 2005 (3): 46–48.

Ronson Branson Quenzer. *Comparative Study on Green Consumption of Chinese and American consumers*. Harbin: Harbin Institute of Technology, 2014.

Song Shuang. *Environmental Education in Japan and Its Enlightenment*. Dalian: Dalian University of Technology, 2007.

Song Xiaoling. Green Financial Policy of Western Banking Industry: Common Rules and Differential Practice. *Exploration of Economic Problems*, 2013 (1): 170–174.

Tan Cheng. *Problems and Countermeasures of China's Green Consumption Legal System*. Guilin: Guangxi Normal University, 2014.

Tang Bohong. Problems and Countermeasures in the Development of Green Finance in China. *Journal of Changchun University*, 2009, 19 (9): 1–4.

Wang Daoming. Current Situation and Countermeasures of Developing Green Consumption—A Case Study of Beijing. *Research on Technology Economy and Management*, 2011 (10): 101–104.

Wang Junhua. On the "Green Revolution" of the Financial Industry. *Ecological Economy*, 2000 (10): 45–48.

Wang Meng. Limitations of China's Sewage Discharge Fee System and Its Reform. *Tax Research*, 2009 (7): 28–31.

Wang Yuanyuan. *Research on Tax System Promoting Green Consumption*. Qingdao: Ocean University of China, 2009.

Wen Tongai, Ni Yuxia. The Rise of Green Financial System and China's Countermeasures. *Citizens and Law*, 2010 (1): 33–36.

Wu Jiang, Jia Lei, Shi Lei. Development History of Environmental Finance in the United States and Its Enlightenment to China. *Environmental Protection*, 2012 (20): 74–76.

Wu Yang. Analysis on the Changes of Environmental Protection Expenditure in the Classification of Government Revenue and Expenditure and Final Accounts. *Modern Economic Information*, 2014 (20): 306–307.

Xie Lanlan. *Research on Fiscal and Taxation Policies to Promote Green Automobile Consumption*. Dalian: Northeast University of Finance and Economics, 2011.

Xu Jinliang, Yuan Tingting, Chang Liang. Empirical Study on Green Procurement by Beijing Municipal Government to Promote the Transformation of Scientific and Technological Achievements. *China Population (Resources and Environment)*, 2014, 24 (11): 161–167.

Yang Tao. Circular Economy Needs "Green Finance". 21st Century Economic Report, July 5, 2006.

Youjie. *Analysis on the Dilemma and Countermeasures of Green Consumption in China*. Shenyang: Northeast University, 2009.

Yu Sulan. *Research on Green Consumption Expansion in China*. Changchun: Northeast Normal University, 2014.

Zang Huiyan. *Research on Environmental Education and Its Legislation in the United States*. Qingdao: Ocean University of China, 2008.

Zhan Liuyang, Ju Meiting, Yang Juan. Suggestions for the Improvement of China's Government's Green Procurement Policy. *Ecological Economy*, 2013 (6): 95–98.

Zhang Chenghui, Tian Hui. Recent International Green Finance Development Trend and Enlightenment [EB/OL]. China Economic News Network. http://www.cet.com.cn/ycpd/sdyd/1474624.shtml. March 2, 2015.

Zhang Ping. *Connotation, Action Mechanism and Practice of Green Finance*. Chengdu: Southwest University of Finance and Economics, 2013.

Zhang Weifeng. *Research on the Legal System of Green Finance*. Zhengzhou: Zhengzhou University, 2012.

Zhang Xue. *Research on Legal Issues of Green Consumption-from the Perspective of China's Current Consumption Tax Law*. Shanghai: East China University of Political Science and Law, 2012.

Zhang Zhenmin. Comparative Study on Green Financial Systems in China, Japan and Korea. *Heilongjiang Social Science*, 2013 (6): 75–79.

Zhang Zhimin. Investigation and Analysis of Green Consumption of Dongguan Residents. *Journal of Dongguan University of Technology*, 2011, 18 (4): 33–37.

Zhao Jing. *Research on Legal Issues of Green Finance-A Case Study of Changsha-Zhuzhou-Xiangtan City Cluster*. Changsha: Hunan Normal University, 2010.

Zou Jiahui. *Research on the Legal System of Green Consumption in China*. Changsha: Central South University of Forestry and Technology, 2009.